Copyright © 2020 by Damian P Myler

Why do we include rude, obscene, and vulg words in this book? These are the words of war, conquest, and anger that help us express our deep-felt emotions. They tend to transcend time and space, war and migrations, as well as mixing and intermingling. How do I know this? Because today, they are almost identical to how they sounded 3,000 years ago.

I also agree with the Oxford Dictionary's reasoning for listing these "types of words": [1, see footnote at bottom of each page.]

I0518007

---

[1]"The role of a descriptive dictionary is to record the existence and meaning of all words in a language, and to clearly identify their status. We include vulgar or offensive words in our dictionaries because such terms are a part of a language's lexicon. However, we label in our dictionaries words that fit into these categories to reflect their vulgar or offensive status and usage in the language."

Table of Contents

4

5

Introduction

Do you remember Neo in the Matrix? Somehow, he found himself in a world, that didn't make sense, a world where many things were hidden from him, the writers called this the Matrix, a systematic control on people so they didn't know the real truth, what if I told you that our reality, is not that far removed from Neo's!

History, archeology, etymology, dinosaurs, giants, ethereal visitors from another realm (aliens), visiting earth and spawning children, even real dragons' all of them really did exist, and within the last 6000 years. I believe etymology, (tracing words back to their origin) proves this.

Neo had to take a pill to properly discover true reality, I am making it easier on you, all you have to do is read my books and investigate my claims yourself – NO BLUE OR RED PILL NEEDED.

Buckle up, folks (or should we say Dorothy), you are about to kiss Kansas goodbye.

Is your seat belt fastened? Are your bags packed and loaded? This journey is about to begin, and it will take you back to the misty dawn of Earth's language. To a time when the very first words were being shaped and spoken. A time of wonders and miracles, when humanity took the simple languages gifted by God and began expanding them—naming not only the animals but plants and places as well. You're about to uncover a hidden treasure of knowledge—the very roots of the words you're reading today!

In a land far, far away, in a lush tropical paradise, we will uncover the ancient language I call **Paleo-English**. Let's rewind to the birth of humanity, where we'll meet our ancestors, witness how they appeared, and discover how they first communicated. Together, we'll explore the extraordinary birth of language, journeying through countless lands, languages, and kingdoms, encountering the one true God, as well as many gods and demons, symbols and idioms. Along the way, we'll trace the raw, primal—some might say

8

primeval—words that lie at the heart of modern English. Buckle up for a journey into the origins of language itself!

We will discover the other languages that contribute to English and how they relate to Biblical roots, all of which combine to create the richest, most diverse language on the planet. Again will encounter real unicorns, giants, aliens, rainbows, and fire-breathing dragons during this enchanting journey.

We will pay homage to the great bastions of Christianity, including William Tyndale, Wilhelm Gesenius, and James Strong. These giants, along with resources like Brown-Driver-Briggs and the King James Bible, will illuminate the foundational pillars of biblical interpretation, hermeneutics, and meticulous scientific study.

Chapter 1

Origins of Language & PIE Connections

In the beginning, was the "WORD", and the "WORD" was with God, and the "WORD" was God (Joh 1.1). It suggests a divine origin for communication itself, with the "Word" acting as a bridge between God the Father and His Son. The implication is profound: He was the Word—to think or to speak means we are using a divine attribute. It implies that there is real power in the spoken word, even in thought, the generation of ideas in our hearing. In fact, Jesus said, "If you have faith the size of a mustard seed, you can say (speak to) this mountain be cast into the sea, and it will happen."

Perhaps examining the Hebrew meaning of "word" can offer deeper insight. Throughout scripture, the phrase "the word of the Lord" appears repeatedly, but what does this recurring phrase truly signify? Another common expression is "and by thy word" or "according to thy word." In each instance, God uses the same Hebrew word—**DaBaR**.

The word **DaBaR** appears over 2,000 times in the Bible and is translated in various ways, with the most common translation being "speech." Interestingly, **DaBaR**[2] also finds a place in Celtic languages. In Old Irish, **dabir** means "word," and the term **bard**—meaning "ancient Celtic minstrel-poet"—is derived from Old Celtic *bardo*, meaning "poet" or "singer."

In English, the word "word" itself can be traced back to Proto-Germanic ***wurda-** (which also gave us Old Saxon, Old Frisian, and Dutch *woord*, Old High German *wort*, and Old Norse *orð*). This, in turn, comes from the Proto-Indo-European root ***were-** (3), meaning "to speak" or "to say." Interestingly, the

---

[2] H1697 דָּבָר dâbâr, daw-baw'; from H1696; a word; by implication, a matter (as spoken of) word (807x), thing (231x), matter (63x), acts (51x), chronicles (38x), saying (25x), commandment (20x), *miscellaneous* (204x). Original connection from Isaac Mozeson "e-word".

English word **verb** also originates from the same root as **DaBaR** (I explore this further in Chapter 3). Additionally, consider the Hebrew word **UWD**, meaning "to speak," "to testify," or "to bear witness."[3]

Linguistics professor Isaac Mozeson, wrote the book "The Word", and believes there are over 80,000 English words from Hebrew, this means that English has more root Hebrew words, than modern Hebrew, WOW!

And this translation/etymology for WORD, comes primarily from him. Etymologist don't now look to Hebrew to trace our etymology, but his and my work clearly shows it does. I don't always agree with his root's he uses a different system from me, he is a Jew and uses Jewish etymology, I am a Brit, and (as I said earlier) use, William Tyndale, Wilhelm Gesenius, James Strong, along with TWOT (Theological Workbook OT) and . Brown-Driver-Briggs, etymologies. I also list my roots with the Strongs Hebrew numbering system, this makes them very easy to trace back. Having said that let us continue to look at DaBaR or DaVaR (Bet/Vet), got truncated, to VaR, and with a hard rolling hard R, we get VaRt; the tongue creates a 'T' sound as it releases and strikes the upper palate, leading to the formation of 'VaRt (note[4]).

There is another DaBaR connection to the Bible; the prophetess, DeBoR'aH, (added "H"), the name comes from the same root and means BEE, in Hebrew, due to its organized motion, its systematic way of doing things The English abbreviation for Deborah, is Debby (d'BEE)[5]. Clearly, BEE comes from this word

---

[3] I think that the English "WORD" fm Proto-Germanic *wURDa fm-UWD? i.e. GIVE or KEEP YOUR UWD (WORD), H5749 עוד ʿûwd, ood; PR to duplicate or repeat; by implication, to protest, testify (as by reiteration, solemnly, stand upright, testify, give warning, (**bear, call to, give, take to**) witness, Judah did swear on oath (UWD) and gave his WORD that Benjamin would not be harmed, under penalty of his life! Oath fm PIE *oi-to-UWD.

[4] Note- Mozeson believes that metathesis created the change DaVaR, became VaRD. While metathesis does sometimes play a role, I do not think it occurred this time.

[5] Deaborah H1682, BEE (*ET) Old English beo "*bee*," from Proto-Germanic *bion (source also of Old Norse by, Old High German bia, Middle Dutch bie), from PIE root *bhei- "bee."

root, but etymologists trace it to PIE root Old Irish *bech* ("bee"), Welsh *bydaf* ("beehive")*bhei-.

The story of Adam naming the animals raises an interesting question. If creation was truly recent, then assigning names would make perfect sense. However, if creation was old and Satan, who was in charge of the earth and its development, had been around a long time, they would have already named all the animals, and God would have downloaded into Adams's brain the understanding of what they were. But the scripture suggests otherwise. Adam, along with his helpmeet Eve, had the task of naming the creatures, implying a more recent creation event.

Initial birthplace of humans and language.

According to the Bible, mankind started with Adam and Eve in the garden of Eden, where God planted vegetables and fruit trees for us to eat (Gen. 2.-3); it is where the tree of life was planted, along with the knowledge of good and evil. The tree of LIFE is where we get the root (CHEER's, L'HIME).

The garden had a geyser that came out, watered the garden, and afterward split into four headwaters (Gen 2:10); this GEYSER was located in Jerusalem and was called **Gishon**[6]; it was perhaps (at the time) a natural hot spring, where Adam and Eve could bath in crystal clear water (Rev.22.1), it is where the tree of life was located. The Garden of Eden was in Jerusalem, and the Temple was built over the threshing floor of the Jebusite on Mount Moria, where Abraham was asked to bind and sacrifice Isaac. It was an area where water was available, i.e., near one of the outlets of the Gishon(GUSH ON) springs (ophel 2Ch 27:3); Solomon also ran a siphon to it from Etam for the temple sacrifices.

---

[6] GEYSER, GUSH, GUTTEN, Gothic giutan, Old English geotan "to pour;" Old English guttas (plural) "bowels, entrails;" Old Norse geysa "to gush;" German Gosse "gutter, drain."H1521 גִּיחוֹן Gîychôwn, ghee-khone'; or (shortened) גִּחוֹן Gichôwn; from H1518; stream; Gichon, a river of Paradise; also a valley (or pool) near Jerusalem:Gihon. From root H1518 GUSH גִּיחַ gîyach,; or (shortened) גֹּחַ gôach; a primitive root; to gush forth (as water), generally to issue, break forth, labor to bring forth, come forth, draw up, take out.

The water had healing properties; it flowed to where the Kidron Valley is today, and it supplied the fortified city of JEBUS (the original name of Jerusalem, Jdg 19:10). King David used a water tunnel to attack Jebus and took the city (2Sam. 5.8). This same spring fed the Pool of Siloam, while another significant pool, Bethesda, also existed in Jerusalem.

King Hezekiah, a forward-thinking ruler, bolstered Jerusalem's water infrastructure. He reinforced the water supply and tunnels; there were even siphon tunnels that had been designed by Solomon to bring in water from far away Etam, this well before the Romans. In fact, Solomon said nothing new under the sun, and siphon water irrigation tunnels were discovered in the Indus Valley (we will speak more About the Indus Valley later).

A powerful image emerges from scripture: the tree of life and abundant water flowing from Jerusalem during God's final temple building. This echoes the divine declaration, "I am the Alpha and the Omega, the beginning and the end" (Revelation 21:6). Just as creation began, so too will there be a renewal, with Jerusalem at its heart.

And he shewed me a pure river of water of life, clear as crystal, proceeding out of the throne of God and of the Lamb. In the midst of the street of it, and on either side of the river, [was there] the tree of life, which bare twelve [manner of] fruits, [and] yielded her fruit every month: and the leaves of the tree [were] for the healing of the nations. And there shall be no more curse: but the throne of God and of the Lamb shall be in it; and his servants shall serve him: [Rev 22:1-3 KJV]

I think God will recreate paradise, in such a way that it will never be destroyed again, and it will be in the exact same place as it was in the beginning.

After the FALL (AUTUMN when red leaves fall as in ADAM[7], see Chap.3), we got pushed out of the Garden and populated the areas, somewhere in the Middle East, between Assyria, Ethiopia (Cush), a land mass called Havilah (Chavilar=circular, for the water encircled the land), which is said to be in Arabia, with the first river Pishon (PISSON[8] H6376, Gen 2.10-14), encircling it. This is an onomatopoeic word, this is produced by the sound it makes like PISS, HISS, other words like this are buzz, ring, and bark. The second river is Gihon (GUSH, GEYSER Jerusalem, also onomatopoeic), the third river Tigris (H2313 חִדֶּקֶל Chiddeqel, Assyrian Idiḵlat, Diḵlat, Old Persian Tigrâ), the fourth is the Euphrates. Many words from our early history are of this type, echoes from our past, like a baby mimicking words from its parents we imitated nature.

---

[7] AUTUMN From Old French autumpne, automne (13c.), from Latin autumnus (also auctumnus, Etruscan, but Tucker "drying-up season UNKNOWN ORIGIN. Red leaves falling, H132 אַדְמֹנִי 'admônîy, from H119; reddish (of the hair or the complexion, red, ruddy Celtic Red Hair, ruddy skin, dmoniy (adom'niy) see Damnonii, אָדַם 'âdam, aw-dam'; to show blood.

[8] Pishon H6376 פִּישׁוֹן Pîyshôwn, pee-shone'; from H6335; dispersive; Pishon, a river of Eden H6335 PUSH, EXPEL POSH (Unknown origin connected to PUSH, proud) פּוּשׁ pûwsh, poosh; a primitive root; to spread; figuratively (PISS), act proudly, grow up, be grown fat, spread selves, be scattered. PIE root *pei(s)-, "to flow" or "to pour," Greek: "pissein" (to sprinkle).

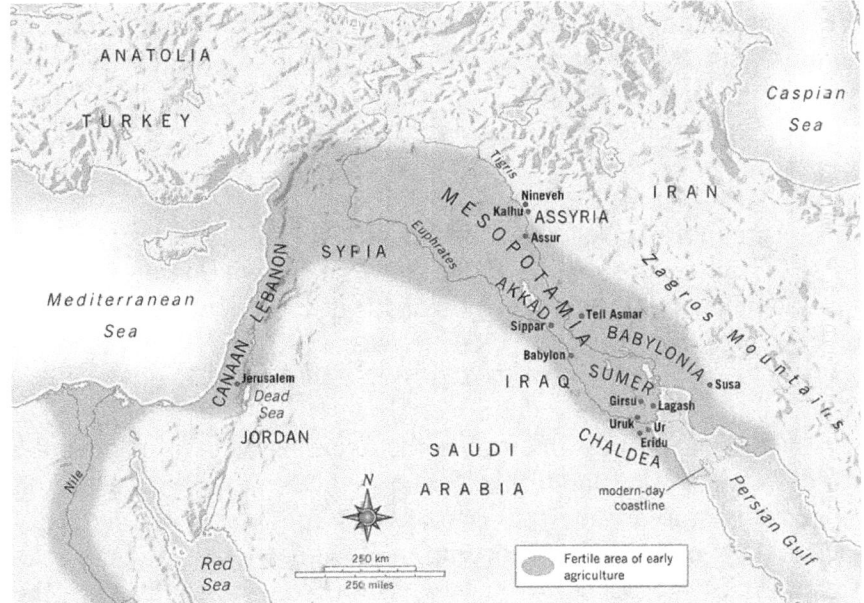

1 FERTILE CRESCENT

While there is much speculation about where the Garden of Eden was, I propose that etymology, specifically the study of place names (toponyms), might hold the key. As stated previously, the garden was encircled with abundant water; I suggest that the main source was the GISHON spring, which still exists today in Jerusalem. It's important to note that the water flowed out of Gishon (Gushon, to Gush forth)[9] and split into 4 headwaters; it was before God created rain; the current Tigris and Euphrates rivers get their source from the mountains, not from a geyser!

Bear in mind that our linguistic journey is estimated to have begun around 6,000 years ago, in the region of the Garden of Eden possibly near Jerusalem. With 1,650 years of development in the

---

[9] GUSH, GEYSER GUSHON, come forth H1521 גִּיחוֹן GîYCHôWN, or (shortened) גִּחוֹן GiCHôUN; from H1518; stream; GuSHon, a river of Paradise; also a valley (or pool) near Jerusalem, Gihon.

GUSH GiYCH IYUC'H SUCK, GEYSER H1518 גִּיחַ GîYaCH or (shortened) גֹּח gôach; a primitive root; to gush forth (as water), generally to issue, break forth, labor to bring forth PUSH, come forth, draw up, take out.

fertile crescent, one might expect significant archaeological remains. But the great flood waters would have destroyed large building projects, like Babel (tower off) and Egyptian pyramids, so all civilizations and towns that have been uncovered are post-flood (2348bc)

An interesting side note is that NOAH should be pronounced No'Ark[10] and means rest; God does have a sense of humor, LOL, he was 600 when the flood came, and on his 601 (7th century) he retired (601), sabbath rest, No'wARK (H1983 וַהֲלָךְ wa·hă·lāḵ. WALK and WORK).

It whispers of a time before the Great Flood, a time when the world was a unified landmass. Some theories propose that during this cataclysmic event, the Earth's tectonic plates dramatically shifted. This movement, according to these accounts, triggered the "fountains of the deep" to burst forth, fundamentally altering the Earth's landscape. The earth became a completely different place with an ice age that followed due to the amount of ash that was in the atmosphere, you can see more on the flood here: LINK.

Noah and the animals (minus the prehistoric creatures) came to rest on Mount Ararat (modern-day Turkey), and his children spawned the three main tribes of man (Tribe comes from three)[11] The Garden of Eden chapter speaks of Haviar,

So please bear this in mind when looking at the proposed PIE origins.

Proto Indo-European root, PIE aka ARYAN root.

The exploration of the Proto Indo-European root, commonly referred to as PIE or ARYAN root, has captivated scholars for centuries. But

---

[10] H5146 נֹחַ Nôach, no'-akh=rest No wARK, to cease work, see walk.

[11] TRIBE, TUATHA, De Dannan Irish "tribe(Tuatha) of the God of Dan H8532 תְּלָת tᵉlâth, tel-awth'; (Aramaic) masculine תְּלָתָה tᵉlâthâh; (Aramaic), or תְּלָתָא tᵉlâthâ'; (Aramaic), corresponding to H7969; three or third, third.

what prompts experts to assert that the origins of the European tongue lie in a Proto-Indo-European (PIE) language, and what are the proposed timelines for its various hypothesized homelands?

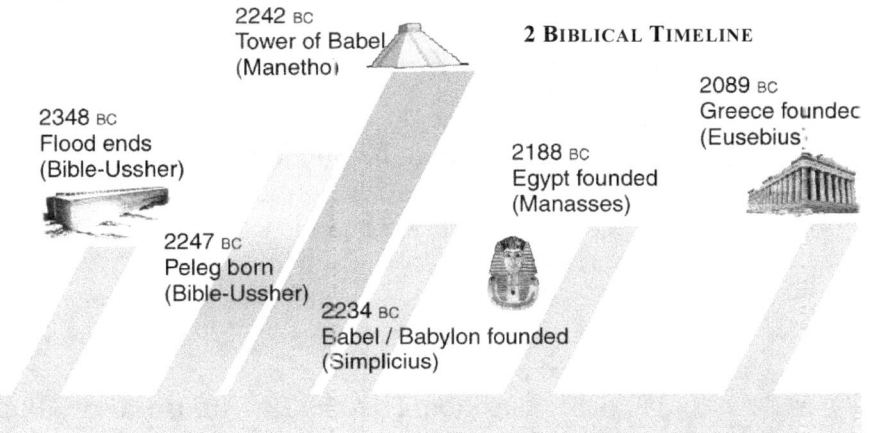

2242 BC
Tower of Babel
(Manetho)

2 BIBLICAL TIMELINE

2089 BC
Greece founded
(Eusebius)

2348 BC
Flood ends
(Bible-Ussher)

2188 BC
Egypt founded
(Manasses)

2247 BC
Peleg born
(Bible-Ussher)

2234 BC
Babel / Babylon founded
(Simplicius)

While there is still much speculation about origins (they are confused Bable[12]), here is the current understanding:

Biblical - Secular timeline.
- Creation 6000 years ago, c. 4000BC
- **Step Pyramid of Djoser** c. 2670–2650 BC (3rd dynasty), Saqqārah necropolis, traditional false date
- Noah (No akh, no wark-rest) 600 when the flood subsided c. 2350BC.
- Peleg, son of Eber, legged it, he split, (Pee and Leg connected to this leg see Pision, Gusher-)[13] 2250BC. (Job 38:25) *cleave* a channel for rain.
- Tower of Babel capital of Babylon, from Hebrew Babel, (confusion) Akkadian bab-ilu "Gate of God" (bab "gate" + ilu "god"). God came down and the elites started talking gibberish 2235BC
- Egypt 1st dynasty 2188 (correct history)

---

[12] Babel, H0894 בָּבֶל Babel baw-bel'; Babylon, Babylonian, Babel- from H1101; confusion; Babel (i.e. Babylon), including Babylonia and the Babylonian empire, Babel, Babylon. H0895 בְּבַל Babel (Aramaic) baw-lal Babylon Babylonian, Babel, H0896 בַּבְלִי Babliy, bab-lee' Aramaic, patr al from H895; a Babylonian, Babylonia.

[13] פֶּלֶג Job 38:25 *cleave* a channel for rain.

- Greece, founding 2090bc

PIE various theories.

1. **The Kurgan Hypothesis**:
   - This hypothesis suggests that the PIE language and culture originated in the Pontic-Caspian steppe. The experts are using various tools to determine who, what, and where these people came from and where they went. Key aspects are as follows: -
   - Male haplo group R1a (Y chromosome) is prevalent due to hunter-gathering and tribal migrations conducted by males. Indicates a Slavic (Russian) and Turkish connection, even though Turkish is not a PIE language, it is a Ural-Altaic Language family and is considered relative to Tungus and Mongolian languages.
   - Horses, wagons, carts, wheels, iron, gold, knives, and daggers, along with the veneration of cows and the use of sheep both in terms of sacrifice and ritual, and they produce, such as wool, meat, and milk are all said to be an intrinsic part of these people, so PIE should be able to piece (link) them together to find the origin of the horse, chariot, wheel, etc. (see Index at end of book for details).
   - The Kurgan culture, associated with this hypothesis, is dated to various phases, with the earliest potentially around 4000 BC and the expansion of these peoples thought to have occurred in several waves, with significant movements happening between 3500 BC and 2500 BC. This hypothesis has many problems in that the dates of archaeological artifacts don't match DNA dates and data. Still, I think the biggest problem is the name, "Kurgan," which is Turkish, and from a completely different language family, i.e., the Altaic family that includes Turkic, Mongolic, and Tungusic language families

and possibly also the <u>Japonic</u> and <u>Korean languages</u> so the PIE origin comes from Kurgan a non PIE root!

2. **The Anatolian Hypothesis**:

   - Proposed by Colin Renfrew, this hypothesis posits Anatolia (modern-day Turkey) as the birthplace of the PIE language. It suggests that the spread of PIE languages coincided with the expansion of farming during the Neolithic period. According to this hypothesis, PIE would have originated around 7000 BC or even earlier, marking it notably older than proposed by the Kurgan Hypothesis.

3. **The Armenian Hypothesis**:

   - This hypothesis suggests that the homeland of PIE was in the Armenian Highlands. It theorizes that the dispersion of PIE languages occurred around 4000 BC or slightly later, with the domestication of horses playing a significant role in their dissemination.

4. **Out of India Theory**:

   - A less mainstream theory proposes that the PIE languages originated in the Indian subcontinent and spread westward. Widely discredited by most linguists and archaeologists due to the lack of substantial evidence, proponents of this theory sometimes date the origin as far back as 7000 BC or around 3000 BC, linking it to Sanskrit and the Vedic period (around 600 BC). However, this theory has been mostly debunked, including claims regarding the Indus Valley civilization and the earliest Brahmi script.

5. **Iran/Aryan Connection**:

   - The connection to Iran specifically pertains to the Indo-Iranian branch of the PIE family rather than the entire family itself. It is believed that the Indo-

Iranians originated in the steppe regions adjacent to the area proposed in the Kurgan Hypothesis, with their languages and culture spreading into the Iranian plateau and the Indian subcontinent. This migration and subsequent differentiation into what would become the Iranian and Indo-Aryan branches are often dated to around 2000 BC or slightly later.

Historians, Archeologists, Linguist and Etymologist, will have a disclaimer like the following: Dates and events are approximate and subject to ongoing research and debate. Advances in archaeological methods, genetic studies, and linguistic analysis continue to refine our understanding of the timelines and movements of ancient peoples, including those who spoke the Proto-Indo-European language.

Anatolian-Hittite, Vedic-Sanskrit, Sanskrit, Greek Kione, Celtic, Germanic, and younger languages like Latin, romance languages, are all said to originate from the Proto Indo-European root (PIE).

The current position of the PIE.

- Despite various theories surrounding Proto-Indo-European (PIE), the linguistic community, particularly etymologists, generally agree on a common root for European languages. This aligns somewhat with the Biblical account of a single, unified language that diversified rapidly at Babel.

- While they propose languages slowly branched from a single root, with extensive timelines to depict this gradual evolution, the assumptions behind this theory are debatable (see previous comment for details).

- They use radiometric dating, believing that it was a consistent decay rate over time; to support this theory they fine tune their instruments using the counting of tree rings. They then use radiometric dating to date the age of the tree. This circular reasoning, has many flaws, for instance tree ring counting, of the bristlecone pine, using older dead pine, along with living pine, and attempt to match tree ring cycles, has been adjusted many times, also there is evidence that tree rings can have more than one season.

- In addition, Carbon-14 dating measures the age of organic materials by comparing the initial and current amounts of Carbon-14, similar to timing with an hourglass. Accuracy depends on knowing the starting conditions' decay rate and ensuring no contamination. If these factors are uncertain, dating results may be incorrect. The various PIE hypothesis uses all three! Radiometric dating issues.

PIE scientists are playing a game of **"pin the tail on the donkey"**; they don't know where the donkey is (which theory is correct), they don't even know what the tail consist of, DNA, Archeological or dating methods. They appear to have thrown the baby out with the bathwater, they are not even using etymology, (word roots) to develop their theories.

For instance, the Kurgan hypothesis, named after a Turkish term for burial mounds, connects these grave sites to a specific DNA signature (R1b) also prevalent in Turkey, but does not connect language, as Turkish is not even considered Proto Indo European, so why use it?

MYLER PIE Hypothesis

While most of the scientist are trying to piece together the story using modern methods, it appears to me they are throwing the baby out with the bathwater. While Dr Jones (father of PIE), did amazing work linking Sanskrit to the Germanic language and somewhat connecting Latin and Greek. The truth is far stranger and one that is told in the Bible.

The cradle of civilization was Mesopotamia, the first city, was built by Nimrod, who was dark skinned, and from Cush (Ethiopia), the real city where the tower of was Babel, was built is most likely Erech (Eridu, Uruk, Iraq), this city is 40 miles northwest of Ur of the Chaldees[14] (,Gen 10:10, 11:31).

Nimrod rebelled against God, and worshiped idols, many reports say Midrash, and book of Jasher) that he, along with, Phut, Mitzraim, Cush and Canaan with their families banded together with Shem and possibly Japhet, to build this tower. Even Terah, (Abraham's father) is involved with Nimrod

The area they worked in was Shiner (Sumer, Sumerians), they rebelled against God and worshiped idols, this is where all the sinners lived in SHINER'town.

MANKIND[15], all worked together and built the "Tower of Babble" Nimrod (from Ham-Cannan had giants), was most likely a giant with mixed seed coming from God and Satan, he built Babylon, and Nineveh and other cities. His name suggest rebellion and he got sons of Shem, and Japheth (along with his own kin) to build a tower a god gate (Akkadian bab ilu means gate of god, bab-ilu=elu El=God).

God came down and confounded the speech (caused us to Babble[16]). The various faction got split off into multiple groups. Most often birds of a feather stick together, the white folks mostly from Shem, (Semites) now had divided tongues and split into multiple group's Medes, Persian, Assyrian etc. they later became known as the Semites, Persians, Medes, Greeks, Romans, Assyrian-Germans, Gaul-Celts.

Sanskrit script, is from Paleo Hebrew (see Chap. 5 The oldest Vedic Sanskrit). Also, the name SANSKRIT, comes from the PIE root *sem, meaning well put together or same, the area of

---

[14] Chaldees was an anachronistic addition like Dan in Gen. 14:14, Abram pursues Lot's captors "as far as Dan." Dan was only established during the time of the Judges (Judges 18:29), the prior name was Laish.

[15] MANKIND, from men-kin(d), 4327מִין mîyn, meen   to portion out; a. species, kind. see H4480. Kind see , KiN Cain H2580

[16] Etymologist unknown- Babble fr H1101 בָּלַל balal, they do trace it to BULL, BLOW.

Mesopotamia was almost completely covered by the SAME, people i.e. sons of Shem, could this be a SIGN, a ZION. Etymologist link of 50 words, to this PIE *SEM root Look at the similitudes, in Biblical Hebrew.

English meaning	Hebrew Word (Transliteration)	Strong's #	Meaning in Context
Symbol	סמל (Semel)	H5566	Symbol, emblem, representation
Image	צלם (Tzelem)	H6754	Image, likeness
Name	שם (Shem)	H8034	Name, identity
Likeness	תמונה (Temunah)	H8544	Form, representation, likeness
Similitude	סימן (Siman)	H226	Mark, sign, token
Garment	שמלה (Simlah)	H8071	Garment, guise, covering
Sign	סימן (Siman)	H226	Mark, sign, token
Mark	סמל (Semel)	H5566	Symbol, emblem, representation
Signpost, sign, mark	ציון (Tsîyûwn)		pillar, sign, title, waymark.
Idol	צלם (Tzelem)	H6754	Image, idol, representation
Shame	שם (Shem)	H8034	Name, reputation, essence
Essence	שם (Shem)	H8034	Essence, core identity
Same (Consider) also HeM)	הם hēm	H1992	They, them, these, ye, same

After Babble, the people of Shiner, along with the Elamites (of Shem) and the Medes were speaking a different language. At this time some from this group would have migrated east to India(H1912 Hindus) and China[17] (Unknown origin-) Much later and possibly

[17] China Qin dydnasty founded in 230 BC, the Qin under King Ying Zheng, Unknown etymology- Bible calls them h5515 סינים Çîynîym, see-neem'; Sinim, a distant Oriental region, possible desert, or thorny wasteland- see h5514 Mount Sinia-baren?

migrated east to India , they would also have mixed with the Median (see fig. 52).

The Medes (middle, median, Mesopotamia)[18], where funding both sides of the war, and they allied to Assyria, Babylon and Persia, each time seemingly gaining more ground till Cyrus the great, (mother was a Median princess), gained power.

Cyrus the great, Darius, and Xerxes[19] were also Persian but the Medes continued to wield, significant influence. The influence on Asia continued to be momentous, and is (I believe) the origin of the Old Indo-Aryan language (Persian-Sanskrit) in the form of Vedic Sanskrit got rolled out eastwards to India and China.

While at a later date many foreigners settled in the country/province of Persia, yet I believe the original settlers of Persian/Aryan/Iranian were Semitic, (Shemite), the founder of which was Elam.[20] Many of the Persian names, come from Hebrew roots Persia=Farci=Pure (pure Aryan root), Aryan=Iran, Persia[21]. If all these names have a Hebrew cognate and identity, then this proves that the Bible and God are correct when he said the language was changed. Shemites / Elamites, where the original Persian, but their language was changed after God confused the tongues.

The Romans where products of or directly from Babylon, and are tied into the Babylonian world system, they are mentioned by Daniel and again in the book of Revelation, and will continue to

---

[18] Middle, Messure, Median – H4077מָדַי Mâday, maw-dah'-ee; (Aramaic) =middle land corresponding to H4075,Median.

[19] Cyrus the Great (559–530 BCE) Darius I (522–486 BCE) Xerxes I (486–465 BCE)

[20] 2 And I saw in a vision; and it came to pass, when I saw, that I [was] at Shushan (Hebrew-Susan lily-H788 שׁוּשַׁן) [in] the palace, which [is] in the province of **Elam;** and I saw in a vision, and I was by the river of Ulai. ... 20 The ram which thou sawest having [two] horns [are] the **kings of Media and Persia.** [Dan 8:2, 20 KJV]

[21] **Aryan=Iran**=compatriot Sanskrit arya- "compatriot;" in later language "noble, of good family." ELAM h5867 (hidden) Aram (H758) and Har (H2022) emphasize elevation, nobility, and highlands, linking to Aryan & Iran ("noble compatriots"). **Persia**=H6539 Pure or splendid, see H1249 בַּר BaR=PURE, clear, sincere , bar; from H1305.

play a role in end time events. Rome's worship of Babylonian gods is well known (again see two Babylon's by Hislop).

The name Rome, Romans, is (said by etymologist to be) unknown, it is mentioned in the Bible in Greek, and is said to mean Strength or make strong (G4514-17). Mozeson, said suggests h7313, or 7315 is the origin for ROAM[22]

The Greeks[23] were from Javan a son of Japheth, but they had many Hebrews scatted amongst them (see WAI). Japheth was also the father of the Medes.

Myler PIE Hypothesis summary.

Tower of Babel as the Cradle of Linguistic Diversity: Humanity, led by Nimrod (a descendant of Ham and likely a giant with a rebellious spirit), unified to build Babylon (Akkadian: Bab-Ilu, "Gate of God"). There are many possibilities for NiMRoD's but the most plausible appears to be EnMaRKaR, Sumerian, Aramaic and Hebrew is mostly a consonantal script (no vowels), so Enmakar would be NMR and KR, where the Kar=hunter in Sumerian, and the D was added to Hebrew to reflect the rebellious qualities of Nimrod[24]. This rebellion against God led to divine intervention, confounding human language and scattering groups across the earth.

Shem's Dominance in Mesopotamia: Prior to Babel, Shemites dominated Mesopotamia. After Babel, distinct linguistic and ethnic groups emerged from Shem, Japheth, and Ham.

---

[22] H7313, rûwm, room; (Aramaic) corresponding to H7311;extol, lift up (self), set up. H7315 רוֹם rôwm, rome; from H7311; elevation i.e. (adverbially) aloft:on high.

[23] H3120 יָוָן Yâvân, yaw-vawn'; probably from the same as H3196; effervescing (i.e. hot and active); Javan, the name of a son of Joktan, and of the race Ionians, i.e. Greeks..

[24] There is a cylinder seal (Old Assyrian period *circa* 2,300 BC) of a hero presenting a new king to the moon-god Sin. The early Sumerian writing in front of the head of the hero (thus labelling him) is KAR.NUN which means the 'Mighty Hunter'. (David Rohl).

It is possible that the sons of Shem, particularly Elamites, migrated eastward and played a foundational role in the development of Vedic Sanskrit, influenced by Paleo-Hebrew.

Sanskrit's Origins: Sanskrit, particularly Vedic Sanskrit, evolved as a structured and sacred language, reflecting its name (sem in PIE, meaning "well-put-together"). This linguistic development reflects the influence of Shemite culture and Hebrew linguistic elements.

Medes as a Central Influence: The Medes (descendants of Japheth), situated in Mesopotamia, acted as intermediaries and power brokers, allying with Assyria, Babylon, and Persia. Their influence extended eastward into India, shaping the Old Indo-Aryan languages, including Sanskrit.

Median influence persisted under the Persian Empire, particularly through rulers like Cyrus the Great, Darius, and Xerxes, despite their Persian lineage.

Rome's Babylonian Connection: Rome, emerging (most likely) from Japhetite peoples, inherited religious and cultural elements from Babylon. This continuity links Rome to the Babylonian world system described in biblical prophecy (Daniel, Revelation).

The worship of Babylonian gods within Rome (Assyrian and Germanic peoples)further emphasizes this connection (as detailed in Alexander Hislop's The Two Babylon's).

Greeks and Japhetite's: The Greeks, descendants of Javan (son of Japheth), inherited cultural and linguistic elements from earlier migrations and interactions with Shemites and Hebrews.

Etymological Observations: The name Rome may derive from Greek (ῥώννυμι, "strength") or Hebrew (רם [RaM], "exalted"). These linguistic roots reflect the city's identity as a center of power and prominence.

For the purpose of tracing PIE, I will focus on the European groups. The Germans aka Assyrians, were bosom buddies with the Romans, this is evidenced by Constantine, setting up second Rome in Germany, namely Trier, which according to tradition is the oldest city in Germany tracing its origin to the Assyrians (see Chap. 6 for more details).

The Assyrian (modern Germans) worshiped all the deities of the Babylonians, actually, they were all Semitic. The Amorites and Canaanites all spoke the same language as the Semitic peoples this is why they are (incorrectly) called Semitic, even though technically they are from Ham[fig52]

Additionally, if you look at the map (Fig. 52) you will notice that the names of the peoples around Babylon, are almost all from the Tribe of Shem, however a team of experts from Ham, Shem and Japhet, seemed to have been assemble, Nimrod (the Ethiopian, Hamite) was the ringleader, they may have assembled to defeat/capture a common foe, a fire breathing dragon, (Seraphim H8314 שָׂרָף sârâph-SeRP'Hnt SERPENT), a physical creature as well as a god worshiped by the Babylonians. Also, the original name of Babble in Akkadian (Semitic tongue) was Bab ilu(to el)=gate of god, it appears that the ziggurat was an attempt to build a portal to the heavenly dimension and God came down and confused the tongue, hence the later name Babble.

The world at this time was unified and sought esoteric knowledge, perhaps Satan and his co-horts, directly communicated with, the folks convincing them to build this portal?

Again, Nimrod appears to be the ring leader and is credited as building Nineveh (Rebellion) and Babylon, (along with other cities) he attempted to get the people to rebel against God. The Hamites were assembled, Shemites, and Japhet, and then God came down divided the speech, i.e. changed their language (Gen 10.2-5).

Eastern and Island peoples are of Japhet, some of Japhet's offspring appear to be white (Russia), others came from Javan, Peleg

(Shem) split into two legs, (he legged it) and the earth became divided at that time ([Gen 10:25](#)).

Cush, Ethiopians, Amorites, Canaanites (Ham), and Shemites, all continued to speak Adamic's (or Edenics, the original tongue).

Again, it appears that most of Shem, Ham and perhaps Japhet, all cooperated in the endeavor to build Babylon, it was so spectacular that even God sat up took notice and said we need to change things up a little.

I believe there was a supernatural element to this, where demons were cooperating to enhance human' knowledge, and perhaps the "tower of Babel" was a gateway to something else? Whatever it was, it caused God to come down and confounded our speech

Is this all there is to it or is there a deeper hidden meaning? My opinion is yes, the Amorites, sons of Ham-Cush-Nimrod, spawned Giants, it is possible that Nimrod himself was a giant and it appears that the seed of Satan, was still in the genetic line of Ham's wife, and some of their offspring were giants (six fingers and toes etc.)

Cush was father of Nimrod (Gen. 10 8), Cush is the father of Ethiopia, which at one point covered a large portion of northeastern Africa. Nimrod was a mighty(giant) hunter. Where did he hunt and gain a famous name for himself? Most likely in north Africa and the fertile crescent's levant an area that encompassed Nile, Euphrates and Tigris rivers. What mighty prey did he hunt? Dinosaurs no doubt, also it appears that Nimrod, ancestors may have set-up Egypt, with some, Assyrian/Elamitic/Shemitic influence.

Early man had many predators that would stalk the earth, is it not only possible but probable that a small number of dinosaurs still existed after the flood. God brought the animals to Noah, he apparently also brought Dragon's, /Dinosaurs, folks in the early days called them DRAGON'S[25] meaning serpent type creature with scales and a tail along with large land creatures although later (19th Cent) they would have been called DINOSAURS[26].

Yes, according to legend, dragons, did indeed survive the flood, (as some were aquatic)[27] many nations tell of encounters with these lizard / snakelike creatures, who were notoriously hard to kill, and

3 SPITTING COBRA - SERPENT

some are said to excrete fire burning their victims. The fire part is still done today, lizard as well as snakes excrete venom, that will burn, and paralyze their victims.

The spitting Cobra, would aim for the eyes and blind their victims, burn their skin and eyes like fire, so to say fire breathing dragons, didn't exist, is just a misrepresentation of the fact. The king James Bible also speaks of Dragon's and fiery serpents, in Num 21:6

And the LORD sent fiery [H8314] serpents among the people, and they bit the people; and much people of Israel died. we Also have for a long time called dinosaurs, dragons, in fact both these terms come from the Bible and the KJ version also calls them

---

[25] DRAGON H 8577 תַּנִּין tannîyr., tan-neen' sea/land monster, see "The word" Moseson.

[26] DINO'SAURS 19th cent H8577, see DINO=DRAGON and SAURUS=H 8317 שֶׁרֶץ sharats, shaw-rats'; a creeping creature, swarmin.

[27] Spinosarus see link.

DRAGON's[28], The Term <u>dinosaurs</u> was coined in 1841, and early dinosaurs were classified correctly as dragons.

Back to Nimrod, it appears that early man had to defend and protect themselves against such wondering beast. If a mighty hunter, had found a way to kill, capture or subdue these creatures he would be in big demand. Also, if you have a common foe people are much more likely to work together.

Dragon-unicorn historical & fossil evidence.

4 DRAGON OF BABYLON

Is there any evidence of dinosaurs/dragons in the upper Nile (Ethiopia) and Babylon?

Rahab, is a sea monster, that God speaks of associated with Egypt, the Nile, and Babylon, symbolic of Satan[29] The Ishtar gate has a depiction of a dragon, with scales like a snake, legs, and body

---

[28] Dragon is a snake, a lion, a flying powerful creature with multiple heads and scales, Satan, SERPENT- 8314 שָׂרָף SâRâP'h(NT), saw-rawf'; PIE *serp- "to crawl, creep". DRAGON H1867 דָּרַךְ dârak, daw-rak' דָּרַךְ ; a primitive root; to, thresh, tread (down). h8577 תַּנִּין tannîyn, H8565; TaN DINO(SAUR) a marine or land monster, i.e. sea-serpent or jackal dragon.

[29]Psa 87:4, Psa 89:10, Isa 51:9

like a lion, paws/claws of an eagle and lion, and mouth of a snake. Amazing as this is we know that Satan is depicted as a snake, dragon, and lion but to roll all these things into a beast before the Bible was written surely this speaks of its authenticity.

Also depicted on the gate are unicorns both these creatures existed in the past both spoken about in the Bible, more on unicorns later.

In 1918, German archaeologist Robert Koldewey, excavator of Babylon, Iraq, observed that the depiction of the fantastical "dragon of Babylon" on the sixth century BCE Ishtar Gate must reference a real animal whose closest relatives would be dinosaurs like the iguanodon.

The search for living dinosaurs was taken up by German-American popular science writer Willy Ley's "romantic zoology" (1941), this led Bernard Heuvelmans (1955), founder of cryptozoology, and later the International Society of Cryptozoologists in Central Africa to find the Mokele-Mbembe, a "living dinosaur. There have been many sightings and reports detailing the exact same creature depicted on the Ishtar gate, are the natives of the Congo, all trying to conspire to make this up? I think not.

What to make of the fact that the Bible claims of behemoth, dragons and dinosaurs, are truly corroborated by scientists, archeology and history. The events of ancient Babylon spoken of in the Bible are true, God came down and confounded the speech of all these folks that came together to build a town. The father of the Romans, Greeks, Egyptians, Hebrews Assyrians Germans were there and most had their speech metathesized (jumbled) see figure 53 and you will see that they all worshiped the same gods but now their names have changed yet the gods' characteristics mostly remained the same. Rome, Assyria and Germany were close allies with Babylon and remained close after the language change. ROME (ROAM), was built on seven hills it is high lifted up, proud, and connected the word GERMAN[30] I talk more about the Roman-Assyrian German connection later, in chapter 7.

Language Test and Connection

In order to prove scientifically whether two languages are connected with a genetic relationship, a structured approach must be followed, notice PIE, originally used this approach with Dr Jones research but current hypothesis, do not use linguistic connection to trace our roots! Talk about throwing the baby out with the bathwater, e.g. the names (Kurgan) they propose for their hypothesis, are not even considered Indo European.

Create Word List Cognates

The objective is to compile a comprehensive list of universally understood meanings, such as "hand," "mouth," and "sky," which form the foundational lexicon across diverse languages. Words are then collected for these meaning slots for each language being considered. Swadesh reduced a larger set of meanings down to 200 originally. He later found that it was necessary to reduce it further but that he could include some meanings that were not in his original list, giving his later 100-item list.

The Swadesh list in Wiktionary gives a total of 207 meanings in a number of languages. Alternative lists that apply more rigorous criteria have been generated, e.g., the Dolgopolsky list and the Leipzig–Jakarta list, as well as lists with a more specific scope; for example, Dyen, Kruskal, and Black have 200 meanings for 84 Indo-European languages in digital form, the list focuses on 200 Hittite words and compares to other PIE, groups with only 100 or less words from each of these compared, it appears that the highest

---

30 ROME ROAM), h7311 רום rûwm, room primitive root; to be high actively, to rise or raise (in various applications, literally or figuratively) bring up, exalt (self), extol, give, go up, haughty. ROAM Old English *ramian "act of wandering about,"possibly related to aræman "arise, lift up." h0758 אֲרָם 'Ărâm, arawm'; highlands of Aram/Syria also grandson of Shem, Possible origin of the word GERMAN, i.e. Aram, (Syria/Damascus).

number of cognates come for Germain and romance languages see below.

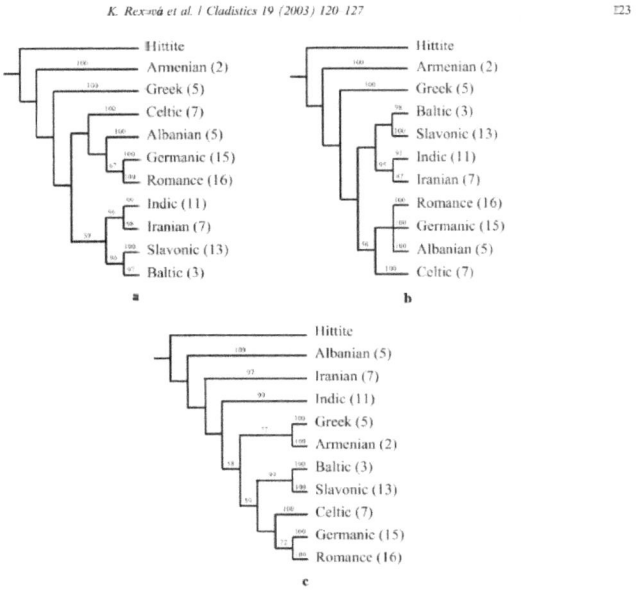

Fig. 1. Phylogeny of Indo-European linguistic groups based on standard multistate matrix (a), altered multistate matrix (b), and binary matrix (c), with bootstrap values indicated above the branches (number of speech varieties per group are in parentheses).

Determine Cognancies

It is thought that a trained and experienced linguist is needed to make cognancy decisions. However, thanks to modern technology, comparing languages has become much more accessible. In the case of Biblical Hebrew, detailed etymology, providing meaning to words, is readily available.

Also many tools are available online to track English word development. Some are in error and don't link words properly; this is clear to me more than ever because I can see words and their use and meaning from 3000+ years ago. This capability proves immensely valuable in establishing cognates.

For instance, all word roots in the Bible link back to 3,2 and sometimes 1-letter roots; out of the 8674 words in the Strongs exhaustive Hebrew concordance, they boil down to about 450-word roots; In fact, of the 8674 current Biblical Hebrew words, there are over 1000 personal names and over 1000 place names, in the Bible. And of the 6000+ other words when the niqqud is removed they reduce to perhaps under 2000 (Niqqud, vowel points added, 7-11th century ad)

When it comes to amateurs delving into cognate research and development, as opposed to trained etymologists, the necessity of formal training might not be as critical, particularly with the assistance of AI and the expanding body of knowledge. Moreover, lexicostatistics does not rely on all the decisions being correct. For each pair of lists, the cognancy of a form could be positive, negative, or indeterminate. Sometimes, a language has multiple words for one meaning, e.g., *small* and *little* for *not big*.

Calculate Lexicostatistic Percentages

This percentage is related to the proportion of meanings for a particular language pair that are cognate, i.e., relative to the total without indeterminacy. This value is entered into an N x N table of distances, where N is the number of languages being compared. When complete, this table is half-filled in triangular form. The higher the proportion of cognac is, the closer the languages are related.

Create Family Tree

The creation of the language tree is based solely on the table found above. While there are several methods for subgrouping, the approach taken by Dyen, Krustal, and Black can be outlined as follows:

- all lists are placed in a pool
- the two closest members are removed and form a nucleus, which is placed in the pool.
- this step is repeated
- under certain conditions, a nucleus becomes a group
- this is repeated until the pool only contains one group

Calculating the lexical percentages of nuclei and groups in this process is imperative.

Applications

A leading exponent of lexicostatistics[31] application has been Isidore Dyen. He utilized it to classify both Austronesian and Indo-European languages with remarkable precision. Dyen, Kruskal, and Black conducted a significant study on Indo-European languages in 1992, employing lexicostatistics to unveil the intricate linguistic tapestry of this language family. Additionally, research has extended to Amerindian and African languages, demonstrating the versatility and applicability of lexicostatistics in diverse linguistic contexts.

Criticisms

Critics, such as Hoijer, have highlighted challenges in identifying equivalents for meaning items, leading to iterative modifications of Swadesh's lists to enhance accuracy and reliability. Gudschinsky raised doubts regarding the feasibility of devising a universal list due to the inherent complexities of linguistic evolution and cultural influences. My personal opinion is that we need to include words of warfare, sex and anger. These words are driven by basic instincts and often travel and retain their original sounds and meaning hence that why I have included them in this work.

Factors such as borrowing, tradition, and taboo can skew the results, as with other methods. Sometimes, lexicostatistics has been used with lexical similarity rather than cognancy to find resemblances. This is then equivalent to mass comparison.

---

[31] **Lexicostatistics** is a method of comparative linguistics that involves comparing the percentage of lexical cognates between languages to determine their relationship

The selection of meaning slots and synonyms remains subjective, further complicating the analysis and necessitating a nuanced approach to linguistic research.

Grimm's and Verner's law

Grimm's and Verner's Law stand as pivotal landmarks in the annals of linguistic development, unraveling the intricate transformations of sound within the fabric of Proto-Indo-European (PIE) and its descendant languages:

Back in the 1820s, one of the brothers, Grimm (yes, of nursery rhyme fame), built on a theory proposed by some of his predecessors. Originally, in 1814, the Danish philologist Rasmus Kristian Rask proposed a connection between European languages. Rask studied many languages and, as a result, started to see a trend where European languages were similar in many respects. In particular, he saw that English *father* and *acre* appear similar to the Latin *pater, ager.* This, and many other examples cause him to think that there was a definite connection between English and Latin and hence Germanic languages and the Latin/romance languages.

Prior to him, the Anglo-Welsh Sir William Jones (1746 – 1794) was perhaps one of the first philologists in the modern era, with the term comparative linguistics coming from his work. He was a gifted linguist and a polyglot (fluent in more than five languages). He proposed a common connection between Germanic, Latin, Greek, and Sanskrit (the precursor to Hindi languages).

In 1786, Oriental Jones, affectionately dubbed "Indi Jones," delivered a seminal address to the Asiatic Society, wherein he articulated the following profound assertion:

More perfect than the Greek, more copious [having more cases] than the Latin, and more exquisitely refined than either, yet bearing to both of them a stronger affinity, both in the roots of the verbs and in the forms of the grammar, than could possibly have been produced by accident; so strong indeed, that no philosopher could examine them all three, without believing them to have sprung from some common source, which, perhaps, no longer exists; there is a similar reason ... for supposing that both the Gothic and the Celtic ... had the same origin with the Sanskrit, and the old Persian might be added to the same family.

What Dr. Jones is saying is that Latin, Greek, and Sanskrit are uniquely tied; he later says that Gothic (Germanic languages), Celtic, and old Persian should be added, since that time the list has increased to 87 languages[32], with Hittite and Tocharian (Chinese) being added.

Dr. Jones is widely regarded as the pioneer of Proto-Indo-European language and comparative linguistics; however, he wasn't the first to conceive of the idea. Nonetheless, he proposed that the language connection stemmed from an invasion into the Indian subcontinent by Aryans (those Germans again).

Grimm's law (also known as the **First Germanic Sound Shift**) is a set of sound laws describing the Proto-Indo-European (PIE) stop consonants as they developed in Proto-Germanic in the 1st millennium B.C. First systematically put forward by Jacob Grimm but first remarked upon by Rasmus Rask. It establishes a set of regular correspondences between early Germanic stops, fricatives, and the stop consonants of certain other centum Indo-European languages (Grimm used mostly Latin and Greek for illustration).

Grimm's Law was the first discovery of a systematic sound change, and it led to the creation of historical phonology as a separate discipline of historical linguistics. The correspondence between Latin *p* and Germanic *f* was first noted by Friedrich von Schlegel in 1806. In 1818, Rasmus Rask extended the correspondences to other Indo-European languages, such as Sanskrit and Greek, and to the full range of consonants involved. In 1822,

---

[32] Albanian, Anatolian †, Armenian, Balto-Slavic, Celtic, Dacian †, Elymian †, Germanic, Hellenic, Illyrian †, Indo-Iranian, Italic, Liburnian †, Ligurian †, Lusitanian †, Messapic †, Paeonian †, Phrygian †, Thracian †, Tocharian †

Jacob Grimm put forth the rule in his book *Deutsche Grammatik* and extended it to include standard German. He noticed that there were many words that had different consonants from what his law predicted, and these exceptions defied linguists for a few decades, but they eventually received an explanation from Danish linguist Karl Verner in the form of Verner's law.

Overview

Grimm's Law consists of three parts which form consecutive phases in the sense of a chain shift.[1] The phases are usually constructed as follows:

1. Proto-Indo-European voiceless stops change into voiceless fricatives.
2. Proto-Indo-European voiced stops become voiceless stops.
3. Proto-Indo-European voiced aspirated stops become voiced stops or fricatives (as allophones).

This chain shift (in the order 3, 2, 1) can be abstractly represented as:

- $b^h \rightarrow b \rightarrow p \rightarrow f$
- $d^h \rightarrow d \rightarrow t \rightarrow \theta$
- $g^h \rightarrow g \rightarrow k \rightarrow x$
- $g^{wh} \rightarrow g^w \rightarrow k^w \rightarrow x^w$

Here each sound moves one position to the right to take on its new sound value. Note that within Proto-Germanic, the sounds denoted by ⟨b⟩, ⟨d⟩, ⟨g⟩, and ⟨gw⟩ were stops in some environments and fricatives in others, so $b^h \rightarrow b$ should be understood here as $b^h \rightarrow b/\beta$, and likewise for the others. The voiceless fricatives are customarily spelled ⟨f⟩, ⟨þ⟩, ⟨h⟩, and ⟨hw⟩ in the context of Germanic.

The exact details of the shift are unknown, and it may have progressed in a variety of ways before arriving at the final situation. The three stages listed above show the progression of a "pull chain," in which each change leaves a "gap" in the phonological system that "pulls" other phonemes into it to fill the gap. But it is also conceivable that the shift happened as a "push chain," where the changes happened in reverse order, with each change "pushing" the next forward to avoid merging the phonemes.

The steps could have also transpired in slightly different manners. An alternative sequence of events might have been:

1. Voiceless stops are allophonically aspirated under most conditions.
2. Voiced stops become unaspirated voiceless stops.
3. All aspirated stops become fricatives.

This sequence would lead to the same end result. This variety of Grimm's Law is often suggested in the context of the glottalic theory of Proto-Indo-European, which is followed by a minority of linguists. This theoretical framework assumes that "voiced stops" in PIE were actually voiceless to begin with, so the second phase did not actually exist as such or was not actually devoicing but a loss of some other articulatory feature such as glottalization or ejectiveness. This alternative sequence also accounts for the phonetics of Verner's law (see below), which is easier to explain within the glottalic theory framework when Grimm's Law is formulated in this manner. Additionally, a change from aspirated stops to fricatives is known to have happened in the transition between Proto-Indo-European and Proto-Italic, so it represents a plausible potential change from Proto-Indo-European to Proto-Germanic.

Improved methods

Some contemporary computational statistical hypothesis testing methods can be seen as enhancements of lexicostatistics, as they employ similar word lists and distance measures.

1. **Computational Linguistics:** Utilizing computer algorithms and computational models to analyze large datasets of

linguistic data, including natural language processing, machine learning, and corpus linguistics.

2. **Cognitive Linguistics:** Examining language from the perspective of how it reflects cognitive processes, such as perception, memory, and categorization, to understand how language is processed and represented in the mind.

3. **Sociolinguistics**: Investigating the relationship between language and society, including language variation and change, language attitudes, and language policy, to better understand how social factors influence language use.

4. **Experimental Linguistics:** Conducting controlled experiments to investigate specific linguistic phenomena, such as language acquisition, language processing, and language production, to test hypotheses and theories about language.

5. **Historical Linguistics:** Using comparative methods and phylogenetic analysis to reconstruct the history and evolution of languages and language families, including the study of language change, language contact, and linguistic reconstruction.

6. **Neuroimaging Techniques:** Employing brain imaging technologies such as fMRI (functional magnetic resonance imaging) and EEG (electroencephalography) to investigate the neural basis of language processing and language-related cognitive functions.

7. **Cross-disciplinary Approaches:** Integrating insights and methodologies from other disciplines, such as psychology, anthropology, computer science, and biology, to gain a broader understanding of language and its role in human cognition and communication.

These enhanced methodologies significantly our comprehension of various aspects of language, spanning its structure and usage to its cognitive and social dimensions.

In summary

Consider the following statement, given to me by AI after an intense discussion on Cognates.

"Two peoples, Aa and Ab, who both stem from the same root A. Over time, Aa and Ab develop distinct languages with different alphabets. Aa writes from right to left, while Ab writes from left to right. Despite these differences, Ab's alphabet retains a closer resemblance to the original alphabet A.

However, the connection between Aa and Ab is not widely recognized by etymologists, leading them to treat Aa and Ab as two distinct languages. Years later, a brilliant researcher named Damian Myler discovers that Aa and Ab have the exact same genetic relationship, tracing back to their common root. When Damian finds words that sound and mean the same in both languages, he would consider them cognates due to their shared origin.

In contrast, standard etymology might label them as false cognates, not recognizing the underlying genetic relationship. This perspective highlights how genetic and historical relationships between languages can reveal true cognates, even when they are not immediately apparent through standard etymological analysis".

I have found during my research that extremely high percentages of cognates are found in the English-Biblical Hebrew comparison. One of my friends believes he has over 80,000, English-Hebrew cognates[33].

Let me give you an example, the word CO'GNATE, comes via the Greek, it means "allied by blood, connected or related by

---

[33] Jew and Linguistic Professor Dr. Issac Mozeson, son of a NY rabbi, who also trained in rabbinical studies, his work "The Word" traces English to Hebrew and he has over 80,000 connections.

birth" (→PIE root *gene- "give birth, beget")   When we trace language back to its ancient beginnings we see that we all came from one man and woman (Adam and Eve), when they had their first blood offspring they called him CAIN, we get the following from this root, KIN, CAIN, GENE, GENE'SIS over 100 words trace to this act H7069[34] (see Cain and Abel chapter 2).

The Celts and Anglo Saxons were brothers, (same tribal members)[35] Additionally, the structural examination of Celtic-Hebrew reveals an abundance of linguistic links, surpassing 23 in number (refer to Chapter 6).

Currently, I have analyzed and documented approximately 4,500 Biblical Hebrew words from the 8,674 words listed in Strong's concordance.

I have noticed that many of our phrases, idioms, and swear words come directly from the Bible, i.e., words we use all the time, swear words, words of war and peace, words of God and good, as well as devil and evil. Words related to farming, agrarian society, woodworking, and construction, also play an important role in language development, in fact the development of the WHEEL, is considered pivotal in transportation and the development of the human race! Guess what it also comes from the Hebrew, I turn my attention to this in Chapter 2.

I contend that these, along with idioms and direct sayings, have transcended space and time, are part and parcel of our language connection, consider the following idioms "you're fired" and "caught between a rock and a hard place" and "drop dead gorgeous,"

---

[34] H7069 קָנָה QâNâH, kaw-naw'; (KIN, GENE) a primitive root; to erect, to have children, i.e. create; by extension, to procure, especially by purchase (causatively, sell);.Gen 4:1 And Adam knew Eve his wife; and she conceived, and bare Cain, and said, I have gotten(birthed, created h7069) a man from the LORD. H7070 קָנֶה QaNE CAIN reed, branch, calamus, cane, stalk, balance, bone, spearmen courtesy *EDN.

[35] Celts and Anglo-Saxons occupied the same territory in Germans, in fact some say that the name German comes from the Celtic root GORIM, -Gar→noisy or , consider H1471 גּוֹי gôwy, go'-ee; rarely (shortened) גּוֹ gôy GoY large group of people, massing easy to see how this developed to noisy, neighbor, see .

phrases nobody can trace, but they come directly from the Bible (see WAI idioms).

Furthermore, consider words like "Jack." Why do numerous names incorporate the term "Jack"? Examples include "Jackhammer," "lifting Jack," "Jackrabbit," and "Jack of all trades." (see WAI for a detailed list) Additionally, our emblems, motifs, coat of arms, royal insignias, flags, and even the Celtic cross serve as undeniable evidence of a genetic language connection.

Later in Chapter 4 we will look at some common words; and at the end I cover others that are currently considered obscene but the Bible uses them, words like Fuxx, Shax, Asshole, Bullshxx, and even the symbols of two fingers and one finger salute, we find these in the Bible also.

Chapter 2

The Story of English

English and Hebrew – are worlds apart, right? But what if there's a surprising connection lurking beneath the surface? While English is undeniably a blend of many languages, could the Bible have played a more significant role than we think?

At first sight, it may seem incredulous to suggest that the origin of English could remotely be connected to Hebrew, but we will find that it is; let's delve deeper.

The earliest settlers in the British Isles are said to be the Firbolg, an aboriginal type people, possibly from Javan[36] Prophecy says Dan will trade with them, Dan who were master mariners and merged with the Phoenicians (see WAI). They came to the British Isles and either merged with or replaced the Firbolg.

According to the chronicles and histories of Ireland (Great Britain), their ancient history goes back to a great flood (Noah) and catalogs the earliest inhabitance of the Islands. The second people, to inhabit this enchanted realm, was the "Tuatha Dé Danann", or its original name Tuatha De, historian and etymologist translated this to mean people or tribe of the God, (of) Danann, being added later. The ancient name was Tuatha De, or Tuatha De Dan, the catholic monks changed the name because it invited a connection to the Danites of the Bible. The name Dan was very prominent in the British Isle and was the name of the ancient hill forts i.e D'N and became every town, and it still survives as TOWN, and DOWN,

---

[36] Gen. 10.4-5says Javan occupied Islands of the Sea , Isa 66.19, said Javan occupied Island far off, and they (Israelites) will decare Gods glory to gentiles will in a distant Island Isa 66.19, also Dan (Tatha de Dannan) will trade together, Ez. 27.9.

even London (lawn'DaN)[37], God instructed Jeremiah to set up hill forts, high heaps, signposts, towns, high pillars (Jer 31:21).

In the Bible the Tribe of Dan's, territory was too small and they ventured out and captured the hill fort of Laish and named it DaN after their father (Jdg 18:29),

In Hebrew and Celtic the meaning of "Tuatha De Dan'ann" means "Tribe (of the) God (of) Dan[38])."

I go into great depth about how they got to Britain in my book "We Are Israel-(WAI).

I would estimate that the Tribe of Dan, along with other Hebrews and Phoenician elements, discovered or perhaps invaded this land pre-Solomonic times (circa 1300-900 B.C.[39]). Deborah recounts in Judges, "*Gilead abode beyond Jordan: and why did Dan remain in ships? Asher continued on the sea shore, and abode in his breaches*" (Jdg 5:17-1235B.C). Furthermore, historical evidence suggests Dan may have been a seafaring tribe from a very early age.[40]

The connection between Israelites and Phoenicians adds another layer of complexity. Dan also interspersed with the Phoenicians, and the Israelites were corrupted by the Phoenicians

---

[37] The Etymology of LONDON, is unknown, it predates the Romans, possibly related to LAND, (Old Irish land, Middle Welsh llan "an open space," - Proto-Germanic *landja) LAWN, (Latin Laudunum, of Celtic origin, Proto-Germanic *landam) appear to be related to LONDON, H3885=luwn, dan=1835ןוול׳luwn D'n luwn D'n Secret dwelling place of Dan, luwn, lodge, murmur, ... the night, abide,
H3885ןול   lûwn,
loon; or לין lîyn; LAND, LANDING, LODGE a primitive root; to stop (usually overright); by implication, to stay permanently
[38] Tuatha-tribe, tribe is from three, three in Hebrew is H8532, תְּלָתָה tᵉlâthâh; (Aramaic), three or third. De is God, German god Tiwaz, old English god Tiw, ie base deiwas, from Hebrew טֵבֵת devath Tê(b)Veth, tay'-beth; Assyrian deity, the tenth Hebrew month, Tebeth. Good (good and god synonymous) H2896 טוב ţôwb, tobe; from H2895 good; Dan one of the Hebrew tribes H1835 דן dân Dan, variant H1839 דָנִי dânî Danite, Dan

[39] Tin ingots found in an ancient ship wreck dating from the time of Solomon and linking Britain with Israel 1300-900BC.

[40] Dan the Pioneer of Israel by Colonel J.C. Gawler

(Semites) and their witchcraft. Another instance of the Israelites-Phoenicians connection was King Ahab, one of the evilest kings of Israel was Ahab. He was married to Jezebel, who was a <u>Zidonian,</u> aka Phoenician.

The Phoenicians, Ashur, Naphtali, and Dan (along with other Israelites) formed the Israelite old navi (O'Ni-and Th'Arish Tharshish)[41]. Their influence extended far beyond their homeland, carrying not just trade goods but also the seeds of their language. But I will not go into the history of the early migrations. At this point, let me summarize the early language. Celtic, Gaels-Gaul's are the French (Reuben). The -Gaulish Normans were Celts) all of them in the ancient past spoke paleo Canaanite-Hebrew-Phoenician-Carthaginian. This fascinating link is explored in greater detail in Chapter 5, providing compelling evidence for the Hebrew roots of the Celtic tongue.

The Celtic people and language are not the only connections to ancient Israel. Our place names, symbols, and idioms also connect us to our ancient past. The Anglo-Saxons, though seemingly distant from the Israelites, also share a surprising connection. As Chapter 7 delves deeper, it reveals that their ancestry can be traced back to Israel, albeit through a period of Assyrian captivity.

I show in the section on the Celts that you can take entire sentences from ancient Hebrew and convert them word for word into Gaelic. While English has undergone significant transformations, shedding vowel structures and prefixes/suffixes of its Celtic and Hebrew roots, a core essence remains. The very framework of these languages and the fundamental "QAL" word root ("daVaRt"), meaning "to speak," persist, fulfilling God's promise to Jeremiah (Jer. 1:7).

---

[41] [41]H590 אֳנִי 'oniy on i-ee, oni(v)ee navy, navy of ships, galley. H8659 תַּרְשִׁישׁ taršîš Tarshish. <u>1Ki 10:22</u>. For the king had at sea a navy of Tharshish [H8659] with the navy of Hiram: once in three years came the navy of Tharshish, [H8659] bringing gold, and silver, ivory, and apes, and peacocks.

Intriguingly, even the English word "word" itself finds its origin in Hebrew – "vart"[42]. This connection strengthens the idea presented in Jeremiah, where God promised Jeremiah that He would make him a BARD and put words in his mouth. He was to form part of the bitter-sweet scroll of Ezekiel and Revelations, where he tore up a nation and kingdom and rebuilt it in another secret hiding place of Yah(see chap. 5). He did this so that the words of God that speak about the kingly line of David, shall never fail (Lia Fail - Stone of Fait), as long as the sun still shines (Jer. 33.17-26). This theme echoes throughout the Bible, even finding resonance in Genesis 28:15.

The story of the English and their people have been a mystery hidden by God for thousands of years, but now God is revealing it to the world (Rev. 10.7). Just as Israel holds a special place in God's heart, the English-speaking world, too, finds itself woven into the divine narrative. He will never abandon us until His grand design reaches its culmination.

Etymology reveals the hidden secrets of English!

The science of etymology uncovers amazing links of where the English and Angles come from.

Let's define the term "English." Traditionally, the narrative goes that "English" is linked to the "Angles," a Germanic tribe who migrated to what is now Britain in the 5th century AD. The word "Angle" itself is believed to be derived from the Old English term "Engle," supposedly meaning "hook" or "land projecting into the sea." This seemingly straightforward connection, however, crumbles under closer scrutiny.

---

[42] Word, debar, Dabar utter var(t) yiddish, wort old German morphed into word in English. H1697 דָּבָר dabar Bard orator Gaelic uwd, (UWᴏrD, WORD, UWt UTTER is also a potential source, 55749 עוּד ʿûwd, ood; a primitive root; to duplicate or repeat; by implication, to protest, testify (as by reiteration); testify, give warning, (bear, call to, give, take to) witness. H5790 עוּת ʿuwth oct'h uwt'h, UTTER, speak.

The French Anglais (Old French Engelsche), and Latin Anglicus, Angle appears to be a modern connection, as the oldest known names for the English are all with an "E."

The venerable (now disgraced) Frisians Bede's in his book on the history of England "*Historia ecclesiastica gentis Anglorum*" *or* "*Gens Anglorum*" for short i.e. the Ecclesiastical history of the English (written in Latin and subsequently translated (731 A.D.). He called the English Anglorum

Intriguingly, the idea that the Angles simply derived their name from a geometric concept just doesn't sit right. There has to be more to it! Let us look closer.

Angles

The familiar terms "England" and "English" have a fascinating origin story intertwined with our Germanic kin. Both terms come from our brothers, the Angels, Saxons, Jutes, and Frisians, who were all known as "Engelisc," i.e., "Engels" or Latinized "Anglican." When we analyze the Latinized version, i.e., "Angles" ," etymologists say it comes from the meaning of "being narrow.". Some say it is from the angle or curve of their land.

In keeping with this theme, Linguistic Professor Isaac Mozeson proposes an origin for the term ANGLE, ie. hook, (hooked land). He correctly links it with ANKLE, and ties it to our patriarch Jacob .

If we look at a foot, the right-angled joint is called the ankle. The origin of the name "ankle" is said to come from the turn or the angle. So, we have the name of the Angles, meaning "curve or bend," and we have the name "ankle," meaning "bend" or "curve."

Angle origin

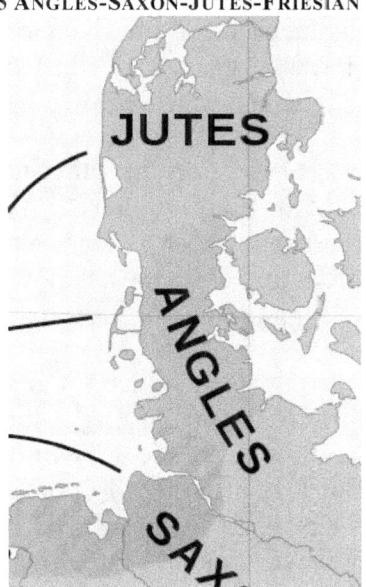

Etymologists, the so called detectives of language history, trace Angle-(Engle) to a Proto-Indo-European (PIE) root, *ang-/*ank- " to bend"[43], let us for a moment accept this premise as being correct, and trace the true origin for ANGLE, ANGLE.

Let's look at Jabo and its etymology. Jacob, also known as Ya'cob, entered the world forever marked by a cunning maneuver. As the story goes, he copped (COP'ed) his brother's heel and, as a result, was called Ya'cob. His name means "deceiver," "supplanter," "to overtake," "to come from behind," "to defraud," or "circumvent." The English equivalent, capturing this essence of trickery, could be "heel" – someone who uses underhanded tactics to "gain an advantage." In addition to ANKLE, and ANGLE, we also developed COP and YANK, from this root, from the father of Israel.[44]

England and English –are pronounced and spelled with an "E," not an "A" as in Angle or Angles, it is said that the word "English "means "of or pertaining to the Angles," from Engle (plural). Here is the problem, the tribe of Angles was never called Angles, they were called Egel, and Engle is the old plural, form. The name Angles is the Latinized form of Egel! Etymologists are tracing a made-up name (latinized form) of Engl and saying that the English comes from the hook or angle of their combined land, this is simply

---

[43] PIE) root, *ang-/*ank- " to bend" (source also of Greek " ankylos limb, " Old English " ancleo – ankle," Old High German "ango – hook")

[44] COP (v) uncertain origin, thought to come from PIE root *kap- "to grasp. YANK to pull or jerk, Etymon root unknown, true origin H3290 יַעֲקֹב Ya'āqôb, yah-ak-obe'; YAnK' KoB-COP from H6117; heel-catcher. עָקַב 'âqab aKoB. ANKLE, ANGLE, PIE root, *ang-/*ank- " to bend" (source also of Greek " ankylos limb, " Old English " ancleo – ankle," Old High German "ango – hook")

wrong. English also was used from the earliest times without distinction for all the Germanic invaders Angles, Saxon, Jutes (Bede's gens Anglorum) and applied to their group of related languages by Alfred the Great!

In addition, other nations, most often, referred to England with an E and not an A[45]. When we look at the origin of the word English, nobody is able to trace it, yet a large part of the Germanic tribes and tongue was known by this name, and it was prior to them settling on the north shores of the Atlantic Ocean, on the Elbe river.

Again we have shown that the name Angles was a Latinized form of the origin Engl, plural Engle, which does not come from the land they occupied, I will explain where Engl comes from shortly. But it is important to point out again that ANGLE ANKLE, even, a'KNUCKLE, KNEE, do have cognates in the Germanic tongue, however none of these begin with an E, but an A. I really cannot stress this enough YOU CANNOT TAKE a LATINIZED version of a word (Engl→Angle) and use angle cognates to determine Engl.

I also delve deeper into this topic in the chapter on Anglo-Saxons (Chapter 6).

The lost ten tribes of Israel and the origins of the Anglo-Saxons (A-S) remain historical enigmas. We will attempt to explain the truth through this book. The Bible reveals that there was an ancient name associated with the northern ten tribes. It's a symbolic name and one mentioned many times throughout the Bible. It is symbolized in the book of Revelations along with Ezekiel, and it is symbolized in the book of Kells and the Celtic cross.

The importance of these symbolic creatures in the Bible is so undeniable that God records them multiple times. In fact, J. Vernon McGee (through the Bible radio) called them the most important prophecy in the Bible. He likened the symbolic representation to the Gospels, Mathew, Mark, Luke, and John. He

---

[45] Dutch - Engelsch, German - Englisch, Danish - Engelsk, French - Anglais (Old French - Engelsche), Spanish - Inglés, Italian - Inglese

was correct in assigning importance to the living creatures; however, he was incorrect in linking them to the Gospels. The images are Man-Reuben, Lion-Judah, Eagle-Dan, and Ox-Ephraim/Manasseh-Joseph. Joseph and his sons were the lead covenant tribes (BRITISH) of Israel, aka Israel.

Contrary to popular belief, the Bible never refers to the Jews as "Israel." Instead, a term/symbol in the Bible connecting Joseph to Aleph (Ox) was the EGEL frisking cows[46]. We speak later in chapter 8 about Joseph and his development of the "aleph-bet." We also cover the Paleo Hebrew, Aramaic Square script, and each letter in depth. I believe the original name for the Engels Saxons, Jutes, and Friesians was Egel[8]. It is recognized that the whole group of Germanic migrants was called Engles. Now, etymology is a science[47]. There is a process to discovering the original root of words. The etymology of English links it with spin. It does not link it with "ankle" or "angle. "I will weave this into the text later. This is important; as I have said the name for England is not the Catholic modified name "Angland," nor do we call the English "Anglish." And while

---

[46] Ox as being the first letter of the alphabet, H504 אֶלֶף 'ELEPH, kine, oxen, family, notice Aleph is not in the Bible it is Eleph.. Egel Egel'ish, notice that the Ayin can be used as A or E, H5695 עֵגֶל 'egel calf, bullock from the same as 5696; a (male) calf (as frisking round), especially one nearly grown (i.e. a steer). Also see, GOAL.

[47] https://www.sciencedirect.com/topics/social-sciences/etymology

The True Origin Of The Engl'ish

Historians and etymologists are unclear about where the Germanic tribes of Angles, Saxons Jutes, and Friesians, came from. They mysteriously showed up in an area that was occupied by the Cumri (Omri H6018)[48] prior to their presence.

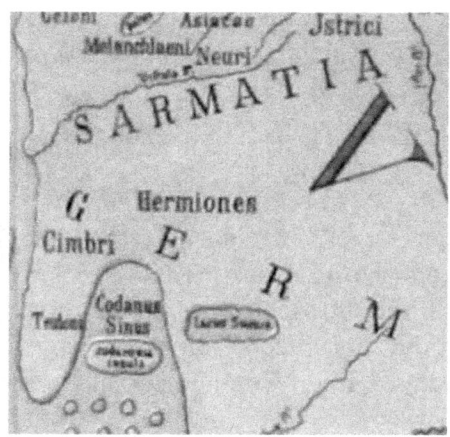

6 POMPONIUS MELA MAP[1]

The term Engl (Engle plural), is again really of unknown origin, the Latinized form is linked to ANGLE and ANKLE, but it's just a theory. In addition, we have another spin applied to Engl's, this involves rotating a moving ball, (put English on it) and while this is a fairly recent term it may have ancient roots.

The ancient Israelites were known as the cowboys, and while almost nobody recognizes this, it is true, as I will explain shortly. Egel H5695 is where we get Engl'land, well at least the first part, with land (I believe) coming from a contraction of LuwnDan, i.e. LuwnD, where the term LAND, LANDING, to take off and LAND, as a pier, jetty, temporary, dwelling, this aligns with Lun in Hebrew with the suffix D being added as in Dan wish is the origin for TOWN and DOWN, LAND temporary dwelling setting DuN for the night! The letter D in Hebrew meant doorway, gate, opening, and entrance, and could indicate why it was added, Etymologist are unsure where LAND came from, and think it's a substratum root

Egel, in Hebrew H5695 (עֵגֶל), is a male calf as frisking round, especially one nearly grown (a steer, bullock). Later we will cover how God speaks of his children and creates a covenant with

---

[48] Omri aka Kumri, see Wales famous king of Samaria H6018עָמְרִי 'Omrîy, om-ree'; from H6014; heaping; Omri, an Israelite

52

them, and how Gods blessing typically falls to the first born, who gets a double portion. The children of Joseph, were the lead covenant tribe, aka BRITISH, (H1285 & H376) and how the symbol of Ephraim (and sometimes Manasseh) is the bull, there are many examples in the Bible of words that we translate as bull, and above I listed the one that we adopted, it is one of our symbols, waymarks, signpost of the providence of God to the children of Israel.

Again, we were the ones who invented the alphabet. Joseph was an amazing man of God and he was very talented (the apple doesn't fall far from the tree, as his father Jacob was a wise Godly man), I am sure he was as Jacked as his father was, and as Douglas Petrovitch discovered when he translated 16 ancient inscriptions Jospeh's sons, Ephraim and Manasseh helped developed this first Alphabet. This means that even the original language came from a Brit![49] It is pretty astounding what God has done with a stiff-necked, bullheaded people!

Back to some more Egel'ish, another derivation of Egel (H5695), is H5696 עָגֹל 'âgôl, aw-gole'; or עָגוֹל 'âgôwl (Ayin, Gamal, Wav/Vav, Lamed)[50] from an unused root meaning to revolve, circular, or round. Also, another interesting point is that when we knock the round circular ball into a net we call it "a goal" (a GOAL of uncertain origin). While we are here let me circle back to the previous word (H5694 עָגִיל 'âgîyl, aw-gheel); (same as H5696); something round, let me put a little English on this billiard ball - aw-gheel' or a wgheel is now a WHEEL[51] (. I hope you're coming around to my way of thinking? We will cover this in more depth later.

---

[49] Brit H1285 בְּרִית berîyth=coveant in Hebrew and was a symbol of Gods providence.

[50] The Ayin ע was one of the letters that formed the early vowel, (see alphabet section) for more details, in this instance, it formed the sound of A or E, depending on its usage

[51] WHEEL is said to come from *Kwel, meaning "revolve, move round; sojourn, dwell" H5696 עָגֹל 'âgôl, aw-gole'; or עָגוֹל 'âgôwl; from an unused root meaning to revolve, circular, round. Pronunciation AGWeL ayin, gimel, wow/vov lamed, truncated to (*kwel) GWeL=Wheel, also root of a GOAL Egahl- see GOAL h5695-matrix at end.

History of the English Language

It was once thought that the Celtic tongue did not survive the blending of languages, however, English has many remnants, of our past, in the form of, Historical Contact, Lexical Borrowings, Syntactical Influence, Toponyms, and Social and Cultural Exchange, in addition the root origin of Celtic and Old English (Anglo-Saxon, A-S) is also from the Hebrew, the A-S came to

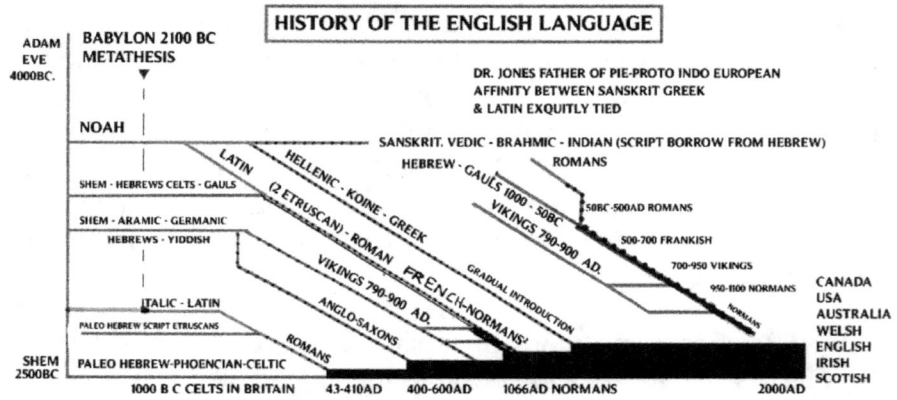

HISTORY OF THE ENGLISH LANGUAGE

ADAM EVE 4000BC. — BABYLON 2100 BC — METATHESIS

DR. JONES FATHER OF PIE-PROTO INDO EUROPEAN AFFINITY BETWEEN SANSKRIT GREEK & LATIN EXQUITLY TIED

NOAH

SANSKRIT. VEDIC - BRAHMIC - INDIAN (SCRIPT BORROW FROM HEBREW)
HEBREW · GAULS 1000 - 50BC · ROMANS
SHEM - HEBREWS CELTS · GAULS
(2 ETRUSCAN) - ROMAN - KOINE - GREEK — HELLENIC
VIKINGS 790-900 AD. — 50BC-500AD ROMANS
SHEM - ARAMIC · GERMANIC
HEBREWS · YIDDISH — 500-700 FRANKISH
700-950 VIKINGS
950-1100 NORMANS
ITALIC - LATIN
VIKINGS 790-900 AD. — FRENCH-NORMANS — GRADUAL INTRODUCTION
PALEO HEBREW SCRIPT ETRUSCANS — ANGLO-SAXONS
SHEM 2500BC — PALEO HEBREW-PHOENCIAN-CELTIC — ROMANS

CANADA USA AUSTRALIA WELSH ENGLISH IRISH SCOTISH

1000 B C CELTS IN BRITAIN   43-410AD   400-600AD   1066AD NORMANS   2000AD

LINES OR DOTS INDICATES HEBREW ALPHABET

SHEM - ASHUR - ASSYRIA PERSIA (LEADER'S - WORSHIPED BARYLONIAN GODS-)GERMANY-ARYAN-VEGAS (SANSKRIT) GERMANIC TRIBES FROM ASSYRIAN CAPTIVITY 721BC.

(1) VIKINGS "DANMARK"- MARK OF DAN (NORSE) - THE VIKINGS (NORSE MEN) MERGED WITH FRENCH TO BE COME NORMANS.

(2) ETRUSCAN - ORIGINAL NAME RASINI - RACE - RESH - HEBREW.CONNECTION

(3) HEBREW - PHOENITIANS GAULS CELTS INTERBRED WHERE OF SHEM AND SPOKE HEBREW.

(4) PERSIAN, IRAN ARYAN HEBREW NAMES. PERSIA= PURE-PARAS-H6540 IRAN ARAM H776 OR ARYAN ARYEN H744 LION ALSO AARON STRONGER NOBILITY IRON, LION, IRANS FOUNDERS WHERE SEMITIC ELAM-H5867

7 ENGLISH LANGUAGE CHART

Britain via a different route, none the less they both contributed to our tongue with its Hebrew root!

God had us sacrifice the Egel for our sins. We worshiped objects that God told us not to, like the golden calf that was also called an עֵגֶל 'êgel, "ay-ghe[52]." This is bad, and we continued this

---

[52] Again notice the A and E interchangeable עֵגֶל 'êgel, ay-ghe H5696 Exo 32:4

evil occupation that was later forced on us by our leaders (sins of Jeroboam-1Ki 14:16).

There were other terms linking this object to us. One of David's wives was called a "g'lah" (H**5698**, a girl). Etymologists don't know where "girl" comes from. The word "gyrle (c. 1300)," or "child," a young person, has the same Hebrew root as Egel(ish) and also relates to a "young calf" and, by extension, a young person, a "girl."[53]

In addition, Sampson called his wife a Heffer (Jdg 14:18), And the men of the city said, *Unto him on the seventh day before the sun went down, What is sweeter than honey? And what is stronger than a lion?*

And he said unto them, *If ye had not plowed with my heifer, ye had not found out my riddle.*

Here, etymology, the science of tracing word origins, becomes crucial by examining how a word is used and its related terms, we can unlock its deeper meaning.

Engel'ish, girl wheel, and goal all connect the origin of Egel. The Americans connect English with a spin! For example, when playing pool, snooker, or billiards, someone might say, "Put some English on the ball." This is also used with other ball games, especially field sports like bowling, tennis, and baseball, and relates to the impressive spinning action. However, some say it's the body English, which appears to come as a result of putting a spin on a ball.

The Hebrew roots offer a massive clue to the origin of "goal." In addition to the meanings already mentioned, the roots are linked in the Hebrew "**to WHEEL**": etymological root *kwel- spin, revolve, move around (GHeeL5694 - circle, ball, spin). **GOAL:** - etymology, narrow, restricted path, hinder, long pole, course. This

---

[53] Liberman (2008) writes: Girl does not go back to any Old English or Old Germanic form. It is part of a large group of Germanic words whose root begins with a g or k and ends in r. The g-r words denote young animals, children, and all kinds of creatures Like H5698 עֶגְלָה 'Eglâh where ah=r

comes from training a heifer for three years using a yoke and plowing a narrow path - (h5696) as in attain, the second noun "to score." Etymon: "place where the ball is" or "object of an effort."

The ox, particularly the young frisking "Egel," played a significant role in Israelite culture. The process of training a bullock to plow took three years, and the young frisking bull (Egel) would be yoked to an older bull for three years. This process is called "goal," and it's where we get the term from. Set yourself a goal, and also kick a circular ball into a net[54]. Again, training a bull for three years was no yoking matter (pun intended).

Symbolically, the ox and the ox head held immense weight, especially for the tribe of Ephraim (mentioned in Deuteronomy 33:17, Numbers 23:8, and Hosea 10:5, 11)[55]. There are a variety of terms linking the bull with Israel/Ephraim and Manasseh, Wheel, hole, goal & frisking bull.

Now, let's go back to the English cowboy connection. The root also identifies the English as cowboys. Wait, hang on just a minute. Americans are known as cowboys because of how they handle cattle, and now you're saying the term English and the sons of Joseph were also known as COWBOYS? Absolutely!

In fact, it got even better. The Celts were also known as cowboys. The elite fighting tribe of Boii, which was in Italy with the Etruscans, occupied the Jutland peninsular and later (after almost complete decimation against the Romans, sees "terror Cimbrian") merged with their brothers from Assyrian captivity. I go into the detail and etymology of the cowBoii's in Chapter 7. The boys (Boii's) almost completely sacked Rome. The Celtic cowboys

---

54 Genesius points out that a young frisking bull would be yoked to an older bull for three years

55 H5694 עֲגִיל 'âgîyl, aw-gheel'; WHEEL from the same as H5696; something round, i.e. a ring, or earring. H5695 עֵגֶל egel calf, bullock from the same as 5696; a (male) calf (as frisking), especially one nearly grown, steer, bullock, calf. Also, see, Goal H5696 עֹגֶל 'âgôl, aw-gole'; or עָגוֹל 'âgôwl; from an unused root to revolve, circular, round Genesius says this term used to train a cow for 3 years GOAL. H5697 עֶגְלָה 'eglah heifer, cow, calf. H5698 עֶגְלָה 'Eglâh, eg-law' 'Eglâh, eg-law'; the same as H5697; Eglah, a wife of David, Eglah GIRL.

H5699 עֲגָלָה 'ăgâlâh, ag-aw-law' same as H5696; something revolving, i.e. a wheeled vehicle, cart, chariot, wagon. H5700 עֶגְלוֹן 'Eglôwn, eg-lawn'; from H5695; vituline; Eglon, the name of a place in Palestine and of a Moabitish king.

56

formed wagon trains that were pulled by oxen, with their women, children, and older family riding inside, while the men mostly rode horses. They would travel thousands of miles in search of greener pastures. They even invaded Greece, and S'AXE'd Greece more on this later.

Returning to the biblical cowboys, the Aleph (ox) symbolized Joseph, and the Sons of Joseph were also known as "UNICORN" (wild ox) and "EGEL" (frisking young bull).

We just showed how the action of a ball spinning and the goal is linked to the bull. Well, guess what the etymon of BALL, BULL, BLOW, BULLOCK, and BALE are all linked with. In fact, PIE links over 100 English words to this root (bhel-2, "blow to swell inflate").

The bull is one of our symbols, waymarks, and signposts of the providence of God to the children of Israel. Again, we were the ones who invented the Alphabet, Joseph was an amazing man of God, and he was very talented (the apple doesn't fall far from the tree). Joseph was jacked with knowledge, just as Jacked as his father, Jack (Jacob), who was a jack of all trades and was really jacked when it came to wrestling.

The noted Professor and Egyptologist Douglas Petrovitch (*The World's Oldest Alphabet*)[56] sheds light on Joseph's inventions which were revealed to him when he translated 16 ancient inscriptions. He also discovered that Ephraim and Manasseh developed the first alphabet.

This, according to the theory, makes the original alphabet (alephbet) a British invention! It's a fascinating notion, highlighting God's work even with those considered stubborn or bullheaded.

Mozeson root בלט H1101 "to flow" or "overflow בָּלַל BaLaL." He links this to "YaBaLL (H2986 יָבַל)," which means "to

---

[56] Dr. Douglas Petrovitch teaches Ancient Near Eastern languages and biblical exegesis, Ancient Near Eastern history (including archaeology, epigraphy, and iconography), Egyptology, and biblical (lower) textual criticism at The Bible Seminary in Katy, Texas.

flow violently." See also "Able, breath and H3999 מַבּוּל, mabbûwl, "deluge."

The Rise of Modern English

We will explore the Celts and Anglo-Saxons. Later (Chapter 6), we'll delve into the fascinating blend brought by the Anglo-Norman invasion. The Anglo-Normans brought an interesting mix (fodder[57]) for the bull-man. It brought Norsemen, Vikings, and Gauls(Celts) that had been intermixed with Latin. It's fascinating that many of the French words link back to old German as well as relate to Roman and Latin.

This continuous blending is what gives English its diversity and strength. It's a language constantly pulled and stretched, with words dropped and new ones added. Scientific, technical, and medical terms often come from Greek, adding a layer of perceived sophistication. Estimates suggest a staggering word count exceeding 100,000.

Many words with 'ph-' prefix are linked to a Greek origin, e.g., *philosophy, physical, photo, phrase, and philanthropy.* Mozeson has linked some of these to Biblical Hebrew[58], remember that Imhotep (Joseph) was a master physician, scholar, engineer, and, stateman, who was deified by the Greeks as the first doctor of medicine, and by the Egyptians (see section on Imhotep Chap. 8).

I want to say the first widely distributed written Bible was the Greek Septuagint (Septuagint→Latin means seventy seviym H7657 Hebrew), written by Jews around 300 B.C. This was the language of all the Jewish synagogues around the world.

The Torah was read in koine Greek, not Hebrew. Scholars agree that Greek, Aramaic, and Latin were the languages of

---

[57]1101 BULL from this (or related root, ie. blow-up) בָּלַל BaLaL, a baw-lal primitive root; (from H1098) to fodder to overflow (specifically with oil.);; to fodder, anoint, confound, mingle, mix. .

[58] E-Word p. 1970 (To)PAZ Pey Zayin, linked to PHOTON, PHOTOGRAPH, PHOSPHATE.

Palestine during the time of Jesus. Hebrew, being a lost language, it appears that the re-writes of the Bible were in Aramaic (with the YHVH written in paleo Hebrews), Greek along with the Aramaic Square Script and some Hebrew, that was only used only liturgically.

Also, in Qumran (Dead Sea Scrolls), it appears that the rewrites of the Bible were in Aramaic and Koine Greek. It is probable that Jesus spoke in Aramaic when he read the words of Isaiah in the temple.[59]

It's even possible that Jesus spoke Greek while reading Isaiah in the temple, and Rabbi Paul's switch to Aramaic when addressing crowds (Acts 21:40 mentions "Chaldee," a dialect of Aramaic) suggests a reverence for the language. The Jews, Rabbis, and learned people think that the script they write in is Hebrew, but it is not. It is called the Aramaic Square Script. It is widely known that Hebrew had been replaced by Chaldee (Aramaic).

In addition, when Jesus alludes to the Scriptures in the Gospels, he usually does so in a manner that agrees with the Aramaic Targum, not the Greek or Hebrew versions. Some examples: In Mark 9:42 50, Jesus warns of judgment by speaking of Gehenna and alluding to Isaiah 66:24, "where their worm does not die, and the fire is not quenched." Notably, "Gehenna" appears only in Aramaic, hinting at the influence of this language on his teachings (further evidence provided later).

This focus on Aramaic highlights the complexities of ancient languages. Because of the difficulty reconstructing the dead language of Hebrew, the Jews (scribes-Rabbis) adopted the niqqud (circa 600ad)-diacritic marks for vowels). This aided their ability to standardize pronunciation. There were three different diacritic systems, all of which caused a deviation in pronunciation. Sephardic (Palestinian), Telmani (Babylonian), and the Tiberian (devised by the Masoretes of Tiberias).

---

[59] The translation of Luke, fits the Septuagint LXX Luke 4:16-19)

In this book, we use the original Paleo Hebrew letters and explore all the forms of the letters. For instance, the Bet (house symbol) can be pronounced as a B or V, and the ayin (eye) takes all 5 vowels, the Yod, Y, J, I, and E, Ian, John, Yon, Eian. The original sound for the Wav was a W, but it also is V. Modern Hebrew lacks the W sound entirely, evident in the pronunciation of "Vodka" (Wodka).

While the New Testament avoids Hebrew citations, Aramaic features prominently. Even Jesus would use it for emphasis (*boanerges, ephphatha, talitha qumi,* (Mark 5:35-43) and *eloi eloi lama sabachthani* (Mat 27:46)).

Much of our English science terms come from the Greek. The man lauded as the father of Greek science, Imhotep, wasn't Greek at all! After his death, he was later worshipped as the God of medicine in Egypt and Greece, where he was identified with the Greek God of medicine, Asclepius. Imhotep wrote extensively on medicine, science, and astrology, so much so that the Egyptians and the Greeks deified him. His name was Joseph, and he was a Hebrew. I speak of him at length in chapter 8.

Yes, the English language is a blend of nations, people, languages, and kingdoms (Rev.10.11).

America, Yank's and Jack.

The term "Jack" holds a surprising connection to American identity. The early English settlers in New England were known as Jacks. It was a common English term for an unknown or lower-class person and may have been derogatory at times. It is still used today in "Every Man Jack." We can also see it in the national flag, the "Union Jack," (union of Jacon) other familiar terms are Jacobite's (Celtic political movement 18c), Jack frost, Jaco lantern, and Jack of all trades. Even the USA and UK Navy were known as "Jack

Tar," interestingly the ancient Israelite navy had a "Tar" in its name, it was a epitaph for a ship, Tar'shish[60].

How did Americans get known as Yanks? Etymologists say they cannot be certain (LOL). There appear to be four contenders (see WAI Yank). After analyzing the four contenders, it has become clear that the most logical explanation is that the New England sellers were called Jack's, and the Dutch traders would call them Yack or Yankle.

Even in Yiddish, "Jacob" is "Yankel," Now, isn't that amazing?

Again this is the origin of ANKLE, ANGLE, YANK, and COP and as supported by Grimm's law (that we discuss in detail later) where sounds produced by the same area of the mouth morph or change over time. These laws show how a "KeL (H6117 עָקֵל 'âqal, the root word from Jacob)" can become "k'hel" and hence a "HEEL."

English is brimming with words linked to our ancestors, the ancient patriarchs. It's no wonder, then, that words associated with Jacob are abundant in English. After all, how many names contain "Jack"? (See WAI for a detailed list).

Who in their right mind would want to associate with being bent or crooked unless they were relating themselves to Jacob's stock?

Good news: There is a much more plausible explanation for the Angle's name. It turns out that the lead British Tribe has a symbol that it uses to signify itself. Its symbol was the ox (a two-horned animal) and the unicorn (a one-horned animal). I will elaborate on these again in WAI in detail. The lead covenantal Tribe of the Brits, Ephraim, is referred to many times in the OT as a bull, and who symbolizes strength and power also happens to be the first

---

[60] H8658Tarshish of unknown etymology, region of stone? king had at sea a navy of Tharshish with the navy (oni-N'I=NavY h590) of Hiram: once in three years came the navy of Tharshish, bringing gold, silver, ivory, apes, and peacocks. [1Ki 10:22 KJV]

letter of the Alphabet (not a coincidence). The aleph is not in the Bible but has been inserted in Psalm 119:1.

"Aleph" itself means "ox" or "bull" in Hebrew. In Deuteronomy 33.13-17, speaking of Joseph, it says, "In majesty, he is like a first-born bull, his horns are like the horns of a wild ox, (unicorn KJV), with them he will gore the nations to the end of the earth."

The term "Israel" and the house of Israel always referred to the northern ten tribes i.e. Ephraim and Manasseh. The term for a frisky bull is "Egel," which is also used when referring to the Brits of the Bible.

A common derogatory English term for a woman is a "cow." It was also used in the Bible. Samson called his wife a "cow" (Jdg 14:18 עֶגְלָה 'eglâh, eg-law' female cow) for revealing the answer to a riddle with which he was testing the Philistines. A few similarities between English American culture and the ancient Hebrews don't automatically mean we are connected. Still, when you add up all the connections that we do have, it's overwhelming evidence.

The term "Angl," or "Aglh," appears in the Bible with a dual meaning. It signifies leaders of the people (Jer 48:34), specifically the people of Israel (Hos. 10:11, Egypt- Jer 48:34, also used for idolatry.

Remember the infamous Golden Calf incident? As the Israelites fled Egypt, they reverted to idol worship. Even while Moses was interceding for us, he was fasting and being disciplined by God himself. We went back to whoring as we did in Egypt. The Golden Calf is called an Egel; even Samaria, with its bull worship, is called Egel.

"He makes them skip like calves, both Lebanon and Sirion. Egel is Hebrew H5695 עֵגֶל ', egel-ay-ghel. It's easy to see how this could also be pronounced "Engl" or "Angle" as in the "Engl'ish, "ish, H376 אִישׁ 'iysh," means man or men in (Psalm. 29:6).

I have surely heard Ephraim bemoaning himself thus: "Thou hast chastised me, and I was chastised, as a bullock H5695 unaccustomed to the yoke… (wild bullock, a unicorn) turn thou me, and I shall be turned; for thou art the LORD my God (Jer. 31:18).

The connection between the Boustrophedon writing style (ox-turning method) and the Israelites is well known in ancient writings, . They believe God foreshadowed this writing method when the Israelites changed their writing direction from the Jews. (It is true that boustrophedon occurred with the English tongue; this is where writing starts from right to left, but when the end of the medium was reached, the writing would turn to left to right form. Hence the ox plow method (boustrophedon) of writing, t n.d.). The calf itself will be taken to Assyria (Hos. 10:6) as an offering to the great king. Ephraim will experience shame; Israel will be ashamed of its counsel (Hos. 10:11). Ephraim is a well-trained calf that loves to thresh, but I will place a yoke on her fine neck. I will harness Ephraim (the ox). Judah will plow; Jacob will do the final plowing. God will use Judah and Ephraim (the Egel'ish) to accomplish his promises, and now we know how he is accomplishing his will. Even in the last book of the Bible, God makes this promise about the Egel'ish:

"But unto you, that fear my name shall the Sun of righteousness arise with healing in his wings, and ye shall go forth, and grow up as calves (h5695 egel) of the stall." (Mal.4.2).

I propose a bold theory: the Angles were our ancestors, descended from Hebrews. My argument hinges on the Assyrian conquest of the northern ten tribes of Israel in 721 BC.

These people migrated westward after successive wars and troubles. They were called by many names: Scythians, Cimmerian, and Gauls until they settled on the angle coast (see previous map). So whether we say their name comes from the right angle (the shape of their land) or we say that it is via their original title, i.e., the egel's (Egel'ish), they are Israelites.

In addition to Joseph developing the Alphabet, along with his sons being known as cowboys and, the Aleph as the first letter (see alphabet), we also have the following symbols linking us to Israel. Therefore I am suggesting that the language of the Hebrews should correctly be called "ENGLISH", (Egel'ish)."

Remember that Jacob made Joseph a coat of many colors, he also blessed his son's before his death. He gave Joseph's sons a double blessing, he did an unusual act, he crossed his arms as he blessed Joe's sons (putting Ephraim above Manassah). I see this process in the name "Coat of Arms"

Coat of Arms first attested to in 11-12th century mid-14c., simply

8 BRITISH COAT OF ARMS

coat (mid-14c.); originally a tunic embroidered or painted with heraldic armorial bearings (worn over armor, etc); see coat (n.) + arm (n.2) and compare Old French cote a armer. Literally an overcoat (surcoat), worn over amour of the knights.

The etymology of "Coat of Arms" comes from the coat (outer garment) and Armour, which was abbreviated to arms.

COAT[61] - Old French cote "Frankish *kottald High ultimate etymologist cannot trace (unknown). From Hebrew H3801 כְּתֹנֶת kᵉthôneth linking to COTTON from Arabic- qutn, a word perhaps of Egyptian.

SURCOAT over amour chain mail - H5630 סִרְיֹן çiryôn, sir-yone' ; for H8302; a coat of mail, brigandine.

ARM, ARMO(U)R, ARMY, HARMONY (PIE *AR) Sanskrit irmah "arm, unit of measurement in Heberew below elbow (H520 Amma), group of skilled people together HARMONY(H525) ARMY (H526-amiy), trained group of people, see also HARD (H714 subdue), in the protective arms of mother (immi army-mama H517).

ROYAL = Is Royal, i.e., Israel means prince, princess, and heir, i.e. ROYALTY to the throne[62]

COAT = Joseph's coat of many colors (H3801 כְּתֹנֶת kutōnet coat, garment, robe)[63]. Crossed Arm = the blessing of Jackob on (See index for names also yad-yard as in the unit of measurement). Arms = the yad, is the (hand), the unit measure, the cubit, which is in Hebrew is H521אַמָּה 'ammâh, am-maw," indicating the arm as a unit of measurement.

The crossed arms refer to the blessing of Jacob on the kids Manasseh and Ephraim, said to be from the St. Patricks and Scottish flags (Gen 48,49).

---

[61] Old French cote "Frankish *kottald High German chozza "cloak of coarse wool the ultimate etymologist cannot trace (unknown). From Hebrew H3801 כְּתֹנֶת kᵉthôneth, keth-o'-neth, or כֻּתֹּנֶת kuttôneth; from an unused root meaning to cover (compare H3802); a shirt, coat, garment, robe, tunic, COTTON from Arabic- qutn, a word perhaps of Egyptian origin, see Aramaic כתן KeeTahN is usually rendered as "flax" or "linen."

[62] HIS ROYAL, ISRAEL from Sarah H8280, H3478 , H3478 יִשְׂרָאֵל Yisra'el yis-raw-ale'; from H8280 (Sarah) and H410; he will rule as God; Jisraël, a symbolical name of Jacob; also (typically) of his posterity, Israel. his royal,highness Jacob and his son's

[63]COAT CLOTH, H5497 סוּת çûwth, cuwth probably from the same root as H4533; covering, i.e. clothing:—clothes. CUT, H5496 כוּת çûwth, cuwth perhaps denominative from H7898; properly, to prick, i.e. (figuratively) stimulate; by implication, to seduce:—entice, move, persuade, provoke, remove, set on, stir up, take away.

The red lion and red hand of Northern Ireland are said to symbolize the Zerah tribe of Judah (see Fig. 13, 14. Some believe the three lions on the Scottish coat of arms represent three "overturns" of the kingdom, starting with Hezekiah and ending with the "Egel'ish" as a final kingdom before the return of the Messiah ("Meshoak," meaning "the anointed one returns").

The unicorn is the wild ox of Ephraim/Manasseh. The harp is the symbol of the house of David; even the name "House of God" in English! Consider "el'bethel," or al Vessel, meaning "holy to God." The chains on the unicorn symbolize servitude to the monarchy. ER is Elizbeth Reigns. Judah became the surrogate father to his son Er, and his name was legally transferred to his son, hence the name Er'ish and Erland.

In summary, the reason the English language is called "English" is due to its connection to the leading tribes of Manasseh and Ephraim, and it is the symbolic representation of the Tribe.

How am I so sure that this symbolic representation is correct and that the people of England are not called "angles" because of an angled piece of land from which they came?

Well, as I have already said, it is the name of the bull that represents Joseph and his sons, along with the emblem or coat of arms of the royal family.

In addition, we have the living creatures of Ezekiel and Revelations, who together symbolize Israel in union with God, partying, having a gig[64] with God for all eternity, in paradise with no pain, suffering, or evil, halleluiah (all hail El-u-Yah), along with the lion, ox, eagle, and man, who altogether represent Israel! (see Fig. 11, Standards of Israel in the desert and the Celtic cross under Chap. 4 the bull's eye section).

Regarding the origins of the British and American peoples, also coming from Shem, I cover the following proofs in this and my other book:- Symbols, idioms, language, culture, artifacts, DNA, archeology, history. mythology, and even the Bible, all point to the fact that "We are Israel" and "English is Hebrew", I summarize these finding in chapter 11

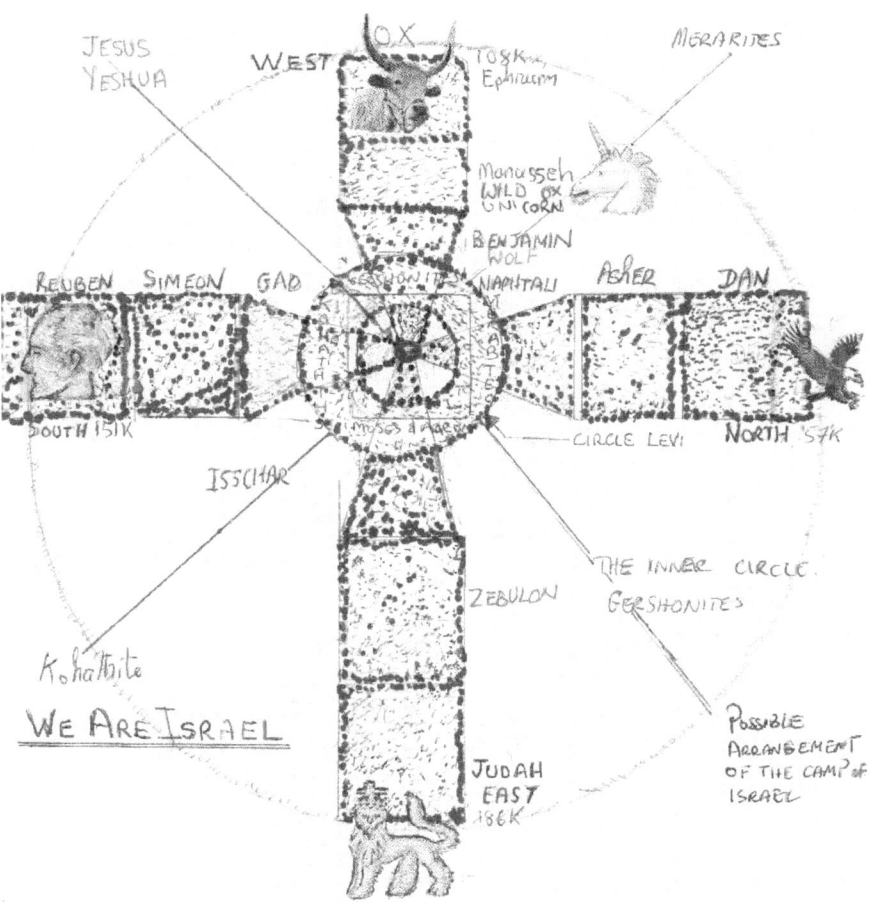

9 NUMBERS 2.2 STANDARDS OF ISRAEL

The scientific, historical, and etymological evidence along with the Bible points clearly to the fact that our original language was Hebrew, and clears up the BABLE, BABBLE that comes from our fearless elites.

Chapter 3

Hebrew - English Names

The next two chapters delve deep into English-Hebrew connections, with so many comparisons it almost resembles a dictionary interspersed with narrative. I haven't been able to come up with a more workable solution!

The Bible suggests a fascinating origin for language – a single, universal tongue spoken by Adam, Eve and their predecessors in its most basic form. God had created all the animals, and he told Adam to name them, so before creation, we didn't have words even for the animals; since God had just created them, this shows that words were very basic and rudimentary; in fact, Strong's Hebrew often identifies words as primitive, like the Hebrew word for sail, gad, about cut, disappear, is, U'ZaL H235 אָזַל ZaL→SAIL[65]
.

The Bible further reveals a world where names hold significant meaning. "Adam" means "red," as in face. He was the first redneck; he was made from the red soil of the EARTH (erets). Also, "dam" is the name of "lifeblood" (blood-red) God says that life is in the blood (Lev. 17:11). Eve's name is not actually in the Bible (like Hebrew); her real name is H2332 חַוָּה(Chet/Het, Wow/Vav, Hey), thought to be pronounced K[H]aVaH and means to show. This is linked to CHEER, and the English toast, CHEERS, (health H2324 Aramaic show, H2421 חָיָה K[H]aYeH, (HiYaH), H1961 HiYaH).

We Brits have a fondness for colorful terms like "dam" and "bloody," and wouldn't you know it, these very words appear in the Bible! "Dam" is where we get the words "dammed" and

---

[65]SAIL→ Dutch zeil, Old High German segal→ZAL H235 U'ZaL אָזַל primitive root to cut-out, to sail, cut from side to side, gad, about, tack to and fro, disappear, other. Etymon unknown suspected PIE root *sek- "to cut," as if meaning "a cut piece of cloth.

"damnation[66]." Aw'dam was the first man to break the covenant of God Brit'am'Yah, and as previously mentioned. Bloodguilt in Hebrew is Mi'damim, "to be dammed"

This connection to "dam" isn't the only British biblical link, Joseph, the chief covenant man (Briton and British), developed the alphabet while in charge of Egypt. This theory is corroborated by Dr. Douglas Petrovich in his book, *The World's Oldest Alphabet.* Petrovich deciphered previously sealed semitic hieroglyphs and determined that Joseph developed the alphabet while in Egypt, and his sons Ephraim (Britain) and Manasseh (America) continued the development. Petrovich deciphered inscriptions that were in the turquoise mines in Seribit, and also inscription off the Farshit road, by the wadi el hol, no joke the Hebrews slaves work in a hell hole, off the far shit road (see chap 9 and 11 for more detail)!

It is also evident from archeology that the prophet Samuel (also British[67]) continued the development; we know this because the script changed from pictograph to Paleo Hebrew. The fascinating and intriguing fact that a Briton not only developed the alphabet but also passed on emblems, symbols, language, culture, and even idioms is certainly a fascinating one.

We will discover the true meaning of many Paleo-English words. Words like "Mary" or "Maria" do not mean "bitterness" or "rebellion" as in "Miriam"; rather, they mean "chosen of Yah," as in "Moriah," marry yah[68] words like "betrothal"[69] come right from

---

[66] DAMN considered an ancient religious term →PIE *dap- "to apportion in exchange, it is bloodguilt from DAM H1818 מִדָּמִים Mi'Damim, (plural Psa 51:14) me dammed

[67] British were Brit, is covenant and ish is man, the lead tribe in Israel was known as the covenant tribe H3050, 5971, h1285 יָה עַם בְּרִית Brit'am'yah Yah am (a) Brit Covenant people of God - h1285 בְּרִית běriyth Brits Covenant people of God - H376 אִישׁ'iysh British man, men, one, husband, any, misc. – Samuel father lived in Ephraim, and was an Ephraimite (1Sam 1.1-2). When the British were kicked out of the promise land that's when the alphabet also stated to leave.

[68] Do anyone believe that the wife of Yah, the chosen of Yah, would be called, bitterness, or rebellion, no they would be called "marry Yah, MARIA, aka MARY, מוֹרִיָה MôWRîYâH, mo-ree-yaw'; or מֹרִיָה Môrîyâh; from H7200 and H3050; Moriah = "chosen by Jehovah"; Morijah, a hill in Palestine, Moriah.

[69] Etymon Be'truth, where Be means surround, enclosure, as in BeYT (BARN BaRley H250 בַּר see alphabet) troth→truth→atroth plural form when two people join, protection, encircling, support→atr

Hebrew, as in "two houses become one," "to crown a royal wedding."

In Ireland, the high kings were crowned on TARA. As I say in "W E Are Israel," The princesses of Zedekiah were brought to ER'land by Jeremiah. One of these married Heremon and was named Teamhair (Tamar, angelized to Tara; Tea is a diminutive of Tamar). Tephi[H6822] is a watchtower (STEPHANY, and STEPHEN)[70] in Hebrew, and a common attribute to castles, both in Hebrew and Celtic use. (see Tea Tephi, index[71]).

TAMAR, and the word. "TIARA" are both Hebrew; the tiara is a woman's crown but is also is a wall of stones, as in "castle".

"Tara", etymologists say is an anglicized form of the Old Irish "Temair" or "Teamhair," which they say is from the Proto-Celtic "*Temris," meaning a sanctuary or sacred space. This word root connects it to the Greek "temenos" and Latin "templum," (TEMPLE), which is of unknown etymology, consider Hebrew H2918 TIRA Castle טִירָה ṭîyrâh, tee-raw'; feminine of H2905; a wall of stones, hence, a fortress or a hamlet, castle, habitation, palace, row, crown, to encircle, wreathe.

The word ALTAR was constructed of dressed or undressed stones (undressed initially for God). Mount Gerizim was a ring of undressed stones that formed the altar and could come from the

---

circle the wagons for protection, H5849 עֲטַר 'âṭar protect/attack crown, see Tiara diadem, crown for a prince or princess (false link → *deru-as "be firm, solid, steadfast") Bet'troth as either a suffix or prefix VSO order changed moving it from a suffix to prefix ie Atroth'bet royal joining of two homes H5854 root is ATaR, for TRUTH, TIARA (crown) & TAR circle, protect encompass.

[70] H6822, צָפָה tsâphâh, (STEPHANY, TEPHI) tsaw-faw' SAW'FAR, (conspicuous SIGN is ZION-H6725 צִיּוּן tsîyûwn, tsee-yoon' Tsee'Yon'der), into the distance, SPhaH, SPY.

[71] H2918 טִירָה tiyrah castle, palace, row, (TIARA same root)habitation h5850 עֲטָרָה 'ăṭârâh, at-aw-raw','ăṭârâh, at-aw-raw'; from H5849; a crown H8559 תָּמָר tāmār Tamar meaning erect, as palm tree (phallic symbol).

Hebrew for a row of stones ATOR[72], where the root TOR[H2905] טוּר means row, and organized arrangement (where we get TOUR from).

Etymologist say ALTAR "to worship, to offer sacrifice, to honor by burning sacrifices to". The process of burning incense and offering prayers to God is called ATaR[H6279] עָתַר.

Note – While it is true that "Tea Tephi" and its story, appear to be a modern construction, yet the ancient bards and histories. like "Annals of the Four Masters", "Ogygia" (O'Flaherty), and Keating's "History of Ireland", (along with others) all echo the same story, i.e. that Tara is connected to Teamhair, as Tea is to Tephi. Which to me appears to be Teamhair=Tamar and Tara=Tara a sacred site, a high mound, a castle, a watchtower (Tephi[H6822]), a place for sacrifice, ALTAR[H6279].

Let us not forget the "Tuatha De" (people of God) of Dan and later Danann, in addition, we still have physical evidence from this history, i.e. Lia Fail, "stone of destiny", that even the curators of Westminster abbey call "Jacob's pillar stone". Is it possible that Etymologist, are completely wrong when they do not look at Hebrew roots?

Even the etymology of ancient places and rivers, and the language connection of Celtic are identical to Biblical Hebrew (see chap. 6) This along with the fact, that our English language boasts thousands of words with direct ties to the Bible. Even holidays, once called "holydays," and the Jewish Holyday Yom (your warm) Kippur, (singular Kapar COVER and CAP) translate directly into English[73].

---

[72] H5849 עָטַר 'âtar, aw-tar'; a primitive root; to encircle (for attack or protection); especially to crown (literally or figuratively, compass, crown. H6279 עָתַר 'ât-har עָתַר 'âthar, aw-thar'; a primitive root from H6281); to burn incense in worship, i.e. intercede, listen to prayer.

[73] YOM is actually from H3117 יוֹם Y'oWM Yud, Wow, Mem used for day, time, chronicles, daily, year etc., Your WarM is the same as Y'WM the Jews added an O. it means to be warmed by the sun. KIPPUR, is the plural, singular KAPHAR, H3722 כָּפַר kaphar and is the day of covering is the origin of the English word KAP and COVER, YOM KIPPUR day of covering. L

71

I will let you be the judge, "Dan" and by the way, the tribe of Dan, means judge in Hebrew, and Dan was prophesized to judge his people (Gen 49. 16-18). The Irish like to get into the police force, the judicial system, and politics, even our current president "Joe Biden" is of Irish descent, who is and was a lawmaker!

God's promises to uproot and replant Israel

The Bible paints a powerful image of God's intervention. God says He will "pluck us up by the roots" and replant us in a new land. A land with a natural border where we will not be disturbed by nations. He promises to pluck his royal bonnie we lads and lassies[74] (Jer. 1:10 KJV). "See, I have this day set thee over the nations and over the kingdoms, to root out (pluck up by their roots)." Over 20 times, God repeats this promise, "to pull up (uproot)," then to "destroy," "throw down," then to "build," and to "plant," but where? The location of this new land remains a lingering question mark, a mystery waiting to be unraveled.

Nineteen times, God speaks about uprooting Israel. "And the LORD rooted them out of their land in anger, and in wrath, and in great indignation, and cast them into another land, as [it is] this day" (Deut. 29:28 KJV).

Even though God uprooted us, he promised not to leave us or forsake us. Why? Because we are His heritage (Joe 3:2, Jer 10:16, Jer 51:19, Isa 19:25, Jer 3:18), we are His portion and His inheritance. He says, "I will not leave you or desert you. I have accomplished everything I have promised" (Gen 28:15). The God is the God of the living, not the dead; he considers Abraham, Isaac, and Jacob to still be alive (Mar 12:26-7).

God designated Ephraim, Joseph's birthright son, as the progenitor of the greatest nation ever, while his brother Manasseh would lead the greatest singular nation (Gen 48:19-20). Ephraim is

---

[74] Binnie H1121 family, Lad-H2056,3206, youth H3208/7, lady, female H5768- וֹלֵל ʻôwlêl, o-lale'; diminutive La'Le LITTLE

a fruitful bull[75]. According to Deut. 33:17 and Jer. 31:18, we will gore the nations to the end of the earth. This, in God's language, is called a covenant (Brit'ish-H1285,376).

The Unicorn and the rainbow are iconic symbols for the English-speaking world. Most people know of the rainbow as a prophecy in the Bible, where God declared that he will not destroy the world by a flood ever again (Gen 9:13. Interestingly, the unicorn symbol appears multiple times in the Bible, representing both fierceness and strength (Nub 23:22, 24:8, Deut. 33:17).

Joseph is also referred to as a cowboy (Egel'ish-H5695), "Joseph is the foal of a wild donkey, the foal of a wild donkey at a spring, one of the wild donkeys on the ridge (Gen.49.17), aka "a cowboy." Where are the sons of Joseph the first to selectively breed, break, and train wild donkeys to become a horse? They appeared on the scene from the region of Arabia at the same time.

We also know that God took Joseph's troubles away when he had his first son— "Manasseh" means "to forget"[76] that God took his troubles away, i.e., out of sight, out of mind.

The Word

"In the beginning was the Word, and the Word (DaBaR) was with God, and the Word was God (John 1:1 KJV)." While this scripture comes to us from the Greek, if it were written in Hebrew, it would use DaBaR.

The spoken word holds deep significance, especially in Hebrew, where God's act of creation involved speaking things into existence. This spoken word is known as "dabar." The Hebrew letter "bet (b)" can also be pronounced as "vet (v)" in German, (Assyrian) which is a Semitic language. The name for "word" in Yiddish is

---

[75] Ephriam fruitful, dual of the masculine form of 672 double fruit; H673 אֶפְרָתִי 'Ephrathiy-e-fruity

[76] H4519 מְנַשֶּׁה MeNaSHsheH "Ma No SHeH," from H5375 נָשָׁא nâsâ', naw-saw, no see, and to, lift off NASA.

"vart," and the older version of this word is "wort." DaVaR truncated to VaR(t), with a hard guttural R, produces a T on release, hence VaR, becomes VaRt, WoRT, then WORDs a probable source of the English origin for "word". Additionally, the Irish words "Dabir" and "brethre" are related to this concept, meaning "word" and "to speak" or "to breathe," respectively. The Gaelic/Irish term "bard" also refers to a speaker or a poet of "da vord" or "da bar[d]. There is a second source that I like better and that is testimony, to give your word, in Hebrew is Ord or Uwd (H5749), this is also bore out in Etymology, German wort, Old Norse orð, Gothic waurd), from PIE *were- (3) "speak, say"[77]

Now we know that WORD comes from Hebrew, but what about the ability "to write"? Now, let's shift focus to the act of "writing.

To write, etymon is said to be from tear, rip, like wripen, but ultimately, they trace it to Proto-Germanic *writan, which means "to tear" or "to scratch," and yet they don't tie it to W/RIPan writa.[78] There is a word in the Bible that fits the bill:- "târaph" seize, TRAP, ensnare, tear to pieces טָרַף T'RaP'H (T) wRiPH RIP, WRITE. [79]

Finally, a touch of symbolism: God declares, "I am the beginning and the end, the Alpha and Omega (A to X [Z])."

And Abram said goodbye to his father's house ta ta[80], goodbye as in the last letter of the Hebrew, the Tav of Ps 119.176 and Gen 20:13, to his family and headed to an undisclosed location over the hills and far away (see WAI page 63-64).

---

[77] Old Irish *Dabir*, Irish: briathar Manx: breear Scottish Gaelic: briathar, meaning word, speech, talk . 2nd option UWD, H5749 עוּד ʻûwd, ood;uwood a primitive root; (Qal) to bear witness, say again and again, to protest, testify, give warning, (bear, call to, give, take to) witness. H1697 דָּבָר DaBaR DaVaR-VaR(t) word, thing, matter, saying, commandment.

[78] To "write "Proto-Germanic *writan, "to tear" W/R'IP RIP or "to scratch," and is also the root of the Old Frisian verb writa, the Old Saxon verb writan, Old High German verb **rizan.** However, the origin of the word outside of the Germanic languages is uncertain. In most Indo-European languages, the word for "write" originally meant "to carve, scratch, or cut," while a few originally meant "to paint."

[79] H2963 טָרַף târaph, taw-raf'; a primitive root; to pluck off or pull to pieces

[80] H8388 תָּאַר ta'ar taw-ar'; H8582/H8376 תָּאָה ta'ah taw-aw' h8582 תָּעָה Ta'ah, Ta'rah

What did the ancient Israelites call their language? Today, we refer to it as Biblical Hebrew or acknowledge its origins with terms like "Paleo-Hebrew script" (explored further in the alphabet section). "Paleo" means ancient or original and reflects the earliest origin of the script and the people of Shem (who wrote it).

In Genesis, it says: "And the whole earth was of one language [H8193-Lip] and of one speech [H1697-daVart-word), Gen 11:1 KJV, see table following."

It wasn't until the Tower of Babel (circa 2200 B.C.), some 1,800 years after creation, that God "confused the speech".

But what was this one tongue/speech called? Based on the fact that today we call the language of the Jews "Hebrew," one would think that this is in the Bible. But originally, there was no specific name given to the language.[81] Abraham was called an IVRI, meaning "he is not from around here, or "over the pond", river or water, its a common theme and term for estuary, gorge, river mouth, like Aberdeen, Avon, Aber'ystwyth, even Inverness it come from the Hebrew root עָבַר 'âbar, (Eber) H5674 origin and meaning of English-Hebrew OVER. The whole land of Cannan spoke the same language, Assyrians, Akkadians, Jews, Phoenicians, and Arabs, all spoke the same language. Later the Canaanite tongue spawned various, offshoots it wasn't until the New Testament that Hebrew also became a language term and it referred to Aramaic(Chaldean), not Hebrew (G1447).

The most common term for God's people in Hebrew is "people," H5971 עַם am. people, nation, folk, Ammi, men, each. This term contrasted with "goy" (H1471 גּוֹי), referencing Gentile nations

---

[81] H762   אֲרָמִי 'Aramiyth Syrian language, Syrian tongue, Syriack (Aramaic-Armenian-Abraham).
H1680   דָּבַב dabab cause to speak,
H1697   דָּבָר dabar word, thing, matter, act, chronicles, saying, commandment, misc, word of God.
H3066   יְהוּדִית Yĕhuwdiyth Jews' language, Jews' speech, first used after the diaspora
H3937   לָעַז la`az strange language
H3956   לָשׁוֹן lashown tongue, language, bay, wedge, babbler, flame, speaker, talkers
H3961   לִשָּׁן lishshan (Aramaic) language
H8193   שָׂפָה saphah lip bank, brim, edge, language, speech, shore, brink, border, side.

and the root of our English words "CROWD" and "CROWDED" and the origin meaning of GWY(dy).

The term "Hebrew" itself appears only 34 times in the Bible (H5680 עִבְרִי `Ibriy or Ivriy) and always designates ethnicity, not language. It is clear that the Bible does not specify that the Israelite tongue is Hebrew. It was a later development. There are times after the diaspora when the Hebrew tongue is called Jewish.[82]

The language of the Hebrews remains a topic of debate. What should we call the language of the Hebrew's? As I mentioned earlier, Joseph developed the alphabet while in Egypt, and the first letter of the Aleph Bet, is his symbol e.g. the OX (aka wild bull UNICORN); the most common term from this was EGEL (5695). I will plow into this later, but I believe that God preordained the English-Hebrew tongue to be called ENGLISH because it comes from EGEL'ISH (cowboy).

Let's look at some more Hebrew-English terms. It is possible that the term "Hebrew" was shortened and truncated to haBri[83], i.e., a bro, meaning kinsman, friend, or companion, in Hebrew.

This theory aligns with the shared structure of English kinship words like "brother," "mother," "father," and "sister." These all follow a base word with the "-ther" or "-ter" suffix, a pattern traceable back to Proto-Indo-European (PIE), the ancestor of many Asian and European languages, including English. The suffixes in these words are related to kinship and family relationships.

For "BROTHER," the base comes from the PIE root *bhrater, which means "brother." This root is also the source for similar words in other languages, such as Latin "frater," Greek "phratér," and Sanskrit "bhrátár."

"Mother" and "father" share a similar origin. The base of "mother" comes from the PIE root *méh₂tēr, while the base of

---

[82] H3066 יְהוּדִית Yᵉhûwdîyth 2Ki 18:26, Isa. 36:11-701 B.C.

[83] H5680 - הָעִבְרִי Ha'Ivri or HaBri(t) patronymic from H5677; an Eberite (he bright, LOL i.e. Hebrew, son of promise) or descendant of Eber.

"father" comes from the PIE root *ph₂tér. Both of these roots feature the "-ter" suffix, which denotes kinship.

Sister stems from the Old English "sweostor" or "swustor," which finds its origins even further back in the Proto-Indo-European (PIE) root *swesor. The "-ter" suffix, in this case, has evolved into "-ster" in Old English and eventually became "-sister" in Modern English.

In summary, the "-ther" or "-ter" suffixes in these English words originate from kinship terms in the Proto-Indo-European language. The similarity in structure highlights the common ancestry and shared roots of these words across various languages.

However, I propose a link to the Bible, considering that "-ther," "-ter," and "-er" suffixes might be derived from a truncated form of the Hebrew words "basar" (flesh) and "sar" (prince or princess, see Sar'ah).

While etymologists say BROTHER comes from Proto-Germanic *brothar and PIE root *bhrater it is clear that the term originated from the Hebrew word "BaSaR" (H1320) it[84], which refers to flesh or kinship! It has the connotation of bringing good news, as a Christian brother, and brotherhood (H1319 בָּשַׂר bâsar, bear, bring, preach, publish).

SHE comes from HE, In Old English, the word for "she" was "heo" or "hio," which was the feminine demonstrative pronoun. In 1300 it transitioned to SHE, the origin is retained in HER→Heo. So just as Eve came from Adam, so SHE→HE. They trace HE, HER, HERE, HIS, IT, SHE, →PIE *ko. Believe it (haha) or not there is an equivalent Hebrew term for this………drum roll please.

---

[84] H1320 בָּשָׂר bâsâr, baw-sawr'; from H1319; compare Arabic بَشَر skin, Syriac axrseb, Assyrian bišru, blood-relation br'er; brethren; brother; bully (n.); confrere; fraternal; fraternity; fraternize; fratricide; friar; friary; pal.

WHO WHOO, hûw', hoo, is the root for SHE THAT, HIM, SAME, THIS, HE, IT, WHICH, WHO, SUCH, WHEREIN.[85] So the SHE→Hio→HE, HER, HERE, HIS, IT, SHE, →~~PIE *ko~~ again traced to Hebrew HUW would have known! [86]

But wait there is more! Just pay shipping and handling and I can supersize this for YE, the masculine plura for H1931 is H1992 הֵם hêm, haym, hêmmâh, or (prolonged) הֵמָּה hêmmâh and form the following English words - THEM, THEMSELVES, THEIR, THEIRS, THEMSELVES, IT, LIKE, HOW, SO, MANY, WHATSOEVER, MORE, AS, SAME, SUCH, THESE, THOSE, WHICH, WHO, WHOM, WITHAL, YE.

Who would have thought that the English term THEM would come from H1992 הֵם hêm, haym, hêmmâh.

How in the world have they kept this hidden from us for all these years, my goodness it blows my mind!

Origin of Language

Language isn't a stagnant pond; it's a vigorous, growing bull. It starts out young and in need of breast milk (מָצַץ H4711 mâtsats, maw-tsats-maw's tits, a primitive root; to suck milk from your mum), and even after it has been weaned, it still needs to be nurtured and fed. Language needed a lot of help in the early days. Adam had to name all the animals and develop names and terms, many of which come from proper names. Language has come a long way since it was first spoken by Adam and Eve some 6,000 years ago.

The naming of all the animals was hard work, so God created a helpmate (Gen. 2.19, an aid h5828). Eve was created. Together, these "two rednecks," as the saying goes ("Two heads are better than

---

[85] H1931 הוּא hûw', hoo; of which the feminine is הִיא hîy' meaning, that, him, same, this, he, she, which, who, such, wherein, most of which is traced to a PIE*Ki or

[86] THEM, THEY, HIM, c. 1200, from a Scandinavian source (Old Norse þeir, Old Danish, Old Swedish þer, þair), originally masculine plural demonstrative pronoun, from **Proto-Germanic *thai.- From Hebrew H1992** הֵם hêm, haym, hêmmâh.

one"), embarked on the monumental task of building human language.

Noam Chomsky, a renowned linguist, proposes a radical theory regarding language origins. He says language did not evolve and did not develop slowly; rather, it jumped suddenly onto the world scene. He basically supports creationism without coming right out and saying it. In *Noam Chomsky-The Emergence of Language*, his YouTube presentation, he says that along with language, there was an explosion of other things, such as astronomical events, that just suddenly appeared.

He basically says that you can take a child from a rural tribe in Africa and bring the child to America, and that person will learn the language and be able to go to university without the need to evolve. Humans have been this way since this massive explosion (he doesn't mention creation but suggests a massive explosion that occurred). In essence, his viewpoint challenges the idea of language evolving over time.

I agree with him that the brain is wired from Day One to speak and communicate, to think, and to develop.

We were made in the image of God, and just as God has the thought and ability to create, so do we. We are unique in the animal world: No other animal can engage in this activity. We did, however, develop language; I differ on using "evolve" here, as it might imply a purely Darwinian process[87].

Religious traditions offer alternative perspectives. Rabbis suggest that Adam was a very primitive and primordial human and that Eve, because she was created from Adam, had a higher intellect. Adam was taken from the red dirt and created. The evidence in etymology does support the view that Adam was a man of few

---

[87] Darwin's theory of evolution by natural selection is God ensuring that the we survive, but to take this and postulate that we all evolved from a primordial soup, is like saying Artificial Intelligence developed by accident by boiling neurons protons and ions, that developed into anodes cathodes, valence bonds, transistors and eventually into printed circuits LOL.

words, whereas it is highly likely (just like today) that Eve did all the talking.

From the word Adam, etymology teaches us that Hebrew was the first language of *erets* (earth) (Gen. 11:1).

And the whole earth was of one language (H8193) and of one speech (Gen. 11.1). Only after the tower of Babble did we start to get other languages (H8193 שָׂפָה sâphâh, שָׂפַת supher suffer and sep'heth, to S'p'h and s'p't, to SPEAK, a speech both come from this root, also SPIT, H8611 תֹּפֶת topheth, to p'het, SPITAL).

While the Bible contains numerous words resembling English terms, it is difficult at times to keep plowing through. In researching this phenomenon, I have done a full extensive root analysis, not just looking at current Hebrew-English cognates, but due to the excessive time required for a full analysis, I offer cognates with the hope that later I can develop a complete Strongs Hebrew-English dictionary, that looks analyses in light of modern etymology.

For now, please see the following words:-

SOD (etymon uncertain origin): "sod" sâdeh, saw-deh, sod, sodded, grass-covered land, soil, h7704 שָׂדֶה sâdeh, *sawd'eh*'; or שָׂדַי sâday; from an unused root meaning to spread out; a field (as flat), country, field, ground, land, soil, wild.

SODOMY SOD and Sodomite, along with Sodomy, are all traced to the Bible. The act of sodomy, spread the shxx around, dirty sod, a clump of grass and dirt, just a piece of dirt, H7704 שָׂדֶה sâdeh, saw-deh, or שָׂדַי sâday; from an unused root meaning to "spread out"; a field (as flat),country, field, ground, land, soil, wild, it's a sad day when God allows wild beasts to invade and sod.

The Book of Genesis, Chapter 10, marks the first appearance of the term "Gentile" (Gowry-:בְּגוֹיֵהֶם bə-ḡō-w-yê-hem. Gen 10.4-5). This reference indicates that God is already distinguishing His people. However, the term "gowry" is where we get the word "crowdy" from because this is the actual meaning (see also H1464 גּוּד gûwd, CROWD, CROWDY).

The term for "tongue" in Gen.10.5 is "H3956 לָשׁוֹן LaShawn, lawsh-own," meaning "your own lash or whip." We have the term tongue-lash, to lash out at someone. The term appears to come from the Hebrew word for Tongue, considered eye lash, from eye and lash.

Adam and Eve

Let's delve into the names Adam and Eve, exploring potential connections to modern English words. With Adam and Eve, we see that Adam was a primitive type of redneck (H120 אָדָם 'Adam aw-dam'; from H119; ruddy, i.e., a human being (an individual or the species, mankind, etc. another, hypocrite, common sort, low, man mean, of low degree, person, *dummy, not very intelligent, red neck, basic type.*

Eve, on the other hand, signifies the "first lady" and the "life-giver." Today, when a woman is pregnant and about to give birth, people hold a baby shower. When a woman's pregnancy starts to become visible, they say she is starting to show. The term "show" in this context, interestingly, shares a root with "shower" (meaning "to rain"), highlighting the metaphorical connection to new life "blooming" or becoming visible.

H2332 חַוָּה Chavvah khav-vaw' *"Chawah"* sound like SHOW'er, or SHOWER" Eve-causatively from H2331חָיָה châyâh, khaw-yaw'; CHEER, CHEERS life-giver; ChaWaH (sometimes pronounce HVaH or angelized to Eve), the first woman, Eve, a primitive root; (compare H2324, H2421); properly, to live; by implication (intensively) to declare or figuratively; causatively, to revive, keep (leave, make) alive, × certainly, give (promise) life, (let, suffer to) live, nourish up, preserve (alive), quicken, recover, repair, restore (to life), revive, (× God) save (alive, life, lives), × surely, **be whole, good health.**

SHOW, CHEER, CHEERS.

81

H7769 שׁוֹעַ shuwa` SHOWER: cry, riches, abundant, libera, opulent tears - from H7768 in the original sense of freedom; a noble, i.e., liberal, opulent; also (as a noun in the derived sense) a halloo, bountiful, crying, rich.

H7778 שׁוֹעֵר or' שֹׁעֵר shôw'êr, SHOW' guard: Someone who made sure that people were clean before entering to see the king, also house of God – active participle of H8176 (as denominative from H8179); a doorkeeper, porter, etc. someone who maintained order before the show commenced, i.e. they got to see the king or access to the Temple, (from the primitive root **to split open, reason out, calculate, reckon, estimate** i.e., can you show me how you did that or got that answer)!

H2324 חֲוָא chăvâ', khav-aw'; CHWA, the vav was anciently a wav, so CHaWA, SHOW (Aramaic) corresponding to H2331; to show, shew.

H2338 חוּט chûwṭ, khoot; CAUGHT, to string together, (Aramaic) corresponding to the root of H2339, perhaps as a denominative; to string together, i.e. (figuratively) to repair, join.

Jewish toast, L'CHAIM, CHEERS.

"L'chaim" (לְחַיִּים) is a Hebrew phrase that means "to life." This celebratory expression is a staple in Jewish culture, uttered when raising a glass. The phrase is composed of two words: "לְ" (l', which means "to" or "for") and "חַיִּים" (chayim, meaning "life"). When raising a glass and toasting, people often say "l'chaim" as a way of wishing **good health**, prosperity, and happiness. This comes from the Hebrew H413 El, ale, in, to, from, here, H0413 אֶל 'êl, ale[88]. Also, there are 6 variants of this word from H408-13:

---

[88] H0413 אֶל 'êl, ale; Preposition-God used everywhere (but only used in the shortened constructive form אֶל 'el); a primitive particle; properly, denoting motion towards, but occasionally used of a quiescent position, i.e. near, with or among; often in general, to:—about, according to, after, against, among, as for, at, because(-fore, -side), both...and, by, concerning, for, from, × hath, in(-to), near, (out) of, over, through, to(-ward), under, unto, upon, whether, with(-in).

See H2332 EVE derivation of the Hebrew word, i.e. life giver comes from H2331חָיָה châyâh, khaw-yaw'; CHEER, CHEERS. CHAIM are said to be from H2425B

H8164 שָׂעִיר sâ'îyr, saw-eer' SHOWER, formed the same as H8163; a shower (as tempestuous), small rain, +other words:

H119 אָדַם âdam, aw-dam'; to show blood (in the face), i.e., flush or turn rosy:—be (dyed, made) red (ruddy) AUTUMN.

H120 אָדָם 'adam aw-dam'; AUTUMN from H119; ruddy, i.e., a human being (an individual or the species, mankind, etc.) another, hypocrite, common sort, × low, man (mean, of low degree), person, *dummy, not very intelligent, red neck, basic type.*

H121 אָדָם Adam aw-dawm'; ADAM, the same as H120; the first man, also of a place in Palestine.

H127 אֲדָמָה 'ădâmâh, ad-aw-maw'; AUTUMN from H119; soil (from its general redness), country, earth, ground, husbandman) land. DEMOCRAT ADaMaH + GHeReTS (Edenics)

H131 אֲדֻמִּים 'Ădummîym, ad-oom-meem'; A DUMMY plural of H121; red spots; Adummim, a pass in Palestine, *A dummy same as H120, low individual, (not smart, i.e., a dummy). Edenics says:-*

H1748 דוּמָם duwmam DUMB, DUMMY, to be silent, quietly wait, dumb.

Hold on, the story gets even more intriguing The "Adummy" becomes the "Aka Dama," or "Akademi," aka "academia." Not so much of a dummy! Through study and meditation, we develop the "Hakah, Dama, AKADEMIA, AKADAMA, AKADAMIAN. "H1970 הָכַר hâkar, haw-kar' primitive root; apparently to injure, by beating, pounding, exploring (see science, to cut open)," dama H1819 דָּמָה dâmâh, daw-maw,

83

imagine, think, silent meditation. So Akadama, akademian comes from the Hebrew to study and meditate[89].

The Fall

The Fall unfolds in the Garden of Eden. The serpent, the most cunning creature God had created, approached the woman with a question laced with deceit: "Did God really say, 'You must not eat from any tree in the garden?'"

The woman said to the serpent, "We may eat fruit from the trees in the garden, but God did say, 'You must not eat fruit from the tree that is in the middle of the garden, and you must not touch it, or you will die."

"You will not certainly die," the serpent said to the woman. "For God knows that when you eat from it, your eyes will be opened, and you will be like God, knowing good and evil."

When the woman saw that the fruit of the tree was good for food, pleasing to the eye, and desirable for gaining wisdom, she took some and ate it. She also gave some to her husband, who was with her, and he ate it as well. The consequence was immediate – the eyes of both were opened, and they realized they were naked, so they sewed fig leaves together and made coverings for themselves (Gen. 3-7).

We ate from the Tree of Knowledge of Good and Evil and got kicked out. But hold on, blame shouldn't solely fall on Adam – Eve was tricked by the serpent, who himself was influenced by Satan (EVIL, H5760 עֲוִיל 'aviy, h5766, 67 עול evell H7843 SATAN שָׂטָן), and God set an angel with a burning sword, that flashed and turned this way then that way and guarding ("GUARDING" comes from "GARDENING" as in fence of trees, hedge about - H1599 גָּנַן GâNaN, gaw-nan'; a primitive root; to hedge about, protect,

---

[89] H1819 דָּמָה Dâmâh , Daw-maw primitive root; to compare; by implication, to resemble, liken, consider, compare, **to think**. Damah'ian to follow God, or to be a student of Yah and grace? Or perhaps to be studious by God's gift? You tell me?

H1598, גִּנְּתוֹן Ginnᵉthôwn, from H1598; GARDENER; *garden town*) the way to the tree of life (H1631, גַּרְזֶן GaRZeN, gar-zen'; from H1629; an axe, wood cutting, also graze, to cut, chew the cud).

Back in the "hedged location" with Adam and Eve, have you pondered the meaning of "engendered"? It's surprisingly common even today, similar to Aw dam.

Please see Chapter 4 crude rude words section for expletives; this is where I will cover words that were commonplace in the Bible up to our expulsion from the Promised Land (721-720 B.C.), words that not only were used every day but that God recorded in the Bible!

Note that back in the primitive past (3,500+ years ago), we were just developing a distinction between ourselves and others, i.e., the way we dressed, Joseph's coat of many colors that later became a plaid and the tartan kilt look (see "We are Israel"-WAI).

Similarly, I think tribal development fostered cultural growth. The term "inner circle" comes from how God set us up in the desert (Nu. 2 also "WAI"). At some point, we developed tribal leaders, and as such, the aristocratic elites were separated from the working class. This was often by our clothes, the way we spoke, our demeanor, etc.

The Aleph (Alpha male) transitioned to mean much more (ALOOF, h441 אַלּוּף 'alluwph) duke, guide, friends, governors, captains, and of course ox. In fact the term to teach comes from the first letter of the Alpha bet, i.e. ALEPH, H502 [90] An alpha male might take the bull by the horns and exert his masculinity.

The Aleph (A) was also numerical and prophetic, = 1, 1000 or multiple thousands. There are a number of times when it pops up, one such incidence was when Abraham and the queen mother Sarah met Abimelech, and he saw how beautiful she was (just like Pharaoh in Gen 15), i.e., how drop-dead gorgeous she was and took her for

---

[90] H502 אָלַף 'âlaph, aw-lof'; (ALPHA in Greek) a primitive root, to associate with; hence, (and causatively to teach)learn, teach, utter.

85

his wife until God gave all his other women "female problems" and shut their wombs. Anyhow, I will not go into all the details here, as I cover these stories in detail in my other book, "WAI." Suffice it to say that Abimelech had a dream where God told him, "You are as good as dead," and Abimelech's response is, "Lord, you know I have not touched her, would you destroy an innocent nation?" This is where we get "drop-dead gorgeous." Notice that Abimelech gives Abraham and ALEPH in response i.e. 1,000 (H505) pieces of silver, so Abraham receives double booty, a double entendre, meaning money, and a lovely wife, I know just another co-incidence (Gen. 20).

And unto Sarah, he said, Behold, I have given thy brother a thousand [H505] [pieces] of silver: behold, he [is] to thee a covering of the eyes, unto all that [are] with thee, and with all [other]: thus she was reproved. (Gen. 20:16 KJV).

We also have a similar situation with Rebekah, clearly, these women were BOOTYFUL!

And they blessed Rebekah, and said unto her, Thou [art] our sister, be thou [the mother] of thousands [H505Aleph אֶלֶף] of millions, and let thy seed possess the gate of those which hate them (Gen. 24:60 KJV).

The Aleph/1000 is a recurring theme and became the symbol of Joseph and his sons Ephraim and Manasseh, but all these events use the same symbol, the ox head, Aleph, the symbol of the tribe of Joseph.

Cain and Abel.

The story of Cain and Abel unfolds in Genesis 4. Cain was the first human to be born. We can pick up the story in Genesis 4.

Adam made love to his wife Eve, and she became pregnant and gave birth to Cain. She said, "With the help of the Lord, I have brought forth (birthed, KIN)[91] a man." Later, she gave birth to his brother Abel.

The narrative opens with a clear distinction between the brothers: Abel tending flocks and Cain working the soil. As time passed, Cain brought some of the fruits of the soil as an offering to the Lord. Abel also brought an offering—fat portions from some of the firstborn of his flock. The Lord looked with favor on Abel and his offering, but on Cain and his offering, he did not look with favor. So Cain was very angry, and his face was downcast.

Then the Lord said to Cain, "Why are you angry? Why is your face downcast? If you do what is right, will you not be accepted? But if you do not do what is right, sin is crouching at your door; it desires to have you, but you must rule over it."

Now Cain said to his brother Abel, "Let's go out to the field." While they were in the field, Cain attacked his brother Abel and killed him.

Then the Lord said to Cain, "Where is your brother Abel?" "I don't know," he replied. "Am I my brother's keeper?"

The Lord said, "What have you done? Listen! Your brother's blood cries out to me from the ground. Now you are under a curse and driven from the ground, which opened its mouth to receive your brother's blood from your hand. When you work the ground, it will no longer yield its crops for you. You will be a restless wanderer on the earth."

Cain said to the Lord, "My punishment is more than I can bear (a fate worse than death). Today, you are driving me from the land (SENTENCE), and I will be hidden from your presence; I will

---

[91] [91] H7069 קָנָה QâNâH, kaw-naw'; (KIN, GENE) a primitive root; to erect, to have children, i.e. create; by extension, to procure, especially by purchase (causatively, sell);.Gen 4:1 And Adam knew Eve his wife; and she conceived, and bare Cain, and said, I have gotten(birthed, created h7069) a man from the LORD. H7070 קָנֶה QaNE CAIN reed, branch, calamus, cane, stalk, balance, bone, spearmen.

be a restless wanderer on the earth, and whoever finds me will kill me."

But the Lord said to him, "Not so; anyone who kills Cain will suffer vengeance seven times over." Then, the Lord put a mark on Cain so that no one who found him would kill him. So Cain went out from the Lord's presence and lived in the land of Nod, east of Eden.

Interestingly, etymology, the study of word origins, offers proof from the fist child born to the human race, we get words like KIN, KIND, KIN'dred, KING, KINGDOM GENE, GEN'ESIS, GENDER, GENERATE GERM, GERMAN (adj.), GERMINATE, PRE'GNANT even COGNATE (CO'GNATE), were birthed by this act of procreation in GENE'SIS. LOL. In fact, etymologists trace over 100 English words from this root. This act of procreation is a smoking gun, direct proof that we didn't come from a primordial soup.

Cain

H7069 קָנָה QâNâH, kaw-naw'; (KIN, GENE) a primitive root; to erect, to have children, i.e. create; by extension, to procure, especially by purchase (causatively, sell);.Gen 4:1 And Adam knew Eve his wife, and she conceived, and bare Cain, and said, I have gotten(birthed, created h7069) a man from the LORD.

H7070 קָנֶה QaNE CAIN reed, branch, calamus, CANE, stalk, balance, bone, spearmen H7014 קַיִן Qayin CAIN, Kenite

H7018 קֵינָן Qeynan Cainan, KENAN

H8423 תּוּבַל קַיִן Tuwbal Qayin TUBALCAIN Gen 4.22 Bronze-Iron age,   *EDN   VOLCANO Tubal-Cain (name) תובל קין [root: VULCAN was the Roman god of fire and metalworking. Vulcan is the source of fiery words like VOLCANO (*EDN) H8423 תּוּבַל קַיִן

G2535 Κάϊν Kaïn CAIN in Greek Bible

G2536 Καϊνάμ Kaïnam land of CANNAN, – to be cained

H7070 קָנֶה qānê reed, branch, calamus, CANE, stalk, balance, bone, spearmen

Many words in the Bible mean KILL, KILLER, consider double entendre at, H3632 כָּלִיל kaliyl (Kiyl) kaw-leel (WHOLE) perfect, wholly, all, wholly burnt, flame, perfection, whole burnt sacrifice, utterly, every whit, whole -from H3634; complete; as noun, the **whole** (specifically, a sacrifice entirely consumed); Wholly acceptable sacrifice that kets KILLED. [92]

Kelly, Jew H3627 כְּלִי kĕliy kel-ee, from H3615-kaw-law-KILLER; vessel, instrument, weapon, jewel, armourbearer, stuff, thing, armor, furniture, carriage, bag, misc, - something prepared, i.e., any apparatus (as an implement, utensil, dress, vessel or weapon), armor (-bearer), artillery, bag, carriage, furnish, furniture, instrument, jewel, that is made of, × one from another, that which pertaineth, pot, psaltery, sack, stuff, thing, tool, vessel, ware, weapon, whatsoever.

KILL THEM, shame them H3639 כְּלִמָּה kĕlimmah kel-im-maw'; from H3637; disgrace, confusion, dishonor, reproach, shame from H3637; disgrace, to wound figuratively, confusion, dishonor, reproach, shame.

HELL, KHELL see KILL H3615 H3622 כְּלוּהַי Kĕluwhay chelluh-c hell from a root meaning to die to pass away, כָּלָה kâlâh, kaw-law' KILL LA h3615

---

[92] *gwelə-, also *gwel-, Proto-Indo-European root meaning "to throw, reach," with extended sense "to pierce." *This made up root forms all or part of*: anabolic; arbalest; astrobleme; ball (n.2) "dancing party;" ballad; ballet; ballista; ballistic; ballistics; belemnite; catabolism; devil; diabolical; discobolus; emblem; embolism; hyperbola; hyperbole; **kill** (v.); metabolism; palaver; parable; parabola; parley; parliament; parlor; parol; parole; problem; quell; quail (v.) "lose heart, shrink, cower;" symbol.
It is the hypothetical source of/evidence for its existence is provided by: Sanskrit apa-gurya "swinging," balbaliti "whirls, twirls;" (see Wheel), Greek ballein "to throw, to throw so as to hit," also in a looser sense, "to put, place, lay," bole "a throw, beam, ray," belemnon "dart, javelin," belone "needle," ballizein 'to dance;' Armenian kelem "I torture;" Old Church Slavonic zali "pain;" Lithuanian galas "end," gėla "agony," gelti "to sting."

Cainine, Arabic pronunciation H3669 כְּנַעֲנִיKĕna`aniy Canaanite, merchant, Canaan, Canaanitess, Canaanitish woman

Cain, get the Cain, humiliate H3667 כְּנַעַן Kᵉna'an, ken-ah'-an; *KNEEL said to be from ANGLE, ANKLE, KnEL from H3665; humiliated; Kenaan, a son a Ham; also the country inhabited by him.

Genetically modified seed H3610 כִּלְאַיִם kil'ayim, kil-ah'-yim; KILLAM, KILL THEM dual of H3608 in the original sense of separation; two heterogeneities, divers seeds (-e kinds), mingled (seed)

Killown: suffer from disease H3630 כִּלְיוֹן KILL'OWN Kilyown kil-yone' a from of H3631; Kiljon, an Israelite, Chilion.

ABEL – Willing and ABLE –

We all know the story of ABEL, he was a giver, he was thankful for the gifts God had given him and he showed it with his sacrificial practices. Doesn't the term "willing and able" captures the sentiments of readiness, capability, and commitment, which can be seen as reflecting qualities like self-sacrifice, love of God, and obedience, that Abel displayed! But surely it's a stretch to link the two? Not if WE ARE ISRAEL and ENGLISH IS HEBREW.

Etymologist don't trace the two words, back to a common root, even though out idiom "willing and able" might suggest a link. The term ABLE is traced from Old French (h)able Latin habilem, habilis "easily handled, apt," " PIE root *ghabh- (ghb-give HabH-HABIT ghABEL) "to give or receive", there are over 40 words from this root, here are a handful, DUTY, EXHIBIT, FORGIVE, GAVE, GIFT, HABIT. Let's put them in a sentence.

ABEL was thankful to God and his GIFT, was a sacrifice, to God, and God FORGAVE him (we all sin) he EXHIBITed his thankfulness with his visible sacrifice. God, in turn GAVE (GIFTed) him peace, and happiness, Able made this a HABIT, his DUTY.

90

Early words stem from actions and historical precedence, it became over time inbuilt, but I think it is more than that, I think it is God-honoring Abel's sacrifice, leaving him a legacy in words!

While the Hebrew word "Abel" does not appear to spawn, the other words, Hebrew words are made up of one-two, and three-letter roots, and ABEL could be split into two words AB'eL, AB[H1] is father in Hebrew as is ABBA, eL[H410] is God and god, ABeL father God, he did send his son as a sacrifice for all, "willing and able" to give his life for US.

An example of a root meaning in Hebrew that comes from the killing of Abel is אבל [H56] mourn, to lament, I'BAWL to cry. We remember the story of Joseph, and his brothers who sold him as a slave into Egypt, and dowsed his coat of many colors with blood and brought it to his father Jacob upon seeing it, "*Jacob rent his clothes, and put sackcloth upon his loins, and mourned[Abel[H56]] for his son many days. [Gen 37:34 KJV]*" We can see that the name ABEL became synonymous with morning.

Etymologist are unsure of the meaning of Abel[H58], they tie it to grassy meadow as in A'BALE, this also could be a metaphor, I suspect Abel was laid to rest in a grassy meadow, and the resting place became synonymous with his grave.

Another version of Abel is HeBeL meaning breath[H1893] הֶבֶל Hebel, HeBLO, BLOW, wind gust, it comes from the root to talk about yourself, vanity, the metaphor "wind bag" (I believe) comes from this root. Did Abel, boast about his relationship with God, to his brother, this sure suggests it? He BELLOWED on and on, till his KIN, CAIN'ed him, he struck him with A'BeLow, (blow) so strong that he sent him BELOW.

The root of the following words are traced to PIE hypothetical root *bhle-, 2 & 3[93] While I think the etymologist have it close on this one I believe the origin is HEBAL or aBel, all of which are linked

---

[93] There is another for of *bhel- (1) which means "to shine, flash, burn," also "shining white", with BLACK and DARK coming from this H1815 דלק d^elaq, del-ak'; (Aramaic) corresponding to H1814, burn.

to "to blow, swell" a surprisingly extensive family, that come from this ancient root, etymologist, trace over 100 words to this root. i.e. HaBeL, or ABeL, here are some BLOW (n) a hard hit with an instrument is of unknown etymology and generally not linked to blow (wind gust of), yet I am saying it is connected in the story of Cain and Abel.

BLOW, BELLOWS, BALL, BALE, BULL, BULLOCKS, BOWL, BAG, BALLOON many, many words are associated with this word. We remember that after Cain, Killed his brother, God stated to him that his BASAR[H1320] BLOOD, cries out from the ground (Gen. 4.10)! From this action we get BLADE, BLEED, BLESS, BLOOD, BLOW. The depth and variety of words associated with "Abel" highlight the fascinating interconnectedness of language.

Abel's Habel, summary:

H56 אָבַל 'âbal, aw-bal'; BAUL,a primitive root; to bewail:— lament, mourn.

H59 אָבֵל 'ABEL aw-bale from H58; a grassy, meadow; A'BALE, ABALE of hay, the name of two places in Palestine, Abel.

H58 אָבֵל ABEL, aw-bale' A'BALE from an unused root (meaning to be grassy); a meadow, plain. Compare also the proper names beginning with Abel. Bale of hay- Aw-bale sees sheaf=bind the hay.

H1893 הֶבֶל Hebel, heh'-bel; (He;BELo-wind, breath) BLOW, BLEW, windbag, the same as H1892; Hebel, the son of Adam, Abel. H1892-הֶבֶל hăbêl; from H1891; emptiness or vanity, **vapor, breath**. H1891, הָבַל hâbal, haw-bal'; a primitive root; to be vain in act, word.

Tubal Cain 3900 B.C. Stone, Bronze, Iron Age.

According to archeologists the Stone, Bronze, and Iron Ages started at different times. In some cases, some areas vastly deviated from the standards that were primarily developed from Europe and the Middle Eastern finds.

Most historians and archaeologists agree that the first true civilizations began to appear around 4,000 BC, with the earliest examples being:

Sumer in Mesopotamia (4,000 BC modern Iraq), is considered one of the oldest civilizations with evidence of writing (cuneiform), cities, and centralized governments.

The Indus Valley Civilization (modern-day Pakistan and northwest India) emerging around 3300 BC with complex urban planning and trade networks.

Ancient Egypt, which also emerged around 3100 BC with the unification of Upper and Lower Egypt, leading to the development of dynasties, monumental architecture, and writing (hieroglyphics).

Göbekli Tepe in Turkey: Dating back to **9600 BE**, this site challenges traditional narratives of early human society, showing that large-scale stone structures existed even before the advent of agriculture. However, it remains an exception rather than the rule, and appears to be an outlier that we cannot currently explain.

The Bible says that man originated 6000 years ago in the Garden of Eden, this view does (mostly) line up with the timelines for man. Around 5900 years ago the Bible records that we had more knowledge and understanding of metallurgy pre-flood.

Tubal-Cain, was born circa 3900BC and the Bible records:

"And Zillah, she also bare Tubalcain, [H8423] *an instructor of every artificer in brass and iron: and the sister of Tubalcain* [H8423] *was Naamah* [Gen 4:22]*"*.

This placement puts him squarely in the Stone Age, which raises some interesting questions.

The biblical passage suggests he possessed advanced metalworking skills that seemingly predate the established timeline for such technology, and it appears that much of what he knew disappeared with him. Perhaps this is why archeologists have such a hard time placing stuff prior to the flood that really wiped out much of the pre-history.

Having said that, we have been lied to—that goes without saying—and you could say, *D'oh*! What was your first clue? Lies about these days, with fake news, but we have a fake history as well. The Founding Fathers of America lived at peace with the Indians and had a peace treaty. The Indians broke the treaty. They also fought with each other and had very inhumane practices, torturous cruel practices, we gloss over this fact. I am not condoning the evil practices of white men, but this country was founded on Judea-Christian principles that many did not live up to.

We also have fake Evolution, and a constructed Proto Indo-European root, that doesn't take Hebrew into account.

Fake-Paleontology

Paleontology, the study of ancient life, including dinosaurs, has captivated imaginations for centuries. The oldest dinosaur fossils are estimated to be around 243 million years old, a staggering timeframe. I have quoted from one of our sterling and most respected institutions, the Smithsonian, an institute that is beyond reproach, right? They would never lie to us or hide any evidence of giants being found in America or elsewhere on the earth, right?

The Smithsonian admits to the destruction of thousands of giant human skeletons, this is a moving target because they keep covering up their tracks. What's all that about? Why would a prestigious institute like the Smithsonian cover anything like this story? I think if we are honest, we all know the answer to that question, which is that the so-called pillars of society have been hiding things from us for a long, long time. Let's take another look at dinosaurs and the evidence found therein. It has been discovered that there was a worldwide flood and that dinosaurs died in mass extinction.

Not only that, scientists have visited every dig site and analyzed the various species found in these millions and millions of year-old strata. Amazingly enough, modern species were found in all the strata levels mixed in with dinosaur bones and absolutely without any evidence of evolution. Check out *The Fossil Record: Proof of Noah's Flood or Evolution*.

Fake-Chronologies

There is no evidence of the Israelites in Egypt. These were done to spawn the idea that the Bible was wrong and no evidence to support the Israelites in Egypt.

Fake-Stone, Bronze, and Iron Age

Below is a statement I found on the web:

The terms Stone Age, Bronze Age, and Iron Age are three classic divisions of history based on the chief material used for tools and weapons at different stages in the history of man.

These eras were first used as classifications for dating artifacts found in Europe. They are not referred to quite as often as they used to be **because, as it turned out, dates varied drastically for the uses of these metals around the world and even among the various parts of Europe more than was first thought** (D'oh, LOL). Some civilizations skipped a period–Sub-Saharan Africa went straight from Stone to Iron, skipping the Bronze Age altogether. American natives never got out of the Stone Age until the era of European exploration.

In *Antiquities of the Jews*, Josephus says, "Tubal exceeded all men in strength, and was very expert and famous in martial performances...and first of all invented the art of working brass." Walter Elwell suggests that his invention of superior weapons may have been the motivation for Lamech's interest in avenging blood.[6]

95

Alternatively, E. E. Kellett suggests that Tubal-Cain may have been a miner.[7]

Ah yes, the lies go deep, but where did they originate? When did the lies start? Let's journey 6,000 years to the Garden of Eden with Adam and Eve in the garden (H1631 גַּרְזֶן garzen-to cut wood GARDENER, GARDEN, h1598 גָּנַן gawnan hedge about-protect).

In those early years, language blossomed from its primitive core. We had a very primitive vocabulary, as stated earlier, and none of the animals had yet been named. Also, many words are interrelated much more than most people think. For example, we will look at the name "Israel." It might hold traces of Sarah ("Sir," Royalty), God's name ("eLl"), hinting at a potential etymology of "I'SiR'AL[94]

Event	Year BC	Year AM
The Creation of the World	4004	1
The World Wide Flood	2348	1657
The Call of Abraham	1921	2083
The Exodus from Egypt	1491	2513
The Foundations of Temple Laid	1012	2992
The Destruction of Jerusalem	586	3421
The Birth of Christ	4	4000

[94] Israel H3478 יִשְׂרָאֵל Yisra'el Israel, Israelites Sarah H8280 H3478, from H8280 (Sarah) and H410; he will rule as God; Israël, a symbolical name of Jacob; also (typically) of his posterity, Israel. his royal, highness Jacob and his son's. Etymon REG, rack stretch H7554 רָקַע râqa', raw-kah' râqa', raw-kah'; a primitive root; to pound the earth (as a sign of passion); by analogy to expand (by hammering); by implication, to overlay (with thin sheets of metal):—beat, make broad, spread abroad (forth, over, out, into plates), stamp, stretch.

Enoch and Anarkim (Anak) giants ANARCHY.

Many folks want are interested in Giant, where they real where they in the Bible, etymology traces them to the ancient Bible reports and reveals hidden meanings "Hididng in plain sight"

Enoch and Anarkim (Anak) giants in the following verses we will discover the origin of the English words: ANARCHY, NECK, CHOKE, CHIN, HANG, JAW, LANKY.

Enoch, a revered figure in the Bible, stands out for his exceptional devotion to God. His life, marked by discipline and righteousness, was so pleasing to God that he bypassed death entirely. The etymology of his name possibly reveals an aspect of his lifestyle.

Enoch = Dedicated (to God). Enoch, see "neck" and choke H2585 חֲנוֹךְ Chanowk khan-oke'; Enoch, Hanoch, Henoch = "dedicated" from H2596; initiated; Chanok, an antediluvian patriarch, Enoch. חֲנוֹךְ Chanowk Enoch, Hanoch, Henoch.

CHOKE ch'(n)'k, Hang, (c)h'n'k -Neck, narrow-train by tasting, see Gesenius H2596 חָנַךְ Chânak, khaw-nak'; a primitive root; (compare H2614) properly, to narrow; figuratively, to initiate or discipline: - dedicate, train up.

HANG, (c)h'n'k, CHOKE-NECK, k'n'k chet nun kuf H2614 חָנַק chânaq, CHAIN (k)haw-nak'; a primitive root (compare H2596); to be narrow; by implication, to throttle, or (reflexively) to choke oneself to death (by a rope), hang self, strangle.

ANARCHY, Anarkim, ananarky, h6062 עֲנָקִים 'Anaqiy – LANKY (giants) an-aw-kee'; patronymically from H6061; an Anakite or descendant of Anak:, Anakim. When a people are not governed by a noble set of laws ANARCHY sets in. The root of anarchy" comes from the Greek word "anarkhia," which means "without rulers."

The word Anakims = "long-NECKED," and long legs, they were a tribe of giants, descendants of Anak, which dwelled in southern Canaan.

10 SUMERIAN SKY GOD-FATHER, AN, AKA, ANU, ANKI.

Anak (a'NeK) means, long NECK עֲנָק 'Ânâq, aw-nawk'; from the h6061 meaning Neck, same as H6060; Anak, a Canaanite.

Anunnaki, Enoch H2585 חֲנוֹךְ cHaNoWKe khan-oke' is said to be the ANUNNAKI referred to in many ancient texts, from H2596; initiated; Chanok, an antediluvian patriarch, Enoch.

FELLER e BULLY, ne phiyl(e) e P'hiy, bully, e fella, aka e fell, bruiser H5303 נְפִיל nᵉphîyl, nef-eel'; or נְפִל nᵉphil; from H5307; properly, a feller, i.e., a bully or tyrant, giant. The etymon of bully said to come from brother lover, is hard to trace. FELL, FALL from great height said to be from *pol PULL down, downfall, downPull.

See also Giants in answers in Genesis this discusses the giants of the Bible.

Noah No Ark =No W'arK

We pronounce the name Noah as "No'ah", but actually the name is Nun Wav Kuf, the closest phonetic spelling is No Ark (H5146 נֹחַ) or No W'arK (H5118 נוּחַ) and means rest. Noah "retired" in his seventh century, paralleling the concept of God's Sabbath rest.

Considering the proven (my book) genetic relationship between Hebrew and English, these connections can be seen as true cognates. Traditional etymology might consider them false cognates due to the lack of a recognized direct linguistic link. However, if these languages share a common root, the phonetic and semantic similarities suggest they are true cognates.

The term 'ark" in English, used in the Vulgate Bible for Noah's ark, means box or chest. It is thought to derive from the Proto-Indo-European (PIE) root *ark- or *arg-, meaning "to hold, contain, guard." The Hebrew word אָחַז ('ArKaZ aleph, chet zayin, H0270), meaning "to seize, to hold, to guard," also illustrates the concept of holding or containing.

Thus, while traditional etymology might not recognize these words as true cognates, a deeper understanding of their historical and genetic connections supports the view that they are indeed cognates.

While this is seen as a satirical play on words interestingly, enough this happens over, and over indicating a deeper connection.

One might argue that metaphors and real words are not cognates, but often real words develop from metaphors, for instance the name for dance in Hebrew is H4234 מָחוֹל mâc'hôwl, MAKE HOLE, dance in a circle, comes from the root H2342 חוּל chûwl, khool (KEL); or חִיל h2427fm-2342 chîyl, CURL, TWIRL, WHIRL, (PIE-*kel=hole) come from this root means spin in a circle, WHEEL comes from a similar root. So dance in Hebrew is a metaphor for make hole mâc'hôwl. I hope you circling around to my way of thinking.

Shem, Semites, and FAME

"Shem was he the father of the white boys? Traditional etymology says he was, although there are indications that other white folks came from Japhet i.e. Russia[95], top of the word, Magog son of Gog- H4031.

The name "Shem" (שֵׁם) held a powerful double meaning: "name" itself and the concept of "fame." The Jews use it as a metaphor for God, The use of הַשֵּׁם (HaShem) and the Tetragrammaton (יהוה, YHWH) in Judaism reflects a deep respect for the sacred name of God. By substituting YHWH with HaShem (the name) in speech and Adonai in prayer. While the earliest texts of the Hebrew Bible show that YHWH was written out and spoken, the tradition of avoiding its pronunciation and using substitutes developed over time. This change became more pronounced after the Babylonian exile and during the time of Ezra, continuing through the post-exilic period into Rabbinic Judaism and onward.

In addition, as time passed, SHEM's name was adopted to refer to the group of people known as 'Semites, i.e. Jews, even though the Assyrian-Germans are Semitic, they instigated the holocaust, as the ancient Assyrians did to the Hebrews.

I believe we get NAME, from SHEM, sHEM, (shin mem, again as most often happens even our current definition of NAME, completely matched the Biblical one

While the Etymon for NAME (v.) is traced via to Old English namian "to bestow a particular name upon, call, mention by name; nominate, appoint," from Proto-Germanic *nōmōjanan Old Frisian nomia "to name, call," to PIE *no-men

We say "make a name" for yourself, the "NAME" is synonymous with "FAME" both of which are embodied in the title

---

[95]Reshe H7220 ראשׁ ROSHe Israelite and foreign nation, ie Russia, see Gesenius..

of one of our father SHEM שֵׁם and the origin of the Semites, a designation encompassing not just Jews, but also Assyrians-Germans[96], (see Chap. 7 for more) however you can make an infamous name for yourself, and bring SHAME, to your Name, SHAM, SCHEME, SCUM are of unknown etymology but also come from this root.[97]

Abram,→Abraham, –

God told Abram, he would be the father of many nations, that his name would be great, and all nations will be blessed by his seed (Gen 12:2). So the question is what names do we have that are derived from ABRAM, or ABRAHAM? Before we discuss this, I want to point out that there are only 8674 Hebrew words cataloged by Strong from the OT, of these there were most likely under 4000, before they niqqud'ed (vowel points-600-1000ad), of the 4000, there are over 2500 place names or people names, this leaves 1500 real root words. Now of the 2500 real names/place names all of which come into English from the original, DAVID דָּוִד D VID H1732, as one example, we have already coved others. Also specific, Hebrew terms have also come directly, or sometimes from the Latin or Greek or both, in addition to the Celtic→Hebrew (see chap. 6) and Old English-Germanic- Aramaic→Hebrew (see chap. 7).

The name Abraham, comes to the Arab's, (Ishmael-Abrahams son) Jews (Judah-keyholder OT)and US directly from the Bible. Now does Abraham's name have any English terms?

---

[96] The Assyrian have had a long connection to Germany, and the Germans also point back to them as their founders (see Trier), etymologically, they cannot properly trace the name German, thought to be from Almany=All Man. The Assyrian, went by Aramaic, and considering that the G or German was an A ARAMAIC, GERMANIC AR MAN'IC H0762 אֲרָמִית'Ărâmîyth,; feminine of H761; (only adverbial) in Aramæan, in the Syrian language (tongue), in Syriac. Another root for German is said to be *ALNAZ said to mean all people, in Hebrew this could translate to king (over all the people) H5387 - Narsai NAZI, , H5387 נָשִׂיא
nâsîy', naw-see'; or נָשָׂא nâsi'; from H5375 (seeNASA);.
[97] H8034 שֵׁם shem name, renown, fame, famous, named, named, infamous, report, a primitive word see H7760 through the idea of definite and conspicuous position; compare H8064 by implication honor, authority, character, a connected word is SUM, SUMMIT, to name to number, collect, pile up as in SUMMIT, H7760 Sum שׂוּם sûwm, soom; or שִׂים sîym; a primitive root; to put (used in a great variety of applications), get, give, **heap up**, , lay (down, up), make (out), mark, **name.**

Abram, means high exulted father, ie. ABBA father. Biblical title of honor, literally "father," used as an invocation of God, from Latin *abba*, from Greek *abba*, from Aramaic (Semitic) *abba* "the father, my father," emphatic state of abh "father." Also a title in the Syriac and Coptic churches.

H48 אֲבִירָם 'Ăbîrâm, ab-ee-rawm'; from H1 and H7311; father of height (i.e., lofty); Abiram, the name of two Israelites, Abiram.H85 אַבְרָהָם 'Abraham ab-raw-hawm'; contracted from H1 and an unused root (probably meaning to be populous); father of a multitude; Abraham, the later name of Abram:— Abraham.

H87 אַבְרָם 'Abram

Sarah, Abrahams wife.

Was Sarah a redhead? We know that she was stunningly beautiful, and the idiom we still use today comes from her and Rebecca, i.e., "drop-dead gorgeous (see idioms)." Interestingly, tradition suggests that Adam and Eve were redheads, and the Israelites are often depicted as fair-skinned. We have already covered that Adam was made from the red clay, his name also means red, as does Edom, in fact, Paleo Hebrew has them as the same word. Esau [H6215] means he'sair he's hair(y), again same meaning in English and Hebrew (what a co-incidence-LOL) the twin brother of Jacob, was also known as Edom (retained in AUTUMN Red Gen 25.25, 30).

Sarah, = "noblewoman" means princes and we got SIR from the root of her name. Sir could include A male or female and comes from SIRE, meaning lord, they connect this erroneously to "SENIOR" meaning old. I does not mean old, one could argue that a noble person could be old, but they are not when they are born! No the word SIR and SIRE come from our queen mother Sarah[H8282] שָׂרָה sârâh lady, princess, queen→H8269 שַׂר sar, sar; (SIR), from H8323, a prince a head person (of any rank or class), captain (that had rule), chief, general, governor, (see ISRAEL, (Is'SiR'eL, son of God, prince of God).

H8282 שָׂרָה SIR'âh, saw-raw'; (SAR is female for SIR, not currently used)feminine of H8269; a mistress, i.e., female noble, lady, **princess, queen**.

H8320 שָׂרֻק sâruq, saw-rook'; from H8319; bright red (as piercing to the sight), i.e., bay, speckled. See H8291.

Could Sarah, scream, or cry a lot, due to her childless state? H8319 שָׂרַק shâraq, shaw-rak, SCRIKE SHRIEK, SCREECH, a primitive root; properly, to be shrill, i.e., to whistle or hiss (as a call or in scorn), hiss, see h7123 קָרָא qᵉrâ', for CRY.

H8163 שָׂעִיר sa`iyr saw-eer' (saw hair); or שָׂעִר sâ'ir, kid, goat, devil, satyr, hairy, rough, scapegoat, from H8175; shaggy; as a noun, a he-goat; by analogy, a faun, devil, goat, hairy, kid, rough, satyr (Esau Gen 27:11).HAIR and HORROR, are cognate's, SCARE is also a cognate, but its unknown please keep reading.

H8177 שְׂעַר sᵉ'ar, seh-ar' (Aramaic) hair→H8181

H8181 שֵׂעָר se`ar say-awr'; (SEE HAIR) or שֵׂעַר sa`ar; (Isaiah 7:20), from H8175 in the sense of disheveling; hair, rough like Esau.

H8185 שַׂעֲרָה sa`arah sah-ar-aw, feminine of H8181, hairiness, breadth of a hair, also hair.

H8175 שָׂעַר sâ'ar, saw-ar, SCARE (unknown origin) a primitive root; to storm; by implication, to shiver, i.e., fear, be (horribly) afraid, fear, hurl as a storm.

ISAAC – Laughter, I's JOKE ?

Abraham was 100 years old. Sarah was 90 and still drop-dead gorgeous.

Isaac was 40 years old *(Gen 25.19)* when he married Rebekah (H7259 רִבְקָה Ribqah Rebekah) after Abraham's servant found her while panning around in Paddan Aram (Armenia), and as was the case with his mother, Sarah. Isaac's wife, Rebekah, was from the white house (33), i.e., her brother was Laban. Rebekah was barren, and Isaac prayed to God for her. Upon which God answered him, and Rebekah became pregnant with twins. God told Rebekah that *(Gen15.16):*

• Two nations are in your womb.
• Two people from within you will be separated.
• One person will be stronger than the other *(which one was naturally stronger, Esau or Jacob?)*
• The older will serve the younger.
• And by his wife Rebekah - *(Gen 24:60) the mother* of thousands of millions.
• Thy seed possess (H3423 יָרַשׁ *yarash*-Irish*)* the gate of those which hate them (Gen 22:17).

Yet, years later, Isaac either forgets, prioritizes one son (perhaps Esau, the elder), or simply makes a poor decision (acting "the fool," as some might say). This act directly contradicts God's earlier instructions. Moreover, we can see *(Gen 25.34)* that Esau despised his birthright *(H1062)* and gave it to Jacob for a bowl of soup — lentil soup!

Isaac knew (I believe) and remembered God's promises, yet he persisted in defying God and wanted to give it to Esau. We can read the story in *(Genesis 27.1,5,28-29)* that even Isaac and his wife told him to give it to Jacob.

• May God give you the dew (Jew) of heaven, the fatness of the earth, and plenty of grain and wine.

• Let people serve thee, and nations bow down to thee: *be lord over thy brethren and let thy mother's son's bow down to thee:* cursed *be* everyone that curseth thee and blessed *be* he that blesseth thee.

God said, "Sarah, thy wife shall bear thee a son indeed, and thou shalt call his name Isaac: and I will establish my covenant (he will be a Brit is a covenant in Hebrew), with him for an everlasting covenant, [and] with his seed after him." Following this divine

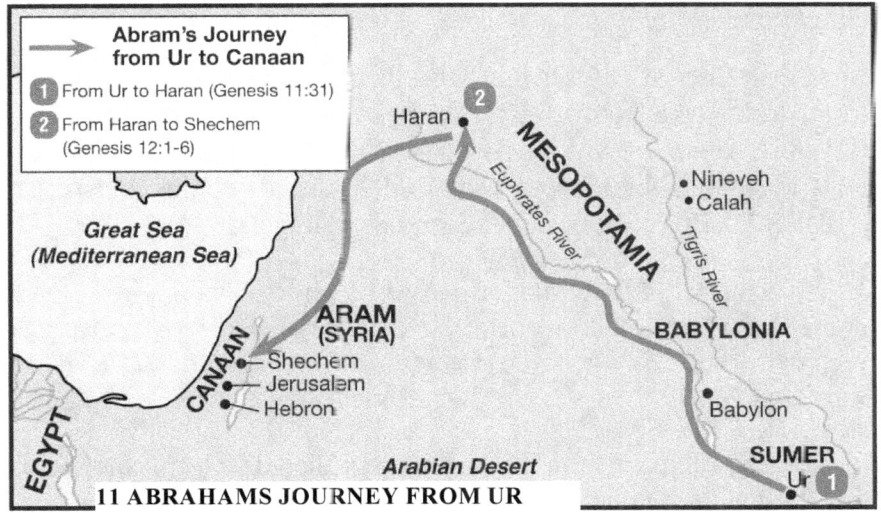

11 ABRAHAMS JOURNEY FROM UR

instruction, Abraham faithfully names his newborn son Isaac, solidifying the covenant established by God.*(Gen 17:19, 21.3 KJV)*.

Abraham was essentially directed to "go west, young man, go west" over (1-Eber H5677) there, clearly from the map Abraham went west.

A divine connection undoubtedly existed between God and Abram from a young age. The call to go from Ur of the Chaldees to Canaan was a westward journey. However, they went up and over (Eber H5677) via Haran. The first message apparently came to Abraham's father, Terah **FIGURE 12: ABRAHAM'S JOURNEY**
(Gen.11.31), but they only got halfway when they landed (H3885 lun(d)) in Haran and stayed there.

God had to give Abraham a nudge and tell him to leave his father and family and keep going *(Gen 12.1)* to Canaan. This renewed call came with specific promises and blessings from the divine.

105

In Genesis 17, God revisits Abram (later Abraham) and presents him with good and bad news (did God ask, *"Which do you want first"?)* The good news is that he is about to become a Brit, and now the bad news is that Abram and all his household has to be circumcised. Ouch!

At the age of 99, Abram received another powerful message from Yah, who reaffirmed his promise of a conditional Brit (H1285). Again, he was the first Brit with skin in the game; God not only made him a Brit but promised his seed would be Brit'ish (H1285, H376), walk before me, and be blameless.

This act of Brit transformed Abram into an exemplar, a focal point for others to draw inspiration. In essence, God's message seemed to be, *"Be my man on earth as a sign and do right by all men (and God)."*

The sign of the covenant was in his flesh, his penis (circumcision, a young shoot or twig of a plant, especially one cut for grafting or rooting, and a descendant of a notable family).

Through this act, God was essentially grafting Abraham and his lineage into his divine family.

The events that unfolded over the following year were nothing short of astounding. Despite the potential pain, Abram, at the ripe age of 99, along with his 13-year-old son Ishmael (who was reaching Bar Mitzvah age) and their entire household, all underwent circumcision.

God also gave Sarah the message and changed their names; they get a hey, the 5th letter of the Hebrew alphabet, representing praise. Abram goes to Abraham, Sarai goes to Sarah (he הַ Ps119.33), it was Sarah's and Abraham's "Hey day," the letter ה was also known as ha, so Abraham and Sarah both get a "Ha," "Ha" and the Bible reveals that both laughed when God told them they were going to have a child. *(Gen.17.17, 18.12).*

In addition, God says your son shall be named Isaac, meaning laughter.

The news of Isaac's imminent arrival hangs heavy. Abraham was very old, and pretty much their lives were over before they had the pleasure of children together; God has told them they would have a child within a year, and now this (as Christians, we experience this a lot, just before a major breakthrough we seem to have to go through hell before we get to heaven)! This event is just before Isaac's birth.

JOKE - from PIE *iok-o- "word, utterance," from root *yek- (1) "to speak" see also yada יָדַע h3045.

ITS JOKE - Isaac, Yits' chak, to laugh H3327 יִצְחָק Yits'chaq, Yits Ch'k, yits-khawk, from H6711

JOKE, J'ke Laugh, H6711 צָחַק tsa'chaq sa'Jaq, laugh, mock, sport, play, Joke, se joke, chuckle chaq(le).

SE JOKE, 6712 צְחֹק ts^echôq, from H6711; laughter (in pleasure or derision), laugh (-ed to scorn).

LAUGH, LAHAG (Laugh) H3933 לַעַג la'ag, lah'-ag, from H3932, laugh, derision, scoffing, scorn (-ing).

Notice that the word "laugh" is almost identical to the Hebrew lahag. If we were to pronounce laug'h phonetically, it would be "laug" and not "laff," as it is today.

Compare H3446. Isaac, ITS JOKE, Yits'chaq, laughter H3446 יִשְׂחָק Yischaq yis-khawk from H7831; he will laugh; Jischak, the heir of Abraham, Isaac. Compare H3327.

Se'JOKE, saw joke H7832 שָׂחַק sachaq, saw-Jak a primitive root; to laugh (in pleasure or detraction); by implication, to play, deride, have in derision, laugh, make merry, mock(-er), play, rejoice, (laugh to) scorn, be in (make) sport. Play, laugh, rejoice, scorn, sport, merry, mock, deride, derision, mockers.

ASSHOLE H2049 הָתֹל hâthôl, hawt'hole, from H2048 (only in plural collectively); derision, mocker.

CHUCKLE chaq(le) 6712 צְחֹק tsᵉchôq, tse-khoke, se-choke from H6711; laughter (in pleasure or derision), laugh(ed to scorn).

Rebekah

Rebekah, H7259 רִבְקָה Ribqah, Ribqâh, R'b-kaw, to block, clog, ensnare, from an unused root probably meaning to clog by tying up the fetlock; fettering (by beauty); Ribkah, the wife of Isaac. She was also known as a cowgirl, i.e., to use a rope to ensnare R'b-kaw, Rip-cow, and rope cow. *See Gesenius.*

The Pillars of the Bible

Abraham, revered as the father of the faithful, serves as a fitting starting point for our exploration. But before delving deeper, let's pause and consider the Bible's foundational figures – their names, their stories, and the spectrum they represent.—the good, the bad (Cain), and the ugly (Esau). These are the people whom God wants to bring to light during the Last Days.

We remember the prophecy that before the great and dreadful day of the lord, Elijah and Moses must come. The Great Day of the LORD…… "Remember the law of **Moses,** My servant, the statutes and ordinances I commanded him for all Israel at Horeb. Behold, I will send you **Elijah** the prophet before the coming of the great and dreadful Day of the LORD. And he will turn the hearts of the fathers to their children, and the hearts of the children to their fathers. Otherwise, I will come and strike the land with a curse."

Esau, Rough, and Hairy

H6215 עֵשָׂו ῾Êsâv, ay-sawv'; ("HAIRY" A'wY) [98]apparently a form of the passive participle of H6213 in the original sense of

---

[98] Hair is actually the truncated form of this word - H8177 שְׂעַר sᵉ῾ar, se har'; s@῾ar (Aramaic) hair (Aramaic) corresponding to H8181; hair.

handling; rough (i.e., sensibly felt), Esav, a son of Isaac, including his posterity, Esau.

H6213 עָשָׂה 'âsâh, aw-saw'; "A SHOW" or "A SAW" a primitive root; to do or make, in the broadest sense and widest application, **to show**, accomplish, advance, appoint, apt, be at, become, bear, bestow, bring forth, bruise, be busy.

Faith and miracles are undeniably intertwined

The Bible defines faith as possessing unwavering confidence in what we hope for, a certainty in things yet unseen.

By faith, we understand that the universe was formed at God's command so that what is seen is not made out of what was visible.

By faith, Abel brought God a better offering than Cain did. By faith, he was commended as righteous when God spoke well of his offerings. And by faith, Abel still speaks, even though he is dead.

By faith, Enoch was taken from this life so that he did not experience death: "He could not be found because God had taken him away." For before he was taken, he was commended as one who pleased God.[6] And without faith, it is impossible to please God because true faith requires believing in God's existence and His reward for those who diligently seek Him.

By faith, Noah, when warned about things not yet seen, in holy fear, built an ark to save his family. By his faith, he condemned the world and became heir of the righteousness that is in keeping with faith.

By faith, Abraham, when called to go to a place he would later receive as his inheritance, obeyed and went, even though he did not know where he was going. By faith, he made his home in the promised land like a stranger in a foreign country; he lived in tents, as did Isaac and Jacob, who were heirs with him of the same promise.

For he was looking forward to the city with foundations, whose architect and builder is God. And by faith, even Sarah, who was past childbearing age, was enabled to bear children because she considered him faithful who had made the promise. And so, from this seemingly infertile patriarch sprung a multitude as vast as the stars and countless as seashore sand.

All these people were still living by faith when they died. They did not receive the things promised; they only saw them and welcomed them from a distance, admitting that they were foreigners and strangers on earth. People who say such things show that they are looking for a country of their own. If they had been thinking of the country they had left, they would have had the opportunity to return. Instead, they were longing for a better country—a heavenly one. Therefore, God is not ashamed to be called their God, for he has prepared a city for them.

By faith, Abraham, when God tested him, offered Isaac as a sacrifice. He who had embraced the promises was about to sacrifice his one and only son, even though God had said to him, "It is through Isaac that your offspring will be reckoned." Reasoning that God possessed the power to raise the dead, Abraham, in a sense, received Isaac back from the clutches of death through his faith.

By faith, Isaac blessed Jacob and Esau in regard to their future.

By faith, Jacob, when he was dying, blessed each of Joseph's sons and worshiped as he leaned on the top of his staff.

By faith, Joseph, when his end was near, spoke about the exodus of the Israelites from Egypt and gave instructions concerning the burial of his bones.

By faith, Moses' parents hid him for three months after he was born because they saw he was no ordinary child, and they were not afraid of the king's edict.

By faith, Moses, having reached adulthood, rejected the privilege of being Pharaoh's daughter's son. He chose to be mistreated along with the people of God rather than to enjoy the fleeting pleasures of sin. He regarded disgrace for the sake of Christ as of greater value than the treasures of Egypt because he was looking ahead to his reward. By faith, he left Egypt, not fearing the king's anger; he persevered because he saw him who was invisible. By faith, he kept the Passover and the application of blood so that the destroyer of the firstborn would not touch the firstborn of Israel.

By faith, the people passed through the Red Sea on dry land, but when the Egyptians tried to do so, they drowned.

By faith, the walls of Jericho fell after the army had marched around them for seven days.

By faith, the prostitute Rahab, because she welcomed the spies, was not killed by those who were disobedient.

And what more shall I say? The list continues! Time wouldn't permit mentioning Gideon, Barak, Samson, Jephthah, David, Samuel, and the prophets, who through faith conquered kingdoms, administered justice, and gained what was promised; who shut the mouths of lions, quenched the fury of the flames, and escaped the edge of the sword; whose weakness was turned to strength; and who became powerful in battle and routed foreign armies. Women received back their dead, raised to life again. Others were tortured, refusing to be released so that they might gain an even better resurrection. Some faced jeers and flogging, and even chains and imprisonment. They were put to death by stoning; they were sawed in two; the sword killed them. They went about in sheepskins and goatskins, destitute, persecuted, and mistreated—the world was not worthy of them. They roamed deserts and mountains, finding refuge in caves and crevices.

These were all commended for their faith, yet none of them received what had been promised since God had planned something better for us so that only together with us would they be made perfect.

The Hebrew word for MIRACLE is MO FAITH, no co-incidence, H4159 מוֹפֵת môwphêth, mo-faith'; wonder, sign, miracle, wondered at[99]

LAG, Laag, :LAG as in delay in speech H3932 לָעַג lâ'ag, law-ag, a primitive root; to deride; by implication (as if imitating a foreigner) to speak unintelligibly, have in derision, laugh (to scorn), mock (on), stammering.

English/Hebrew Sports Terms

While the Bible makes no mention of organized sports, we do know that our Jack was Jacked! Yes, Jacob worked out big time; you could say he was the first Jock. He was scared to death of his brother Esau *(Gen,32.7)*, and he remembered well the promise his brother made to kill him; the next time he saw him, Esau had an army that had taken out kings in the past*(Gen.14.14-17, Gen.27.41, and was not a foe that could easily be defeated).*

His twin brother was not cut from the same cloth as our Jack *(Gen.27.16)*, but Jacob's trickery didn't go down well. The fear of his brother made him work harder, train, and pump iron so that he was physically fit as a fiddle. This dedication didn't go unnoticed. Remember the story of Jacob wrestling with a mysterious figure (an event foreshadowing Jesus, perhaps)? Still, Jacob prevailed and, as a result, was given the name Israel *(Is'royal, his royal sons of the king).*

And he said, Thy name shall be called no more Jacob, but Israel[H3478] for as a **prince** hast thou power with God and with men, and hast prevailed Gen 32:28.

The world's Oldest Football, from 1540 A.D., is found in 12 © SMITH ART Stirling Castle, Smith Art Gallery and Museum, GALLERY AND MUSEUM, STIRLING

---

[99] H4159 מוֹפֵתmôwphêth, mo-faith'; or מֹפֵת môphêth; from H3302 in the sense of conspicuousness; a miracle; by implication, a token or omen:—miracle, sign, wonder(-ed at).

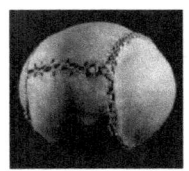 Stirling. Crafted from cowhide and inflated with a pig's bladder, this fascinating relic measures half the size of a modern football. However, the sport is much older than that. Indications are that the Egyptians (and Hebrew slaves?) played many ball games, like hit and catch, for example, a type of baseball. Many nations have loved sports as a way of diversion and challenge; no doubt that the Israelites loved it as well, especially the northern ten tribes, while the Jews, on the other hand, tended to focus more on intellectual pursuits.

See also wheel, H1523 גִּיל gîyl, gheel, as in rotation, to spin, and euphemism, euphemistically be giddy gi'yel.

I would have loved to see a match between the northern kingdom (Israel-Brits) and the southern kingdom (Jews). Somehow, I don't think the Jews would win; they do not appear to be very good soccer players. Having said that, moving beyond the game, many Jews, along with their brothers from another mother, did intersperse among the nation and comprise Europe today, such as Danmark, southern Ireland (tribe of Dan), Er'ish (northern Ireland-Zarahites and Brits), Kumri (Omri Welsh), France (Reuben), Portugal (Gad), Spain—has many Jews, with the area of Zaragoza and many surnames of Perez.

A GOAL

13 SOCCER BALL- COWS UDDER

A GOAL or aw gowl (H5696 עָגֹל 'âgôl, / aw-gole' עָגוֹל 'âgôwl), or ma gowl (aw-gole' my goal, also right of redemption, i.e., to have a goal h1353 גְּאֻלָּה ge'ullâh, gheh-ool-law'). From this comes the term "ga'al," i.e., GIRL,  H1350 גָּאַל gâ'al, gaw-al, a primitive root, to redeem (as in kinsman redeemer).

H5696 עָגֹל 'âgôl is from an unused root meaning to revolve, and also used by God when they installed revolving (soccer) balls in

113

the Temple. It is also used for cows that are trained. The training takes three years, hence the term "to have a goal." The similarity to a cow's udder is certainly noticeable, but it's more likely a coincidence. Did we make footballs from the circular (Fig 13) udder of a cow and use it to play games in ancient Israel?

As Solomon says, there is nothing new under the sun, and we would make it into a soccer ball (football), something we kicked (with our foot) and knocked into a net[100] N5414 N'TaN gain something, captured, delivered, food, net profit, or enemy even, score "A gole"! Sounds Egel'ish to me). Notice that many soccer balls resemble the markings of a British Friesian cow, this is said to be for black and white tv.

The original soccer ball may have started as cow, or pig udder and then to improve durability it was at some point covered by leather (cowhide.

Music

As mentioned in my other book "We Are Israel", it has a large section on bagpipes the harp along with other musical instruments. The musical traditions of Ireland and Scotland, with their prominent bagpipes and the Irish love of the harp, hint at a possible connection to ancient Israel. It appears that King David invented the bagpipes, they are upto two term that relate to bagpipes in the bible, 1- nebel[H5035], and 2- סוּמְפֹּנְיָה cuwmpowněyah-h5481 root of Symphony, a bag pipe, music, from Greek mousikē-G3451 (technē) to mix sounds, in a melodious harmonious way consider מָסַךְ mâçak-H4537, maw-sak'; a primitive root; to mix, MASH , MIX[101]. Even seemingly unrelated terms like "GIG" and "GIDDY" hold surprising biblical roots.

---

[100] N5414 used in a wide varierty of terms most common of which is give, deliver, yield NET profit, collect fish, Etymologist are unshure where NET comes from – I am saying grain, to aquire something a net is a tool to gain food, enemy etc.

[101] *meig-, PIE root meaning "to mix." It forms all or part of: ADMIX; ADMIXTURE; IMMISCIBLE; MASH; MEDDLE; MEDLEY; MELANGE; MELEE; MESTIZO; METIS;

GIG, GIDDY and GAG H'G'G, ha gig. H2287 חָגַג ᶜhâ'gag, h'GG ᵏhaw-g'g', a primitive root, to reel to and from drunkenness to observe a festival (originally religious); by implication, to be giddy, celebrate, dance, (keep, hold) a (solemn) feast (holiday), reel to and from drunkenness, (compare); properly, to move in a circle, i.e. (specifically) to march in a sacred procession. This is supported by the known etymology, which can trace it to "spinning top"giddy girl".

Music H4537 מָסַךְ mâçak, maw-sak primitive root; to mix, especially wine (with spices):—mingle.

G3451 μουσικός mousikos moo-sik-os'; from Μοῦσα Moûsa (a Muse); "musical", i.e. (as noun) a minstrel, musician, musician.

The music is a blend, a melody, a symphony of sound. That is what is expressed here because the music comes from a variety of different pipes.

Does Amos 6.5, suggest that King David invented the bagpipes *"That chant to the sound of the viol*(nebel H5035)*, [and] invent to themselves instruments of musick, like David"*; sounds like a strong possibility, but even if he didn't, the bagpipes were played in ancient Israel, and it was a tradition. We know this from the instances where the device is mentioned.

There is another term for bagpipe, one that was used in the timeple of King David, and the Jews call this Chamat Chalalim, see Mishnah for more information.

MISCEGENATION; MISCELLANEOUS; MISCIBLE; MIX; MIXO-; MIXTURE; MUSTANG; PELL-MELL; PROMISCUOUS. It is the hypothetical source of/evidence for its existence is provided by: Sanskrit misrah "mixed;" Greek misgein, mignynai "to mix, mix up, mingle; to join, bring together; join (battle); make acquainted with;" Old Church Slavonic mešo, mesiti "to mix," Russian meshat, Lithuanian maišau, maišyti "to mix. mingle," Welsh mysgu "to mix.

The Mishnah

(Keilim 20;2) mentions a Chamat Chalalim, which is a bag of pipes or musical bagpipe as an instrument that does not become ritually impure.

In Modern Hebrew, the word "bagpipes" is translated as Chamat Chalalim (plural). Chamat (according to Jastrow) means the stomach of an animal.

The Classical Commentary on the Mishnah of Rabbi Obadiah bar Tenorah (1465-1550) says: # Chamat Chalalim. An inflated animal stomach into whose opening pipes are inserted and wind emitted through holes in the pipes results in the sound of a song. # The Mishnah was written down in about 220 CE but is derived from Oral Traditions reaching back all the way to the Second Temple Times, the Period of Ezra, and beyond into the Biblical Era. [102]

NAG, harras

NAG, Nag'n, a constant beating of a drum, a tune, a melodious beat, H5059 נָגַן nâgan NAGGIN.

Nag, harass, tyrannize, distress, driver h5065 נָגַשׂ nâgas, naw-gas - Nawg's, harass, tyrannize, distress, driver primitive root; to drive (an animal, a workman, a debtor, an army); by implication, to tax, harass, tyrannize, distress, driver, exact(-or), oppress(-or), × raiser of taxes, taskmaster.

---

[102] Courtesy of Brit Am..org

Chapter 4

Hebrew / English Names of God

In my previous book, I offered extensive evidence suggesting the USA and Great Britain fulfill biblical prophecy. While compelling, in "We Are Israel", I discuss the following:

God promises a kingly line that shall not end but continue even as God takes out the last king of Judah (WAIp.326); Yehovah even repeats his promise to Jeremiah as he is taking the last king of Judah out. God says the following: David will never fail to have a man sit on the throne of Israel (Jer. 31.35-37,33.17-26). Therefore, we must look for the fulfillment of this because God never lies, and his promises are yah and Amen.

The rock the builder has rejected has become the chief cornerstone – the first temple builders rejected Jacob's pillar stone, and it became the foundation for the thrones of Ireland, Scotland, and Britain (Stone of Scone, WAI. p.213).

Evidence of tin that was mined in Cornwall has been linked to Solomon and the Hebrews (Tin, WAI-p.175.

Toponyms or Place-name etymological links, include, London, rivers Tamar, Thames, Avon, Alban, Hebrides, Britany, Britain, etc. (WAI-p.192, etc.)

Idioms, with over 100, traced directly to our forefathers, e.g., drop dead gorgeous, always darkest before the dawn, your fired, to hold out, etc. (WAI-p.267-283).

Our language's roots intertwine with Hebrew, Celtic, and Anglo-Saxon influences. This connection extends beyond the alphabet and even touches our greetings. Now, let's delve into the fascinating realm of names for God. Yes, the Hebrews of old (HeyBros H5676 עֵבֶר 'êber, lǝ·'eḇ·rōw) are represented by the two chiefs of the nations countries USA and Britain (Jer .31.7)

117

But before exploring this further, let's address a curious question: Did God ever offer specific instructions on how to greet one another?

This is what the Bible says; we can pick up the story in Exodus 3.14:

And God said, "I will be with you. And this will be the sign to you that it is I who have sent you: When you have brought the people out of Egypt, you will worship God on this mountain."

Moses said to God, "Suppose I go to the Israelites and say to them, '**The God of your fathers** has sent me to you,' and they ask me, 'What is his name?' then what shall I tell them?

God said to Moses, **"I am who I am**: Say to the Israelites **I am** has sent me to you.

How do we pronounce "I am that I am"? in Hebrew "Hayah a'sir Hayah"[H1961] [H834], wow is it just me or do you see the English in this phrase too? I am in Hebrew is HiYaH and means praise Yah, in Hebrew and it is exactly how we greet each other today. God told Moses what to do, and we (English speakers) still use it today, that's profound I think.

Another way we greet someone is with a warm handshake or a hug and sometimes a kiss when it is a sincere greeting (something Judas, knew all too well yet he used it to betray Jesus). The symbol for a handshake is the Yud[103] (Yod) ⟋⟍ Yud (AKA, H520 אַמָּה 'ammâh, arm), and cubit original 18". There was also the long cubit, which was 21 "now 24" (see Chap. 10 Alphabet Yud).

And the next fascinating question arises: How do the Jews address each other today? They pretty much use the term Shalom for hello and goodbye, (see greeting section of this chapter).

---

[103] See alphabet section, Benner says the Yud, is a closed hand, I don't see that, clearly it looks like a handshake in paleo Hebrew.

So the Brits just happen to have a Hebrew name (British), and English just happens to be Hebrew (Egel'ish cowboy or the bull tribe), and we just happen to greet each other the way that God told us to in the Bible. We also just happen to use all the emblems, idioms, etc. of the Bible. If you sound like a duck, walk like a duck, quack like a duck, and fly like a duck, there's a pretty good chance YOU'RE A DUCK! Hello, LOL, even a fifth-grader can see it! But back to the story.

God and good etymology.

Where did we get the name "GOD" and "GOOD" from and are they linked?

Well, according to etymonline.com, good used to be spelled god! Old English gōd (with a long "o") "excellent, fine, valuable, desirable, favorable, beneficial, full, entire, complete of abstractions, actions, etc.", "beneficial, effective, righteous, pious" of persons or souls, "righteous, pious, virtuous"; probably originally "having the right or desirable quality" from Proto-Germanic *gōda - "fitting, suitable" (source also of Old Norse goðr, Dutch goed, Old High German guot, German gut, Gothic goþs), a word of **uncertain origin**, suspected to be from PIE root *ghedh- " "to gather, to take up together").

Etymologists say God is of uncertain derivation, they say GOOD and GOD are not linked yet they say that GOD is linked to virtue, which itself is to be GOOD. GOOD and GOD used to be spelled the same. They say that GOD is Old English god "supreme being, deity; the Christian God; image of a god; **godlike person**," from Proto-Germanic *guthan (source also of Old Saxon, Old Frisian, Dutch god, Old High German got, German Gott, Old Norse guð, Gothic guþ), which is of **uncertain origin**; perhaps from PIE *ghut- "that which is invoked"

Since time immemorial, all the nations have poured out libations (given sacrifices) to their deities, whether it has a large G or small g. All GOD's were approached to seek their welfare, consider the following:-

119

Worship and Positive Outcomes:

Appeasement and Favor: Worship Practices: In many ancient cultures, people worshipped gods to gain their favor and ensure good outcomes. This could include offering libations, sacrifices, prayers, and other rituals.

Deity Roles: Deities were often associated with specific domains, such as rain, fertility, war, or health. Worshipping these gods was believed to bring blessings and avert disasters.

Libations and Sacrifices: Purpose: Libations (pouring of liquids) and sacrifices were common practices to honor gods, seek their protection, and secure their goodwill.

Good Outcomes: The ultimate goal of these rituals was to promote positive events, such as abundant crops, victory in battle, or overall prosperity.

So GOOD and GOD do have an intrinsic role to play together, and while some gods have malicious intent the GOD does not and is holy. In fact Jesus himself calls GOD by this name, i.e. GOD, the supreme creator is GOOD. We can see this from the lord's Prayer (Matt 6.9).

"Our Father in heaven, *hallowed* be your name"....

Jesus here is saying not that God's character, is holy, but his name is literally HOLY, this is the true origin of the words GOD and GOOD and is confirmed by the term GODDESS, a phrase also from the Bible and refers to a shrine prostitute, someone devoted to a pagan god. There was a plate on Aaron's head that read "holiness[H6944] to the lord" (Exo 39:30 KJV), ie. GOD'S.

GoD'S Kuf, Dalet, Sin H6944 קֹדֶשׁ QoDeS, holy, sanctuary (holy, hallowed) things, most holiness dedicated hallowed consecrated misc.

GODS -H6942 קָדַשׁ qadash, sanctify, hallow, dedicate, holy, prepare, consecrate, appointed, bid, purified.

GODDESS, god's a she -H6945 קָדֵשׁ qâdêsh, kaw-dashe'; from H6942; a (quasi) sacred person, i.e. (technically) a (male) devotee (by prostitution) to licentious idolatry, sodomite, unclean.

SAVE, SAFE, SAVIOR, SALVATION.

Etymologists trace the following words to the hypothesized root *sol - CATHOLIC; CONSOLIDATE; CONSOLIDATION; HOLISM; HOLO-; HOLOCAUST; HOLOCENE; HOLOGRAM; HOLOGRAPH; INSOUCIANT; SAFE; SAFETY; SAGE (n.1) kind of herb; SALUBRIOUS; SALUTARY; SALUTE; SALVAGE; SALVIFIC; SALVO "simultaneous discharge of guns;" SAVE (v.) "deliver from danger;" save (prep.) "except;' SOLDER; SOLDIER; SOLEMN; SOLICIT; SOLICITOUS; SOLID; SOLIDARITY; SOLIDITY; sou. They say this means "whole, well-kept". PIE *SOL= whole, The terms "save," "savior." and "salvation" were translated from Koine Greek, the common dialect used during the Hellenistic and Roman periods. Koine Greek differs from Classical Greek in its simplified grammar and syntax, making it more accessible for everyday communication and religious texts. This facilitated the spread of Christianity and its teachings across the Eastern Mediterranean and beyond.

SAVE, SAVIOR, SALVATION, SAFE, SAFETY, all said to stem from the root SAVE (v), i.e. *sol. The etymology of the words is traced to Greek and are as follows:-

G4982 σώζω sōzō SAVE, make whole, heal, be whole, etc.
G4991 σωτηρία sōtēria SALVATION, the (one) be saved, deliver, health, saving, that (one) be saved
G4992 σωτήριος sōtērios SALVATION, that brings salvation
G4990 σωτήρ sōtēr SAVIOUR, The word "savior"

The words SAFE, SAFETY, and SAFLEY, are said to derive from SAFE, Old French sauf " saved spiritually, redeemed, Latin salvus "uninjured, in good health, safe all, redeem, from PIE *solwos from root *sol- "whole, well-kept".

The first time SALVATION, is used in the Bible, was by Jacob, as he was giving his blessing to his sons[Gen 49:18], the next time the Bible uses it, is when we and Moses were caught between the devil and the deep blue sea, Moses said to stand still and see the salvation of JOEY [יהוה(H3068)], fear ye, not the Egyptian, for they are here today but gone tomorrow, never to be seen again (Exo. 14.13)! And yes it is where we get our idioms, I have over 100 directly from the Bible.

Save and safe, to hide, to protect, to save. ʦaʼphan and protect, tˢoughen.

H6845 צָפַן tsaphan: tsaw-fan (toughen-protect) to hide, treasure up '; a primitive root; to hide (by covering over); by implication, to hoard or reserve; figuratively to deny; specifically (favorably) **to protect**, (unfavorably) to lurk, esteem, hide, (den one, self), layup, lurk (be set) privily, (keep) secret(-ly, place).

SAFE, secure, out on a limb, on a CLIFF, safe from predators but not safe, also divide.

H5586 סָעַף çâ'aph, saw-af', (**saw off**) a primitive root; properly, to be safe on a branch or top of a tree, i.e., leaders -also metaphor-yet God says **you can run, but you can't hide** from him-divide up; but used only as denominative from H5585, to,

Behold, the Lord, the LORD of hosts, shall lop H5586 the bough with terror: and the high ones of stature shall be hewn down, and the haughty shall be humbled Isa 10.33.

H5585 סָעִיף çâ'îyph, saw-eef'; CLIFF SAFE, from H5586; a fissure (of rocks); also a bough (as subdivided), (outmost) branch, clift, top on an inaccessible craggy rock metaphor for safe.

Here is the exact word root recorded in the Bible by Moses

122

H3444 יְשׁוּעָה Ye SHaVaH[104] so Moses said "stand still and
See Ye Saviour" Wow English is Hebrew and We are Israel! It gets
even clearer with the long form of Joshua יְהוֹשׁוּעַYᵉhôwshûwa',
again a valid transliteration is Ye how ShaVA[105], "ye our saviour"

We all know as Christians that Jesus is our spiritual savior, in fact,
he is the savior of the world, the Jews, gentiles, Arabs or anyone
who God calls is saved through grace and the redeeming act of Jesus
on the cross. God is not limited to a certain Christian mantra, he
saved, David, Noah, and Enoch, and some of these were saved
before the Torah was written.

HOW TO BE SAVED

If you feel touched by God, by reading this, you do not need a
Pastor, Rabbi, imam khatib, Mullah or even a Myler, all you need
is to call on YE'our Saviour (Joshua), in your language and he will
hear you!

Seek and you will find, knock and the door will be opened, ask and
Ye shall receive, this is God's promise to all, these are all verbs by
the way, and they all require action on your part, if you would like
to know more go to my website Jerubbaal (YeRebel) aka
rebelministry.com.

Back to some more saving words, the etymologist say all the
saving words mentioned earlier come from *sol meaning whole,
whole, well-kept" like the Hebrew SHALOM[H7965]. I mentioned the
Greek and the English-Hebrew but there are other connections, that
are almost identical to the proposed PIE root i.e. *SOL, with a

---

[104] Yᵉshûw'âh is the standard translation, but Ye ShaVaH, is also a valid transliteration H3444 יְשׁוּעָה
Ye SHaVaH,
[105] H3091יְהוֹשׁוּעַ Yᵉhôwshûva', yeh-our-sha-vah; or יְהוֹשֻׁעַ Yᵉhôwshu'a; from H3068 and H3467
Jehovah-saved; Jehoshua (i.e. Joshua), the Jewish leader. Compare H1954, H3442. H3467 יָשַׁע yasha'
[ya sha(v)] means to save, savior, to deliver, to help, preserve, salvation.

suffix aM meaning people at peace, peace on a nation[106]? See greeting and salutation sectiôn, toast to health. Irish, English, and Hebrew are all related to SOL (slàinte from slán, (shalom) meaning "whole, healthy"

    H7999 שָׁלֵם SoL'M, shaw-lam'; a primitive root; to be safe (in mind, body or estate) whole body, (nation people)
    H7951 שָׁלָה shâlâh, shaw-law'; or שָׁלוּ shâlav; (Job 3:26), a primitive root; to be tranquil, i.e. secure, SAFE, SECURE, successful, be happy, prosper.

HOLY, WHOLE, HEAL, HEALTH.

    The Old Testament holy is what today we call God; we covered this earlier, H6944 קֹדֶשׁ qodesh, holy, sanctuary, but where does the word HOLY, WHOLE, HEAL, HEALTH trace to the following:

    Old English halig "HOLY, consecrated, sacred, godly, ecclesiastical", from Proto-Germanic *hailaga- (source also of Old Norse heilagr, Danish hellig, Old Frisian helich "holy", Old Saxon helag, Middle Dutch helich, Old High German heilag, German heilig, Gothic hailags "holy"), from PIE *kailo- "whole, uninjured" (see health). Adopted at conversion for Latin sanctus.

    Etymologists connect HOLOCAUST, to "whole sacrifice, burnt offering", remembering all things work for the good of those that love him and are called according to his purpose.

    Again etymologists say HOLY, WHOLE, HEAL, HEALTH → PIE *kailo- "whole, uninjured"

    HOLY H3632 כָּלִיל kâlîyl, kaw-leel'; from H3634; complete; as noun, the whole (specifically, a sacrifice entirely consumed); as

---

[106] H7999 Phoenician שלם Arabic سلم be safe, secure, Muslim, and infinitive Islām properly submission to God; Assyrian šalâmu, be complete, unharmed.

adverb, fully, all, every whit, flame, perfect(-ion), utterly, whole burnt offering (sacrifice), wholly, HOLOCAUST.

HOLY, WHOLE, HEAL, HEALTH from Hebrew -H3606 כֹּל kôl, kole; (Aramaic) corresponding to H3605, all, any, (forasmuch) as, be-(for this) cause, every, no (manner, -ne), there (where) -fore, though, what (where, who) -soever, (the) WHOLE.

CHASTITY, CHASTE.

The origin is said to be cut, castus (castrate) "cut off, *kes- to be pure from faults see SACRED, but consider the following.

CHASTE, holy, ha saint, cha ciy (t) d H2623 חָסִיד (chaciyd khaw-seed, from H2616; properly, kind, i.e. (religiously) pious (a saint), godly (man), good, holy (one), merciful, saint, (un-) godly. Saints, holy, merciful, godly, good, godly man, Holy One, holy one, ungodly.

SACRED

The origin of "sacred" is a fascinating etymological puzzle. Traditionally, it's traced back to the Proto-Indo-European root "sak." meaning "to sanctify, consider the Biblical Hebrew term "Zak." signifying purity and often used in reference to God.

Looking deeper, the late 14th-century English word "sacred" emerged from the past participle of the obsolete verb "sacren," meaning "to make holy." From Old French sacrer "consecrate, anoint, dedicate" (12c.) or directly from Latin sacrare "to make sacred, consecrate, hold sacred, immortalize, set apart, dedicate". From sacer (genitive sacri), "sacred, dedicated, holy, accursed". From Old Latin saceres. From PIE root *sak- "to sanctify".

SACRED *sak PIE, ZaK(red) H2134 זַךְ zak(red) from H2141 clear, clean, pure, used for things of God (see edenics.net).

125

CHRIST

The term "Christ" boasts a rich lineage, journeying from its Greek origins to become a cornerstone of Christianity. So we get the terms like Christian, Christ like Christ kind.

Christ (n.) "The Anointed" is synonymous with and translated to Greek. In Hebrew, it means mashiah (see messiah). This title, signifying a chosen and divinely appointed individual, was bestowed upon Jesus of Nazareth. Old English Christ (by 830, perhaps 675); from Latin Christus; from Greek khristos meaning "the anointed," noun use of verbal adjective of khriein" meaning to rub, anoint" (from PIE root *ghrei- "to rub").

In the early Church, "Christ" functioned as a title, always accompanied by the definite article ("the"). But from an early period, it was used without it and regarded as part of the proper name of Jesus. It was treated as a proper name in Old English but not regularly capitalized until 17c. Pronunciation with long -i- is the result of Irish missionary work in England, 7c.-8c. The ch- form, regular since c. 1500 in English, was rare before. Capitalization of the word begins at 14c. But it is not fixed until 17c. Notably, the Latin term "Christ" supplanted the Old English term "Hæland" ("healer, savior") as the preferred way to describe Jesus.

As an oath or strong exclamation (of surprise, dismay, etc.) attested by 1748. Even more curious, the 17th-century Familist sect experimented with using "Christ" as a verb, with "Christed" meaning "made one with Christ." Christ-child "Jesus as a baby" (1842) translates German Christkind.

G5546 Χριστιανός Christianos Christian
G5547 Χριστός Christos Christ
G500 ἀντίχριστος antichristos antichrist

CHOSEN KOCHEN

The concept of the "Chosen One" resonates deeply in religious traditions. In Christianity, it refers to Jesus, the Messiah (מָשִׁיחַ, mâshach, meaning "anointed with oil"). The term "chosen" could also mean someone who has been picked. It was the term given to the High Priest, a similar term was used to depict a prophet, a seer, a star gazer according to the Hebrew etymology.

CHOSEN comes from Old High German kiosan, German kiesen, Old Norse kjosa, Gothic kiusan "choose," Gothic kausjan proposed root *geus- "to taste, test", this appears to line up with KOSHER, the Jewish term for acceptable; (chosen) food. And while Kosher does not directly mean to taste or test food, it does mean *accept, or approve*, which is also implied with Kosher.

KOSHER, (CHOSEN) Is the Jewish name for acceptable food, ritually fit or pure, clean, lawful, the origin of CHOSEN? H3787 כָּשֵׁר kâshêr, kaw-share'; a primitive root properly, to be straight or right; by implication, to be acceptable; (figuratively CHOSEN) also to succeed or prosper, direct, be right. Sanskrit jus- "enjoy, be pleased;" Avestan zaosa- "pleasure," Old Persian dauš- "enjoy;" Old High German koston "try,"

CHOSEN is from choose, which means to test, taste, try; this appears to be identical Kosher (H3787). The high preist of israel was also a KOSHER (chosen) instrument of God, an acceptable, lawful representative of God on earth. He also wore the breastpalce, indicating the twelve tribes of Israel.

This is called H2833 חֹשֶׁן chôshen, kho'-shen comes from the high priest's, and again this could line up metaphorically with "a chosen one". We should also look at VISION, GAZE (coming up).

MARY CHOSEN ONE

Intriguingly, Mary is also referred to as "chosen." Experts say that the Greek Moriah comes from the Hebrew Miriam, which means bitterness (H4813 מִרְיָם). Do you think that God would choose a woman to be his wife and deliver his child and call her name Miriam-bitterness? Or is it more likely that the chosen one of God, i.e., Mary, would have a name meaning chosen of Yah? Just like Mount Moriah (H4179)[107] was the location chosen of Yah to build the temple.

HALO

Where does HALO, come from? 1560s, "ring of light around the sun or moon," from Latin *halo* (nominative halos), from Greek halos "disk of the sun or moon; ring of light around the sun or moon" (also "disk of a shield"); "threshing floor; garden," of unknown origin.

Halo comes from the threshing floor, the exact location of God's temple was the threshing floor[108] of the Jebusite and it is where the English halo comes from, do you remember the calling of anyone from his threshing floor, did Gideon have a HALO on? comes via the Greek (G257 ἅλων halōn, hal'-ohn) and the Hebrew. HALO, חָלָה châlâh, khaw-law'; a primitive root (compare H2342, H2470, H2490); properly, to be rubbed or worn treat, lay to, put to pain, pray, make prayer, And while we are thrashing HALO (courtesy *Edn).

let us look at the threshing floor in Hebrew it is H1637 גֹּרֶן gôren, CORN; from an unused root meaning to smooth; a threshing-floor (as made even); by analogy, any open area, (barn, corn, threshing-) floor, (threshing-, void) place. This lines up with the etymon of CORN, aKERNAL that was winnowed and ground on the threshing floor. Additionally we have the following from this root, GRAIN, CORN, GRANARY (storage place for grain) even GRANITE, FILIGREE; GARNER; GARNET;;; GRANGE;

---

[107] Maria= Moriah=h4179 chosen of Yah, marry=mah'r (i)=h4117, to be engaged, endowed, promised in marriage, not Marah=h4784 bitterness, or Miriam, rebellion H4813 מִרְיָם Miryam meer-yawm'; the name of Moses sister).

[108] H1637 – גֹּרֶן gôren, go'-ren; from an unused root meaning to smooth; a threshing-floor (as made even); by analogy, any open area (barn, corn, threshing-) floor, (threshing-, void) place.

GRANGER;; GRANULAR; GRANULE; GRENADE; GRENADINE; KERNEL; POMEGRANATE.*gre-no-

VI'SION, ZION, HAZY, GAZE, SEE,

A VISION (see ZION), is a HAZY, GAZE, a glassy view with an almost imperceptible picture of the future, this is true most of the time, perhaps sometimes we have a dream and when we wake up we don't remember the dream, sometimes the dream might include items that don't seem connected. Is it possible that all these items could be connected? I think that Hebrew etymology appears to connect them.

CHOOSE, PIE root *geus- "to taste; to *choose*." It is unknown which semantic root is prominent but consider. Used as a prophet chosen by God, for a vision.

H2374. חֹזֶה chôz'eh, kho-zeh'; K'h'ZH CHOOSE, GAZE (to choose and to see kho'zeh) from H2372; a beholder in vision: also a compact (as looked upon with approval), agreement (act of choosing), prophet, see that, seer, (star-) gazer.

HAZY (unknown origin), GAZE, SEE, sawon, SAW (see past tense from sawon), (Boutkan No certain PIE etymology) H2372 חָזָה châzâh, khaw-zaw'; a primitive root; to (how-zaw) gaze at; mentally to perceive, contemplate (with pleasure); specifically, to have a vision of, behold, look, Prophecy, provide, see ZION.

A VISION (see ZION) is a HAZY, GAZE, with an almost imperceptible view of the future.

SIGN Latin signum "identifying mark, token, indication, symbol; proof; military standard, ensign; a signal, an omen; *sign* in the heavens, constellation." Etymologist Watkins, literally "standard that one follows," from PIE *sekw-no-, from root *sekw- (1) "to follow." De Vaan has it from PIE *sekh-no- "cut," from PIE root *sek- "to cut". Often the etymologist really stretches out the connection/s, here is the true connection.

SIGN, ZION H6725צִיּוּן tsîyûwn, tsee-yoon' (YONDER from, Old English geon "that over there"), from the same as <u>H6723</u> in the sense of conspicuousness (compare <u>H5329</u>); a monumental or guiding pillar, sign, title, waymark. See watchtower (tephi), spoken of earlier - H6822, צָפָה tsâphâh, (STEPHANY, TEPHI) tsaw-faw' SAW'FAR, to peer into the distance; SPY, TzP'HaH, proposed root *<u>spek</u>- with over 64 English words proposed from this root.

One more that I should "spek" of (sorry could not resist that one), *"And it shall come to pass afterward, [that] I will pour out my spirit upon all flesh; and your sons and your daughters shall Prophecy, your old men shall dream dreams, your young men shall see visions[H2384] ".*(Joe 2:28, Acts 2:17, KJV)

H2384 חִזָּיוֹן chizzâyôwn, khiz-zaw-yone'; (kidz saw vision) from H2372; a revelation, expectation by dream, vision

H2377 חָזוֹן châzôwn, Chet Zayin, Vav Nun khaw-zone'; from H2372; a sight (mentally), i.e. a dream, revelation, or oracle, vision.

God's a Limey

Here is another interesting modern English, old Hebrew (English) connection - The actual name for God in the Bible is Elohim, and the letters are אֱלֹהִים a LHYM. Interestingly, "Limey," a slang term for Britons, shares some phonetic similarities. Coincidence? Perhaps. But the connection goes deeper.

Let me give you the actual name of God (or god) as I read it: eLo'him, abbreviated it would be a form of greeting in ancient Israel. This would be eLo, hello (<u>H430</u>).

YHWH as JOEY

H3068 יְהֹוָה YHVH or YHWH (the original) JOEY, Yĕhovah LORD, GOD, JEHOVAH, variant yeh-ho-vaw'; from H1961; (the) self-Existent or Eternal; Jeho-vah, Jewish national name of God:— Jehovah, the Lord. Compare H3050, H3069.

Lion of Judah

The powerful imagery of the "Lion of Judah" has deep roots in the Bible. God himself is declared the "Lion (Lyion)" of the tribe of Judah in scripture.

We can see the original use of the term for Lion in Genesis. 49.9 Judah [is] a lion's (Ariy) whelp: from the prey, my son, thou art gone up: he stooped down, he couched as a lion (ariy) and as an old lion (labiy) who shall rouse him up? h738 אֲרִי 'ariy (T'Ariy-tear-young lion from H717) h3833 לָבִיא labiy' (old lion-from H738), לַיִשׁ layish, lah'-yish; from H3888 in the sense of crushing; a lion (from his destructive blows),(old) lion.

H717 אָרָה ârâh, aw-raw, a primitive root; to pluck, gather (g-awraw), pluck.

H3833 לָבִיא lâbîy', law-bee, or (Ezekiel 19:2) לְבִיָא lᵉbîyâ irregular masculine plural לְבָאִים lᵉbâ'îym; irregular feminine plural לְבָאוֹת lᵉbâ'ôwth,

H3612 כָּלֵב Kaleb Calᵉ(b), dog, collie=Calᵉ(b) also Lab as in Labrador C'leb

The word lion (n.) boasts a rich etymology, with roots stretching far back in time. Late 12c., from Old French lion "lion" also figuratively "hero" (12c.), from Latin leonem (nominative leo) "lion; the constellation Leo", from Greek leon (genitive leontos), a word from a non-Indo-European language, perhaps Semitic (compare Hebrew **labhi "lion** h3833 לָבִיא labiy") plural lebaim; **Egyptian labai,** lawai "lioness"). Old English had the word straight from Latin as Leo (Anglian lea).

The Latin word was borrowed throughout Germanic (compare Old Frisian lawa, Middle Dutch leuwe, Dutch leeuw, Old High German lewo, German Löwe); it is also found in most other European languages, often via Germanic (Old Church Slavonic livu, Polish lew, Czech lev, **Old Irish leon, Welsh llew (Cymru Cmri pre-Roman name-Omri=pupil of Jehovah H6018).**

131

G3023 λέων leōn lion A lion is a brave person.

Lion in Yiddish is *leyb*, corresponding to h3833 לָבִיא *labiy'* Old High German lewo (as in Leo the Lion)

YES, IS.

Etymologists say that the words YES, and IS originated in the following way.

YES (adv.) Origin: Old English "gise, gese," likely from "gea, ge" (meaning "so") + "si" (meaning "be it!"). Derived from Proto-Germanic *sijai- and PIE *si- (optative stem of ***es- "to be"**). They also say YES is from is YEA with SE added so YEA'SI as in " yea see" yea (adv.)[109] and comes from Proto-Germanic *ja-, *jai-, a word of affirmation (agreement).

IS (v.) third person singular present indicative of be, Old English is, from Germanic stem *es- (source also of Old High German, German, Gothic ist, Old Norse es, er), from PIE *es-ti- (source also of Sanskrit asti, Greek esti, Latin est, Lithuanian esti, Old Church Slavonic jesti), third person singular form of root *es- "to be." Old English lost the final -t-.

The Hebrew word YESH[110], can mean YES, shut the front door, wow yet another word that sounds and means the same in English and Hebrew..There are 37 different words said to stem from the root *es[111]YES and IS -Gesenius and Mozeson say that these

---

[109] YEA (adv.) Old English gea (West Saxon), ge (Anglian) "so, yes," from Proto-Germanic *ja-, *jai-, a word of affirmation (source also of German, Danish, Norwegian, Swedish ja

[110] Y**esh** H3426 provides an affirmation of existence or truth—similar to how "yes" can affirm something in English. yaysh; perhaps from an unused root meaning to stand out, or exist; entity; used adverbially or as a copula for the substantive verb (H1961); there is or are (or any other form of the verb to be, as may suit the connection), there are, (he, it, shall, there, there may, there shall, there should, (which) hath, (I, shalt, that) have, (he, it, there) is, substance, it (there) was, (there) were, ye will, thou wilt, wouldest.

111 ***ES-** Proto-Indo-European root meaning "to be." It forms all or part of absence; absent; am; Bodhisattva; entity; essence; essential; essive; eu-; eucalyptus; Eucharist; Euclidean; Eudora; Eugene; eugenics; eulogy; Eunice; euphemism; euphoria; euthanasia; homoiousian; improve; interest; is; onto-; Parousia; present (adj.) "existing at the time;" present (n.2) "what is offered or given as a gift;" proud; quintessence; represent; satyagraha; sin; sooth; soothe; suttee; swastika; yes.

words come from H3426 Yesh, 1. Entity, 2. used adverbially or as a copula for the substantive verb (H1961). As Gesenius says, it is used in place of the yes of English.

In everyday conversation, a simple "YES" can be surprisingly complex. Take the phrase, "Do you want a drink?" Responding with "Yes" goes beyond simply agreeing; it becomes a substitute for the entire action ("drink"), essentially meaning "give me one, please." Some argue that "yes" functions as an adverb here, modifying the meaning of the question from inquiry to action. An alternative perspective sees "drink" morphing into the infinitive "to drink" upon receiving the affirmative "yes."

Again it is generally thought that there is no Biblical Hebrew word for "yes" or "no," and the same goes for the old Celtic language (Irish and Welsh). In Biblical Hebrew, when a question is asked, the answer is generally given by repeating the question.

And he said unto them, Know [yada H3045] ye Laban the son of Nahor? And they said, we know [H3045] [him]. [Gen 29:5 KJV] The actual reply was yā·dā·ʿə·nū. יְדָעְנוּ׃ - we know him (yada e nu, ya we know). Clearly, it is easy to see why Wiliam Tyndale said English agreeth 1000 times more with Hebrew than doeth Latin or Greek! "Yada e nu" means "ya I know"

H3045 יָדַע yada` which means know, known, knowledge, perceive, shew, tell, wist. understand, certainly, acknowledge (ya), acquaintance, consider, declare, teach, misc.

The Hebrew word "Yada" (יָדַע) carries a strong connotation of agreement, similar to saying "yes" in specific situations. There are other related words, like "yes," "aye," and "h'n" (הֵן H2005), used for affirmation (as explored by Gesenius) that I won't delve into here.

Having said that, the Holy Spirit convicted me of the connection between God: Hi, hiYah, Hello, Yahway (for quite some time. However, it has taken quite a bit of digging to uncover that this is exactly where our Yes, Yah comes from: to be, is, self-existent one, to be in agreement.

Isn't that enlightening? This potential connection offers a new perspective on the origins of our word "yes" and its link to the concept of being and existing. For further exploration, check out my YouTube channel, which delves deeper into the idea that English has Hebrew roots and we share a connection to Israel.

H3069 יְהֹוִה YHVH or YHWH -Yĕhovih Ye hovah, H3068 יְהֹוָה YHVH or YHWH -YĕhovahYe hovah).

The simple act of saying "yes," in all its variations – ya, yeah, yah – carries a deeper meaning than mere agreement. It could represent a connection to both the divine and the earthly. For the scholarly mind, the linguist, or anyone seeking a deeper dive, here is a path to explore further cross-references.

Professor of linguistics at Yeshiva University in Israel, Isaac Mozeson of Edenics.net, agrees with me and says the following: "*Yes*" does trace to H3045 יָדַע yada along with, along with *yes, sure*.

However, traditional linguistics offers a contrasting view. The Anglo-Saxon "gese" or "gise" (meaning "yes") is believed to stem from a reconstructed (guesses at) Indo-European root, "es," signifying "to be." This highlights the ongoing debate surrounding the etymology of "YES."

I propose that PIE*es is actually H1961 which has 120 different variations in the Bible[112](יְהִי YHY, YHE- YES, i.e. "to be" is in Hebrew and Just as Moses asked God what his name was his reply was I

"I am that I am" in Hebrew this is hiya sir hiya היות (H1961[113])YOAS or (He)YOAT is **"to be"** (*Genesis2:18*). Other

---

[112] Hebrew hes suffix, prefix, and infixes that change the basic form, Strongs Hebrew lists the base root for all these variants, a common form of variant is seen in Gen 1.3 when God said "Let **there be** light" יְהִי: Yud Hey Yud could be pronounced Y'eH

[113] H1961 to be, become, come to pass, exist, happen.

like-sounding words that speak to the affirmative sense of YES include יש YaiYSH (there is – Genesis 18:24 – see IS). יאות YayEOOS (properly, rightly) is in Jewish Aramaic (Targum Genesis 27:36). יישר YaSHahR means straight, even, right, correct – see JURISDICTION.

An affirmative response to the question: "Do you have it?" would be יש YaiSH (H3426)[114].

The third person present of "to be" is traced to Greek *es-ti*, Sanskrit *as-ti*, and the Indo-European "root" *es* (to be).

יש YAISH means "there IS..." "All the earth shall know that *there is* a God in Israel: - (*1Samuel17:46*). (See IOTA for the Yod = I equation.) היות HeYoW(S) means "to be" in *Genesis2:18*.

MIRACLE

In another amazing twist of fate, the word miracle, in Hebrew means more faith, Jesus alluded to this when he said"

"*I tell you, if you have faith as small as a mustard seed, you can say to this mountain, 'Move from here to there,' and it will move. Nothing will be impossible for you.*" Matt 17.20 more faith= miracle.

Miracle mo faith, H4159 מוֹפֵת mowpheth, mo faith mo-faith'; or מֹפֵת môphêth; from H3302 in the sense of conspicuousness: a miracle; by implication, a token or omen, miracle, sign, wonder (-ed at).

---

[114] H3426 יֵשׁ yêsh, yaysh; perhaps from an unused root meaning to stand out, or exist; entity; used adverbially or as a copula for the substantive verb (H1961); there is or are (or any other form of the verb to be, as may suit the connection):—(there) are, (he, it, shall, there, there may, there shall, there should) be, thou do, had, hast, (which) hath, (I, shalt, that) have, (he, it, there) is, substance, it (there) was, (there) were, ye will, thou wilt, wouldest.

THEE, THY, THYSELF

Dont thee thy me, thee thy thyself and see how thy likes it – Growing up in the northwest of England, near Wigan (a place made famous by George Orwell and Myles Standish) we often used this phrase, it was a sound that was not easily replaced by the standard Latin alphabet, anf the TH was represented by the A-S thorn (þ)[115], but where did they get it from? The A-S, scholars generally agree that the runic alphabet came from the Etruscan. Etruria was a vassal of the Phoenicians (see Pyrgi Tablets). So they both came from the Paleo Hebrew.

The symbols thorn (þ) voiced and voiceless "th" sounds (like θ and $\eth$) these symbols come from the Paleo Hebrew the 9th letter of modern Hebrew Tet/Tov.

Biblical "Hebrew to English" Alphabet
Hebrew is the first and oldest alphabet: 1859 BC

Pictograms		Phonograms		Echograms	Aramaic Hebrew	Masoretic Hebrew
Egyptian Hieroglyphics 1859 BC		Mosaic Hieroglypic Hebrew Alphabet 1859 - 550 BC		English Modern	Square Hebrew 550 BC - 70 AD	Vowelled Hebrew 600 AD - present
Gardiner's Sign List #	Sounds Like	First Hebrew Phonogram Alphabet 1859 - 1100 BC	Paleo-Hebrew 1100-550BC	English	First Century	Vowels, dots, dashes were invented by Masoretes (600 AD) did not exist before.
(F35)	D	Tov Good — Sinai 112 — Sinai 357	⊗	Th	ט	Th as in Thin
M42	Wn	Tayis Male goat WH2 Sinai 249 Sinai 92 Sinai 351 376	X †	T,Th	ת	ת T as in Time (dot) ת Th ans in Theme

14 TH, T, TET, TOV, TAF

The sound was so prominent in the Semitic language that when the Jews changed it from TH to T (this started after the northern ten tribes were taken away by God 721bc.) both the Arabs and the Persians(ث thā ث th)[116] brought it back into their alphabet.
Having said that the origin all point to the Tav/Tov, it is important to point out that THIS with Yod

---

[115] If you would like to know a little more about the thorn in my side please click this link (pun intended).

[116] **Arabic and Persian Alphabets:** The Arabic alphabet, with its ث (thā') representing the voiceless *th* sound (/θ/), does have a character for this sound, suggesting it was important in Semitic phonology. Persian, derived from Arabic, maintained the ث (th) sound, reinforcing the idea that this particular phoneme (common in Semitic languages) was significant enough to be included and represented in later scripts.

Greetings and Salutations

HI, HIYA, HELLO.

HI, HIYA variant of HELLO unknown origin, linked to call, attention, like, "hey you" HELLO, HOLLA, HALLUEN call to attention, made popular by the telephone, greeting, but not thought to connect with.

In English we have several ways to greet each other, it appears that HI, HIYA, is connected to HELLO. I find this fascinating that time after time I come across cognates (words that mean the same in two tongues), people early on recognized this and called them true cognates but now we reject this idea because we cannot understand how we are genetically connected to ancient Israel.

I hope this book along with "We Are Israel" helps explain this. But for now, lets just imagine that "We are Israel" and that English springs from Hebrew roots. If we can accept this premise then it starts to make sense that ancient phrases, that we used to use and that God told us to use are actually being used.

How should we greet one another is there anything in the Bible indicating this? After hundreds of years in slavery, we Hebrews are crying out to God because of the oppression of the Egyptians. And God (at the appropriate time) appears to Moses and tells him to address the Hey'Bro's with Hiyah sir Hiyah, sound familiar!

[14] *God said to Moses, **"I am who I am.**[c] (a metaphor for the Eternal One) This is what you are to say to the Israelites: 'I am (Hiyah)has sent me to you.'"*

hI, hiya, Hello

The complete etymology is unknown, Middle English: Halouen (to shout in the chase) indicates an early use of shouting, a call to attract attention. Old High German: Hala, Hola (emphatic imperative of fetching or calling) – used for hailing, especially ferrymen. Middle Dutch and Old Norse: Similar forms and uses indicating greetings or calls to attract attention. Modern English: Emerged as a common greeting in the 19th century, popularized by telephone use.

HIYA, HIYAH the Hebrew term comes from הָיָה hâyâh, [117] when we look at the paleo Hebrew and see the true meaning of הָיָה Hay, Yud, Hey (יְהֹוָה see H3068), experts agree that the Hey means praise or look here, (see Hey in alphabet section). Etymologist and Hebrew experts agree HaYaH or HIYA means attention look here, or praise with hands high (see halal Halleluia). The Yod is recognized by Rabbi's, and Jewish scholars as representing God, so in paleo Hebrew HiYaH means praise God (see Hey alphabet section).

And it's the way God told us to greet one another HIYA, sir HIYA.

Consider that the supreme God was called ELO HIM, a term also used for Judges magistrates, eLo, hello (H430 אֱלֹהִים 'elohiym elo hyim,- Aleph is considered a gutteral stop , **strong silent type**), or אֱלֹוהַּ'ĕlôwahh, el-o'-ah; (shortened) אֱלֹהַּ 'ĕlôahh; probably prolonged (emphatic) from H410; a deity or the Deity, God, god, H430. A greeting paise Yah, praise Elo him, GOD day, God evening, see Yah, English has God in many of our greetings, a coincidence?

Halleluiah, HAIL, and YELL, El u Yah.

YELL, Proto-Germanic *gel PIE root *ghel- (1) "to call."

---

[117] H1961châyâh, haw-yaw primitive root (compare H1933); to exist, i.e. be or become, come to pass.

HAIL (v.1) "to greet or address with 'hail!,'" also "to drink toasts," c. 1200, heilen; to call to from a distance," hæil "be healthy" (see Halleluia and health).

Hallelujah, a phrase we love to sing at church, that celebratory cry of praise might surprise you with its origins. As a single phrase, it appears in Revelations 19. *"And after these things I heard a great voice of much people in heaven, saying, **Alleluia**; Salvation, and glory, and honour, and power, unto the Lord our God: [Rev 19:1 KJV]"*

In the Hebrew Bible, the closest version appears in Psalms (see Ps. 104.35) it is made up of two compound words praise, HaLaL[H1984] and Ya(h), Lord[H3050], i.e. "Praise (ye the) Lord"[118], rendered Halleluiah in English.

But, that is not what Hall'el'u'iah means in Hebrew and English, there is another word nestled in there, can anyone see it? It is EL, this is significant, this term is retained in the Hebrew word, full meaning is Hail El u Yah, Praise God who (is) YaH. El is an unused English term for God, except in the phrase "El Yeah",

ELIJAH[H452] and means אֱלִיָּה'Êlîyâh, El i YaH, God, I YaH and is retained in the English in the strong affirmation/agreement phrase "HELL (i)'YAH", used whenever someone, emphatically wants to agree with you, (see the introduction, Hell and Elijah).

Why is this important? Because it means the same in English and Hebrew, and it comes to us direct phrase from the Bible

---

[118] Hallelujah, from praise=HaLaLH1984 and Ya(h)=LordH3050, i.e. "Praise (ye the) Lord", the word in Hebrew is הַלְלוּיָהּ HaLaL with a suffix ו Wav/Vav transliterated as ○U=who and YaH Lord. הַלַל=Praise○=who יָהּ=Lord.

Toasts Jewish, British, Welsh

Jewish toast to life - lock hyme, L'chiam, לְחַיִּים, is the plural form of the Hebrew H2416, (חַי, chay) L means "to" and Chaim means "life". In England, we say cheers, which matches the Hebrew (H2421 חָיָה chayah), a primitive root (compare H2331, H2421); "to live". Shut the front door, wow, again we use a word, that parallels what the Jews use and is in the Bible.

CHEERS, is a toast to good health, longlife its Biblical cognate is H2421 חָיָה chayah, Etymology Online c. 1200, trace it now to "the face, countenance,", especially as expressing emotion, from Anglo-French chere "the face," Old French chiere "face, countenance, look, expression", from Late Latin cara "face" (source also of Spanish cara), cherry-face, they try to link it to drinking from horn's and hence from Greek kara "head", from PIE root *ker- (1) "horn; head". As early as mid-13c, it had the meaning of "frame of mind, state of feeling, spirit; mood, humor".

While the Greek word for HORN, Kara, has a Hebrew root, H7161 קֶרֶן qeren, keh'-ren, →H7160; a horn (as projecting); by implication, a flask, cornet; by resemblance, a drinking vessel. This is not the correct link, rather I will argue that my first entry is the more correct etymon i.e. CHEERS→ chayah "to live" H2421 חָיָה

So CHEERS to everyone, early settlers in Providence Rhode Island (1636) would greet the Algonquin Indians with a "What Cheer!". It became a very important phrase, so much so that the Indians adopted the phrase into their language.

And we have cheerio good day.

The Hebrew term for greeting is where we get the English term, yell, shael, or hail, to desire, or proclaim H7592 שָׁאַל shâ'al, shaw-al **shâ'êl** desire also salute (greet)'; or שָׁאֵל shâ'êl; a primitive root; to inquire; by implication, to request; by extension, to demand, ask (counsel, on), beg, borrow, lay to charge, consult, demand, desire, × earnestly, enquire, greet, obtain leave, lend, pray, request, require, salute, × straitly, × surely, wish.

Welsh (Cumry-Omri H6018 עָמְרִי) word for cheers is yekidah spelled, <u>iechyd da,</u> .

LOVE, and its variant LUV.

Another very British phrase and anyone who has visited or spent some time in Britain will be familiar with it, often folks would call individuals LOVE or LUV, it is a gesture of affection. The term can also mean to enjoy something, both in a none sexual, and sexual sense. Example "Would you like to take a walk", "I would LOVE to" The term means "to care, desire, love." The proposed root is PIE *leubh-.

A phrase in Hebrew would be I would "love it" if you would do something for me. H3863 לוּא luVA, pray thee, if, would God, O that.

We also relate the heart to love, consider[H3826] לִבָּה LeBaH, also L'V'H, the heart, deep seated LOVE[119]. Sexual love is driven by the heart!

would it might be- today often used as endearment with thank you added. This appears to be the origin; I haven't scanned all the Hebrew words for a match, but it's possible that this could be the source. Other types of usage are "Hi luv, bye luv, etc." See dad for the seat of love.

Other Hebrew / English terms for love

SHACK-UP, to lodge with someone for sex, SHACK, lien, or securing a claim, from Hebrew shackup, shawk ab. Abimelech

---

[119] H3825 לְבַב leˈbab, leb-ab', (Aramaic) corresponding to H3824, heart from H3824 לְבָב lêbâb, ay-bawb'; from H3823; like H3820 the heart (as the most interior organ) bethink themselves, breast, comfortably, courage, (tender-) heart(-ed), mind, understanding.

shacked-up with Sarah he liened on her (Gen. 26.10), and while in the end he didn't touch Sarah, but, he did get a wake up call.

SHACK-UP H7901 שָׁכַב' shâkab, a primitive root; to lie down (for rest, sexual connection etc.) at all, cast down, (lover-)lay (self) (down), (make to) lie (down, down to sleep, still with), lodge, take legal possession (lien see Gen. 26.10) ravish, take rest, sleep, stay.

DAD PAPA DAID

DAD etymolohy - Welsh tad, Irish daid, Lithuanian tėtė, Sanskrit tatah, Czech tata, Latin tata "father," Greek tata, used by youths to their elders). Compare PAPA French papa, from Latin papa, originally a reduplicated child's word, similar to Greek pappa (vocative) "o father," pappas "father," pappos "grandfather, POP (n.2) US version of PAPA" The native word is daddy; colloquial diminutive of dad, with -y

Basically, they are saying that DAD, DADDY, PAPA, POP, TATA, TETE, all developed from baby talk.

DUDE, originally a fastidious, person (attention to detail perhaps overly protective). The current meaning of DUDE is a casual term used to address or refer to a person, often a friend or acquaintance. unknown origin but sound like the Irish for dad DAID H1730 דּוֹד dowd beloved, uncle, love(s), father's brother, well-beloved.

DAVID H1732 דָּוִד DoD daw-veed'; rarely (fully); דָּוִיד Dâvîyd; from the same as H1730; loving; David, the youngest son of Jesse, from דּוֹד dôwd, dode; or (shortened) דֹּד dôd; from an unused root meaning properly, to boil, i.e. (figuratively) to love; by implication, a love-token, lover, friend; specifically an uncle, (well-) beloved, father's brother, love, uncle.

DAD, El dad, (he DAD) God has loved H419 אֶלְדָּד 'Eldad el-dad'; Eldad from H410 and H1730; God has loved; Eldad, an Israelite, Eldad. Or whom God loves

DAD, A dad, shall love H111 אֲדַד 'Adad Hadad, mighty man = "I shall move softly: I shall love" probably an orthographical variation for H2301; Adad (or Hadad), an Edomite, Hadad.

The name "dad" means breast and the seat of love. We cover this elsewhere in the text, but it's like PAPS and Pappy or Pops, all are the same origins, see Ma(s) TITS, 4711 מָצַץ 'mâ'tsats, that ye may milk out,[H4711] and be delighted with the abundance of her glory.

Israel, Yis/His Royal

What does the name Israel really mean? We remember that Jacob fought against God and won, and his prize was a new name, Israel[(H3478)], and it means "He will rule as God" In Hebrew it literally means ROYALTY son or prince of the king in this case Gods adopted son. Let's break it down YSHRaEL יִשְׂרָאֵל (H3478) Yud Sin, Resh, Aleph, Lamed, the Y-Yud prefix שָׂרָה Sarah (H8280) to rule or have power as a prince and EL, אֵל =God and (I cover these later in more detail).

The name ROYAL and ROYALTY come from mid-13c., "fit for a king;" late 14c., "pertaining to a king," from Old French roial "royal, regal; splendid, magnificent" (12c., Modern French royal), from Latin regalis "of a king, kingly, royal, regal," from rex (genitive regis) "king," from PIE root *reg- "move in a straight line," with derivatives meaning "to direct in a straight line," thus "to lead, rule."

Celts would call a king Ra, **Rí**, or commonly **ríg** (genitive), is an ancient Gaelic word meaning 'king'. It is used in historical texts referring to the Irish and Scottish kings, and those of similar rank. While the Modern Irish word is exactly the same, in modern Scottish Gaelic it is *righ*, apparently derived from the genitive. Cognates include Gaulish *Rix*, Latin *rex/regis*, Spanish *rey*, French *roi*, Sanskrit *raja*, and German *Reich*.

RA, is an ancient anek for a diety or king, Amun Ra, was king of the Egyptian gods, and was the God of life.

143

Let me give it to you in English "Ye is Royal" comes from the queen mother Sarah whose name means prince or princess (child of the king), royalty. You mean to tell me Yisra'el is Ye is Royal yes! Hello Eloohim!

H3478 יִשְׂרָאֵל Yisra'el is-raw-ale'; Israel, Israelites from H8280 and H410; **he will rule as God;** Jisraël, a symbolical name of Jacob; also (typically) of his posterity, Israel also means "God prevails".

G2474 Ἰσραήλ Israēl Israel, **"he shall be a prince of God."**

H8280 שָׂרָה sârâh, saw-raw'; a primitive root; to prevail, have power (as a prince). H8282 שָׂרָה sârâh, saw-raw'; feminine of H8269; a mistress, i.e. female noble, lady, princess, queen. We remember Sarah has a Hey added to Her name, the same time Abram did, it was their Hey day. Sarah's original name was Sara (SaR) and is where we get the term SIR from

H3479 יִשְׂרָאֵל Yisra'el (Aramaic) Israel corresponding to H3478:

H3481 יִשְׂרְאֵלִי Yisrĕ'eliy Israel, Israelite, patronymically from H3478; a Jisreelite or descendant of Jisrael, of Israel.

H3482 יִשְׂרְאֵלִית Yisrĕ'eliyth Israelitess feminine of H3481; a Jisreelitess or female descendant of Jisrael, soldier of God, to fight for what you believe in.

G2475 Ἰσραηλίτης Israēlitēs Israel, Israelite, feminine of H3481, a Jisreelitess or female descendant of Jisrael.

Dad – seat of love

Dad – Breast's – as in papa, and pap's - And it came to pass, as he spoke these things, a certain woman of the company lifted up her voice and said unto him: Blessed is the womb that bare thee, and the PAPS which thou hast sucked. But he said, Yea rather, blessed are they that hear the word of God, and keep it (Luke 11:27-28).

Dad- seat of love, i.e., mum's breasts (H1717 דַּד dad), a sign of ownership, he's the dad, her breast belongs to him "breasts", same

144

as Pap's and pops meaning dad's / breasts! Strong's definition says:-
דד dad, the same as H1730; the breast (as the seat of love, or from its shape), breast, teat.

"[Let her be as] the loving hind and pleasant roe; let her breasts [H1717] satisfy thee at all times; and be thou always ravished with her love (Prov 5:19 KJV)."

Yah, Yes, and See Yah

The name Yah, as in Lord, is used H3050 יָהּ Yahh, LORD, JAH

Yah is where we get yes from, and it means to be in agreement, i.e., with God.

Yes (adv.)

Old English gise, gese "so be it!" probably from gea, ge "so" (see yea) + si "be it!" from Proto-Germanic *sijai-, from PIE *si-, optative stem of root *es- "to be." Originally stronger than simple, yeah. Used in Shakespeare mainly as an answer to negative questions. As a noun from 1712. Yes-man was first recorded in 1912 in American English.

See you

See Yah. Achiyyah H281. אֲחִיָּה, אֲחִיָּהוּ Achiyyah, a see yah brother, or worshiper of Yah", from H251. ach and H3050, Yahh; brother (i.e., Worshipper) of Jah; Achijah, the name of nine Israelites - Ahiah, Ahijah.

But wait, can "we see you" or "we'll see you" really be in the Bible? Well, actually, yes, it can, and the first time it was used was in

145

12 And the earth brought forth[H3318-we see u] grass, [and] herb yielding seed after his kind, and the tree yielding fruit, whose seed [was] in itself, after his kind: and God saw that [it was] good. [Gen 1:12 KJV]

31 And Terah took Abram, his son, and Lot the son of Haran, his son's son, and Sarai his daughter in law, his son Abram's wife; and they went forth[H3318] with them from Ur of the Chaldees, to go into the land of Canaan; and they came unto Haran, and dwelt there. [Gen 11:31 KJV]

These quotes I presented showcase the Hebrew verb **yatsa (qal)**. However, when used in a sentence, the verb undergoes modifications, as you can see in the examples. Check below, and you can click the link to the complete Bible reference.

H3318 וַיֵּצְא֣וּ <u>way·yê·ṣə·'ū</u> weye se u yâtsâ', yaw-tsaw'; yaw saw, (se u-goodby) a primitive root; to appear, to go (causatively, bring) out, in a great variety of applications, literally and figuratively, draw forth.

Let's not forget a very similar-sounding name, O Shea Yah:

H1954 הוֹשֵׁעַ hôwshêa', how-sha (v)-yah; *(our savior and O'sha'yah)* from H3467; deliverer; Hoshea, the name of five Israelites, Hosea, Hoshea, Oshea. God go with Yah.

And this would not be completed with a goodbye from Jack!

H3167 יַחְזְיָה Yachzᵉyâh, yakh-zeh-yaw from H2372 and H3050; Jah will behold; Jachzejah, an Israelite, Jahaziah, i.e., See you, Jack. Or Josh< I know you're coming back because Yah will behold, or do you prefer Yesh see yah, i.e. see Yah, יַחְזְיָה Yach'zᵉyâh.

h8454 תּוּשִׁיָּה tûwshîyâh, too-shee-yaw'; or תֻּשִׁיָּה tushîyâh tûwshîyâh too-shee-yaw Take care of yourself, be wise, "see yah" wisdom, sound knowledge, success, sound or efficient wisdom, abiding success, the wise know they will see Yah.

146

This also cometh forth from the LORD of hosts, [which] is wonderful in counsel, [and] excellent in working. [H8454] [Isa 28:29 KJV]

The LORD'S voice crieth unto the city, and [the man of] wisdom[H8454] shall see thy name: hear ye the rod, and who hath appointed it. [Mic 6:9 KJV]

Ta Ta, Ta Ra

Another way to say goodbye is ta ta or ta ra. It is used commonly in northern England and surprisingly widespread as a parting phrase in India, Surely this cannot be in the Bible, right? Well, let's take a peek; we can pick up the story in Genesis 20:13:

And it came to pass, when God caused me to wander(h8582 Ta ah) from my father's house, that I said unto her, This [is] thy kindness which thou shalt shew unto me; at every place whither we shall come, say of me, He [is] my brother. [Gen 20:13 KJV]

H8582 תָּעָה Ta'ah, taw-aw' (*ta and ta'wa, ta ra*) Goodbye as in the Tav of Ps 119.176 see also ta ta, but do we also get the English "to err" (Tav Ayin Hey t'ah, the Ayin can also be represented with an e as in ta e'h, to err, see alphabet section). The Ayin is the ancient eye and is used for a, i, e, and some say g, so it's possible that ta e'h. - To see ah (T Aeyin-eye H praise God.

H376 Abraham said goodbye to his father's house (Gen 20:13).

"If you meet your enemy's ox or his donkey wandering [H8582] away, [H8582] you shall surely return it to him. [Exo 23:4 NASB].

The wicked have laid a snare for me, yet I have not gone [H8582] astray [H8582] from Your precepts. ... 176

I have gone [H8582] astray [H8582] like a lost sheep; seek your servant, for I do not forget your commandments. [Psa 119:110, 176 NASB]

Here, we have the use Ta' ta and Ta'eh (ayin used for a, e, to wander away, or go away astry, to leave, i.e., ta ta or ta ra.

We also have the British term tits up, i.e., to err תָּעִיתִי tā-'î-tî, and err by failing for a prostitute (Ps 119.176)

Despite their similar sounds, "ta ta" and "ta ra" appear to have distinct meanings. "Ta ta" seems more commonly used to imply going astray, while "ta ra" might simply signify departure.

DRAW, BE DRAWN, (SKETCH).

DRAW, tawar, H8388 תָּאַר ta'ar taw-ar' a primitive root, to delineate, reflex, to extend, **be drawn**, mark out (*i.e., draw*), (Rimmon-) methoar (by union with H7417).

Draw, Taah, taw-ah Tav, Aleph-aandw in this case, Hey T'w'H אָה ta'ah taw-aw' Alphabet is A-X, x being the last letter, X = Ta or mark - a primitive root; to mark off, i.e. (intensively) designate, point out. The tav is the last letter of the Hebrew alphabet. We British also use it to finish off, i.e., goodbye ta ta, a ra

KILL

KILL from Old High German quellan "to suffer pain," German quälen "to torment, torture"), from PIE root *gwele- (from Hebrew- kawl-awm' H3637) "to throw, reach," with extended sense "to pierce." They from all or part of the following words - ANABOLIC; ARBALEST; ASTROBLEME; BALL (N.2) "dancing party;" BALLAD; BALLET; BALLISTA; BALLISTIC; BALLISTICS; BELEMNITE; CATABOLISM; DEVIL; DIABOLICAL; DISCOBOLUS; EMBLEM; EMBOLISM; HYPERBOLA; HYPERBOLE; KILL (V.); METABOLISM; PALAVER; PARABLE; PARABOLA; PARLEY;

PARLIAMENT; PARLOR; PAROL; PAROLE; PROBLEM; QUELL; QUAIL (v.) "lose heart, shrink, cower;" SYMBOL.

Kill them. H3637 כָּלַם kalam kawl-awm' a primitive root; properly, to wound; but only figuratively, to taunt or insult, be (make) ashamed, blush, be confounded, be put to confusion, hurt, reproach, (do, put to) shame. shame, confusion, dishonour, reproach, ashamed, confounded, blush, hurt, reproach, confusion

Killer, Kala, restrain someone H3607 כָּלָא kâlâ', kaw-law'; a primitive root; to restrict, by act (hold back or in) or word (prohibit):—finish, forbid, keep (back), refrain, restrain, retain, shut up, be stayed, withhold.

Killer, Kalah, finished, your finished, life over, perish H3615 כָּלָה kâlâh, kaw-law'; a primitive root; to end, whether intransitive (to cease, be finished, perish) or transitive (to complete, prepare, consume):—accomplish, cease, consume (away), determine, destroy (utterly), be (when... were) done, (be an) end (of), expire, (cause to) fail, faint, finish, fulfill, × fully, × have, leave (off), long, bring to pass, wholly reap, make clean riddance, spend, quite take away, waste.

RAW, RED RAW, Skinned Flesh.

Raw aw, meaning raw food gone bad, and skinned flesh. [the Aw or ah (Ayin) on the end turns it bad?] H7489 רָעַע râ'a', raw-ah, a primitive root; properly, to spoil (literally, by breaking to pieces); figuratively, to make (or be) good for nothing, i.e., bad (physically, socially or morally), afflict, associate selves (by mistake for 7462), break (down, in pieces), displease, (be, bring, do) evil (doer, entreat, man), show self friendly (by mistake for 7462), do harm, (do) hurt, (behave self, deal) ill, × indeed, do mischief, punish, still, vex, (do) wicked (doer, -ly), be (deal, do) worse.

Various Hebrew/English Terms

Plagues on Egypt

There were ten plagues in Egypt; God starts in Exodus 7 by saying that unto Pharaoh Moses would be a god (h430 אֱלֹהִים 'elohiym).

The first sign was Moses staff that turned into a snake; of course, the Egyptians sorcerers were able to duplicate the event and produce their own snakes. But ours came back to bite them (Ex. 7.8-13)! All of this was to harden Pharaoh's heart, as God had said it would.

From here, we had the plague of blood, which the Egyptians themselves attempted to replicate. This hardened Pharaoh's resolve. Then we had the plague of frogs, which the Egyptians were able to duplicate; with the same result, Pharaoh got tougher, even though he asked Moses to pray for the frog removal. After the frogs then came the gnats (Exo 8.16).

The Gnats and the Glies

The story takes a fascinating turn when the Egyptian sorcerers fail to replicate the plague of gnats. Interestingly, the magicians tell Pharaoh that *"this is the finger of God"* In the early going, the Egyptians must be thinking to themselves, "HA HA--who is this God, and who does he think he? We can do exactly what he does!"

16 And the LORD said unto Moses, Say unto Aaron, and Stretch out thy rod, and smites the dust of the land, that it may become lice throughout all the land of Egypt. 17 And they did so; for Aaron stretched out his hand with his rod, and smote the dust of the earth, and it became lice in man, and in beast; all the dust of the land became lice throughout all the land of Egypt. 18 And the magicians did so with their enchantments to bring forth lice, but they could not: so there were lice upon man, and upon beast. 19 Then the magicians said unto Pharaoh, This [is] the finger of God: and

Pharaoh's heart was hardened, and he hearkened not unto them; as the LORD had said. [Exo 8:16-19 KJV]

The gnats or flies plaguing Egypt were associated with the goddess Uatchit. Egyptians revered her as the protector of the Lower Nile, the "Queen-of-Cobras," and a powerful magician ("Great-in-Magic"). Interestingly, her name "Uatchit" phonetically resembles a rather vulgar term ("u a shit"). Some also connect this plague with the scarab deity. Who would roll up balls of dung?

This is a slap in the face for the Egyptians. One of their deities, who is great in magic and goddess of flies, cannot produce flies. Wow—this is nothing more than the finger of God, it seems to me. They think God is giving them the middle finger like FU. The Bible is unclear at what point the gnats appear.

Maybe they use the term "finger of god" as a general term for miracles? Despite my research, I haven't found a definitive answer. In modern terms, we might say "hand of God" to convey a similar meaning.

Finger of God

We can pick up the story in Exodus 8:19. Again, the magicians said unto Pharaoh, **this is the finger of God:** and Pharaoh's heart was hardened, and he hearkened not unto them; as the LORD had said.

The phrase "finger of God" remains a captivating metaphor, but I haven't found any relevant references in ancient Egyptian records. However, we can (through the process of examination and empirical data) establish the following.

Our fingers have served as a powerful communication tool for millennia in a non-verbal way, when one cannot communicate verbally due to background noise or perhaps other restraints, we would use our hands.

After the Tower of Babble incident, the language of Earth got scrambled, and we really had to use our hands a lot when trying to communicate with a person or with a group whose language we did not understand.

A hand in our face means stop.

A pointing finger could mean go there or look there, or it's you.

A wagging index finger means, "don't do that".

Despite its seemingly straightforward meaning as an insult ("up yours!"), the middle finger gesture has a more complex history.

A single or split v sign symbol thrust at you means FU. Or you turn it around, and it means peace. Also, the same v sign aleph when you beat your chest with it means "I love you." Remember that Joseph was in charge of Egypt circa 19th century B.C., was the Imhotep, the non-Egyptian or commoner that created the granaries for storage of grain during seven years of plenty that immediately was followed by seven years of drought. Everything points to this fact. Also of note is that Imhotep slogan or catchphrase was "One who comes in peace." I argue that the Aleph of the Alphabet had much more significance than just a starting point. See Aleph details for more information.

A finger or a thumb turned upside down means you are going down or not good.

A thumb pointing straight up means great, I agree; good job.

Which finger do you think the Egyptians got from the message?

The use of fingers represents disdain, war, acceptance, and selection, and it's also used for peace. This practice of imbuing hand gestures with meaning stretches far back into the mists of time.

The Index Finger

To Which Finger Were They Referring?

Typically, the middle finger is used as a form of the phallic symbol. When Pharaoh realized that God was metaphorically giving him the finger, so to speak, it hardened his heart. God knew this would happen; this is the first instance in the Bible for this term.

Later, we have many instances where the horns of Ephraim and Manasseh would gore the nations to the end of the earth. God said that he would drive them to the end of the world where they would gore the nations: *"I said I would scatter them and blot out their memory from mankind"* (Deu. 32.26). Their origin would be blotted out until God was ready to reveal them and speak of Joseph's birthright son, Ephraim. v33:17 In majesty (Israel - His Royal Highness), he is like a firstborn bull; his horns are the horns of a Unicorn; with them, he will gore the nations even to the ends of the erets.

His glory [is like] the firstling of his bullock, and his horns [are like] the horns of unicorns: with them, he shall push the people together to the end of the earth: and they [are] the ten thousands of Ephraim, and they [are] the thousands of Manasseh. [Deu 33:17 KJV].

All the horns of the wicked also will I cut off; [H1438] [but] the horns of the righteous shall be exalted. [Psa 75:10 KJV]

Fear not, thou worm Jacob, [and] ye men of Israel; I will help thee, saith the LORD. and thy redeemer (Gael Gaelic), the Holy One (Qod'osh God, good. i.e. sanctified) of Israel.

Behold, I will make thee a new sharp threshing instrument having teeth: thou shalt thresh the mountains and beat [them] small, and shalt make the hills as chaff. [Isa 41:14-15 KJV]

We are now aware (see "We are Israel") that the symbols of Ephraim/Manasseh (and to some degree Benjamin Num.2. also

153

wolf) are the Ox, i.e., Egel'ish or cowboy, and that the first letter of the Alphabet depicted this (Ƿ Ɐ A), the Unicorn being depicted by the middle finger. See the alphabet for more details.

H2651 חֹפֶן chophen hand, fist, handful, grab a handful and then ho p'hen (open) and H'Ph'n high Phen, high five.

And God sent Moses, *And the LORD said unto Moses and unto Aaron, take to you handfuls[H2651] of ashes of the furnace, and let Moses sprinkle it toward the heaven in the sight of Pharaoh. [Exo 9:8 KJV].*

I think this is a clear indication of the origin, don't you?

Hip-Hip-Hurrah

h8597 תִּפְאָרָה tip' harah, tip harah, hip' harah-first letter chet (h) to acknowledge someone's - beauty, bravery, glory, honor, majesty. **Hip hip hooray** (also **hippity hip hooray**; *Hooray* may also be spelled and pronounced **hoorah, hurrah, hurray,** etc.) is a cheer called out to express congratulation toward someone or something in the English-speaking world and elsewhere.

By a sole speaker, it is a form of interjection. In a group, it takes the form of call and response: the cheer is initiated by one person exclaiming, "Three cheers for...[someone or something]" (or, more archaically, "Three times three"[1][2][3][4]), then calling out "hip hip" (archaically, "hip hip hip") three times, each time being responded by "hooray" or "hurrah".

TITS

Tits - Tits - maw's tits. H4711 – matsats מָצַץ ' mâtsats, (pronounced-maw-tsats) maw' tsats. That ye may suck, and be satisfied with the breasts of her consolations; that ye may milk out, [H4711] and be delighted with the abundance of her glory. (Isa 66:11 KJV)

צִיץ (from the root צִיץ)—(1) *a shining plate*, on the forehead of the high priest, Ex. 28:36—38. Compare Ps. 132:18.

(2) *a flower*, Job 14:2.   Plur. צִצִּים (for צִיצִים comp. זִקִּים, זְיקוֹת) 1 Ki. 6:18.

(3) *a wing* (compare at the root נָצַץ), Jer. 48:9.

(4) [*Ziz*], pr. n. of a town, only once, 2 Ch. 20:16.

Tits – צִיץ Tsîyts, tseets, 16 To morrow go ye down against them: behold, they come up by the cliff of Ziz;[H6732] and ye shall find them at the end of the brook, before the wilderness of Jeruel. (2 Chr 20:16 KJV), the same as H6731.

LABAN, L'B'N

Jacob worked at the white house and got his 4 wives from the white house, this was LaBaN[120], his etymology is retained in ALBION the original name for the British Isles, along with the following LEBANON(white mountain) ALP's, ALPINE region, St Albans takes its name from the first British saint, Alban. How is it possible that so many names come from a non-indo European root?

Albion is an alternative name for Great Britain. The name for Scotland in most of the Celtic languages is related to Albion: *Alba* in Scottish Gaelic, *Albain* (genitive *Alban*) in Irish, *Nalbin* in

---

[120] H3837 Laban = "white" son of Bethuel, brother of Rebekah, and father of Leah and Rachel, proper locative noun a wilderness encampment of the Israelites

Strong's Definitions [?](Strong's Definitions Legend) לָבָן Lâbân, law-bawn'; the same as H3836; Laban, a Mesopotamian; also a place in the Desert , Laban.

Manx and *Alban* in Welsh and Cornish. These names were later Latinised as *Albania* and Anglicised as *Albany*, which were once alternative names for Scotland.

Albania Greek Albania,IE word *alb "hill" (also proposed as the source of Alps) or from the PIE root *albho- "white" (see alb). Albania also was a sometime name for Scotland. Related: Albanian (1590s). Old English elfet "swan," literally "the white bird; ALBINO.

late Old English albe "white linen robe" worn by priests, converts, etc., from Late Latin alba (in tunica alba or vestis alba "white vestment"), fem. of albus "white," from PIE root *albho- "white" (source also of Greek alphos "white leprosy," alphiton "barley meal;" Old High German albiz,

POOR

The English term POOR, can be used metaphorically as something weak, lacks strength, or easily broken, it also means to have nothing, or very little, it is the hypothetical source of the following words - *pau- (1) Proto-Indo-European root meaning "few, little." The Jewish feast of Purim means a lot that is cast the lot it is also from the same root. Almost like gambling (casting a lot) will make you poor, there is perhaps a lot of truth in that.

It forms all or part of: catchpoll; encyclopedia; filly; foal; few; hypnopedia; impoverish; orthopedic; Paedophryne; paraffin; parvi-; parvovirus; paucity; Paul; pauper; pedagogue; pederasty; pedo-; pedophilia; poco; poltroon; pony; pool (n.2) "game similar to billiards;" poor; poulterer; poultry; poverty; puericulture; puerile; puerility; puerperal; pullet; pullulate; Punch; Punchinello; pupa; pupil (n.1) "student;" pupil (n.2) "center of the eye;" puppet; pusillanimous; putti.

H6331 פּוּר puwr poor a primitive root; to crush:--break, bring to nought, X utterly take.

156

H6332 **פּוּר** Puwr pᴄor also (plural) Puwriym {pooreem'} or Puriym {poor-eem'}, poor him from h6331; a lot, **פּוּר** pûwr, poor; a primitive root; to crush, break, bring to nought. Pur, Purim.

HEAVENLY TERMS.

ASTRONOMY

c. 1200, "astronomy, astrology, the scientific or occult study of heavenly bodies", from Old French astrenomie "astronomy, astrology", from Latin astronomia, from Greek astronomia, the abstract noun from astronomos, literally "star-regulating", from astron "star" (from PIE root *ster- (2) "star") + nomos "arranging, regulating; rule, law", from PIE root *nem- "assign, allot; take", perhaps originally with reference to mapping the constellations or movements of planets.

ASTRONOMY, along with over 30 other astronomical terms come from STAR, that etymologist trace to *ster. Here is the list - ASTER; ASTERISK; ASTERISM; ASTEROID; ASTRAL; ASTRO-; ASTROBIOLOGY; ASTROBLEME; ASTROGNOSY; ASTROID; ASTROLABE; ASTROLATRY; ASTROLOGY; ASTROMANCY; ASTRONAUT; ASTRONOMY; ASTROTURF; CONSTELLATION; DISASTER; ESTELLA; ESTHER; INSTELLATION; INTERSTELLAR; LODESTAR; STAR; STARDUST; STARFISH; STARLET; STARLIGHT; STARRY; STELLAR; STELLATE. In that list is the Biblical figure ESTHER, correctly pronounced A'STAR, (Persian for Star, see star), she did actually saved the Jewish race from the evil HAMAN, who was hanged on his own gallows, the Jews commemorate this event with PURIM (casting of lots, see POOR).

STAR, ISHTAR.

The name STAR comes to us from the Germanic link, Old English steorra Dutch ster, Old High German sterro, they trace it to a PIE root *ster- (2) like ASTEROID, aSTER, some believe Akkadian istar "venus," Is also linked. The PIE *ster- is linked to over 30 entries[121] one of them being the Biblical figure **Esther aka, a'Star H635** אֶסְתֵּר 'Eçtêr, Aleph Samech, Tav, Resh A'STaR, of Persian derivation; Ester, the Jewish heroine.

Next, we will look at the Hebrew king and queen, Ahab and Jezebel (H348 אִיזֶבֶל 'îzebel), they worshiped Ashtar[122] and Baal. Ashtar is the Phoenician sex goddess meaning A STAR, it is and the actual word is Ashtoreth[123] Hebrew full name.

ASTARTE, ASHTORETH

Semiramis, Ishtar, and Astarte - Legends describing Semiramis have been recorded by writers including Plutarch, Eusebius, Polyaenus, and Justinus. She was associated with **Ishtar and Astarte** *(I'ShTaR, A'STaR'te, the origin of the English star)* since the time before Diodorus. [11] The association of the fish and dove is found at Hierapolis Bambyce (Mabbog), the great temple which, according to one legend, was founded by Semiramis, [19] where her statue was shown with a golden dove on her head.[20]

GODDESS INANNA

Goddess Anna Inanna, Ishtar, Phoenician, Assyrian, Venus, and eight-pointed stars Inanna[a] is an ancient Mesopotamian goddess associated with sex, war, justice, and political power. Inanna, originally revered in Sumer, later found devotion from the Akkadians, Babylonians, and Assyrians under the name Ishtar[b]. She was known as the **"Queen of Heaven"** (e.g. A'STAR) and was

---

[121] aster; asterisk; asterism; asteroid; astral; astro-; astrobiology; astrobleme; astrognosy; astroid; astrolabe; astrolatry; astrology; astromancy; astronaut; astronomy; AstroTurf; constellation; disaster; Estella; Esther; instellation; interstellar; lodestar; star; stardust; starfish; starlet; starlight; starry; stellar; stellate.

[122]H6253 עַשְׁתָּרוֹת 'Ashtârôwth, ash-taw-roth'; or עַשְׁתָּרֹת 'Ashtârôth; plural of H6251; Ashtaroth, the name of a Sidonian deity, and of a place East of the Jordan:—Asharoth, Astaroth. See also H1045, H6253, H6255.

[123] H6253 עַשְׁתֹּרֶת 'Ashtoreth, Ashtoreth=star, probably for H6251; Ashtoreth, the Phoenician goddess of love (and increase).H6251 עַשְׁתְּרָה 'asht°râh, ash-ter-aw'; probably from H6238; increase, flock.'âsâr, aw-sawr'; for H6235; multitude of stars? sixscore thousand, + twelve(-th).

158

the patron goddess of the Eanna temple in the city of Uruk, which was her main cult center.

With the planet Venus as her celestial domain, this Mesopotamian goddess was often depicted with powerful symbols like the lion and the eight-pointed star. Her husband was the god Dumuzid (later known as Tammuz), and her sukkal, or personal attendant, was the goddess Ninshubur (who later became the male deity Papsukkal).

EASTER

Easter (22,March-25 April),is well known as the time we celibrate, Jesus's death and resurrection, however it is a makeover of a pagan holiday, and before the time of Bede, we called it Pascal (Passover-from Hebrew root paws'akh' H to jump, or hop over HOP"to spring, leap; to dance; to limp," from Proto-Germanic *hupnojan). There is much to unpack regarding Easter, it is linked to Esther and A'Star, Asteroid, Venus, Ishtar, and Ashtarte some say its origin comes from Etuscan see also linked to Proto-Germanic *austron-, "dawn," & PIE root *aus- (1) "to shine, "dawn". It echos the death burial and resurrection of Jesus, bringing a new dawn, and beginning, and covenant. Which occurred in the spring, April is also related, perhaps from Apru, an Etruscan borrowing of Greek Aphrodite.

There are many names that relate to Easter, sunrise, dawn, easter bunnys, many pagan traditions that were made over into Chritiasn Holidays by Satanically inspired rulers many of whom have controlled Religion and Countries. This one word "Easter" and all its links speaks volumes.

METEOR

Meteor, late 15c., "any atmospheric phenomenon," from Old French meteore (13c.) and directly from Medieval Latin meteorum (nominative meteora), from Greek ta meteōra "the celestial phenomena, things in heaven above," plural of meteōron, literally "a thing high up," noun use of neuter of meteōros (adj.) "high up, raised from the ground, hanging," from meta "by means of" (see meta-) + -aoros "lifted, lifted up, suspended, hovering in air," related to aeirein "to raise" (from PIE root *wer- (1) "to raise, lift, hold suspended") ἀμήτωρ amḗtōr, am-ay'-tore; from G1 (as a negative particle) and G3384; motherless, i.e. of unknown maternity, without mother.

Names of little gods fallen angels

Hell, Yeh, Hell No

How art thou fallen from heaven, O Lucifer [H1966], son of the morning! [how] art thou cut down (H1438) to the ground (earth, hell), which didst weaken the nations! [Isa. 14:12 KJV].

Behold, the Lord, the LORD of hosts, shall lop the bough with terror: and the high ones of stature [shall be] hewn down, [H1438] and the haughty shall be humbled. [Isa 10:33 KJV]

Lucifer H1966 הֵילֵל heylel hay-lale' Hey, Yud, Lamed, Lamed HYLL Hell as in the Devil, (in the sense of brightness); the morning-star, from H1984 hail or Yell.

HAIL, YELL HALLO H1984, 1985 הָלַל hâlal, haw-lal'; (HAIL here comes the king, from where do you hail, also Yell and perhaps Hallo) a primitive root; to praise, to be clear (orig. of sound, but usually of color); to shine; hence, to make a show, to boast; and thus to be (clamorously) foolish; to rave;, rage, renowned, shine.

HELL the abode of the Devil, a term that is no longer used for God, it was used for the God and the Devil. H426 אֱלָהּ 'elahh (Aramaic) el'ah God, god =לְ and ה =Praise therefore eloh = praise i.e., God see H1985.

ALE, etymology unknown, strong drink, intoxicating, H410 אֵל '(a)el ale (now used for might drink Ale), Originally used for both God and Devil now only dEvil - God, god, power, mighty, goodly, great, idols, Immanuel, **might, strong.**

160

HELL is the abode of the DevEL Hell Elah is a term that is no longer used for God H426 אֱלָהּ 'elahh (Aramaic) el'ah

Devil, Evil, Awful

But what about the English word Devil? While the origins of the English word "devil" are fascinating, let's delve deeper into four possible Hebrew words that may have contributed to its development.

DEVIL, EVIL, AWFUL, H5760 עֲוִיל 'aviyl aw-val'; a primitive root; to distort (morally), deal unjustly, unrighteous.

EVIL, AWFUL, AVIL H5765 עָוַל 'ăval aw-val' a primitive root; to distort (morally), deal unjustly, unrighteous.

EVIL, AWFUL, AVIL H5766 עֶוֶל 'evel, eh'-vel; or עָוֶל 'âvel, and (feminine) עַוְלָה 'avlâh; or עוֹלָה 'ôwlâh; or עֹלָה 'ôlâh; from H5765; (moral) evil, iniquity, perverseness.

EVIL H5767 עַוָּל 'avvâl, av-vawl intensive from H5765; evil (morally), unjust, unrighteous, wicked.

Satan, Parade, Proud, Sod.

Satan H7853 שָׂטַן sâṭan, saw-tan, primitive root; to attack, (figuratively) accuse, (be an) adversary, resist.

Satan h7854 שָׂטָן satan saw-tawn, from H7853, an opponent; especially (with the article prefixed) Satan, the arch-enemy of good, adversary, Satan, withstand.

Stick chest out proud-zed and parade H2086 זֵד zêd, zade parade, proud, pomp From H2102; arrogant, presumptuous, proud.

Sod, you sod, to be insolent seethe, זִיד zîyd H2102 זוּד zûwd, zood, or (by permutation) זִיד zîyd; a primitive root; to seethe; figuratively, to be insolent, be proud, deal proudly, presume, (come) presumptuously, sod.

Sodom, Sodomite, sodomy, see doom.

H5467 סְדֹם Çᵉdôm, sed-ome, from an unused root meaning to scorch; burnt (i.e., volcanic or bituminous) district; Sedom, a place near the Dead Sea, see doom, destruction and that's what happened and our etymology speaks of it a burnt mess of towns, completely destroyed!

Goddess, and god's

H6945 קָדֵשׁ qadesh kaw-dashe'; "god's a she" from H6942; a (quasi) sacred person, i.e. (technically) a (male) devotee (by prostitution) to licentious idolatry, sodomite, unclean. sodomite, unclean.

Wait, so a male prostitute is a "god a she", an idolatrous act, what should be a sacred event, i.e., God's what is devoted and holy to God is called "God's" (Holy H6944 קֹדֶשׁ Godes), comes from "to consecrate to God", or to burn up, to sacrifice, as in God ash, a sacrifice, that gets burned up, its where we get ash from.

H6948 קְדֵשָׁה qĕdeshah ked-es-haw god'es whore, a goddess, a whore Temple prostitute, feminine of H6945; a female devotee (i.e., prostitute), harlot, whore.

Wikipedia says the following:

The noun *goddess* is a secondary formation, combining the Germanic *god* with the Latinate *-ess* suffix. It first appeared in Middle English from about 1350.[2] The English word follows the linguistic precedent of a number of languages—including Egyptian, Classical Greek, and several Semitic languages—**that add a feminine ending to the language's word for *god*.**

The term for a male or female devotee today is "I'm God's" like God'es, God's, H6942 קָדַשׁ qâdash, kawdash or God's, to set apart as sacred.

It's clear that the English term "goddess" comes from the Bible, H6945 קָדֵשׁ qadesh kawd'ashe,

And she comes from H1931 הִיא HeeYE, (s)HeeYe but we also have H0802 אִשָּׁה 'ishshah wife, woman, one, married, female, misc.

The term for mankind is H0582 אֱנוֹשׁ 'ĕnôwsh, en-oshe'; "e'now'she" from H605; mankind, he and she remember that Eve came from Adam, i.e. the modern translation of this word is mortal meaning mankind.

Ghoul, Goal

Ghoul, Goel, H1352 גֹּאֵל gô'el, go'-el, from H1351, profanation, defile. -גָּאַל (H1351) notice it is "go el" where el means god, or demon, or evil spirit

Ghoul, Goel, gaw al H1351 גָּאַל gâ'al, gaw-al' a primitive root, (rather identified with H1350, through the idea of freeing, i.e.; repudiating) to soil or (figuratively) desecrate, defile, pollute, stain.

With a handful of intriguing words explored, let's be clear: this project isn't intended to be a comprehensive dictionary or lexicon – perhaps that's a future endeavor, God willing. However, to whet your appetite for the etymological journey ahead, here are a few examples of the rich tapestry of English words we'll encounter: girl, gal, goal, Gael, gail, and gwheel. Each holds its own unique story waiting to be unraveled.

Crude/Rude Biblical Hebrew Words

Caution! This section contains Hebrew words that are considered crude and rude by modern-day standards.

Why do we include rude, obscene, and vulgar words in this book? These are the words of war, conquest, and anger that help us express our deep-felt emotions. They tend to transcend time and space, war and migrations, as well as mixing and intermingling. How do I know this? Because today, they are almost identical to how they sounded 3,000 years ago.

I also agree with the Oxford dictionary's reasoning for listing these "types of words"[124]

The etymology of the rude words like "SHIT" and others is somewhat obscure and disputed due to its vulgar nature and the consequential historical reluctance to document it. Nonetheless, rude words are generally considered to be of Germanic origin, with cognates found in several Germanic languages, which can help us see how or if they have changed much over time.

The Bible starts with the following words: *[In the beginning, God created the heaven and the earth Gen 1:1 KJV]*. The English phrase "In the beginning" is a translation of one Hebrew word H7225 רֵאשִׁית re'shiyth, beginning, first fruits, first, chief, misc. The Bible employs a very primitive version of the early English language. In this instance, the correct pronunciation of reshiyth is בְּרֵאשִׁית bə-rê-šît, meaning "In the beginning," as opposed to re-shiyth, meaning first fruits or beginning.

This analogy is akin to the idea of creation ex nihilo (from nothing) – God starting with a "baresheet." We also know this as the basic building blocks of life, to start, to grow something, for it to be fruitful, it must have organic matter that fuels the growth.

The technical definition for the Hebrew word for beginning is H7225 רֵאשִׁית rê'shîyth, ray-sheet is the basic verb (Qal), Bereshit

---

[124]"The role of a descriptive dictionary is to record the existence and meaning of all words in a language, and to clearly identify their status. We include vulgar or offensive words in our dictionaries because such terms are a part of a language's lexicon. However, we label in our dictionaries words that fit into these categories to reflect their vulgar or offensive status and usage in the language."

is the preposition-b noun, feminine singular (Prep-b | N-fs) in this sentence and it means in the beginning, the firstfruits, first, chief.

SHIT

Perhaps it is a strange coincidence that the sound and meaning are so similar to the English bare shit? Let's look at where we get, Sit, Set, Shit, Shity, Shitfaced (drunk), shithouse, (a worthless piece of shit). They are all in the Bible and are all intertwined around each other because English is Hebrew.

H8352 שֵׁת Shêth, shayth, from H7896; put or sit. i.e. substituted; Sheth. third son of Adam, Seth, Sheth and he replaced Abel.

H7896 שִׁית shîyth. sheet'h; a primitive root; to put, set, place, mark(in a very wide application), apply, appoint, array, bring, consider, lay (up). let alone, × look, make, **mark**, put (on), regard, set, shew, be stayed, × take.[Gen 3:15 KJV] 15 And I will **put (set)** enmity between thee and the woman and between thy seed and her seed; it shall bruise thy head, and thou shalt bruise his heel.

H8357 שֵׁתָה shêthâh, shayt-haw, from H7896; the seat (cf the person) buttock.

H4960 מִשְׁתֶּה mishteh, mi-sht-he (me shitty) from H8354, drink, by implication, drinking (the act); also (by implication) a banquet or (generally) feast, banquet, drank, drink, feast((-ed), -ing).

H8358 שָׁתָה shâthâh, shaw-thaw primitive root; to imbibe (literally or figuratively). assuredly, banquet, × certainly, drink(-er, -ing), drunk (× -ard), surely. (Intensive proposition of H8248.)

H8354 שָׁתָה shâthâh, shaw-thaw, a primitive root; to imbibe (literally or figuratively):—× assuredly, banquet, × certainly, drink(-er, -ing), drunk (× -ard), surely. (Intensive proposition of H8248.)

H8359 שְׁתִי shthy shet-hee' from H7896 a fixture, i.e., the warp in weaving, the warp (Lev 13:48 KJV) 48 Whether [it be] in the warp, [shet'hee] or woof; of linen, or of woolen, whether in a skin or in anything made of skin.

Wow, did you get that all those very English terms are right in our own Bible today? Words spoken by the ancient Hebrews in their daily lives have survived for over 3,000 years and remain nearly identical in our modern usage.

In the beginning, God created the Heaven and Earth from nothing but bare sheets. In plain Egel'ish, this means bare, unadorned, simple, unembellished, plain, basic stuff. Things that the Bible calls shit שִׁית Shin-SH, Yud-I, Tav-T, don't shoot the messenger. Synonyms for shix are dung, waste, manure, muck, fertilizer, slurry, and excrement. The perfect building blocks of life, Hello! God started with a clean slate, then added fertilizer, water, seedpods, the sun, the earth, and the moon at the absolute perfect position in the universe and <u>walla</u> (ala אָלָה H422 to swear, take an oath before God).

BULLSHIT

The term Bullshit is a common expression for an English speaker, but where did this pungent word originate? That's a question worth digging into. The term has become synonymous with insincere talk; it's all bull or bull-crap, it is made up of bull and xxx and shit, we have briefly touched this and will cover more extensively later. Bull has three meanings:-

1-Bull – male castrated bovine animal

2-Bull-"Papal edict, the seal on a document from the Latin bulla, said to come from the Gaulish, and etymologists say PIE beu. They also think much, great, many, bumps, blisters, Lithuanian lule (buttocks), middle Dutch payl (bag), and Latin bucca (cheek) all come from this root.

3-Bull insincere, or dishonest talk, old French bole modern Icelandic bull (nonsense).

166

The original word is thought to come from the PIE root bhel, to blow or swell, we covered this earlier, but we talk about it again below..

Interestingly, the Bible might offer an echo of this etymology in the story of Cain and Abel. Recall the narrative: Able's sacrifice was pleasing to God, but Cain's wasn't. Cain was mad as hell. In fact, he was made at El (God), and he allowed hatred to come into his heart (eL-satan-god)

The noun Etymologist thinks it is in insincere talk (Bull). Etymologists are uncertain where it's from; they think maybe it is linked to the Old French bole but appears to be connected to a bolder variant of Middle English bulder ston "stone worn round, cobblestone" (c. 1300), from a Scandinavian source akin to Swedish dialectal bullersten "noisy stone" (large stone in a stream, causing water to roar around it), from bullra "to roar" + sten "stone." Or the first element might be from *buller- "round object," from Proto-Germanic *bul-, from PIE root *bhel- (2) "to blow, swell." The specific geological sense "large weather-worn block of stone standing by itself" is from 1813.

Remember Nabal (5036)נָבָל foolish hand his foolish talk to David, also a tower of Babel, (h894 בָּבֶל Bâbel, baw-bel'; from H1101; confusion) Babylon confused speech,

The Aleph is the horned bull, and that is no buwl Shit.

BALL, BAWL BALLS, BLOW, ABEL, BELLOWS-see edenics 1895 הֶבֶל Hebel heh'-bel; Abel-= "breath" as in a Bellohs, from H58; a meadow, the name of two places in Palestine.:—Abel. the same as H1892; Hebel, the son of Adam:—Abel. Ball, as in spherical object, is a diminutive of the testicle

Bull from Blow, belloe, Ball Aball H59 הֶבֶל Hebel heh'-bel; Abel-= "breath" as in a Bellohs, from H58; a meadow, the name of two places in Palestine.:—Abel. the same as H1892; Hebel, the son of Adam:—Abel.

167

Bull, buwl bool Rain/ 8th Month H945 בּוּל bûwl, bool; "increase: produce "the same as H944 (in the sense of rain), Bul, the eighth Hebrew month

Horeb-Bull, buwl bool food stock H944 בּוּל bûwl, bool; from H2981; produce (of the earth, etc., food, stock

Bull, buwl bool food stock H944 בּוּל bûwl, bool; from H2981; produce (of the earth, etc.):—food, stock

Bull, buwl bool Rain/ 8th Month H945 בּוּל bûwl, bool; "increase: produce" the same as H944 (in the sense of rain), Bul, the eighth Hebrew month

Horeb-Bull, buwl bool food stock, H944 בּוּל bûwl, bool; from H2981; produce (of the earth, etc.):—food, stock

Horeb-Bull, buwl bool Rain/ 8th Month H945 בּוּל bûwl, bool; "increase: produce" the same as H944 (in the sense of rain), Bul, the eighth Hebrew month

Bullshxx, h944-5, h7848 שִׁטָּה, בּוּל Buwl, shittah bull-shittah Land, and produce hurting lack of rain, God caused the land to shittah, to Buwl, shittah!

Horeb-Bullshxx, h944-5, h7848 שִׁטָּה, בּוּל Buwl, shittah bull-shittah Land, and produce hurting lack of rain, God caused the land to shittah, to Buwl, shittah!

Buck, and run down trample, H947 בּוּס buwc tread..., polluted, loath-a primitive root; to trample (literally or figuratively), loath, tread (down, under (foot)), be polluted.

Blush, ashamed, embarrassed H954 בּוּשׁ buwsh boosh ashamed, confounded, shame, all (inf. for emphasis), confusion, delayed, dry, long, shamed

Bush, show bush, i.e. naked, ashamed, embarrassed see blush H954 בּוּשׁ buwsh boosh ashamed, confounded, shame, all (inf. for emphasis), confusion, delayed, dry, long, shamed.

ASSHOLE, ARSE, Backside, WHORE.

Everyone has heard the term "you're an Asshole" meaning a mocker, to deride someone to say something that is very wrong. Consider the following:

H2048 הָתַל hâthal, hawt-hal' (ASS HOLE) a primitive root; to deride; by implication, to cheat, deal deceitfully, deceive, mock. The term is metaphorical, and means piece of SHIT, anus, or a despicable person and is said to come from ASS and HOLE

ASSHOLE and ARSEHOLE are said to come from ARSE & HOLE, where ARSE means "buttocks, hinder part of an animal," Old English ærs "tail, rump," from Proto-Germanic *arsoz from PIE root *ors

H811   אֶשְׁכּוֹל 'eshkôwl, ASSHOLE esh-kole'; or אֶשְׁכֹּל 'eshkôl; used to describe a bunch of grapes or testicles, prolonged from H810;.

Man's testicle "his SACK" H810 אֶשֶׁךְ 'eshek, eh'-shek (ASS ball-sack,), from an unused root (probably meaning to bunch together); a testicle (as a lump), stone.

Notice that the spelling of this Hebrew word has a Kaf for the final letter K (Aleph, Sin/Shin Kuf), this may have been changed, from a Kuf.

SACK even etymologist are now tracing this to Hebrew, "large oblong bag," Middle English sak, from Old English sacc from Proto-Germanic *sakkiz, Hebrew, Phoenician saq "sack, cloth of hair, bag, mourning-dress" H8242 שַׂק (Sin Ku)SaQ, from H8264; properly, a mesh (as allowing a liquid to run through), i.e. coarse loose cloth or sacking (used in mourning and for bagging); hence, a bag (for grain, etc.), sack.

WHORE (n.) Etymology

The 1530s spelling alteration (see wh-) of Middle English hore, from Old English hore "prostitute, harlot," from Proto-Germanic *hōran-, fem. *hōrā- (source also of Old Frisian hor "fornication," Old Norse hora "adulteress," Danish hore, Swedish hora, Dutch hoer, Old High German huora "prostitute"; in Gothic only in the masc. hors "adulterer, fornicator," also as a verb, horinon "commit adultery"), probably etymologically "one who desires," from PIE root *ka- "to like, desire," which in other languages has produced words for "lover; friend".

"WHORE" itself might be a Germanic euphemism, a substitute word for a term lost to time. The natural evolution of Old English vowels would have resulted in the pronunciation "*hoor," which persists in some dialects even today. It might have shifted by the influence of the Middle English homonym hore, "physical filth, slime," also "moral corruption, sin," from Old English horh. The wh- form became current 16c. A general term of abuse for an **unchaste or lewd woman** (without regard to money) from at least c. 1200. Of male prostitutes from the 1630s. Whore of Babylon is from Revelation xvii.1, 5, etc. In Middle English, with occasional plural forms horen, and heoranna.

BELCH or Beoch, foul-smelling odor? H889 בְּאֹשׁ bĕ'osh be'osh or be(l)' och, God causes us to shittah, and the smell out of the hind quarters was bad!

BLUSH, ashamed, embarrassed H954 בּוּשׁ buwsh boosh ashamed, confounded, shame, all (inf. for emphasis), confusion, delayed, dry, long, shamed

SHITTY.

Shitty, not good, bad workmanship, H8359 שְׁתִי shthiy shet-hee' from H7896; a fixture, i.e. the warp in weaving:- warp (Lev 13:48 KJV) 48 Whether [it be] in the warp,[H8359] or woof; of linen, or of woollen; whether in a skin or in anything made of skin.

SHIT TOWN.

shit town, leader, ruler in Babylon H7984 שִׁלְטֹן shiltown (Aramaic) shilt-one'; (Aramaic) or שִׁלְטֹן shiltônlemma שִׁלְטֹן missing vowel, corrected to שִׁלְטֹן; corresponding to H7983, ruler. Foreign ruler of a town where we are slaves!

SHITFACED.

Shit (faced) Shithiy, to get drunk h8358 שְׁתִי shᵉthîy, shet-hee' from H8354; intoxication, drunkenness. (Eccl 10:17 KJV) 17 Blessed [art] thou, O land, when thy king [is] the son of nobles, and thy princes eat in due season, for strength, and not for drunkenness [H8358]!

What is the Hebrew term for someone who greatly feared God?

And they journeyed: and the terror[H2847] of God was upon the cities that [were] round about them, and they did not pursue after the sons of Jacob. [Gen 35:5 KJV]

SHITTAH, CHATTER, SHATTER.

H2847חִתָּה chittâh, khit-taw', (SHITTAH, themselves) from H2865; fear, terror.

H2865 חָתַת châthath, khaw-thath'; (SHATTER) a primitive root; properly, to prostrate; hence, to break down, either (literally) by violence, or (figuratively) by confusion and fear, abolish, affright, be (make) afraid, amaze, beat down, discourage, (cause to) dismay, go down, scare, terrify.

H2851 חִתִּית chittîyth, k'hit-teeth';(CHIVER?) from H2865, fear, terror.

SHAG.

Shag ah H7686 שָׁגָה shâgâh, shaw-gaw, a primitive root; to stray (causatively, mislead), usually (figuratively) to mistake, **especially (morally) to transgress,** by an extension (through the idea of intoxication) to reel, (figuratively) be enraptured, (cause to) go astray, deceive, err, **be ravished, sin through ignorance,** (let, make to) wander shâgâh shag' [Pro 5:20 KJV] 20 And why to wilt thou, my son, be ravished (Shag ah) with a strange woman, and embrace the bosom of a stranger? Still don't think English is Hebrew, I have thousands, but I can't fit them all in this book.

This term was also used for making love with your wife: *Let her be as* the loving hind and pleasant roe; let her **breasts (dad, whose ya daddy-lover) satisfy thee at all times**; and be thou ravished (shagah) always with her love, (Prov 5:19, 20).

The finger symbols, the middle and two fingers.

ﬖ ﬗ A , We have been communicating with our hands since the origin of the world, in fact, we probably used them more then than we do today, also after Bable when the language got metathesis we really needed to communicate this way. In addition during war when two opposing armies would greet they would shout and jeer at each other and use symbols to communicate their intention.

The hand the arm and the fingers played a vital role in this communication, here we will uncover the origin of the Middle Finger (used predominantly by the USA) and the two fingers (peace war signs used by the British)

The two-and-one-finger salute has appeared many times throughout history. It was a symbol (digitalis-impudicus) used in ancient Greece and Rome as a sign of contempt and insult; it is said to represent the phallus or penis and means FU.

172

The index finger and ring finger (beside the middle finger), in more contemporary periods, have been likened to represent the testes.[2] (Wikipedia)

A curious geographical divide exists when it comes to the middle finger. In the United Kingdom, Ireland, Australia, and New Zealand (and potentially other Commonwealth nations), a two-finger salute reigns supreme as the go-to gesture of insult. Meanwhile, across the pond in America, the middle finger takes center stage as the most recognizable symbol of disrespect. Is it possible that the Bible not only predicted these symbols but also caused them to function as a marker between USA and UK.

First we will set the stage, we will travel back 3,500 years to ancient Egypt, Moses, and 40 years wandering in the desert, where he and God were tagged as Scotts (Succots). We see in Deuteronomy 33 that Moses prophesied and says that Ephraim (E Phruity - double fruit-E' fruity) and Manasseh (Me'nas'seh-me no see, "*out of sigh out of mind*", trouble gone) are predicted to gore the nations to the end of the earth with their horns, and in other instances, we are depicted as ox, calves, eleph'ants even the unicorn, the bull tribe, or cowboys!.

In Egypt when Moses is trying to prove to Pharoah that God wants them to leave. Pharaoh then asked for a sign (Exo.7.9)

The initial display involved a transformed staff becoming a snake, but the Egyptian magicians replicated the feat. However, Aaron's snake devoured theirs, showcasing a clear difference. Then we have Blood, but Pharoah can duplicate this also; then we have frogs, but the magicians could also produce them. Then we have gnats or lice, and the Egyptians can not reproduce them, and they say, "This is the finger of God" (Exo.8.19).

A strange saying. "the finger of God." I think it is a sign of God's power and majesty, but they took it as a sign of contempt. But can we find the use elsewhere in the Bible?

In Isaiah it says the following:

"Then shalt thou call, and the LORD shall answer; thou shalt cry, and he shall say, Here I am. *If thou take away from the midst of thee the yoke, the putting* **forth of the finger**, *and speaking vanity"* (Isa 58:9). This is repeated other places in the Bible. *"who winks maliciously with his eye, signals with his feet and* **motions with his fingers**"(NIV Pro 6:13)

As the LORD had said: "The finger of God," to which finger were they referring? Typically, the middle finger is used as a form of a priapic symbol. A symbol that would enrage an opponent and harden their heart, is it possible that God used this finger?

While Pharaoh may have interpreted the plagues as a divine insult, a metaphorical "giving of the finger" from God, this response only hardened his heart. God knew this would happen; this is the first instance in the Bible of this term.

COME old English Cuman/Cum

The English word COME to oneself, recover; arrive; assemble" CUMEN, (past participle), from Proto-Germanic *kwem, from PIE root *gwa- "to go, come."

Cumeth from, the Hebrew h6965 קוּם quwm küm, Come to be, cum about, to rise up, come up, get up, etc.a primitive root; to rise (in various applications, literal, figurative, intensive and causative), abide, accomplish, × be clearer, confirm, continue, decree, × be dim, endure, × enemy, enjoin, get up, make good, help, hold, (help to) lift up (again), make, Gen 17:7 come brit zera (seed).

COUGH   H6958 קיא qow'PH kow'ph, vomit, spue, or קָיָה qâyâh; (Jeremiah 25:27), a primitive root; to vomit, spue (out), vomit (out, up, up again).

COUGH, to vomit - cough, see cough, H6892 קָא qe'kay; vomit-or קיא qîy'; from H6958; vomit, vomit.

174

Chapter 5

English is in the Bible

Prophecy predicted English-Hebrew

Previously, I have listed many cognates, (words that sound and mean the same in two languages), and at times I have done an in-depth analysis of how they trace back to Hebrew.

In this section under Ezekiel (and Jeremiah's) message(s), God speaks directly to us, telling us, that a hidden language is Hebrew, but what is this hidden language? This will be explored shortly.

Part of the hidden link (if you like) is explored in "We are Israel" (which is available anywhere books or e-books are sold, but also on my website (Rebelministry.com) for free. This book traces the physical transitions of the lost ten tribes of Israel to the British and American peoples, again this is a point that is clearly shown in Prophecy.

What does it take to link a nation to a different nation, one that was hidden and disappeared from view 2700 years ago? Forging a direct link between nations separated by three millennia is undeniably challenging. Because nations rise and fall, they get conquered and deported, and they move from place to place, they merge with other people, their language gets corrupted and will surely change over time, and even their culture can change also. But through all of this it is evident "birds of a feather flock together", "strength in numbers", we would always migrate in groups, it's safer that way. These reasons along with our culture, and language (even though it can change we had a distinctive style and pronunciation), for these and prophetic reason I believe we mostly stayed together.

We know from the Bible that God cast Israel out of his sight 721 BC, this means the inventors of the aleph bet, (alphabet), aka Israel, aka Samaria, aka OMRI (CYMRY see Wales next chapter), left Cannan 721 BC. This lead tribe, was the head of the covenant, the tribe prophesied to receive God covenant promises, and blessing, this was Joseph, who Jacob made into two tribes Ephraim and Manasseh, these tribes had a covenant symbol of the OX, hence the first letter of the Aleph bet, Aleph=ox or Unicorn, bet=house. We brought our symbols with us and still use them today, (see alphabet section Chap 10. for details).

The term covenant was a very important phrase to the ancient Hebrews, and it's one more ZION (SIGN see index at end), that we retained as indicated by our name Britain, British and rule Britannia Brit am=covenant people in Hebrew, British=covenant man in Hebrew Britannia= covenant people of God in Hebrew (see index, last section for details).

Two main prophest's Ezekiel and Jeremiah.

These two speak of the demise of Israel[125] and indeed Judah, even though Israel was taken out 721BC, still Ezekiel and indeed Jeremiah both are sent to the lost 10 tribes.

In WAI (see abbreviation list), Chap.9 I list the various attempt listed in the Bible of when Israel tried to breakaway firstly from Egypt and subsequently from the land of Israel, we have the story of Danaus, son of Bela (Bilha H1090 בִּלְהָה was Dan's mother), whose brother was ruling Egypt (Joseph), flees from Egypt to Argos, in Greece. Hecataeus of Abdera (quoted by Diodorus Siculus), speak of Cadmus and Danaus, fleeing Egypt after ten plagues hit the country.

Cadmus is credited with being a Phoenician and bring the first alphabet to Greece. There are many parallels in Greek mythology, quasi-historical quotation, for instance Hercules, was a

---

125 Judah was never called Israel, in the Bible, when it speak of Israel, it gererally speaks of the northern ten tribe and the sons of Joseph specifically, i.e. the coveant men.

176

hero from Argos (the place where Danite settled). Samson (the exact same figure) was a Danite, (See WAI chapter Greece for more details).

In addition Denmark, Dnieper, Danube, are linked with Danaus, and the Celtic founder Tuatha de Danaan (people of the tribe of Dan) as we mentioned earlier.

Essentially during the time of Solomon as king of the world (at the time) the Phoenician and Hebrew navy would have joint expedition and would be gone for 3 years at a time, we know from forensic evidence that tin ingots found in a ship wreck off the coast to Israel dating to king Solomons time were from Britain, off the river Tamar (a Hebrew name see Chap.6). Many of the Israelites left early during the troubles with Assyria and, they formed the Celts / Phoenician / Carthaginians. The Etruscan's where vassals to the Phoenicians.

This formed the early migrations of the Israelites, the later migrations came via Assyrian, Babylonian, Persian and Median captivity.

The Bible states that the ten northern tribes from Assyrian conquest, where taken to Halah, **Habor**, Hara, the Gozan River and the cities of Media,[126] and they are there till this day, Josephus indicated that the ten lost tribe where an immense multitude beyond the Euphrates. I must point out that the proponent of PIE, say that

---

126 2Ki 17:6, 2Ki 18:11, 1Ch 5:26. **Halah (חֲלַח/ Strong's H2477):** A city or region associated with the Assyrian Empire. It is often identified near **Calah** (modern-day **Nimrud**) in **northern Iraq**, an important Assyrian administrative and cultural center. **Habor (חָבוֹר/ Strong's H2249):** Refers to the **Khabur River**, a tributary of the **Euphrates**, in modern-day **northeastern Syria**. This region served as a prominent area for Assyrian resettlement policies and is repeatedly mentioned as a place of exile. **Hara (הָרָה/ Strong's H2024):** A less certain location, **Hara** may refer to a mountainous region within the Assyrian Empire or adjacent territories. It is thought to be in **modern-day Iraq** or a nearby area known for its rugged terrain. **Gozan (גּוֹזָן/ Strong's H1470):** Refers to a region near the **Habor River**, corresponding to **Guzana (Tell Halaf)** in **modern Syria**. Guzana was an important Assyrian administrative center where exiles were likely settled. **Cities of the Medes (מָדַי/ Strong's H4074):** Refers to settlements in **Media**, a historical region in **modern-day Iran**. The Medes were an Indo-Iranian people allied with the Assyrians, and later the Babylonians and Persians. These cities became important areas for Israelite exile communities. (*2 Kings 17:6, Isaiah 13:17*).

177

Persian and Median is part of Proto Indo European (see Chap. 1, but more on this shortly).

Jeremiah started Prophecy 627-570BC? while still a boy, some suggest as young as 13 - 17 years of age, and Ezekiel who starts 593–571BC, both well after Samaria was exiled.

Ezekiel is by the Kebar River, he was taken in the second wave of Jewish captives. The name Kebar, which is also known as, **Habor** (Harbor) where the northern ten tribes were taken. Ezekial, was sent to the tribes in exile the British. Remember that Prophecy is often dual or multifaceted, God likes to repeat himself so we get the message.

Ezekiel was told that You are not being sent to a people of strange speech, God repeats it twice but why? Let's read it and find out –

And he said unto me, Son of man, go, get thee unto the house of Israel, (always the northern ten tribes Ephraim and Manasseh) *and speak with my words unto them.*

*For thou art not sent to a people of a strange speech and of an **hard language**, but to the house of Israel;*

*Not to **many people of a strange speech and of an hard language, whose words thou canst not understand**. Surely, had I sent thee to them, they would have hearkened unto thee. Eze 3:4-6*

As Identified, this is Israel (northern ten tribes), who are now speaking a language that seems foreign, but God says it isn't, and repeat's it 4 times wow – 721 to 593 (Ezekiel Campagne started) = 128 years, It takes 1+ generation before the kids start speaking the new native language (Chaldean- Aramaic-AGrmanci). Ezekiel is told there is a great multitude (Josephus said the same 600 years later). They intermingled and married, again Persia was originally Semitic i.e. son of Shem Elam, the Medes, assisted the Assyrian's and extended their empire, they also turned on them, and assisted the Babylonians when they conquered Assyria, they also assisted

178

Persia when they conquered the Babylonians. In fact Cyrus the great's mother was a Medeian princess[127].

It was from this melting pot that the Germanic languages came, it has Hebrew roots with Persian and Median structural changes along with loan words, Sanskrit was an early version of these changes that also originally employed the Paleo Hebrew alphabet that morphed into Vedic & Brami.

Chaldean [a type of Catholic version of Assyrian]-Aramaic-had Persian and Median mixed in. The Persians were originally Shemite (of Shem), but since BABBLE (mixing) they speak a different language, but their rulers retained their heritage hence the etymology of Persia and Iran/Aryan being Hebrew/Aramaic. Also mixed in as where the Assyrian (Chaldeans), the Medes

Ezekiel, begins his prophecy in Babylon remembering Psalms 137 "By the waters of Babylon", and he is giving a message to the remnant in Jerusalem. 1st sacking of Jerusalem is in 606BC and Daniel was taken at this time, i.e. the 3rd year of Jehoiakim 609-598 in the first expulsion(Dan 1.21).

Whereas the 2nd sacking was during the reign of Jehoiachin 598-597 BC, only 10,000 people were taken during this time (2Kin. 24.11-12). There would be a third and a fourth and final destruction of Jerusalem still to come.

---

[127] **Cyrus the Great (559–530 BCE) Not a Mede** but had a significant connection to the Medes: Cyrus was of **Persian** descent but united the **Medes and Persians** to form the Achaemenid Empire. His mother was a **Median princess**, making him a descendant of the Median royal family. Cyrus defeated his grandfather, **Astyages**, the last king of the Median Empire, and incorporated the Medes into his empire.

2. Darius I (522–486 BCE)Not a Mede but of **Persian** descent:Darius was part of the Persian Achaemenid dynasty.His inscriptions emphasize Persian ancestry, particularly his lineage from **Achaemenes**.However, Darius relied on Median nobles and traditions to stabilize his rule and strengthen ties with the Medes.

3. Xerxes I (486–465 BCE)Not a Mede but of **Persian** descent:Xerxes was the son of **Darius I** and **Atossa**, the daughter of Cyrus the Great.Through Cyrus, Xerxes had a Median lineage on his maternal side, but he identified primarily as Persian.

3rd sacking of Jerusalem - 597 B.C. Jerusalem falls at the hand of Nebuchadnezzar of Babylon. Nebuchadnezzar captures Jehoiachin and takes him as a prisoner to Babylon. Zedekiah is set up as a puppet king over Judah (Jer. 24.1).4th and final destruction of Jerusalem - 586 B.C. King Nebuchadnezzar lays siege to Jerusalem. He destroys the city and burns the temple.

The destruction of the temple starts on the 9th of Ab (Hebrew month) and completes on the 10th. The 9th of Ab will also be the day Jerusalem's SECOND temple (Herod's temple) will be completely destroyed in 70 A.D, what a coincidence, it must be a, mother nature, or karma thing (true believers know it's a God thing).

JEREMIAH'S COMMISSION.

The book of Jeremiah is especially unique because Jeremiah was the son of Hilkiah (Jer. 1.1) and during Josiah's reformation, Hilkiah the kohen gadowl (High Priest), found the book of the law, the Bible says Jeremiah's father Hilkiah the priest came from Anathoth and does not clarify if the two Priest are one and the same, although I feel it highly likely.

God identifies Jeremiah as a special child, one that the Spirit of God has known (in dwelt) even before he was born (Jer. 1.4) Yah has a very special job for him, Jeremiah says he can't even speak because he is so young when God called him, (Jer. 1.6).

Perhaps his public speaking was a problem he was nervous but the calling and Jeremiah's age were important, God had a huge task for him, "Today I appoint you over nations, and kingdoms to uproot and tear down to destroy and overthrow, to build and plant" (Jer. 1.10).

The Bible paints a powerful image of God's intervention. God says He will "pluck us up by the roots" and replant us in a new land. A land with a natural border where we will not be disturbed by nations. He promises to pluck his royal bonnie we lads and lassies[128] (Jer. 1:10 KJV). "See, I have this day set thee over the nations and over the kingdoms, to root out (pluck up by their roots)." Over 20 times, God repeats this promise, "to pull up (uproot)," then to "destroy," "throw down," then to "build," and to "plant," but where? The location of this new land remains a lingering question mark, a mystery waiting to be unraveled.

Where did Jeremiah take the king's daughters, where did Jeremiah continue the kingly line, with three overturns till Christ comes the second time to take ownership?

Astonishing Promises of God reiterated: -In the midst of saying that he will cast Israel and Judah from his sight, God makes this astonishing promise

'The descendants of Israel will NEVER cease to be a NATION before me, and call's the sun, moon, stars and earth (erets) as witness only if you can measure the foundations of the earth or the heavens can be measured, will I reject all the descendants of Israel. God said I will watch over them to build and plant (Jer. 31.28), he calls Ephraim an unruly Calf, is not Ephraim my dear son in whom I delight, I have great compassion for him… "set up road sign's, put up guideposts, take note of the highway, the road you take return O Virgin Israel return to your towns" (Jer. 31.9, 18-21).
"Because I am Israel's father and Ephraim is my first-born son (the covenant [Brit] goes to the firstborn).
Hear the word of the Lord O nations; proclaim it in a distant coastland, he who scatters Israel and will gather them and watch over his flock like a shepherd. He who commands the sun and moon and stars…will the decedents of Israel ever cease to be a nation before me" (Jer. 31.35-37, Ps. 19).
Israel had a habit of setting up pillars, heaps (Gen. 28.22, 31.13,45, 52, 35.14), signposts, memorials, tombstones, even God led Israel by a pillar (Ex. 14.19) of cloud and a post of fire, and as we see above God instructed Jeremiah to set up Pillars. 'Set thee up

---

[128] Binnie H1121 family, Lad-H2056,3206, youth H3208/7, lady, female H5768- עֹלֵל 'ôwlêl, c-lale'; diminutive La'Le LITTLE

waymarks (see yonder-H6725 TARA), make thee high heaps(Tamar-erection-pillar h8564) set thine heart toward the highway, even the way which thou wentest: turn again, O virgin of Israel, turn again to these thy cities.' (Jer. 31:21)

Again God is turning our hearts back to him, our roots, and our origins(Mal. 4.6). Three prominent Tamar's in Britain, the river Thames(anciently Tamar), river Tamar in Devon (tin mining area), and Tara the ancient seat of kingly lines (two thousand years) and power. I know the plans I have for you, declares the Lord, Plans to prosper you and not to harm you plans to give you hope and a future!(Jer. 29.11), lest we forget, the Lord is the same yesterday to day and forever (Heb.13.8).

Believe it Believe it, it's true! And he does not forget the promise to David, Israel and the Levites – (Jer. 33:17-26 NIV) "For this is what the LORD says: 'David will never fail to have a man to sit on the throne of Israel'. v22 'I will make the descendants of David my servant and the Levites who minister before me as countless as the stars in the sky and as measureless as the sand on the seashore'. v23 The word of the LORD came to Jeremiah: v24 Have you not noticed that these people are saying, 'The LORD has rejected the two kingdoms he chose'? So, they despise my people and no longer regard them as a nation. v25 This is what the LORD says:

'If I have not made my covenant with day and night and established the laws of heaven and earth, v26 then I will reject the descendants of Jacob and David my servant and will not choose one of his sons to rule over the descendants of Abraham, Isaac and Jacob. For I will restore their fortunes and have compassion on them.

KEY TO FINDING ISRAEL

Below I have listed some keys we will be using to find Israel:
-1All nations of the earth shall be blessed by your seed (Gen.12.3).

-2. I will make you a great nation and a great company of nations (Gen. 48.19-20). If God says they will be great, I think it's a sure bet that he means the greatest ever

-3. The two Nations will be great brothers i.e. Ephraim and Manasseh (Gen. 48.17-20). And again - May god make you like Ephraim and Manasseh (Gen. 48.20). In other words, something outstanding and worthy of praise.

-4. Vast natural resources and a great climate for growing and abundant water (Gen. 49.22-28, Ez.17.5, Gen. 27.28).

-5. You shall never fail to have a man sit on the throne of Israel, A long kingly line that traces back to David, in other words, a kingly line that has existed for thousands of years and can be traced back to King Da'vid (Gen. 49:10).

-6. Israel will have a natural border (2Sa. 7:10).

-7. House (Nation) built on a rock and a church and kingly line tied to the rock, Jacob's pillar stone (Gen. 28:22, Gen. 31:45, 2Ki 23:3, a rock that the builders rejected has become the chief cornerstone (Psa. 118:22, Isa. 28:16, Mat. 21:42).

-8. Strong bow sign of strong military sustained by God – But his bow abode in strength, and the arms of his hands were made strong by the hands of the mighty God of Jacob; (from thence is the shepherd, the stone of Israel, Gen. 49.24).

-9. Remnant of Israel prophesied to come from Islands of the sea, the western coast and also known as Kitty and Chittam(H3794) they will form part of the holy covenant.

Ezekiel's bittersweet message.

What did God say to Ezekiel (Eze 3.4)? The Bitter Sweet truth is that "We are Israel" and "English is Hebrew."

[3] Then he said to me, "Son of man, eat this scroll I am giving you and fill your stomach with it." So I ate it, and it tasted as **sweet as honey in my mouth**.

[4] He then said to me: "Son of man, go now to **the people of Israel** and speak my words to them. [5] You are not being sent to a people of obscure speech and strange language, but to the people of

Israel— [6] not to many peoples of **obscure speech and strange language**, whose words you cannot understand. Surely, if I had sent you to them, they would have listened to you. [7] But the people of Israel are not willing to listen to you because they are not willing to listen to me, for all the Israelites are hardened and obstinate. [8] But I will make you as unyielding and hardened as they are. [9] I will make your forehead like the hardest stone, harder than flint. Do not be afraid of them or terrified by them, though they are a rebellious people."

Prophecy is often dual and while Ezekiel is being sent Israel by the Kedar (Harbor) river, he is also sent to a people in the distant future who appear to have no connection to the Israelites, (you and I) but God says, no, that is incorrect.

We know that the event is mostly future (Eze.2-3.15), because it is reiterated in Revelation, where the Apostle John speaks about the bitter-sweet message again. This time, the exiles are no longer in Babylon, but they are now in Europe (95a.d.) and later America, but the Book of Revelation is about the last days, i.e., today, so Ezekiel and John are really being sent to YOU and ME!

The Book of Ezekiel spans a significant timeframe, with many chapters, like the Valley of Dry Bones (Chapter 36), seemingly referencing the end times. The book clearly is a message for us today, just as most of the prophetic messages relate to the last days. It has been calculated that ¼ to 1/3 of the Bible is prophetic, again the majority of which deals with the last days. Again Ezekiel's message, is sent to a people who seem to speak a different language is being sent primarily to the house of Israel, who now speak Egel'ish and whose roots come from the Hebrew. Joseph, aka house of Israel and his sons, Ephraim, Manasseh, and the tribes associated with us will join Judah (who now have returned to their ancestral homeland), and we will choose one leader and fight the battle of Armageddon (Hos.1.11).

ZION's SIGN's

Ok, now back to the signs (Zion's [H6725]) that God left us to indicate our origin, the high heaps and waymarks[129]; God covenanted the kingly line, and he also promised that the descendants of Israel would never cease to be a nation before him, where was this fulfilled?[130] It was surely fulfilled and is still being fulfilled. All the things just mentioned are true, but God designed a roadmap that would help us. He told us to set up high heaps, waymarks.

- British Symbols, coat of arms, animal symbols etc. -
- Artifacts – Jacob's pillar stone
- Folklore Myths and Legends
- Idioms
- religion, war, and peace, sex and food, etc., music and drinking, Language Connection
- Sports, Goal, Net
- Ancient Place names – etymology
- Food, cows, fish, birds, diet, etc.

History

Great Britain has been occupied by the same people for upward of 3,000 years. This fact is attested to by Celtic place names and old maps, which date back to at least 500 B.C.).

According to modern Linguistics, a Proto-Indo-European (PIE) is the root system as the common ancestor for many European languages, including Celtic tongues. Language does not exist and

---

[129] Jer. 31:21-22H1567, H8564 Tam-roor-erection, and Zion's, sign post H6725.

[130] Thus saith the LORD, which giveth the sun for a light by day, [and] the ordinances of the moon and of the stars for a light by night, which divideth the sea when the waves thereof roar; The LORD of hosts [is] his name:If those ordinances depart from before me, saith the LORD, [then] the seed of Israel also shall cease from being a nation before me forever. [Jer 31:35-36 KJV]

is a construct made by linguists to fill the void, and the real connection is to Hebrew, as we will soon discover.

The Gaelic tongue is said to be similar to Sanskrit, a language that also has been lost. Experts believe they can piece together the fragments by analyzing the variety of different languages and develop/infer from them one root word, most of which are bizarre and don't appear to link back. However, there's a counterpoint: the Hebrew Bible, some believe, preserves the true roots of our linguistic past.

If we for one moment take the premise that Europe came from Sanskrit, that itself came from ancient MEDIA, where the ten tribes were taken captive. This is where the language of SANSKRIT developed, and it developed from Hebrew. Also their script was borrowed from Paleo Hebrew.

Sanskrit-Brahmic Text or script:

"The oldest known Sanskrit is said to be Vedic Sanskrit (1500-1000 B.C.). This is considered an Indo-Aryan subgroup of the Indo-European family group (remember Hitler correctly identified the Germans as Aryan); It was an oral language and the Brahmic script is the oldest known Sanskrit text (circa 600B.C.). The script looks very similar to Paleo Hebrew / Phoenician and while there has been difficulty tracing it back, most scholars believe that it does come from Hebrew/Phoenician.

SANSKRIT etymology.

The word Sanskrit and its etymology are important clues to its origin, as Etymologist piece together linguistic tapestries, that show how one language connects to another. The word SANSKRIT, the verbal adjective *sáṃskṛta-* is a compound word consisting of *sáṃ* ('together, good, well, perfected') and *kṛta-* ('made, formed, work').[45][46] It connotes a work that has been "well prepared, pure and perfect, polished, sacred.

The ancient consider writing to be scared, this was true of Hieroglyphics (hieros "sacred [Hero] and glyph) which are also

186

from Hebrew. Cuneiform was introduced to us by Sumerians and later Akkadians (Semitic) but some form of writing/script was antediluvian (I have no doubts), and while the sons of Noah were their contemporaries (still alive) because the tower of Bable, occurred only about 110 years after the flood.

Sanskrit holy writing, the name is **Old Persian** San, fm **Sam**=same, Avestan (Darius 1), hama "similar, the same, **skrit** Old Persian kunautiy "he makes;" from PIE root *kwer- This is what etymologist say not me, I am just repeating and agreeing with it, they link Sanskrit directly with old Persian at the Biblical time of the Medes And Persian of Daniel.

After which the great masses dispersed to the west, (Germanic tribes) and to the east (India). Following is a more detailed explanation of Sanskrit writing.

Brahmi, Encyclopedia Britannica (1999), Quote: "Brāhmī, writing system ancestral to all Indian scripts except Kharoṣṭhī. Of **Aramaic derivation or inspiration**, it can be traced to the 8th or 7th century B.C., when it may have been introduced to Indian merchants by people of Semitic origin. (...) a coin of the 4th century B.C., discovered in Madhya Pradesh, is inscribed with Brāhmī characters running from right to left."

SANSKRIT –SHEM'S SCRIPT-(Hebrew).

The Etymology of Sanskrit, says it's a holy script/writing, the name Shem in Hebrew is used in place of God's name by Jew's they do not pronounce YHVH or YHWH, rather they say HaShem (the name), both have the connotations of holiness. I could explore this topic and write for pages on Name, Abrabic word for Shem, ism إسم, and sam-same and its ties to Ets-SEM[131] the proposed PIE route of same *sem, which also ties it to SAME or SHEM'SCRIT (Sanskrit), this connection is linguistically, entomologically, metaphorically, and historically a match.

---

[131] Ets-SEMיצמע, עצם [E]TSeM, [A]TSMeeY mean self and selfsame (Genesis 7:13).

187

The earliest (indisputably dated) and best-known Brahmi inscriptions are the rock-cut edicts of Ashoka in north-central India, dating to 250–232 B.C.". [132] this shows that it was well after the Assyrians captured the ten northern tribes, aka Israel 721b.c. And many of the Paleo Hebrew characters can still be identified in the Brahmi script. And while they are used for different sound's, it appears they modified them to match words/sounds in their language.

(handwritten annotations on chart) TA SA — KAPH — ⊗TH — Greek TH. — Bet — YHY — LAMED — YAD

+ ka [ke]	1 kha [kʰe]	Λ ga [gə]	gha [gə]	[ṅ [ŋə]
d ca [ca]	cha [cʰa]	ja [ja]	jha [jʰa]	h ña [ɲə]
ta [tə]	0 tha [tʰa]	da [də]	dha [ɖʰə]	I ṇa [ɳə]
ta [te]	0 tha [tʰa]	da [da]	dha [dʰə]	na [nə]
pa [pə]	pha [pʰə]	ba [bə]	bha [bʰa]	ma [ma]
ya [jə]	ra [rə]	la [lə]	va [və]	
sa [ɕə]	sa [ʂə]	sa [sə]	ha [hə]	

(handwritten): STRONG INDICATION THAT THIS WAS BORROWED earlier from paleo Hebrew.

15 Brahmi Alphabet- Hebrew

Despite the fact that the original Sanskrit tongue has clear Semitic links, the experts refuse to acknowledge it; rather, they say Hebrew is a Hamito-Semitic (aka Afroasiatic, north Africa as in Ham, Shem, Japhet). I will delve deeper into this debate later in the text.

While some believe Sanskrit originated in India, the evidence suggests a Mesopotamian birthplace, the cradle of civilization itself. Yes, the fertile crescent was very close to where Noah landed the ark (Mount Ararat, Turkey). Also of note is that people settled in Egypt in the fertile Nile delta shortly after the flood. Scientists now say the birth place of the first humans was

---

[132] Courtesy of Wikipedia

Johannesburg, South Africa; it's important to bear in mind that after Noah jumped in the ark with all the African animals.

Re-arranged the entire earth, opened up the floodgates of heaven, and the waters that were deep below the earth also erupted along with volcanic and tectonic activity where the earth's mantle shifted. Indeed, all the ash that was spewed up into the atmosphere caused the one and only ice age; this is now claimed by scientists to be the reason for the ice age, just as God and the Bible say!

Scholar and archaeologist Raymond E. Capt proposes a link to ancient Mesopotamia, the homeland of the Hurrians. The Hurrians spoke a language that was neither Semitic nor Indo-European. They occupied an area that would later be Assyrian territory, the Assyrians and Medes, adopted some of their culture, gods **Tesh'**ub -i.e.Tues'day, may prove to come from them, the Hurrians also worked closely with the Mede's who introduced horse-drawn chariots for the first time in Mesopotamia. The origin of the term chariot might help us with its origin; the name is Semitic and is used in the Bible. The Bible uses a different term for Chariot, but the English term Chariot comes from the Bible.

Etymologist say Chariot comes from Old French charriot "wagon" (13c.), "car," PIE root*kers- "to run."

CHARIOT, H2742 חָרוּץ chărûwts, khaw-roots'; or חָרֻץ châruts; fm H2782; properly, incised or incisive; hence a trench (as dug), gold (as mined), a threshing-sledge (having sharp teeth). The Bible lists many names for chariot; however it predominantly uses this one root words see below.

Mecab a Cab, (my cab) a saddle h4818, note that most of the Hebrew words that are used for chariot, use the root H7392 רָכַב râkab, raw-kab'; could be the origin of CAB see also H6906 (6989) קבה as a Cab, an enclosure, covering, hollo.

Both these roots offer connections to the Pie root and connections to Cab, Car and chariot, clearly there is a connection here that need to be investigated more.

Chapter 6

Proof the Celtic Language Is Hebrew

Dr. Davies Welsh's Lexicon.

Dr. John Davies of Mallwyd was a prominent Welsh scholar and clergyman during the early 17th century. He is best known for his contributions to Welsh lexicography and grammar, and his efforts significantly impacted the preservation and study of the Welsh language.

The affinity between Hebrew and Welsh was mentioned by Dr. Davies (amongst others) and in the preface to his Welsh Grammar there was a poem to the effect that.

"He gladly deigns his countrymen to teach;
By well-weigh'd rules, the rudiments of speech;
That when the roots first of our own we gain;
The Hebrew tongue we thence may soon attain"

The link between Hebrew and Gaelic has been known for some time. The similarities are so striking that they prove a true language connection.

 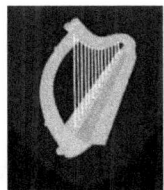 

16 SCOTTISH AND ISRAELI FLAGS   HARP OF DAVID - NORTHERN IRELAND FLAG

This chapter dives into the connection between Celtic and British people with ancient Israel and Egypt. While hundreds of linguistic experts propose such a link, I've narrowed the focus to seven for a more concise exploration.

Let's remember that Joseph married an Egyptian, our mother Asenath daughter of Potiphera priest of On (Gen. 41.50, see Chap. 8 Egyptian connection). So yes, we do have a connection to Egypt and ancient Israel. See also Dr Worrell

If scholars in the 19 and 20th centuries started to come to a realization that "We are Israel" and "English is Hebrew" why is it mostly unknown, why do the etymologists point to Sanskrit as the original tongue?

Even though I point out that there are language experts who know the truth, mainstream etymologists does not even look for a connection between Biblical Hebrew and Gaelic

One of the earliest dictionary's, listed many English words with Hebrew connections[133], so what happened? If we have a number of folks coming out with the truth, why is it that we are more in the dark than ever before?

Well, it is a systematic effort by atheistic professors who not only don't want to look at any connections between God, history, language, archeology etc. but actively covers up many such connections and attack conservative Christian. It's a common thread these days and now more than anytime we can see the left absolute hatred of God, patriotism and the white boy ancestry.

But that's not the full story, in reality, it ultimately comes down to God the creator hiding these things. Because if God is for revealing it who can be against it? Well, the whole world could be, because Satan's in charge of the world. However, that wouldn't matter, that's why alien race of giants is still no match for people who are blessed and protected by God. So even though the left and Satan are waging a war against the white man, by destroying our country and promoting racism by putting every other race (especially black people) above the whites in our own countries, I

---

[133] "Universal Etymological English Dictionary" by Nathan Bailey, first published in 1721

don't need to give all the college scholarship and business development programs for everyone except the white man.[134]

The process of hiding the true identity of the Celts, Germanic, and Gaulish peoples started over 2500 years ago. It all began when God cast Israel out of sight and untimely out of view for the nations, in 927 BC Jeroboam, (sins of 2Ki 10:29) and Rehoboam (sins of sin 2 Chr.12) came on the scene.

Jeroboam was allowed to take the northern kingdoms of Israel from Rehoboam (Solomons's son), in doing so he was afraid that they would at some point go back and worship God in Jerusalem, so he took God out of the schools, government, and even worship, he appealed to Israel's vanity and set up golden calf worship (Calf was the symbol of Ephraim/Manasseh) in Bethel and Dan. His brother from another mother was no better, but God took Rehoboam to the wood shack early, he gave him a shellacking by "Sheshak" the Egyptian (2Ch 12:1-16)

This was the beginning of the end. It culminated in God casting Israel out of his sight in 721 BC, ever since this date speculation and prophetic statements of who they are and when they will reconnect have been proposed.

The idea that there are still hidden secrets in the world/Bible are again perpetuated in the book of Daniel and in the book of Revelation chapter 10 the meaning of the bitter sweet little scroll is sealed up, until the time of the end. Daniel and the Apostle John are told not to reveal but seal up (Dan. 9.24, 12.4,9, Rev. 9.24, Rev.10.4). Today I am revealing what these books mean.

I point out in my first book (WAI) that we are in the last days when the mystery of God will be revealed and the covenant people Ephraim and Manasseh, (stick of Ephraim) who God hid his face from will once again come together with the stick of Judah as nations and chose one leader and fight in the battle of Armageddon (Isa.8.11,16-18)

---

[134] Women's Business Enterprise WBE, ABE, BBE, MBE.

April 8th i.e. Nisan 1, was a pivotal ecliptic eclectic, electric, and ominous, date. And is the date that God started revealing hidden information, the testimony that was sealed, is now being revealed by Zion's,(H6725) symbols and wonders. All of which points to my two books which are filled with signs and symbols all throughout.

God allowed Satan to deceive the whole world (Rev.19.9, 2Cor.4-3-4), but I don't think he realized he was doing the work of God, now the time is here for God to reveal the true identity of Israel, and Satan is mad as EL (H410 אֵל 'ēl god). Trust me this has to happen

If you can read this with an open mind and set aside any prejudice you might have, I assure you, you will not be disappointed.

Remember, NOAH WAS CONSIDERED A CONSPIRACY THEORIST -then it rained.

Moses was telling lies, using smoking mirrors and spreading misinformation –Till the death anger passed over and the Hebrews were saved by the blood of the lamb!

Back to more proofs that "We Are Isael" and English is Hebrew"

Linguistic Experts British-Israel link real.

In the following section, I outline seven leading language experts who all agree that the people of the British Isles, had centuries of significant integration/exposure to Hebrew, some go so far to say Celtic is Hebrew.

When we put this together with all the other evidence, it is clear and unmistakable evidence that "We are Israel" and English is Hebrew. Remember God prophesied this!

Jeremiah's commission was to teardown, uproot and replant the kingly line, with its root intact and that's what he did in the British Isles.

194

Ezekiel was sent to the Israelites yet their language was not readily identifiable as Hebrew "(For thou *art* not sent to a people of a strange speech and of a hard language, *but* to the house of Israel-Eze 3:5).

It is the last days and Israel (not the Jews) are still in exile from the promised land of Israel, they are unwilling to listen even though God is sending THIS MESSAGE. Ezekiel is in solitary confinement and they tie him up. They do not give him water to drink and he cannot speak out (cau dy geg 3.25,26). Till the time is right for God to allow him to speak, this mystery is sealed till the last days, this time is now!

The bitter-sweet message of Ezekiel chapter three is reiterated in chapter 10 of Revelations, the little scroll with writing on both sides, indicates the mystery of God, a message of peoples, nations, languages and kings (Rev.10.11)

1. Pritchard: A leading English language scholar **1857.**

A 19th century etymological language expert who founded modern anthropology and single handedly put ethnology on a scientific basis the English physician and ethnologist was among the first to assign all the human races and ethnic groups to a single species.

His name was **James Cowles Pritchard** and in 1857 he wrote a book titled, *"Eastern Origin of the Celtic Nations"* after a detailed study into the subject he concluded that the Celtic (Keltic) tongue

"forms an intermediate link between [the Indo-European] and the Semitic, or perhaps indicates a state of transition" from Semitic to European languages. (p.349), in another area, he states,

"it does not appear probable that the idioms of North Africa are even so nearly related to the Semitic, as the latter are to the Indo-European languages."

Here he goes against the prevailing authorities and boldly states the Semitic language is closely related to the Celtic tongue.

As mentioned elsewhere in the chapter Carthaginian (Phoenicians who spoke Canaanite aka Hebrew) and also used the Ibri alphabet could easily spread around to every continent on earth.

The joint task force would be gone for 3 years at a time 3000 years ago when the ThArish sailed together 1000-600 BC) and Gaelic were identical, this again is bore out in a story he retells in his book.

Essentially, he speaks of a British (Gaelic speaking) crew landing in a Tunisia (north African) port and being able to understand the language of the natives who spoke Carthaginian, a Hebrew dialect!

Prichard also saw how the Celtic language completely mimics Biblical Hebrew in the way words were formed and the adding of suffixes and prefixes (p. 380), as we will show with whole sentences and phrases later in the chapter.

2. Professor-Dr. Worrell-Semitic Scholar 1927

Distinguished language scholar, **William H. Worrell,** Associate Professor of Semitics at the University of Michigan, proved that the Celtic language evolved in some way from both the Hebrew and Egyptian languages. In his 1927 book, *"A Study of Races In The Ancient Near East,"* he says,

"In the British Isles certain syntactic phenomena of insular Celtic speech have led to the inference that in this region languages were spoken which had some relation, however remote, to the Hamitic-Semitic family… the Insular Celtic languages, particularly colloquial Welsh, show certain peculiarities unparalleled in Aryan languages, and these remind one strongly of Hamitic and Semitic." (p. 46, 50)

196

In very scholarly chapters, Dr. Worrell shows that the structure of the Hebrew, Egyptian, and Celtic languages is related. He says, *"...we find that the Celtic languages of the British Isles, particularly in their spoken forms, differ from all other Aryan languages, and in a way to suggest the Hamitic or Semitic tongues... "* (p,40)

How could the Celtic people exhibit language characteristics in common with both Hebrew and Egyptian? The eminent scholar theorizes that the ancestors of the Celts, before coming to the British Isles, had dwelt for a time in North Africa near Egypt, where they came into contact through trade with both the Hebrews and Egyptians. However, occasional trading would not change the entire structure of their language! A much greater intimacy with both the Hebrews and Egyptians is indicated.

Would it not make more sense that the ancestors of the Celts were themselves Hebrews who escaped from Egyptian bondage westward? The Israelites were in an extended captivity in Egypt and thus would have had a solid mixture of both languages in their vocabulary, exactly as, the Celts had. Dr. Worrell comments on the ancient Hebrews:-

"We fancy we can almost follow them across into Europe, and imagine them the builders of Stonehenge and the dolmens of Brittany. Perhaps they were the people of Druidism. It may be that Caesar's soldiers heard in Aquitania [France] the last echoes of European Hamitic speech; and that Goidels and Brythons learned from Pictish mothers the idioms of this pre-Aryan British tongue. And may not this have been, indeed, the language of the whole Mediterranean race?" (pp. vii-viii)

Many years of scholarship, and many pages of evidence, prove that Dr. Worrell was not far from the truth.

3. Hjelmslev: A Danish language scholar 1970.

Danish scholar, **Dr. Louis Hjelmslev,** completed independent research into the root structure of languages. In his book, **"Language: An Introduction"** (University of Wisconsin Press, 1970), he pointed out the great influence of the Semitic tongue upon the Indo-European languages. He states:-

"Even a language like Greek, which is considered one of the purest Indo-European languages and which plays a greater role than any other in comparative Indo-European studies, contains only a relatively small number of words that can be genetically accounted for on the basis of Indo-European." (p.63)

Dr. Hjelmslev states that most European words are borrowings from non-Indo-European languages. In fact,

"a genetic relationship between Indo-European and Hamito-Semitic [i.e., Egyptian-Hebrew] was demonstrated in detail by the Danish linguist Hermann Moller, using the method of element functions." (p. 79)

This is an important point. The similarity between Hebrew and English goes far beyond the mere resemblance of similar-sounding words. The element functions represent a *"genetic relationship"* between English and both Hebrew and Egyptian. (p.83) These languages are therefore related in their very root structure, showing a common origin. Given these facts, a group of Danish language scholars has proposed eliminating the separate language categories of Semitic and Indo-European, combining them into one new category called, **Nostrati.**

"Nostratic, a name proposed by Holger Pedersen for the languages related to our **own,"** namely Hamito (Egyptian) and Semitic (Hebrew). Interestingly, the word, *'nostratic,'* is taken from the Latin word, *"nostras,"* meaning, *"our own countrymen." (p. 80)* Yes, the Semites, he says, are our own countrymen, because both language streams indicate a common origin in their very root structure.

4. Blodgett: An American language scholar 1982

Dr. Terry Blodgett, chairman of the Southern Utah State College Language Department, received international attention in 1982 as a result of his research, which discovered **"a *major Hebrew influence"*** in the roots of the English language. A newspaper report commented:-

"Recent discoveries concerning the Germanic languages suggest there must have been extensive Hebrew influence in Europe, especially in England, Holland, Scandinavia and Germany during the last seven centuries of the pre-Christian era [700 B.C. to Christ].
"

These dates take us back to the conquest of the *"lost"* ten tribes of Israel, who were removed from Palestine by Assyria and dispersed to other lands between 845 and 676 B.C.

Dr. Blodgett's doctoral dissertation was on **"Similarities In Germanic and Hebrew "** which deals with these discoveries. He states that his research has ***"traced various tribes of Israel into Europe."*** Dr. Blodgett presented his research in seminars in America, Germany, and Switzerland during the 1980's. For more information about the migrations of the dispersed Israelite tribes, ask for our tract, **"The Real Diaspora."**

5. Mozeson: A Hebrew scholar 1989, and 1995

In his encyclopedic work, "The Word, The Dictionary That Reveals the Hebrew Source of English."

Hebrew language scholar, Dr. Isaac Elchanan Mozeson, gives many tens of thousands of English words with a Semitic origin. I consider him a personal friend and he has told me the count today is around 80,000.

I don't always agree with his voluminous work because he sometimes uses metathesis to draw a connection from Hebrew to English, metathesis is a process whereby words get jumbled up due to a variety of reasons. This may be the case in a smaller number than he purports. One reason for a metathesis is boustrophedon, i.e ox-plow method of writing where words could be written from left to right then right to left.[135]

Metathesis is most likely the primary cause of the confusion in the city of Babylon (i.e. babble), where God confused the speech, however, God left Hebrew intact.

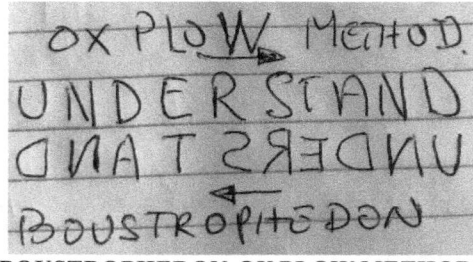

17 BOUSTROPHEDON-OX-PLOW METHOD

To babble is to speak incoherently Etymologist do not know where it comes from, they offer mid-13c., babeln "to prattle, utter words indistinctly, talk like a baby," akin to other Western European words for stammering and prattling (Swedish babbla, Old French babillier, they also say" Greek barbaros "non-Greek-speaking" but the meaning here is an uncouth foreigner and does not mean jumbled or mixed up.

In Welsh babble is baldorddi. It clearly came from Bable h867 בָּבֶל Bâbel, baw-bel'; from H1101; confusion; Babel. BeL (BULL) of Babylon, became Baal of Cannan[136]

Anyhow enough of my babbling on, back to Prof. Mozeson, he undoubtedly amassed an amazing treasure trove of English-Hebrew connections, and perhaps someday we could collaborate on

---

[135] Bird - Originally in Old English, it was "brid.", Horse - Old English had "hros." Wasp - In Old English, it was "wæps." Aks (or "ax") - This is an older form of the word "ask." Some dialects still use "aks" today. Thriteen - This Middle English variant of "thirteen" shows metathesis of the 'r' and the vowel. Comfort - The Middle English form "comforten" shows metathesis when compared to its Latin root "confortare." Third - Old English had "þridda," where the 'r' and the vowel were switched in positions.

[136] H1078 בֵּל Bêl, bale; by contraction for H1168; Bel, the Baal of the Babyloniansl.

200

a joint work, and Brit and a Jew working together again would be awesome!

Dr. Mozeson teaches the English language at Yeshiva University and completed his linguistic thesis at NYU. His conclusion was *"that English and Hebrew are profoundly connected.*

6 Professor Theo Vennemann Linguist and scholar

It has been an enigma for a long time, to try and figure out where the Basque people are from but now, it is clear they are Celtic. The German historical linguist, Professor Theo Vennemann is known for his controversial theories of a "Vasconic" and an "Atlantic" stratum in European languages, published since the 1990s. He drew a connection between Basque and the Celts and consider a vast area of Britain, Ireland as well as France, Spain and Portugal to be part of a group he calls the A "Vasconic" language family.

It is the Area where the lost ten tribes went and were commonly known as the Iberian Peninsula, a name from one of our ancestors they were the children of Eber Hebrews, ibri aka ivri, iber and means not from around here, i.e. he's from over there OVeR-English and ABaR-Celtic עֵבֶרh5676).

Professor Theo Vennemann believes that "Semites" from Canaan and the Middle East settled in western and northern Europe on at least two occasions. The first time they introduced Megalithic Monuments and changes in the language. The second time they brought the Runic Script and additional cultural influences.

Etymology of the region agrees with Vennemann (see "We are Israel") The "Iberians" (Hebrews) had long established, trading settlements along the Ebro (Hebrew) river. The Carthaginians,

Greeks, and Romans, knew this and called them **IBERES** (Hebrews)[137].

Even the word SPAIN[138] is Hebrew, said to mean Island of Rabbits, from the Phoenician/ Hebrew word shâphân (SPaN hyrax-rabbit). The word means hidden one (as a burrowing animal, rock rabbit) there is an indication that this word, may come from a similar word tsâphôwn also meaning hidden metaphor for "northwest" Even the word CELT, is said to mean hidden one

In those days the house of Judah shall walk with the house of Israel, and they shall come together out of the land of the north[H6845] (literally Spain/Europe) to the land that I have given for an inheritance unto your fathers. [Jer 3:18 KJV].

The Zarahite branch of Judah was there, but it is difficult to pinpoint the exact location " in the Ebro Valley, some connect it to Zaragoza, this region is also known as ARGON, which means river, and is also Hebrew (ARNON).

---

[137] **IBERES** (Hebrews) from Latin Iberia from Greek Iberes, believed to be related to that of the River Ebro

[138] SPAIN H8227 שָׁפָן shâphân (SPaN hyrax-rabbit) from the root H8226 שָׁפַן sâphan, however Mozeson believes they got it wrong but that its actually from H6828 צָפון tsâphôwn, or צָפֹן tsâphôn; from H6845; properly, hidden, i.e. dark; used only of the north as a quarter (gloomy and unknown)north(-ern, side, -ward, wind).

Zaragoza was originally known as <u>Sedetani</u>, and another area was called <u>Edetani</u>, there are many tribes[139] from this region with a suffix, Ani or Tani which comes from the Hebrew "ammi[H5971]" meaning (God's) people, we also have Celt'iberi, Iberian, peninsular, and Ebro rivers the Ibri, the original word meaning Hebrew[140](the Jews call it Ivrit).

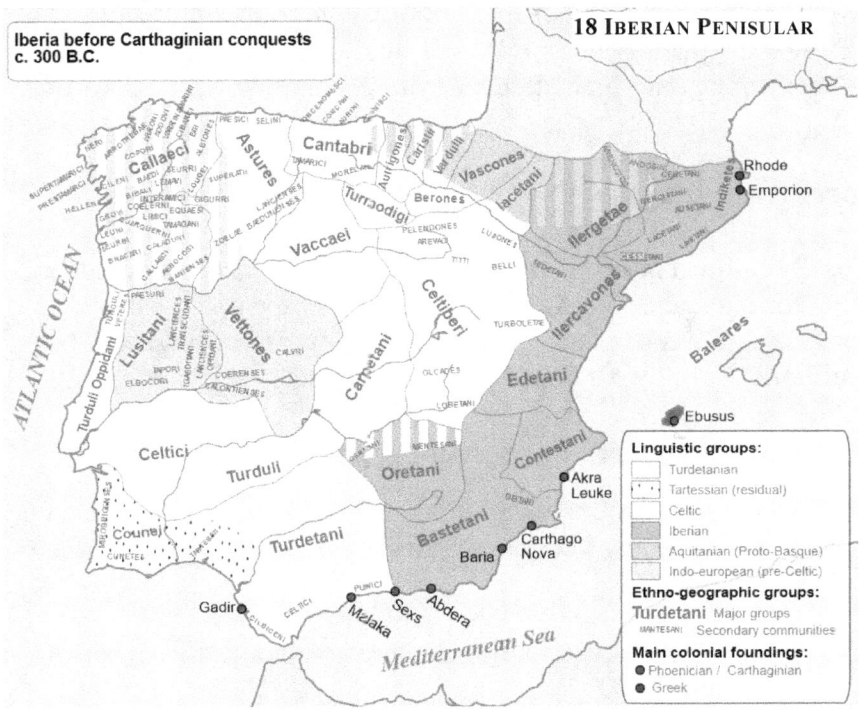

According to the Irish chronicles, the Jews (aka Zarahrite branch) migrated from Spain (<u>Zaragoza</u> region) to Ireland and are known as sons of Mil aka Milesians or sons of the Prophecy(מְלֵא H4390-6), because of the severe drought in Spain a vision was given them of Ireland, a place that was well watered and good grazing

---

[139] Laceitani, Bastetani, Cortestani, <u>Ammi; H5971</u> . A variant of AM Hebrew people, tribe, group (of Israel)

[140] H5680 עִבְרִי'Ibrîy, ib-ree'; patronymic from <u>H5677</u>; an Eberite (i.e. Hebrew) or descendant of Eber, Hebrew(-ess), woman). From H5677 OVER, AVaR, עֵבֶר'Êber, ay'-ber; the same as <u>H5676</u>; Eber, the name of two patriarchs and four Israelites, Eber, Heber

land. They followed and fulfilled the prophecy, hence the name Mil, (Mael, Male) aka Milesians (see We are Israel).

There is also the possibility that this is a patriotic name, coming from Mahol[H4235] *For he was wiser than all men; than Ethan the Ezrahite, and Heman, and Chalcol, and Darda, the sons of Mahol: and his fame was in all nations round about. [1Ki 4:31 KJV],* where Ethan, Heman, Chalcol, and Darda as Zerahites (or Ezrahites), indicating their descent from Zerah, one of the sons of Judah.

7 Jorgensen Langfocus a language expert 2016.

Paul Jorgensen Langfocus is an English teacher who has a passion for languages, he was able to learn and speak almost fluent Tagalog in one week. Clearly, he is a very impressive linguist who has millions of followers on his youtube channel.

In the section following Paul along with a lady called Rachel posted similar findings, I combined their thoughts along with mine and others into the following table.

Amazing link between the structure and indeed the words of Hebrew and Celtic.

1- The VSO order is the same i.e. verb subject object "Jumped Jack river"
2- Inflected prepositions for person and number.
3- Inflected Prepositions for Possession
4- Inflected Prepositions for Obligation i.e. "to have"
5- Presumptive pronouns in relative clauses
6- Definite article and no indefinite article
7- Constructive case genitive – when two nouns are together the first noun alters the second.
8- The use of the word "and" with subordinate meaning, circumstantial.
9- The use of the word "and" also creates contrastive meaning.

10- *Nouns have singular, dual, and plural forms.*

11- *Definite article and no indefinite article.*

12- *There are different rules for labial consonants.*

13- *Lenition of consonants.* (Bet/Vet)

14- *Pluralization results in vowel changes earlier in the word.*

15- *There are several sorts of guttural consonant sounds.*

16- *There is an unchanging 'infinitive particle' with different positives and negatives.*

17- *Prepositional pronouns.* - conjugated preposition.

18- *Cognates*, many cognates exist, I believe in the thousands[141].

19- *General syntax.* Take any sentence in Paleo Hebrew, translate it word for word and the structure stays the same in Gaelic. You will have the correct idiomatic structure / syntax and meaning[142].

20- *Aspiration* - Speaking of the CELTIC use of the HEBREW rule of "ASPIRATION." (shandhi-Sanskrit) Dr. Meyer says, "The assuming of the guttural aspiration on the part of the consonant, under the influence of the preceding vowel is the kind of change regularly adopted in IRISH, whereas in WELSH, the vocalization of the mute is now the general rule. It is now unquestionable, however, from the gradual and even now only partial adoption of this rule in WELSH, that the IRISH usage is the MORE ANCIENT of the two, as is still further proved by its striking analogy with that of the DAGHESH LENE in HEBREW." (Dr. Charles Meyer – liguistin dissertation page 312, 1847).

21- *Consonantal language.* Most language experts say that Biblical Hebrew is mostly a consonantal script (no vowels). Many say the same about the Welsh language. This may appear to be correct when you see these Welsh town names without vowels, like the following: Bwlchgwyn, Rhydymwyn, Ysbyty Ystwyth, Bryn, Cwmtwrch,

---

[141] The Affinity between the Hebrew Language and the Celtic, looks to the grammar similarites and list cognates, by Thomas Stratton 1872

[142] See Play Poenulus of Plautus

Cwmystwyth, Mwnt, Cwm, Plwmp, Rhyl, Ysbyty Cynfyn, Tywyn (pronounced tuh-winn), Ynysybwl.

As if that wasn't enough, I have much more to prove the language link is real.

To summarize, we have covered linguistic expert testimony, along with actual structural analysis of Gaelic and Hebrew. But if they are the same people and language wouldn't there be complete sentences and many cognates?

Sure there would but a language that has been separated and moved in different directions for 2500 years would surely still be difficult to trace? Indeed we would think so, especially since most etymologists can't trace words back beyond a few hundred years and then they analyses cognates in different languages (that appear related), to come up with a fake Proto Indo European (PIE) root.

Well as you are aware (if your read my first book "WAI") I have already amassed damming, nah dam breaking evidence to support this claim.

POENULUS OF PLAUTUS.

Around 200B.C. an ancient Roman dramatist, Titus Maccius Plautus wrote a play, called The Poenulus (Latin for "The Carthaginian", in which he placed the current Phoenician (Phoenicians spoke Canaan i.e. Hebrew) into the speech of one of his characters.

Phoenician of Plautus
Byth lym mo thym nociothii nel ech an ti daisc machon
Ys i do iebrim thyfe lyth chy lya chon temlyph ula.
Early Irish Gaelic
Beth liom' mo thime nociaithe, niel ach an ti dairie mae coinne
Is i de leabhraim tafach leith, chi lis con teampluibh ulla.

This happened 2220 years ago (200B.C.) and the example is said to show Phoenician Punic and early Irish, being identical, it was a position that actually goes back hundreds if not thousands of years and was promulgated by individuals who knew the truth.

In the 18th through 19th century scholars, such as Gen. Charles Vallancey, Lord Rosse, and Sir William Betham, also wrote on this subject. Vallancey, for instance, speaks of, *"The great affinity found in many words, nay whole lines and sentences of this speech, between the Punic* [Phoenician] *and the Irish."*[143]

When I go into a Google translator and put in the Punic tongue, it recognizes it as Welsh, this is no surprise to me as the two are so close to one another.

Welsh Journalist – Israeli spy's

Two Welsh speaking Journalist were held in a Libyan jail because they were suspected of spying for Israel.

They had Welsh writing on their medical supplies and the officials thought it was Hebrew! They were so convinced that they jailed them for weeks before the Libyan Interior Ministry finally released them. The article quoted above was written by the independent, news organization and also stated:-

In 1821, the journal The Cambro-Briton noted the "affinity between the Hebrew and Welsh tongues". "The many points of resemblance between the languages in question have been noted by several learned writers," it noted, adding that this was "not merely in a coincidence of particular words, but in a general agreement of idiom and structure".

Wales, Welsh origin of the Cymry people.

If the Welsh are Hebrew were do their names come from? This is a fair question, surely place names rivers tribal names must point to their origin and background. I go into this is depth in "WAI".

---

[143] George Rawlinson, *Phoenicia*, p. 327.

Eber means crossing, over there, it's a metaphor i.e. "not from around here", it was used of with Abraham and Jospeh (it was used for river crossing in the Bible or mouth of a crossing, other side (Gen 50:10), in Welsh Aber, Scottish, aber and inver, Aberdeen, Inverness (mouth of the river Ness), Old Irish *indber, inbir, inber*. There are thousands of place names that use this prefix or suffix, even Ebro river in Spain, Ebredees (Hebrides'), Hibernia, and IBERIAN peninsular, all from our Eber roots.

Let us not forget that God promised Abraham to make his name great and his name is revered by Jews, Christians and Arabs, but Abraham was also called a Hebrew (Gen.12.1-3), Also considered of the lineage of Shem, Semites. God keeps his promises, he really does!

The name Wales and Welsh is a relatively modern name, it was what the Angles called the Celts, from Wealh, Walh "Celt, Briton, Welshman" the Welsh called themselves Cymry.

In Romanina, *Ţara Galilor*, literally "Country of the Gauls" In French, Welsh is *gallois*, while for Gaul it is *gaulois*

In Raymond Capt's book 'Missing Links Discovered in Assyrian Tablets', he actually points out that the name Kimri is listed in Assyria and tied to the Hebrew, he also points out that the name comes from Omri (H6018, Khumri). As he states, the name Omri begins with the consonant 'y' called Ayin which is pronounced with a guttural 'h' and is represented in Assyrian transliteration as 'Gh' or 'Kh'.

Omri = 'pupil of Jehovah' or heaping, from the root (עָמַר H6014) meaning to **gather grain or bind sheaves**. Perhaps now we realize the significance of the statement, remember the dreamer? Joseph and his dream of the sheaves bowing down to him (Gen 37:7), and he finally came into his **'Hay day'** and we Brits-Samaritans have the saying **'make hay while the sun shines'**, in other words, when God give you an opportunity, take it.

When we know the sheaf's background and the symbolism, it's easy to see the benefit of the name Omri, as well as a title **pupil of Jehovah.** Omri's parents wanted so much for their son, unfortunately, Omri did not live up to his name he was a very bad king, yet militarily he was strong and while he did not follow God's laws he was a highly respected and looked up to leader.

Let's take a look at what happened. In 930 – 909 B.C., Jeroboam (2Ch 9:29) was given the Northern ten tribes. He ended up using human reasoning and Jerry took God out of the schools, removed God from worship and destroyed the monuments and symbols of God. He was afraid that the people would go back to Jerusalem and worship the true God and allow Solomon's son Rehoboam to rule over Israel (2Ch 9:31). Long story short, he gerrymandered the tribes, yes. He re-drew the political and spiritual boundaries of the nation.

Years later, in 885 – 874 B.C., along comes Omri. He was one bad Hombre, one of the worst kings that Israel had and he was the father of the worst king ever Ahab (see chap. 7). However, we must remember that Israel was already apostate and had abandoned the one true God.

Omri set up Samaria, he bought the hill on which Shemah had lived and built a city and called it Samaria (1Ki 16:24). Look at the Brit'ish name for Samaria (**H8111**) *Shomerown – Shome r own so Omri* (Khimri-Cymry) *bought the hill and built himself a home and called it sHome r own,* sounds Egel' ish to me.

He set up Beth Omri 'the statutes of Omri' and superseded Gods statutes. Basically, more and more liberalism wanted God out of the picture, which just invites evil. Remember, God is our Magen, and exceeding great reward, when we take God out, we lose our shield. That's what's happening today in Israel: open borders, lawlessness, lies on both sides, honesty and truth seems to have been taken out, take God out of the schools and look at what's happening!

For the statutes of Omri are kept, and all the works of the house of Ahab, and ye walk in their counsels; that I should make thee a desolation, and the inhabitants thereof a hissing: therefore, ye shall bear the reproach of my people (Mic 6:16).

The ancient name of *Wales* was *Kumri*. It's Hebrew, as are many the names in these Is' lands (H336 we added luwnD-London, to the end of everything).

There are hundreds of books that I know on this subject most likely the number is in the thousands, one amateur etymologist Tony Daccre Barat has been studying the subject for over 30 years and has amassed over 1500 books that speak to the link.

Barber's Suggestion of Ancient Britons shows that the Cymry language was Hebrew, and they were called 'The People of Jehovah'. We noted earlier that the name Omri meant student of Jehovah. The term Britannia phonetically could be represented as Brit am yah (see index).

Taliesin, the Welsh bard of the sixth century, tells us his 'lore is written in Hebraic' (i.e. wisdom is Hebrew).

Aylett Sammes, 1676, said, he would call us Hebrew from our language, but we must be Phoenician. We have already shown the striking similarity between ancient Welsh Gaelic and Carthaginians in the Phoenician of Plautus. Aylett should call us Hebrew, because we are!

The Rev. Eliezer Williams (b.1754) wrote several works on the Celts and made several remarks (quoted by Roberts p.23): "In the Hebrew...which the ancient British language greatly resembles..." "The roots of most of the ancient British, or real Welsh, words may be regularly traced in the Hebrew..." "Scarcely a Hebrew root can be discovered that has not its corresponding derivative in the ancient British language... but not only. the words...their variations and inflections afford a much stronger proof of affinity.

The plural number of nouns likewise is often formed in a similar manner in the Celtic by adding in (a contraction of -IM which is the suffix used in Hebrew to form the masculine plural)...in

210

the formation of sentences, and in the government of words...the same syntax might serve for both...."

Davies in "Mythology of the Ancient Druids" (p.94) asserts that "Taleisin, the chief Bard, declares that his lore had been detailed in Hebraic..."

It follows from all the above that though the language of the British Celts may have superficially conformed to an Indo-European type, it had enough Semitic and Hebraic features to confirm the notion that Hebrew had been their original tongue. This explanation fits best of all the facts in our possession taken from all disciplines concerned with the subject.

The Welsh language Is 80% Hebrew

It is said that over 80% of the Welsh Gaelic came from Hebrew, another writer did a word-for-word comparison and he found many words were almost an exact match (Ref. link) hs name was "Glas" he submitted a list of Welsh words with Hebrew origins in 1832. The writer remarked that, "But the best proof of the Eastern descent of the ancient British is the close resemblance and connection existing between the Welsh and Hebrew languages, even at this day. As a proof of this we have extracted the following vocabulary of words in both tongues, so closely resembling each other in sound and sense as to leave no doubt whatever on the subject.

Many of these words, it will be found, have been transmitted from the Welsh, through the Anglo-Saxon into our modern English. It would be easy to swell their number..."

> Aeth: He went, he is gone; hence - Athah
> Aml: Plentiful, ample -Hamale
> Ydom: the earth -Adamah
> Awye: air, sky - auor, or
> bu: it came to pass = bo
> boten, or potten : belly = beten.
> brith: bright = barud

cas: hatred = caas (anger).

dafnu: to drop, or distill by drops = nataph, taph.

In 1675 Charles Edwards ("Hanes y Fydd") published A number of Welsh Cambro-Brittanic Hebraisms in which he shows that whole phrases in Welsh can be closely paralleled by whole phrases in Hebrew...

From the list of Charles Edwards, L.G.A. Roberts (1919) made a selection and we have selected examples from Roberts after slightly modernizing the Hebrew transliterations : It should be noted that when account is taken for likely and known dialectical changes of pronunciation the examples given in effect show identical Welsh parallel phrases for the Hebrew original.

Welsh: Gael hedd (Gen.31:47) meaning Geledd i.e. heap of testimony.

Hebrew : GaLAeD (גלעד Could this be the origin of the word Gael and Gaelic)?

Welsh: Bagad meaning "A troop cometh" (Gen.30;11)

Hebrew BaGaD h1409 בגד BaGāD

Welsh : Anudon meaning "Without God"

Hebrew: Aen Adon, (אין אדון).

Welsh :Yni all sy dda meaning "I am the Almighty God"

Hebrew: Ani El Saddai (אני אל שדי Gen. 17;1).

Welsh : Llai iachu yngwyddd achau ni meaning "Let him not live before our brethren" (Gen.31;32)

Hebrew Loa yichei neged acheinu (לא יחיה נגד אחינו).

Welsh Ochoren ballodddi hoc-dena meaning "After I am waxed old shall I have pleasure?" Gen.18;12).

Hebrew : Acharei belothi hedenah (אחרי בלתי היתה לי עדנה)

Welsh Bebroch fra am beneu ach ef, dyfet Deborah mam ianceth Ribecah

Hebrew :Beborcho mpnei achiv vetamath Deborah mayneceth Ribecah.
meaning "When he fled from the face of his brother . but Deborah Rebecca's nurse died" (Gen. 35;7-8)

Welsh: Yngan Job   yscoli yscoli cynghaws i (Job 6;1,2
Hebrew: Veya(g)n Eyub ....shocol yishocal ca(g)si

Welsh: Amelhau bytheu chwi a bythau holl ufyddau chwi [Gen. 10;6].
Hebrew: Umalu bathechoh and bathei col avedochoh (ומלאו בתיך ובתי כל עבדיך). meaning "And they shall fill your house and the houses of all your servants"

Welsh   Iachadd ni, means "Thou hast healed me"
Hebrew: hechiyatni (דחיתני).

Welsh   Nesa awyr peneu chwi .(Psalms 4;6.).
Hebrew: Nasa aor panechohmeaning (נסה אור פניך) "Lift thou up the light of thy countenance"

Welsh   An annos meaning "None did compel"
Hebrew: ain ones. (אין אנ Esther 1;8).

Welsh   Be heulo, luerferfo
Hebrew: behilo, leoroe, (בהילו ..לאורד). (Job 6;4) meaning "When his candle shined ..... and by his light.."

Welsh   Bwgythieu   in   gwarchaeni
Hebrew: Biu(g)thi elohai   ya-a(g)rchuni (בעותי אלוה יערכוני).
(Job 6;4 "The terrors of God set themselves in array against me).

Welsh   As chwimwth meaning "an angry man"
Hebrew ish chamas (איש חמס) (Psalms 140:12 Proverbs 16:29 meaning a wickedly-violent man).

I am convinced that the Brits are the Brits of the Bible, that the English are the Egel'ish of the Bible and that Luwn Dan is the secret hiding place of Gods people. There are many, many proofs here in this book that show our connection to Jacob, and it is clear

213

from a little research that I was not alone in uncovering this connection.

There have been many learned people through the ages that have written about this connection, including the language connection, and to dismiss this idea because we have some arrogant, condescending attitude is not one that I think God supports.

The Bible says 'The truth shall set you free', and it's time for the cover-up of our sacred past to be revealed and for the fathers, leaders, ruling class to wake up and to turn to their children and tell the truth, and for the children to turn to their fathers (Abraham, Isaac, Jacob, Ephraim, Manasseh and David).

Now this is important because in Jeremiah we read this - Gaelic, *before me"* (Jer. 31.35-37, Ps. 19). Israel had a habit of setting up pillars, heaps (Gen. 28.22, 31.13, 45, 52, 35.14), sign posts, memorials, tomb stones, even God led Israel by a pillar (Ex. 14.19) of cloud and a post of fire, and as we see above God instructed Jeremiah to set up Pillars.

'Set thee up waymarks (see yonder-H6725), *make thee high heaps* (Tamar-erection-pillar h8564) *set thine heart toward the highway,* even *the way (direct me-derek h1870)* which *thou wentest: turn again, O virgin of Israel, turn again to these thy cities.'* (Jer. 31:21) Again God is turning our hearts back to him, our roots, and our origins (Mal. 4.6).

Three prominent Tamars in Britain: the river Thames (anciently Tamar), river Tamar in Devon (tin mining area), and Tara, the ancient seat of kingly lines (two thousand five hundred years) and power. I know the plans I have for you, declares the Lord, plans to prosper you and not to harm you plans to give you hope and a future!

Chapter 7

Anglo-Saxons, and Germans.

The Romans' occupation of Britain, started AD 43-87 under Emperor Claudius, it lasted just over 300 years, the Romans's final withdrawal was in 410 AD, when the last Roman settlements were ordered out of Britain, this undoubtedly left a void, as no unified leadership existed, and the land was fragmented under local landlords who were answerable to petty tribal chiefs.

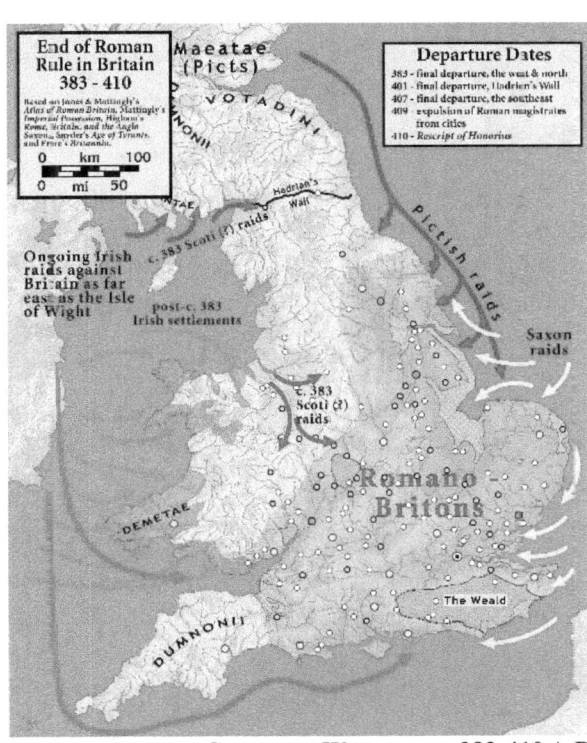

19 ROMAN BRITAIN COURTESY WIKIPEDIA –383-410 A.D.

This status made protecting the land against well-armed and trained raiding parties very difficult. Groups would form and raid England from Scotland, Ireland, and Scandinavia.

Departure dates based on Jones and Mattingly's Atlas of Roman Britain, Imperial Possession, Higham's Rome, Britain and the Anglo-Saxons, Snyder's Age of Tyrants, and Frere's Britannia.

383 A.D.-final departure, the west, and north
401 A.D. final departure, Hadrian's wall
407 A.D. final departure, southeast

409 A.D. Expulsion of Roman magistrates from cities
410 A.D. Rescript of Honorius telling the Roman cities to see to their own defense, a tacit acceptance of temporary British self-government.

Most of our knowledge about the Anglo-Saxons largely stems from the writings of the monk Bede (672–735 AD), who in turn drew from the accounts of monk Gildas (500-570 AD). The problem for historians is that their accounts have been tainted and brought into question.

The Anglo-Saxons peacefully migrated to England from northern Europe and settled in England during the 5th and 6th centuries. According to the Anglo-Saxon chronicles and modern archeology large swathes of A-S, came and settled in England after being invited

Vortigern (king of the British, according to Bede), invited **Hengist and Horsa** to Britain in 449 A.D. to fight the Picts and Scots (Irish).

Eventually, they rebelled against Vortigern and set up their own government. Again, most of the Anglo-Saxon (A-S) settlements appeared to be peaceful migrations; the A-S were mostly farmers, and they had an agrarian society much the same as the ancient Hebrews.

Though initially a collection of smaller groups scattered across various kingdoms, the Anglo-Saxons eventually coalesced into a single political entity called the Kingdom of England. This unification occurred under the reign of King Æthelstan, who ruled from 924 to 939 AD.

The Anglo-Saxons suddenly appear?

But where did the Angles, Saxons, and Jutes, come from? They suddenly appear near the Jutland peninsular, (circa 300 AD) in an area previously occupied by the CYMRI (see Mela's map), all are said to be Germanic, (Teuronic) they coalesce after the Cymri

216

(OMRI[H6018])leave, and fight the Roman's, (and as mentioned in Chapter 3), the Celts were also known as cowboys.

The elite fighting tribe of Boii, which was in Italy with the Etruscans, occupied the Jutland peninsular and later (after almost completely decimating the Romans, sees "terror Cimbrian") appeared to have partially merged with their brothers the Anglo-Saxons.

The Celtic cowboys (cow Boii's), formed wagon trains that were pulled by oxen, with their women, children, and older family riding inside, while the men mostly rode horses. They would travel thousands of miles in search of greener pastures. They even invaded Greece, and S'AXE'd Greece.

Modern historians and archeologists know very little about the A-S, before they arrived in England circa 5th century, some say they came from Sythia, and others say achiology and DNA testing do not line up with the Sythian hypothesis. The oldest known archeological evidence dates back only to 2nd century AD.

I have analyzed the etymology of names, such as CELTS, GAULS, and GODOL[144] (Old Irish Goidhel) under chapters 2, and 3, you can also check out the English Hebrew dictionary available on my website.

The term German and Germanic is a general term used by the Romans, and it applies to all of the tribes in the region, I discuss this shortly. Under maps see how the map of Pontonius Melae showed that they believed the region where the A-S come from was called Cumri, Cumbri; it is what the Welsh people call themselves Cymry. As we can see, the Jutland peninsular was named.

---

[144] H1419 גָּדוֹל gâdôwl, gaw-dole'; or גָּדֹל gâdôl; (shortened) from H1431; great (in any sense); hence, older i.e. "got old"; also insolent.

Maps

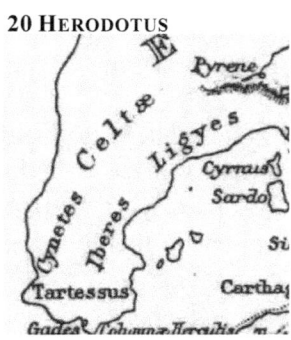

Herodotus map shows that the Celts were in the known world during Herodotus' time (450 B.C.). We also know that the British Islands were known to Solomon and Th'Arish[145] navy. This dates back to 1000 B.C. [146]

We can also see from the map provided by Pomponius Mela that 45A.D (see full map Fig.6a). The area of land where the Angles, Saxons, and Jutes were known as the Cimbri is the original name of the Welsh and links back to Omri, a king of Samaria. Again, we can see the Cimri Cimbri; it also shows Ireland to be Juvernia[147], aka Iber'nia Island of Hebrews, and another ancient name for Israel.

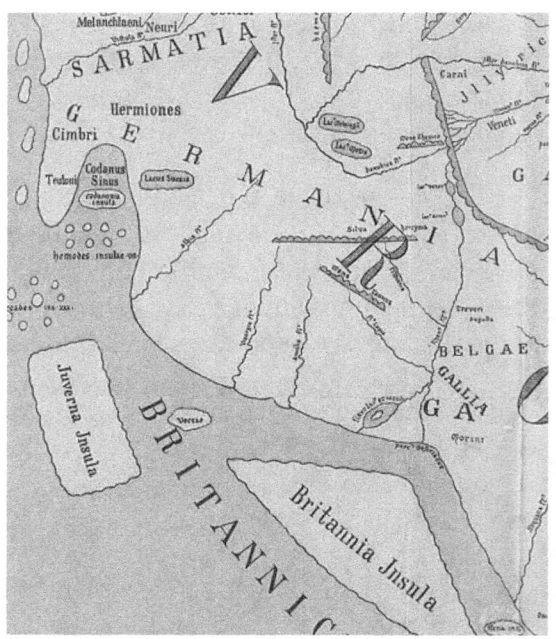

21 POMPONIUS MELA MAP

---

[145] Tarshish or Th'Arish, location, a distant port, site not certainly known (Wkl^Altor. Forsch. see 445); most *Tartessus* in Spain Thes (after older authorities) Ges^Is i. 719 Mey^Geschichte. d. Alt. i, § 281; other views are: *Tyrseni* (Etruscans) in Italy.

[146] Tin ingots found off the coast of Israel that date back to Solomons time and came form England.

147 Etymology of "Ivernia"/"Hibernia", "Ierne" in Greek to "Ivernia" and "Hibernia" in Latin, and finally to "Ireland" in English.

218

Albion (white house from Laban) in the later map by Ptolemy c. 140A.D., it shows that the Jutland peninsular where the A_S came from was called Cimbri (Welsh) and still occupied the area where the Anglo-Saxons came from. The reason for this is that many ancient writers linked them together. Strabo (VII.i,2) links the Cimmerian, calling them genuine Galatae, i.e., cimbri[148].

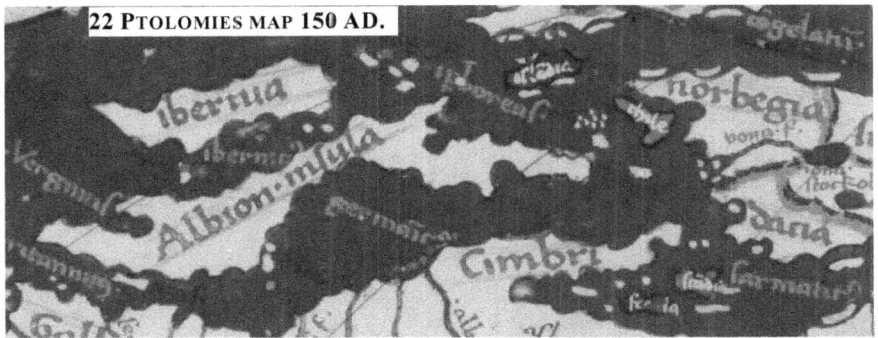
22 PTOLOMIES MAP 150 AD.

Ptolemy, in his map, calls them Cimbri.

These people fought against the Roman forces many times in 101 BC. The Cimbri moved out of what is now Denmark and into the Jutland peninsular. There, they swelled in numbers and fought against Rome, and they had victories in 113, 109, and 107, and the Romans were slaughtered at the Battle of Arausio on the Rhone River suffering a humiliating defeat in 105 BC. Inexplicably the Cimbri and Teutones failed to finish the job and allowed the Romans to re-group.

The Romans elected General Gaius Marius, for an unprecedented five continuous years as consul beginning in 104 B.C., with the mandate to create a new army. Which he did and attacked the Cimbri in 102 BC and later to finally crush the Cimbri threat.

148Missing Links Capt p.171, Starbo VII, I,2, Strabo, c. 64 bc-21ad, Greek geographer and historian.

At times many of the Germanic tribes fought as mercenaries with the Romans. The names Germany (adj.), Germanic, Germain, and GENE are said by etymologists to come from the PIE *gene[149].

Again, maps from Pomponius Mela and Ptolemy show Cimri and Samatian. We learn later that the Jutland peninsula and the area of the Elbe are where the Saxons, Angles, Jutes, and later Northmen (Normans) come from. The Romans referred to these people as "Germani," a term signifying kinship or family. The truth is that the Celt Gauls and Assyrians, along with the lost ten tribes of Israel and the Jews, are of the same stock; we are Semites from the lineage of Shem.

As I point out in this and my previous book, there are many historians, scholars, and linguists who agree. A valuable resource for connecting this information is "Missing Links Discovered in

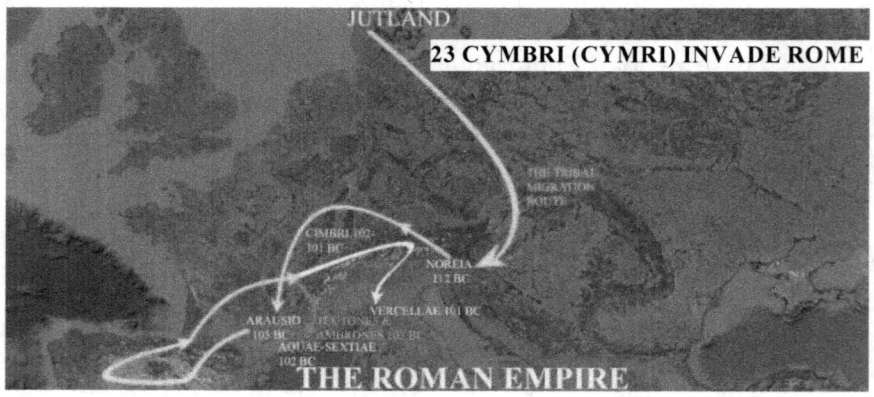

Assyrian Tablets"[150]. The Saka or Sakka (Saxons), Cimri (Welsh-Omri), he points out that the Sarmatians rode horses and lived in wagons drawn by oxen, and their dress culture customs were similar to the Scythians[31]. It further argues that the Scythians, also known

---

[149] I trace PIE root GENE to Kin and Gene (genee) H7014, relates to family, possession, by extension tribe, kinfolk, etc. H7018 קֵינָן Qeynan, kay-nawn'; from the same as H7064; fixed; Kenan, an antediluvian, Cainan, Kenan. h7014 קַיִן Qayin, kah'-yin; the same as H7013 (with a **play upon the affinity** to H7069); Kajin, the name of the first child, also of a place in Palestine, and of an Oriental tribe, Cain, Kenite(-s). H7069 קָנָה qanah, kaw-naw' to bear, possessed, to create (also of God) buy, get, purchased, buyer, possessor, owner, recover, redeemed, misc.

[150] "Missing links discovered in Assyrian Tablets" Raymond Capt 1985 -Sarmatians customs p. 168

for their wagon-dwelling lifestyle and inhabiting areas identified as Sarmatian territory, were actually Scythians and, surprisingly, of Hebrew stock descended from Assyrian captivity.

The etymology of <u>Saxons</u> speaks of it, meaning to cut as (s)axe knife, or sword. Old Norse sax "knife, short sword, dagger,' Old High German Saxnot, name of a Frisian war-god[151].

The origin of "Anglo" remains shrouded in mystery. While some theories suggest a connection to "angle," "ankle," or "angling," these terms lack resonance in folklore or burial practices, unlike the revered axe (a Saxon symbol). The wagon, however, was revered. In Hebrew, the wagon is linked to Joseph and Ephraim; the name is ăgâlâh[152] , and is the name for the wagon. The English is said to be from Proto-Germanic *wagna*; they are close, but the correct word is *agalah.*

Who are the current Germans?

There is a great multitude of people who call themselves Germanic including the Dutch, Belgium, Sweden, Denmark, Norway, Great Britain, and indeed the German plus others. No one knows where these people come from, but as we have seen in this book, the etymology of English (80% of commonly used English words are Anglo-Saxon), is Hebrew. Now let's look at the words GERMAN, and GERMANIC. The word GERMANIC originated in 1630s, "of Germany or Germans," from Latin Germanicus. from Germani, the word GERMAN (n),

---

[151] Modern English axe, Middle English sax, Old English seax. Other Etymons for the root science, axe, scissors, ski, split (skit). SKIN SCIENCE -SAXON-knife-cut-divide/ knowledge to split truth from fiction, to divide, to cut from knife? H7915שַׁכִּין sakkîyn, sak-keen'; to cut, divided as a knife-intensive perhaps from the same as H7906 in the sense of H7753; a knife (as pointed or edged), knife. ETM say split comes from flint Sword, Sore as circumcised by a sharp rock, also knife SWORD (d))H6864 צֹר tsôr, tsore from H6696; a stone (as if pressed hard or to a point); (by implication, of use) a knife, flint, sharp stone.

[152] H5699 עֲגָלָה 'ăgâlâh, ag-aw-law' from the same as H5696; something revolving, i.e. a wheeled vehicle, cart, chariot, wagon from Egel' a symbolic name for Ephraim/Manasseh.

Germani, from GERMAN (n), "a native of Germany," 1520s, from Latin Germanus (adjective and noun, plural Germani), first attested in writings of Julius Caesar, who used Germani to designate a group of tribes in northeastern Gaul, yet the word is of unknown origin.

Germani is considered to be neither Latin nor Germanic. Perhaps originally the name of an individual tribe, but Gaulish (Celtic) origins have been proposed, from words perhaps originally meaning "noisy" (compare Old Irish garim "to shout") or "neighbor" (compare Old Irish gair "neighbor"). Middle English had Germayns (plural, late 14c.), but only in the sense of "ancient Teuton, member of the *Germanic* tribes." I believe the word Irish garim "to shout" or "neighbor comes from the Hebrew Gowy[153] CROWD, a mass of people, it's a metaphor for noisy like a host of grasshopper. Irish Garim- Goyim = "nations"

Another option they say is the earlier English word Almain (early 14c., via French; see Alemanni). Shakespeare and Marlowe used the name Almain for "German; some think, Almain means all-man? Allemagne Germany, Alamannic refers to the ancient tribes and their language.

German, Germanic, Aramean, Aramaic?

Is it possible that the name German could come from Aram[154], as Germaic, could come from Aramaic, actually there is an ancient connection between Aramean's and Germans.

ARAMAIC, GERMANIC AR'MAN'IC H0762
אֲרָמִית’Ărâmîyth,; feminine of H761; (only adverbial) in Aramæan, in the Syrian language (tongue), in Syriac. Another root for German

---

[153] H1471 גּוֹי gôwy, go'-ee; rarely (shortened) גּוֹי gôy; apparently from the same root as H1465 (in the sense of massing); a foreign nation; hence, a Gentile; also (figuratively) a troop of animals, or a flight of locusts, Child of Abrahm/Israel, heathen, nation, people.

[154] Aram H758 אֲרָם ’Ărâm, arawm'; from the same as H759; the highland; Aram or Syria, and its inhabitants; also the name of the son of Shem, a grandson of Nahor, and of an Israelite, Aram, Mesopotamia, Syria, Syrians.

is said to be *ALNAZ said to mean all people, in Hebrew this could translate to king (over all the people) see AMRAM[155], high exalted people.

The Syrian (short form of Assyrian) people were sons of Shem they founded Nineveh along with Nimrod. The Assyrian Empire. Shem's suns Ashur (Assyria) and Aram (German) were present when building the tower of Babbel.

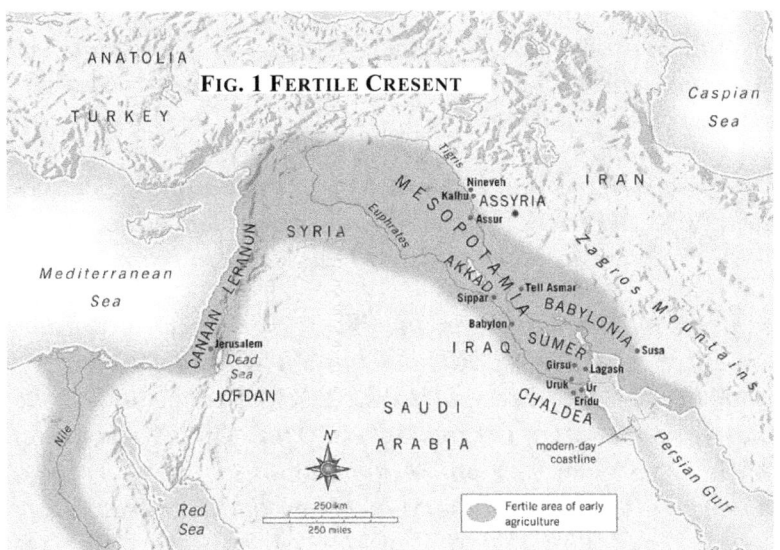

FIG. 1 FERTILE CRESENT

While the word NAZI[156], is an acronym for Nationalsozialist. I find it strange that this name would also be used by Assyria and Israel, as its meaning similarly meant high exalted one.

---

[155]H6019 עַמְרָם 'Amrâm, am-rawm'; probably from H5971 and H7311; high people; exulted people (nation) Amram, the name of two Israelites.

[156] H5387נָשִׂיא nâsîy', naw-see'; or נָשִׂא nâsi'; from H5375; properly, an exalted one, i.e. a king or sheik; also a rising mist.

Germany-Trier, Aryan-Aramean.

It is hard to believe that the citizens of one of the world's greatest and most enduring empires should fade almost completely from worldview. Over the course of nearly 2,000 years (up until around 600 b.c.), the Assyrians had been one of the largest and most significant forces shaping the ancient world. What happened to them?

A small, crushed minority survive to this day, living stateless in their Mesopotamian homeland. Those still living in modern-day Iraq number around 1 million.

But the history of man is the history of migration. We cannot expect the entire Assyrian people to have remained in the same territory—nor to have just been limited to the Mesopotamian region.

A medieval inscription in the West German city of Trier proudly declares that "Before Rome, Trier stood for 1,300 years." The construction of Trier is said to have taken place under the direction of Trebeta, son of the ancient Assyrian King Ninus (Josef K. L. Bihl, In Deustchen Landen*). According to the story, Trebeta had been driven out of Mesopotamia by his mother, Semiramis. He left with a "great multitude of Assyrians (Armans-Aryan)" and established the city of Trier in modern-day Germany. Thus we see textual reference to Assyria's fingerprints into Europe and specifically Germany as early as 2,000 B.C.*

Historical references show that after the Assyrians' defeat around 600 B.C., populations labeled as "Assyrian" were found all around the Black Sea region (as noted by Sylax, Diodorus Siculus, and Pliny the Elder). This follows along with a Bavarian tradition that their Germanic peoples came from the region of Armenia, near the Black Sea. The Scythians had in fact retreated to this location, after conquering the Assyrians. They evidently would have brought many Assyrian captives with them.

The historian Jerome wrote in the fourth century A.D. about Indo-Germanic tribes that during his time were invading into

Europe. He stated to them: "Assur [the Assyrian] also is joined with them" (note Psalm 83:8)—the Assyrians during the fourth century were pushing into Europe! For a more in-depth analysis of the Assyrians' migration to modern-day Germany, see here *and* here*.*

Leonard Cottrell wrote in Anvil of Civilization *(1957):*

In all the annals of human conquest, it is difficult to find any people more dedicated to bloodshed and slaughter than the Assyrians. Their ferocity and cruelty have few parallels save in modern times.

It thus should not be surprising that those perpetrators of modern "bloodshed and slaughter" (penned just after World War II) are themselves *the descendants of the Assyrians. It is also fitting that the once-great city named after the Assyrian forefather— Assur—has been chiefly excavated by German archaeological teams.*

The Bible does not end with descriptions only of Assyria's past. It also contains many prophecies of Assyria's—or Germany's—*future. You can read our detailed progression of them.*

While there's more to explore on this topic, connections between Assyria, Nimrod, deities, language, and even Rome have been proposed. Alexander Hislop's book, *The Two Babylons*, delves deeper into these ideas, he says their gods were the same and the Romans worshiped Nimrod and his wife Semiramis.

[Isa 7:17, 20 KJV] 17 The LORD shall bring upon thee, and upon thy people, and upon thy father's house, days that have not come, from the day that Ephraim departed from Judah; [even] the king of Assyria. ... 20 in the same day shall the Lord shave with a razor that is hired, [namely], by them beyond the river, by the king of Assyria, the head, and the hair of the feet: and it shall also consume the beard.

[Isa 11:11, 16 KJV] 11 And it shall come to pass in that day, [that] the Lord shall set his hand again the second time to recover the remnant of his people, which shall be left, from **Assyria**, from

225

Egypt, from Pathros, from Cush, from Elam, from Shinar, from Hamath, and from the **islands of the sea**. ... 16 And there shall be a highway for the remnant of his people, which shall be left, from Assyria; like as it was to Israel in the day that he came up out of the land of Egypt.

[Isa 19:23-25 KJV] 23 In that day shall there be a highway out of Egypt to Assyria, the Assyrians shall come into Egypt, the Egyptians into Assyria, and the Egyptians shall serve with the Assyrians. 24 In that day shall Israel be the third with Egypt and with Assyria, [even] a blessing in the midst of the land: 25 Whom the LORD of hosts shall bless, saying, Blessed [be] Egypt my people, and Assyria the work of my hands, and Israel mine inheritance.

[Isa 20:6 KJV] 6 and the inhabitant of this isle shall say in that day, Behold, such [is] our expectation; whether we flee for help to be delivered from the king of Assyria: and how shall we escape?

[Isa 27:13 KJV] 13 And it shall come to pass in that day, [that] the great trumpet shall be blown, and they shall come, which were ready to perish in the land of Assyria, and the outcasts in the land of Egypt, and shall worship the LORD in the holy mount at Jerusalem.

[Isa 36:13 KJV] 13 Then Rabshakeh stood and cried with a loud voice in the Jews' language, and said, Hear ye the words of the great king, the king of Assyria.

[Jer 50:17 KJV] 17 Israel [is] a scattered sheep; the lions have driven [him] away: first, the king of Assyria hath devoured him; and last this Nebuchadrezzar king of Babylon hath broken his bones.

[Eze 23:7 KJV] 7 Thus she committed her whoredoms with them, with all them [that were] the chosen men of Assyria, and with all on whom she doted: with all their idols she defiled herself.

[Hos 7:11 KJV] 11 Ephraim is also like a silly dove without heart: they call to Egypt, and they go to Assyria.

[Hos 8:9 KJV] 9 For they are gone up to Assyria, a wild ass alone by himself: Ephraim hath hired lovers.

[Hos 9:3 KJV] 3 They shall not dwell in the LORD'S land, but Ephraim shall return to Egypt, and they shall eat unclean [things] in Assyria.

[Hos 10:6 KJV] 6 It shall also be carried unto Assyria [for] a present to king Jareb: Ephraim shall receive shame, and Israel shall be ashamed of his own counsel.

[Mic 5:6 KJV] 6 And they shall waste the land of Assyria with the sword, and the land of Nimrod in the entrances thereof: thus shall he deliver [us] from the Assyrian, when he cometh into our land, and when he treadeth within our borders.

[Mic 7:12 KJV] 12 [In] that day [also] he shall come even to thee from Assyria, and [from] the fortified cities, and from the fortress even to the river, and from sea to sea, and [from] mountain to mountain.

[Nah 3:18 KJV] 18 Thy shepherds slumber, O king of Assyria: thy nobles shall dwell [in the dust]: thy people is scattered upon the mountains, and no man gathereth [them].

[Zep 2:13 KJV] 13 And he will stretch out his hand against the north, and destroy Assyria; and will make Nineveh a desolation, [and] dry like a wilderness.

[Zec 10:10-11 KJV] 10 I will bring them again also out of the land of Egypt, and gather them out of Assyria, and I will bring them into the land of Gilead and Lebanon, and [place] shall not be found for them. 11 And he shall pass through the sea with affliction, and shall smite the waves in the sea, and all the deeps of the river shall dry up: and the pride of Assyria shall be brought down, and the scepter of Egypt shall depart away.

Names associated with our northern enemies.

- The land of Ninevah (Assyrian capital set up by Nimrod).

- BabbleH1167 בַּעַל ba`alman, owner, husband, have, master, man given, adversary, archers, babbler, bird, captain, confederate, misc

- Babble H3956 לָשׁוֹן lashown tongue, language, bay, wedge, babbler, flame, speaker, talkers

- Babylon, Babylonian, BabelH894 בָּבֶל Babel Babylon, Babylonian, Babel

- Babylon H895 בָּבֶל Babel (Aramaic) Babylon

- BabylonianH896 בַּבְלִי Babliy (Aramaic) Babylonian

- Shinar, Babylonish H8152 שִׁנְעָר Shin`ar Shinar, Babylonish, = "country of two rivers" makes me think of sinner. Let's see if we have something similar.

- Shager H7683 שָׁגַג shagag err, flesh, sin ignorantly, deceived, went astray

- Shager H7686 שָׁגָה shagah err, ravished, wander, deceiver, cause to go astray, sin through ignorance, go astray, deceived

- Sinner, zanahH2181 זָנָה zanah...harlot, go a whoring, whoredom, whore, commit fornication, whorish, harlot, commit, continually, great, whore's.

- Sin own zanuwnH2183זְנוּנִיםzanuwn, whoredoms

- Sinerth zěnuwthH2184זְנוּתzěnuwth, whoredom

- Sin H8133שְׁנָאshna' (shen-aw') alter, change, *(often in a bad way)* (be) diverse [(Aramaic) corresponding to H8132] Root(s): H8132

- Shine H8132שָׁנָאshana (shaw-naw') to alter [a primitive root] KJV: change, (shine Ecc 8:1, Lam 4:1).

- Nineveh Ashur son of Shem created Ninevah, Asshur H804 H5210נִינְוֵהNiyněveh, nee-nev-ay of foreign origin; Nineveh, the capital of Assyria, Nineveh.Nineveh

- Nimrod, him rood, rude H5248 נִמְרוֹד Nimrôwd, nim-rode or נִמְרֹד Nimrôd; Nimrod = "rebellion" or "the valiant" probably of foreign origin; Nimrod, a son of Cush, (crush-. Rude Rude, to lord it over someone, to trample H7300 רוּד ruwd rood a primitive root; to tramp about, i.e., ramble (free or disconsolate), have the dominion, be lord, mourn, rule. The etymology of rude is not able to trace it, but they say its possible from to rudnes as in red

- Asshur H804רוּשַּׁא 'Ashshûwr, ash-shoor or רֻשַּׁא 'Ashshur; apparently from H833 (in the sense of successful); Ashshur, the second son of Shem; also his descendants and the country occupied by them (i.e., Assyria), its region and its empire: —Asshur, Assur, Assyria, Assyrians. See H838.
- Assyria, A rabble, rebble, rebuke a contentious crowd H3377 בֵרָי Yârêb, yaw-rabe ya'wabe(l) from H7378; he will contend; Jareb, a symbolical name for Assyria, Compare H3402.
- The name Nazi is ancient Assyrian Narsai (Pahlavi), "potent utterance".

Chapter 8

Egyptian Connection

Were did the Brits come from? Well, our parents tell us we came from our mummy's belly, right? But where did she come from? New DNA studies of Egyptian mummies show that 70 percent of the UK is related to the ancient Egyptians! What the heck! So our real mummy is really a mummy—shut the front door!

How in the world could this have happened? Do the Egyptians look like Europeans? (Pharaohs had red hair). Well, actually many experts believe the Egyptians may have initially possessed a Caucasian look, later integrating with North African populations.

The early Egyptians, according to some theories, possessed European features. This suggests they were either a white, blond, or red-haired population themselves or intermixed with such a group. The reaction of both kings (Pharaoh and Abimelech) to the genetic look of both Sarah and Rebekah suggests it was something more than just good looks.

The Bible hints at an early instance of interbreeding with the Egyptians. Nearly 4,000 years ago, Joseph, referred to as "the Brit" in some traditions, married an Egyptian woman (Genesis 41:45). This marked the beginning of a long relationship.

During Joseph's time and afterward, we were in Egypt for over 400 years and many subsequent sojourns; even the Hyksos kings were said to be Semitic. We built a replica of the Temple in Upper Egypt, the area known as Elephantine island; the Temple appears to have been built circa 7th century B.C.

Solomon further solidified the bond by marrying into the Egyptian royal family. There is a long history of economic, military, and social interaction with Egypt, so much so that when Jeremiah was taking out Israel, God warned them not to flee to Egypt, where many Jews lived (Jer.42. 19, 44.).

Again DNA evidence from Egypt corroborates the close relationship between the "Brits" and ancient Egyptians, aligning with both biblical and Irish historical accounts. What's more is that we are Hebrews; our language, idioms, artifacts, standards, ancient place names, music, etc., all point to this fact!

Yes, the first G.I. Joe was the ruler of Egypt, and the king gave Joseph an Egyptian wife named Aseneth, and they had two children: Ephraim (e phruity-he fruity-double fruit-Britain) and Manasseh (Ma'na'sseh-ma no see, out of sight out of mind-causing to forget, *troubles*). And yes, our mummy was Egyptian, hello.

Imhotep and Pharaoh Djoser

There's some debate surrounding the exact chronology of Imhotep's life. Traditionally placed around 2580 B.C.E., he's credited with constructing the first pyramid-style tomb for Pharaoh Djoser. This groundbreaking structure, with its distinctive square base, marked a significant shift in funerary architecture.

Imhotep *Jj m ḥtp He who comes in peace*

Imhotep by Joshua J. Mark, published on 16 February 2016

Imhotep (Greek name, Imouthes, *c. 2667-2600 B.C.E) was an Egyptian polymath (a person expert in many areas of learning) best known as the architect of King Djoser's Step Pyramid at Saqqara.*

24 IMOTEP JOSEPH

His name means "He Who Comes in Peace"  *and he is the only Egyptian besides Amenhotep to be fully deified, becoming the god of wisdom and medicine (the Bible suggests Joseph was the physician that delivered his grandchild Am'Makir-Am'merica (and according to sources Imhotep was the god of science, medicine and architecture). Imhotep was a priest (remember he married Asenath, the daughter of the priest of On), vizier to King Djoser (and possibly to the succeeding three kings of the Third Dynasty), a poet, physician, mathematician, astronomer, and architect.*

Although his Step
Pyramid is considered his greatest achievement, he was also remembered for his medical treatises, which regarded disease and injury as naturally occurring instead of punishments sent by gods or inflicted by spirits or curses. He was deified by the Egyptians in c. 525 B.C.E and was equated with the demi-god of healing Asclepius by the Greeks. His works were still extremely popular and influential during the Roman Empire, and the emperors Tiberius and Claudius both had their temples inscribed with praise of the benevolent god Imhotep.

Imhotep is a commoner like Joseph.

Imhotep was a commoner by birth (the Hebrew Slave, Yosaf) who advanced to the position of one of the most important and influential men in Egypt through his natural talents.

There are many accounts detailing the amazing similarities between Imhotep and Joseph, including the fact that he built huge granaries to store grain during the seven years of plenty and the seven years of famine. Yes, Yosaf kept the faith through thick and thin! (Remember Pharaoh's dream of 7 thick cows and seven lean cows)

The famine stele tantalizingly hints at a connection to the Joseph story despite containing embellishments and inaccuracies. Imhotep was none other than Joseph, a commoner, a Hebrew slave, who rose to the title of Governor of all Egypt, built granaries to hold the grain for the 7 years of plenty, and supplied the known world with food stock for the 7 years of drought. The similarities are such that this can be none other than the Biblical Yosaf! Next is an interesting article saying that Jozer's tomb at Saqqara was the first to be ornately decorated with hieroglyphs.

Saqqara pyramids | The Step pyramid

*"It was the first **pyramid** where **inscriptions** were found to be decorating the walls of the burial chamber! **There** are more than 700 incantations, which are supposed to help the dead king throughout the afterlife, and they are known as the **Pyramid** Texts."*

Many secular historians and Egyptologists seem determined to cast doubt on the Bible's historical accuracy yet readily accept unproven accounts from secular sources. The following article states that according to the Bible and some historians, Joseph was alive during the 7th century B.C.—that's just crazy talk! 10 century B.C. David was fighting Goliath in the Promised Land. Joseph's (Imhotep) tenure in Egypt was circa 1800 B.C. 18/19th century.

Also, as David Rohl and the Patten of Evidence movie (and others) point out, the Northern and Southern kingdoms often had co-regency. This, along with the arguments put forth by David Down, suggests a possible 18th-century B.C. timeframe for both Joseph and Imhotep, placing them as contemporaries.

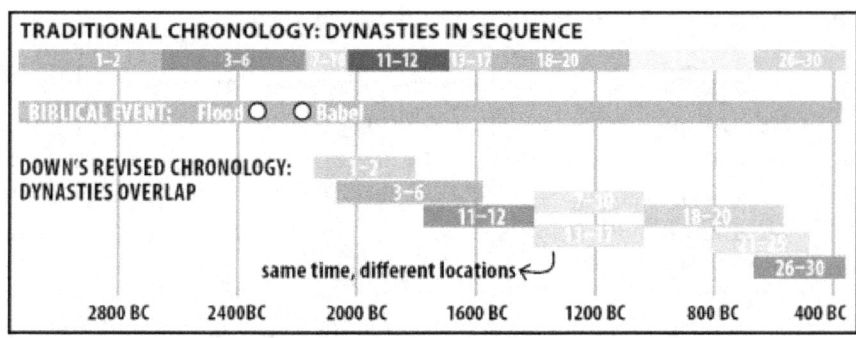

26 DOWNS REVISED CHRONOLOGY

This chronology aligns closely with David Rohl's revised chronology and his book, *The Pattern of Evidence*, particularly regarding the Exodus and subsequent migrations. This is where Dr. Rohl's real focus is, i.e., the new kingdom (NK 18-20 dynasties). It is important to note that the new kingdom has now arrived after the devastation of the plagues in Egypt and the exodus of the Israelites.

234

Also, new evidence shows that this kingdom actually has Semitic burial sites in Goshen.

We can see below that the 3rd Dynasty, where Joseph was, now overlaps his tenure in Egypt.

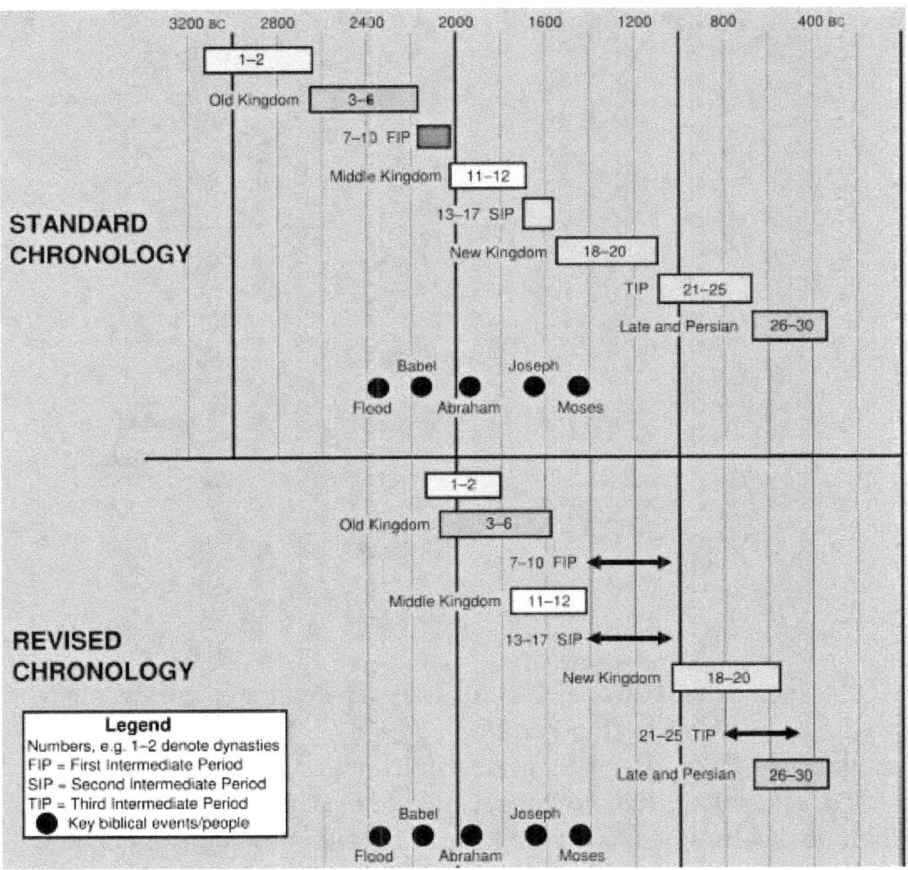

27 DAVID DOWNS TIMELINE - FROM CREATION.COM.

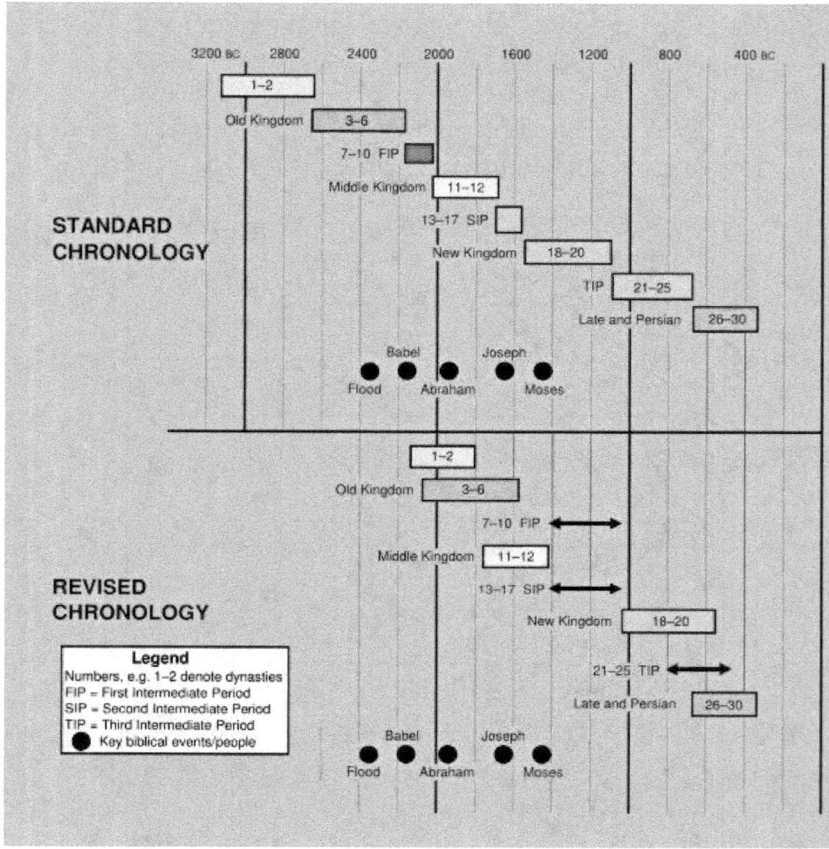

The date of 2670 B.C.E for Imhotep cannot be correct since we had a worldwide flood around 2350 B.C. The Egyptian dating method is "Fake History," like many things that are fake in this world. The powers that be can get most of the sheep to go along with their nonsense. Just look at the fake Trump–Russian conspiracy that caused the majority of people to believe it, even though there was no evidence found after thirty-two million dollars and in-depth investigations by the FBI and Mueller.

We really need to wake up! The Bible's portrayal of Satan as a deceiver (Revelation 12:9) underscores the importance of critical thinking. While a healthy dose of skepticism is crucial, it shouldn't lead to distrusting all leadership. Discernment is key – independently verifying information and holding leaders accountable are essential steps in navigating today's complex world.

So, the great man of Egypt, Imhotep, was Joseph. He lived in the 3 dynasties, while Egypt had some technology and, undoubtedly, some hieroglyphs before that time. Joseph (God) did enhance them; it was the Hey Bros, i.e., Joseph, that God gave the "tō·w·rat — 47 Occ. (וְתוֹרֹתָי H8450, 51 and52 - to, it was also known as the Ox [Tora]. The bull, i.e., Tora, seems [157]תוֹר synonymous with Torah!

Egyptian Hieroglyphs – Alphabet

Where did the alphabet come from? It is said that it came from Egyptian symbols, i.e., their hieroglyphs.

The Egyptian hieroglyphic script, a system for representing the ancient Egyptian language,

28 HIEROGLYPH – PALEO-HEBREW

captivated early observers like Herodotus. These Greeks, struck by the hieroglyphs' pictorial beauty, believed them to be sacred and dubbed them "holy writing." And the word hieroglyph comes from the Greek *hiero* 'holy' and *glypho* 'writing'. Hero[158] is also said to come from the Greeks via Latin. And means a GOoD-man. In the ancient Egyptian language, they were called *medu netjer*, which

---

[157] H8450
(Aramaic)oxen, bullock,
תּוֹרָה towrah to-raw
from H3384; a precept or statute, especially the Decalogue or Pentateuch:—law.

תּוֹר   towr
H8451
,   Law,

[158] Hero of superhuman strength or physical courage," from Old French heroe (14c., Modern French héros), from Latin heros a demi-god, illustrious man," from Greek hērōs Perhao of uncertain orign, others speculate its from "defender, protector" and from PIE root *ser- (1) "to protect" Hero in Hebrew it is H543אָמֵן'amen, be a man, is what I say. I would also offer h2220עָוֹרֶן zᵉrôwaʻ, zer-o'-ah; Aother possiblility is Goven, H3559כֹּוּן kûwn, koon; a GoVN is a distinguished man, a warrior(IM)..

237

translates to "god's words," reflecting their belief that writing was a divine invention.

Indeed, it was God who gave it to Joseph; you might say he received the "Word" (decipher[159] scriptorium Gen.41.37) from God. The Jews believe that the Aramaic Square

29 FRAGMENT OF A WALL DECORATION FROM TOMB OF SETI I

THE HIEROGLYPHIC ALPHABET

a — VULTURE	a — ARM	b — FOOT	kh — PLACENTA	d — HAND	f — HORNED VIPER
g — POT STAND	h — COURTYARD	h — CANDLEWICK	i, y — REED LEAF	dj — COBRA	k — BASKET
l — LION	m — OWL	n — WATER	o, w — KNOTTED ROPE, QUAIL CHICK	p — MAT	q — HILL
r — MOUTH	s — FOLDED CLOTH	sh — POOL	t — LOAF	tch — ROPE	z — DOOR BOLT

Script is holy, and they go to great lengths to pontificate on the script, especially the Yud and even the niqqud (added 600 A.D.). However, it's important to acknowledge that the earlier Paleo-Hebrew alphabet served as the foundation for the modern Hebrew script we use today.

The first decipherable script was composed of three types of signs: logograms representing words, phonograms representing sounds, and determinatives aiding comprehension. Sir Alan Gardener categorized over 750 of these symbols, with the total exceeding 1,000.

Unlike Hebrew, Egyptian hieroglyphs are read either in columns from top to bottom or in rows from the right or from the left. The image itself often provided clues about the reading direction.

As stated earlier, the Egyptian chronologist got it all wrong! Which leads us to misdate other areas. It's a circular problem. We date one area based on another area. If we get one area wrong, well,

---

[159] Write to Scribe, cipher and decipher writing, h5608 Cifer H5608 סָפַר caphar çiphar, scribe, tell, declare, number, count, shew forth, writer, speak, accounted, commune, told out, reckon, penknife, shewing, talk

then everything has to be rewritten, and the powers that be are loathed to do that. Additionally, secular humanist educators at these institutions often go beyond skepticism of religion (including the Bible). They actively distort truth by promoting falsehoods (like evolution being a fact) while denying God's existence.

With the timeline corrected and Imhotep being Joseph as identified in the famine stele, then early Egyptian writing developed alongside ancient (paleo) Hebrew. If this was the case, perhaps Joseph helped develop Egyptian writing along with Hebrew. After all, Egyptian accounts credit Joseph with creating the first alphabet.

Hebrew was the first alphabet developed by Joseph in Egypt. I am sure Joe used many of his family's pictographs and helped transform some of Egypt's pictographs. This is why I believe that some Egyptian hieroglyphs look similar to the earliest Hebrew, which I call Egelish (English). Joseph developed the first alphabet in 1859 B.C. Joe and his sons created the first alphabet. Yes, the Brits created the first alphabet! It's true!

30 HEBREW PICTORGRAPH

Hebrew block letter	Projected Proto-Hebrew original letter	Middle-Egyptian hieroglyphic exemplar
א		
ג		
ה		
מ		
ע		

The Middle Kingdom of Egypt thrived between the 14th and 18th centuries BC. A collection of 16 previously translated ancient inscriptions lay in museums for 100 years but have now proven that Hebrew is the very first Alphabet in Earth's history, from which all other alphabets, including English, Latin, and Arabic, are derived. Dr. Doug Petrovitch adds another layer of intrigue, stating, *"We know that God used this Hebrew Alphabet at Sinai in 1446 B.C. in the written Law of Moses."*

Canadian researcher Dr. Douglas Petrovich is the first person in history to translate these 16 inscriptions, and it all started when he realized that they were in ancient Hebrew. This refutes the previous notion that.

Phoenician was the first alphabet, and it proved beyond doubt that, Phoenician was derived directly from Hebrew, which is, in fact, the true Proto-Canaanite alphabet. Douglas Petrovitch's book, "The World's Oldest Alphabet," (Fig.23), explores these complexities. Another interesting, article from the Jerusalem Post talks about Hebrews (Jews) adapting the alphabet creating vowels (link), this person was in fact Samuel who was also British (covenant man) from the tribe of Ephraim (Sa 1:1).

Now therefore, if ye will obey my voice indeed and keep my covenant (H1285 בְּרִית *bĕriyth* pronounced Brit with ish meaning man in Hebrew), then ye shall be a peculiar treasure unto me above all people: for all the eret (EARTH) *is* mine (Exo. 19:5).

God is our portion, and we are God's potion. And God did not abandon the northern ten tribes when Assyria came in and sacked the land in 722-721 B.C.

But does anyone question that the land of Israel was only the start of the promises of God? God intended that Jacob was to inherit the high places of the earth. *"When the Most High divided to the nations, their inheritance, when he separated the sons of Adam, **he set the bounds of the people according to the number of the children of Israel**[160]. For the LORD'S portion is his people; Jacob is a lot of his inheritance" (D**eut. 32:8-9**).*

[Thou art] my portion, O LORD: I have said that I would keep thy words. [Psa 119:57 KJV]. Hiyah (hey).

---

[160] http://biblehub.com/deuteronomy/32-9.htm

I cried unto thee, O LORD: I said, Thou [art] my refuge [and] my portion in the land of the living. [Psa 142:5 KJV]

Chapter 9

Alphabet British-Hebrew.

It is well known that the Romans reintroduced the English alphabet during their occupation (43A.D.-410A.D.) It is called the "alphabet" because that is what the Greeks called it. The Geeks added an "a" to the end of "aleph" because they rarely end a word on a consonant. "Beta" is the second part of the word. Yet it transitioned to us as "alphabet" and not "alphabeta." Today, it's widely accepted that the Greeks, in turn, derived their alphabet from the Hebrew "alephbet," the first two letters of the Paleo-Hebrew script.

Greek alphabet

Various localized versions of the Greek alphabet were utilized across ancient Greece during the archaic period and early classical era. This diversity persisted until around 400 BC, when a standardized 24-letter alphabet, the one we know today, emerged. The foundation for all Greek alphabets was the 22-character Phoenician/Hebrew alphabet, except for the letter Samekh. The Greek equivalent of this, Xi (Ξ), appeared only in a subset of Greek alphabets. A common addition across these alphabets was Upsilon (Y), representing the vowel /u, ū/.

These local alphabets, known as 'epichoric', exhibited several differences, such as the usage of consonant symbols X, Φ and Ψ; the implementation of innovative long vowel letters (Ω and H); the presence or absence of H in its original consonant role (/h/); the application or omission of certain archaic letters (F = /w/, Q = /k/, M = /s/); and numerous variances in individual letter shapes.

The Greek alphabet, as we recognize it today, is a 24-letter system and was initially the regional variant used by the Ionian cities in Asia Minor. This specific system gained official recognition in

Athens by 403 BC and eventually became the standard across most of the Greek world by the mid-4th century BC.

It's noteworthy that the Greek alphabet's emergence from the Phoenician/Hebrew system marked a pivotal shift in ancient Greece. It signaled a move from a primarily oral culture to one embracing written communication.

The Greek innovation of adding individual vowels was critical as well, as it led to one of the earliest complete vowel alphabets. These developments had profound impacts, facilitating cultural exchange and communication across different regions, thus playing a crucial role in the dissemination of Greek literature, philosophy, and science, and significantly shaping the trajectory of Western civilization."

All of this was made possible by Joseph, the original inventor of the Aleph Bet. Also, even though the Etruscans, along with the Greeks, developed individual vowels, these sounds were in the original Hebrew, albeit using letters like Aleph, Hay, Waw, Vav, Yod, and Ayin, which produced the following sounds: Aleph = A, E, I, O, U. the Hay = H, HE, HA, HI, the Wav/Vav = W, V, I, 0, U, Yod, = Y, I, J, E and the Ayin = A, E, I, O, U. See alphabet section for more information.

Joseph was also a Hero (Hieroglyphs-writing of the gods/God) to the Egyptians as well as the Greeks, who readily embraced his medical and scientific skills (Imhotep-Egypt-Æsculapius-Greece)[161].

---

[161] **Imhotep**, Greek **Imouthes**, (born 27th century BC, Memphis, Egypt), vizier, sage, architect, astrologer, and chief minister to Djoser (reigned 2630–2611 BC), the second king of Egypt's third dynasty, who was later worshipped as the god of medicine in Egypt and in Greece, where he was identified with the Greek god of medicine, Asclepius. He is considered to have been the architect of the step pyramid built at the necropolis of Saqqārah in the city of Memphis. The oldest extant monument of hewn stone known to the world, the pyramid consists of six steps and attains a height of 200 feet (61 metres).

Etruscans

Who were the Etruscans – The Etruscans were quite the mystery for some time. While ancient writers offered diverse theories about their origins, their frescoes hint at a darker complexion, suggesting possible intermarriage with lighter-skinned populations.

A veil of mystery shrouds the origins of the Etruscans, a powerful pre-Roman civilization that thrived in present-day Italy. It has been the subject of long-standing debate among historians and archaeologists. The theories regarding their origins come from several ancient authorities:

1. **Herodotus:** Herodotus, the Greek historian, proposed in the 5th century BC that the Etruscans were from Lydia in Asia Minor (present-day Turkey). According to him, a prolonged famine led the Lydians to send out half of their population under the leadership of Tyrrhenus to look for a better land, which led them to Italy. This explanation is known as the Lydian hypothesis.

2. **Dionysius of Halicarnassus:** A century later, another Greek historian, Dionysius of Halicarnassus (1st century BC), vehemently disagreed with Herodotus. He argued that the Etruscans were native Italians, "autochthonous" people with deep roots in the region. This opposing view is called the autochthonous hypothesis.

3. **Xenophanes:** Xenophanes, a Greek philosopher and poet from the 6th and 5th centuries BC, suggested that the Etruscans might be from the region of Lemnos based on certain similarities he noted between the Lemnian and Etruscan languages.

Modern scientific research, including genetic studies, seems to suggest that Herodotus is correct.

A genetic study published in 2007 by a team of Italian and Spanish scientists compared the DNA of cattle from the Tuscany region of Italy, where the Etruscans lived, with cattle from various areas around the world, including Turkey. They found a close genetic match between the Tuscan and Turkish cattle, suggesting a possible common origin.

Another study, published in 2013, examined the mitochondrial DNA (which is passed down through the maternal line) from Etruscan burial sites and compared it with the DNA of modern-day Tuscans and Anatolians (from modern-day Turkey). The results revealed a significant overlap between the Etruscan and Anatolian samples, once again suggesting a potential link between the Etruscans and the region of modern-day Turkey.

Others have drawn a language connection between Etruscans and Phoenicians (see Pyrgi Tablets, section).

Etruscan origin

It appears that the ancient Etruscan spoke an ancient form of Hittite.

We have robust evidence both historical and DNA that links, the Etruscans with the Hittites (Heth H2845 son of Canaan, Gen 10:15, they spoke Proto Hebrew or Early Northwest Semitic).

1. The Ancient historical figure Herodotus connects Etruscans with Anatolia (Hittites).
2. DNA Evidence linking cattle and ancient Etruscan DNA to Anatolia (Hittites).
3. Pyrgi Plates/Tablets, circa 500BC these, show that the Phoenicians and the Etruscan not only shared the same deities (Asarte-Phoenician, Uni-Etruscan, Mary in Roman Catholicism), they also copied their alphabet.
4. Language, early vowel usage ("i", "e", "a," and "u") linking Etruscan, Lydians and other languages in the Lemnian region, namely Hittite and Akkadian (Semitic), all of which

had similar four-vowel systems, again suggesting an early connection.

The Hittites and Phoenicians shared ancient ties. Sidon, a major port originally settled by Sidonians, was considered Canaanite territory, just like Heth (the land of the Hittites)[162]. The major sea port of Sidon was eventually absorbed by the Phoenicians, who predominantly functioned out of Tyre, Sidon (1Ch 1:13), also with an eastern sea port of Eziongerber. The Sidonians were Hittites; they were sons of Ham (Egypt, Ethiopia, Canaan 1Ch 1:8). The Hittite language is considered an archaic form of Indo-European; it is proto-Semitic. In fact, the name for water is water in Hittite. I do not think there are enough known words to build a solid connection. However, Dr. Zaidan believes there is a connection.[163]

Etruscans and their influence on the Romans

The Etruscans, a powerful and wealthy civilization, flourished in ancient Italy from the 8th to the 3rd century BC. Their domain, Etruria, encompassed modern-day Tuscany, western Umbria, and northern Lazio. Their culture, politics, and technology significantly influenced the ancient Romans, who eventually absorbed or pushed out the Etruscan civilization. The ancient's believed them (at some point) to be pirates because they were great navigators and ship builders.

Political Structures

The Etruscans, mirroring the city-states of ancient Greece, boasted a unique governing structure. They had a form of government that included a monarch, a council of nobles, and an

---

[162] Gen 10:15 And Canaan begat Sidon his firstborn, and Heth H2845 חֵת Chêth, khayth; from H2865; terror; Cheth, an aboriginal Canaanite, Heth- They spoke a very early primeval form of Hebrew, as indeed the Canaanites did. Ezekiel 27:8 The men of Sidon and Arvad were your oarsmen. Your men of skill, O Tyre, were there as your captains.

[163] Dr. Zaidan Ali Jassem, Professor at Department of English Language and Translation, Qassim University, KSA (2012a-f, 2013a-q, 2014a-k, 2015a-g) has shown in forty one studies so far that Arabic, English, German, French, and the so-called Indo-European languages in general are genetically related very closely phonetically, morphologically, grammatically, and semantically or lexically to such an extent that they can all be regarded as dialects of the same language

assembly of citizens. This system had a profound influence on early Roman political structures. For example, the Romans adopted the concept of "rex," or king, from the Etruscans, which was later replaced by the Republican system.

Military Tactics and Strategies

The Romans borrowed heavily from the Etruscans in the realm of military organization. The Etruscans pioneered the use of the phalanx, a formation that the Romans later adopted and modified. Additionally, the tradition of the "triumph," a celebratory parade for victorious generals, found its roots in Etruscan practices.

Religion and Divination

The Etruscans were deeply religious, and their beliefs significantly influenced the religious practices of the Romans. They had a pantheon of deities, many of which were assimilated into the Roman pantheon. Furthermore, the Romans adopted Etruscan religious practices, particularly their methods of divination and the art of interpreting the will of the gods.

Infrastructure and Urban Planning

The Etruscans were skilled builders and engineers. Their knowledge in constructing fortified walls, drainage systems, aqueducts, and roads was passed onto the Romans. Even the design of the Roman Forum, the heart of their city, bears the mark of Etruscan architecture, which itself likely drew inspiration from Phoenician and Hebrew ingenuity (a topic we'll explore further – see Hiram, the Phoenician master builder of Solomon's Temple).

Art and Symbolism

Etruscan art, rich with symbolic meaning, played a vital role in shaping Roman artistic sensibilities. From Etruscan sources, the Romans adopted the arch, the use of terracotta in sculpture, and the concept of depicting narratives in frescoes. Etruscan mastery of bronze work, particularly in crafting mirrors, vessels, and statues, also left a lasting impression on Roman art.

Language and Alphabet

The Etruscan language significantly influenced the development of Latin, the language of the Romans. In addition, the Romans adopted the Etruscan version of the Phoenician/Hebrew aleph-bet, which eventually developed into the Latin alphabet used in the Western world today.

Phoenician / Hebrew / Celtic connection

While many scholars postulate that the Etruscans got their alphabet from the Greeks, the **Pyrgi** Tablets tables tell a different story.

Pyrgi Tablets

The Pyrgi Tablets, also known as the Pyrgi Gold Plates, are three gold leaves that bear an inscription detailing a dedication made around 510 BC by Thefarie Velianas, king of the city of Caere in Italy, to the Phoenician goddess Ashtart. Their discovery in 1964 at Pyrgi, an ancient port city for Caere (now Santa Severa), serves as a tangible reminder of the vibrant cultural exchange between the Etruscans and Phoenicians.

Language and Inscription

Two of the tablets are inscribed in Etruscan, while the third is inscribed in Phoenician/Paleo Hebrew. The Phoenician text commemorates a temple dedicated to Ashtart, a powerful goddess. The Etruscan inscriptions mirror this devotion, referencing their own equivalent, Uni. Interestingly, the tablets suggest that the Etruscan king was operating under a form of Phoenician suzerainty (dominion, power, dominance), highlighting the fact that the alphabet in 500B.C. was common knowledge to the Etruscans, including the Phoenician religion in Etruria.

I believe that Etruscans who called themselves RASENNA (*rasna,* possibly RACE, a term that comes from RESH, as in head)[164] were a mixed race, that had many Hebrews and Phoenicians in their ruling class.

Further enriching the picture are the shared practices of divination among the Phoenicians, Etruscans, and Ancient Hebrews (particularly during Elijah's time). These cultures held deities like the Phoenician goddess Ashtoreth ("star," "the bright one") in high esteem.[165], along with BAAL worship abounded so much so that Elijah called them out and had a contact between 850 prophets (Baal 450 and Asherah 400) to one (1Ki.18.33). The word ASTEROID, STAR, and possibly TAROT comes from Astarte.[166]

The narrative doesn't end there. Carthaginians (Phoenicians) allied and even subdued the Etruscans, and for hundreds of years, they worked together to control the Mediterranean Sea[167]. The Phoenicians came under increasing pressure from a variety of sources, namely the Assyrians (circa 720BC) and later the Persian empire, where they lost Tyre and Sidon (circa 600BC). This event marked Carthage's rise to independence and its efforts to forge new

---

[164] RACE "people descended from a common ancestor, class of persons allied by common ancestry," from French *race*, earlier razza "race, breed, lineage, family" (16c.), possibly from Italian razza which is of unknown origin (cognate with Spanish raza, Portuguese raça), it comes from the Etruscan-Phoenician-Hebrew, H7218 רֹאשׁ   rô'sh,
roshe; H7217, from head Ra's rash, firstborn of Israel, race Resh, - from an unused root apparently meaning to shake; the head (as most easily shaken), whether literal or figurative (in many applications, of place, time, **rank**, etc.):—**band (of men)**, beginning, **captain**, chapiter, **chief**(-poor, principal, ruler, sum, top. H7217 רֵאשׁ   re'sh
(Aramaic) head, sum, **chief**.

[165] Astarte name of a Phoenician goddess identified by the Greeks with their Aphrodite, from Greek Astarte, from Phoenician Astoreth (plural Ashtaroth), equivalent to Assyrian Ishtar. Apparently properly a virginal goddess of the moon or the heavens, but she has been frequently confounded since Biblical times with the sensual Ashera (see Asherah).

[166] ASTEROID, STAR, TAROT (Tarot a word of unknown origin), H6253 עַשְׁתֹּרֶת 'Ashtoreth, ash-to'reth; Ashtoreth=star, probably for H6251; Ashtoreth, the Phoenician goddess of love (and increase). (/əˈstɑːrti/; Greek: Ἀστάρτη, Astártē) is the Hellenized form of the Middle Eastern goddess Astoreth (Northwest Semitic), a form of Ishtar (East Semitic), worshipped from the Bronze Age through classical antiquity. The name is particularly associated with her worship in the ancient Levant among the Canaanites and Phoenicians. She was also celebrated in Egypt following the importation of Levantine cults there. The name Astarte is sometimes also applied to her cults in Mesopotamian cultures like Assyria and Babylonia. See also H6251 עֲשְׁתְּרָה 'ashtᵉrâh, probably from H6238; increase, flock, make rich. See H6240, asar ten only in combination.

[167] See Carthaginian Empire by

alliances. The name "Tyrrhenian Sea" might even be a legacy of the Phoenician presence.

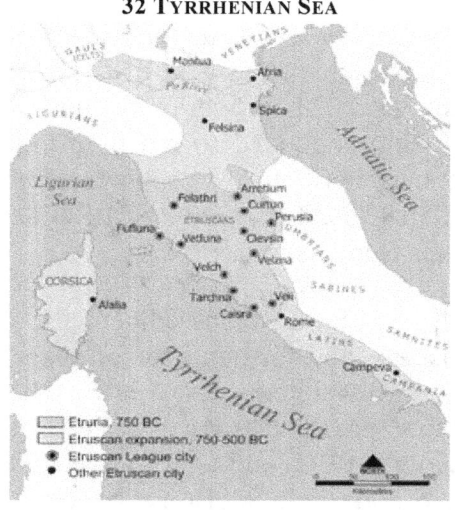

Etymologists trace the name "Tyrrhenian Sea" back to the Etruscans. The word itself has a fascinating lineage, and means "pertaining to the Etruscans," from Latin Tyrrheni, from Greek Tyrrenoi "Tyrrhenians," from tyrsis "tower, walled city" (cognate with Latin turris "tower"). Earlier Tyrrhene (late 14c.). TOWER, pre-Indo-European Mediterranean language. Meaning "lofty pile or mass."

The Tyrrhenian Sea is from TYRE[168] as the walled towering island city of the Phoenicians, and this is from the Hebrew in H6865 צֹר Tsôr lofty pile, rock, (cognates SOAR TOWER over). Other related words are TYRIAN, TARTAN. The royal tradition of tartans is traced by etymologists back to Tyre and Tyrian purple, which has been known for a long time as a color of royalty. However, the concept of a multicolored fabric symbolizing royalty might have even older roots. The story of Jacob gifting Joseph a "coat of many colors" around 1898 BC (Genesis 37:3) offers a possible earlier instance. Even the kilt (tartan) dress of the Romans was copied from the Phoenician/Hebrews.

Etruscan and Latin Alphabet

It is generally believed that 21 of the 26 archaic Etruscan letters were adopted for Old Latin from the 7th century B.C., either

---

[168]SOAR, TOWER, Phoenician fortress H6865 צֹר Tsôr, tsore; or צוֹר Tsôwr; the same as H6864; a rock; Tsor, a place in Palestine, Tyre, Tyrus

directly from the Cumae alphabet or via archaic Etruscan forms, compared to the classical Etruscan alphabet retaining B, D, K, O, Q, and X but dropping Θ, Ś, Φ, Ψ, and F. (Etruscan U is Latin V; Etruscan V is Latin F) Link.

Clearly, these Greeek Θ, Ś, Φ, Ψ symbols were not in the Etruscan, Roman, Phoenician or Paleo Hebrew alphabet, and the Phoenicians/ Etruscans had close ties. The fact that they left them out increases the probability that they got it directly from the Phoenicians/Hebrews.

I also point out in WAI that many early Greek locations were plied by the Phoenicians, Hebrews, and Celts, who all spoke the same language. One example is how the Greeks embraced Joseph (Imhotep) and idolized him. Also, the Danites struck out early while still in DANUS and CADMUS, along with Lacedemonians and DANONI, even the early settlers TUATHA DE DANANN, who had a short stint in Greece before going to Ireland, as noted by Irish, Greece, and Roman historians.

We covered this earlier, the "Tuatha de Danann" -- literally, the Hebrew word Three, Tre, and Tuatha (Hebrew for three)[159], the etymology of "tribe" comes from "three" and is via Celtic and Latin, via Etruscans[170].

De means God; see etymology for Tue'sday (De and TU are the same), Danaan=Dan, the tribe of [171].". The Greeks called them the Danoi, and the Romans called them Danaus.

Conclusion

---

[169] H8532   תְּלָת tᵉlấth,
tel-awth three in Hebrew,

[170] Old French tribu or directly from Latin tribus " one of the three political/ethnic divisions of the original Roman state" (Tites, Ramnes, and Luceres, corresponding, perhaps, to the Latins. Sabires, and Etruscans), etymologist done know the origin but I have it see reference above.

[171] H1835 דָּן dān, H1839 דָּנִי dānî.

Despite their eventual absorption (destruction or assimilation) into the Roman Republic, the Etruscans left an indelible mark. From political systems and military tactics to religion, infrastructure, and art, the Etruscan influence can be seen in many aspects of Roman civilization. Without the Etruscan contributions, Roman society would have developed differently, potentially altering the course of Western civilization.

However, the Etruscans themselves weren't entirely self-taught. It's abundantly clear they drew heavily from the knowledge and, crucially, the alphabet of the Phoenicians (Hebrews). What is also sure is that Etruria was under the direct control or a vassal of the Phoenicians, possibly from the 7th century BC, but evidence shows that by the 7th century, they most definitely were (see Pyrgi Tablets).

Introduction to the alphabet

When we talk about the alphabet script, most people think of cuneiform as the oldest, and indeed, it is. This type of writing uses wedges to signify consonants and vowels in each pictograph. It often has one vowel and one consonant. Egyptian hieroglyphs, too, rely on pictographs, albeit arranged linearly, to narrate stories. But here's where things get interesting.

Both cuneiform and hieroglyphs, along with many other scripts, utilized a combination of alphabets and pictographs. Imagine "Aleph" (an ox-head) representing the sound "A" or "Bet" (a house) signifying "B." Also, the direction of reading of both scripts (and others) can be discerned by looking at the direction of the object's face(see Boustrophedon), like E means writing is left to right and means right to left.

Ǝ

The cuneiform script, with its wedge-shaped symbols representing syllables (one consonant and one vowel), stands as the oldest writing system we know of. Hieroglyphics, with their pictorial representations encompassing consonants, vowels, syllables, and even entire concepts, follow closely as the second-oldest. The alphabet invented and developed by Joseph and his sons is the third oldest script and the first known alphabet, again the first one that used symbols-letters to sound out a word.

The Paleo Hebrew, or should I say the original alphabet, started with pictures (Pictograph-H6600 and H6599 פִּתְגָּם pithgam, Pit'h'gam) that were used to produce a letter (sound). This is not disputed.

33 SUMERIAN PICTOGRAPH

The earliest word pictures, some argue, emerged on Sumerian tablets a staggering 5,000 years ago (though some claim even earlier origins). We know from the Bible that Enoch prophesied about God and the fallen angels because Jude (Jesus's brother) said so (Jde. 1:14).

Did this message travel through pictographs, oral tradition, or perhaps both? I believe it was pictographs, as there is evidence of pictographs being used pre-flood, and Joseph used some of the symbols to create the alphabet. In Raymond Capt's book *Missing Links Discovered in Assyrian Tablets,* he states that a Semitic civilization influenced the Sumerian people at Kish in a region called Akkad. They spoke Hebrew (a Semitic language) and were known as "Akkadians."

He states that it was these people who took over the Sumerian city of Kish (P. 23). This would make sense because God was the word, and it's logical for Him to give the first written alphabet (language) to His own people, the Semites.

I am the Aleph and the Ta (the alpha and omega), I am the beginning and the end, and Ephraim is my first born (son of Joseph, Jer 31:9). Again, in John 1.1, "In the beginning was the word and the word was with God and the word was God." This clearly indicates the relationship between the written and spoken word and God and his people.

34 MOSAIC SCRIPT

The word, the written word, was, I believe, given to God's people (later known as the Israelites-sons of Jacob). It is clear that pictographs and oral traditions were handed down from generation to generation. Akkad was a Shemitic (Semitic, sons of Shem) city, so it is feasible that we did know and use pictographs prior to the development of the alphabet.

In my other book, *We Are Israel*, I delve deeper into this concept, citing newly deciphered inscriptions from the Egyptian turquoise mines at Serabit el-Khadim (interpreted by D. Petrovich in *The World's Oldest Alphabet*). These inscriptions, according to my analysis, suggest that Joseph played a pioneering role in the development of the alphabet.

The first letter of the Alphabet is the Aleph (ox head). One of the earliest mentions of the Aleph is in Genesis 24:60: "*And they blessed Rebekah, and said unto her, Thou art our sister, be thou the mother of thousands H505 of millions, and let thy seed possess the gate of those which hate them* (see also Gen 20.16, circa 2026 B.C.)." This suggests that the symbol was attached to blessings and later became the symbol of Ephraim and Manasseh.

I don't think the word was given to the Egyptians to pass on to Joseph. No, the covenant people of God (Britannia-Brit'am'yah) had been taught aspects of the word until God inspired Yosafe to develop the first alphabet.

The fact that God so intricately associates Himself with speech and the written word suggests that speech has power and even written words have power, and I think God rewarded the Israelites with knowledge, understanding, and power. It just doesn't make sense to me that God would give this to the Egyptians so that they would give it to Joseph. No, God positioned Joseph, the "alpha male" of Egypt, to save the world and also gifted them with the alphabet – a tool for us to comprehend history and preserve His commandments.

The original order of the Alphabet.

How do we know the order of the original alphabet? And what objects do they represent?

The original order is slightly different from our modern English. One source for the order is the Bible, and we find each of the alphabetic names written in the margins (not actually written in the Bible). They are as follows.

1 -A, ALEPH-Ox, (Psa. 119:1).
2 -B, BETH-House, (Psa 119:9)
3 -G, (C)GIMEL ג -Camel (Psa. 119:17), 1580 [e]
4 -D, DALETH-Door, (Psa. 119:25)
5 -H, (E)HE-Praise, (Psa 119:33).
6 -V, VAU-hook-Peg, support, pillar, (Psa 119:41)
7 -Z, ZAIN-Psa 119:49
8 -C, CHETH-Psa 119:57
9 -T, TETH-Psa 119:65
10-J, JOD-Psa 119:73
11-C, CAPH-Psa 119:81 Salvation
12-L, LAMED-Psa 119:89
13-M, MEM Psa 119:97
14-N, NUN-Psa 119:105
15-S, SAMECH-Psa 119:113
16-E, AIN-Psa 119:121
17-P, PE-Psa 119:129
18-T, TZADDI-Psa 119:137
19-K, KOPH-Psa 119:145

20-R , RESH-R-Head, first, top, start Psa 119:153
21-S, SCHIN-Psa 119:161
22-T, (X)TAU-Psa 119:169

Psalms 119 and its acrostic[172] poetry

Examining the Psalms revealed a fascinating poetic technique. I, at one point, analyzed each of the Psalms to see how they were used, and the Psalmist used poetry to weave each line and verse. They weaved the appropriate letter into each verse, but what they didn't consistently do was explain or list the original pictogram meaning. In other words, the original Hay is a picture of a man with hands raised (I believe) in worship ⱳ but the Psalmist does not (now) record the original meaning (Praise, or look here -see alphabet section).

Praise words are Halleluiah and Halal (origin of HAIL and YELL)[173], where Halal forms the first part of Hall (All and HAIL) EL=God, U= who = YAH, the personal name of God.

English-Hebrew Alphabet, Jews-Aramaic.

Will the real script of the Hebrews please stand up and take a bow? As we said in the introduction, the real language and script of the ancient Hebrews started to leave the Promised Land when the northern ten tribes (aka Brit'ish-covenant man) were attacked and later completely absorbed by the Assyrians.

Around 800 BC, the northern ten tribes, also known as the "Brit'ish-covenant man," faced Assyrian attacks and eventual assimilation. This culminated in the capture of Samaria (sHome-

---

[172] An acrostic is a poetic arrangement of letters in which (most commonly) the first letter of each line begins with the next letter in the alphabet.

[173] H1974 הַלּוּל hillûl
praise, make merry H1984 הָלַל hālal

256

ron) in 721 BC. From this time, Aramaic (Ashurit) started to become the vernacular of the entire region, and it ceded only to Arabic in the ninth century A.D. Interestingly, the Arabic script, like all alphabetic scripts, finds its roots in Paleo-Hebrew, further solidifying the interconnectedness of written languages.

The original alphabet script isn't used by the Jews today. It's what the Jews call *Ketav Ashurit (כְּתָב אַשּׁוּרִית)*. We (the Brits) call this Paleo-Hebrew . The modern Jews call "Hebrew" "Avrit" (or aBrit-where the "Bet" can be a "Vet"). Get that? A Brit!

ketav Ivri "Hebrew script" (H3791 כְּתָב kathab writing/scripture Hebrew=H5680 עִבְרִי 'Ibrîy, ib-ree), also called Phoenician or Proto / Paleo-Hebrew. This script was still widely used during the age of the Mishnah (Mishnah oral traditions of the Jews 536B.C.-70AD) and was well known to the sages.

The other script, *Ketav Ashurit (כְּתָב אַשּׁוּרִית)* ("Assyrian script" H804 אַשּׁוּר 'Aššûr Assyria), is the one we know today as the Hebrew alphabet.

The earliest inscriptions in the Aramaic language use the Phoenician alphabet.[2] Over time, this script evolved into the distinct form we recognize today. Aramaic gradually became the *lingua franca* throughout the Middle East, with the script at first complementing and then displacing Assyrian cuneiform as the predominant writing system. This happened because the inventors of the alphabet were displaced.[174]

---

[174] Courtesy Wikipedia

Ashurit	ך/כ	י	ט	ח	ז	ו	ה	ד	ג	ב	א
Ivri											

Ashurit	ת	ש	ר	ק	צ/ץ	פ/ף	ע	ס	נ/ן	מ/ם	מ/ם
Ivri											

35 ASHURIT/IVRIT

Rabbinical circles hold lively debates about the origin of writing. The Talmud, a cornerstone of Jewish scholarship from Babylon, even features this discussion, presenting three distinct viewpoints on the primacy of specific scripts.

1- Torah was given to Israel in Ivri letters, and this is the sacred (Hebrew) language/script. Later, in the times of Ezra, the Torah was given in the Ashurit script and the Aramaic language, and eventually, this replaced the original Ivri script/language.

2- It was taught. Rebbi said: "Torah was originally given to Israel in Ashurit script. When they sinned, it was changed to *roetz* (Ivri script). When they repented, Ashurit script was reintroduced."

3- R' Shimon ben Elazar said in the name of R' Eliezer ben Parta, who said in the name of R' Elazar Hamoda'i: "This writing was never changed [i.e., it was always in Ashurit script]."

It is clear to anyone who looks at the archeological evidence! All the early writing found in ancient Israel was written in different forms of *ketav Ivri*, i.e., Paleo-English, not Ashurit (modern Aramaic square script Hebrew), so the correct script of the ancient

258

Israelites is the Paleo-Hebrew Alphabet. One that is still in use today by the English-speaking world.

36 Mirror image of original Paleo Hebrew

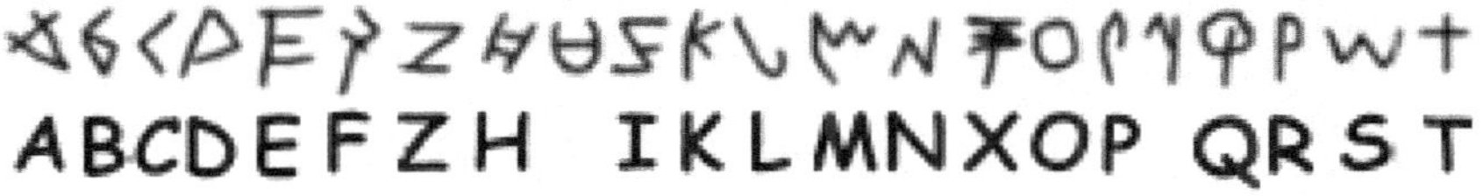
ABCDEFZH IKLMNXOP QRST

Above is the mirror image of the original Paleo Hebrew against the English version. Despite a separation of over 3,000 years, the resemblance is undeniable.

However, Paleo-Hebrew met its demise around the destruction of the Second Temple in 70 A.D. With the exception of inscriptions on a handful of ancient Jewish coins, no other traces of Paleo-Hebrew survived. The Babylonian Talmud (*Sanhedrin 21b*) has a pertinent discussion about these two forms of Hebrew writing:

Mar Zutra[3] *or, some say, Mar Ukba said: Originally the Torah was given to Israel in Ivri (Paleo-Hebrew) letters and in the sacred Hebrew language. Later, in the times of Ezra,*[4] *the Torah was given in Ashuri script and Aramaic language. Finally, they selected for Israel the Ashuri script and Hebrew language, leaving the original Hebrew*[5] *characters and Aramaic language for the ignorant people. Rebbe Yose said: Why is it called Ashuri (Assyrian) script? Because they brought it with them from Assyria.*[6]

This theory aligns with modern archaeological discoveries. Around 1,800 BC, Egyptian hieroglyphics are believed to have sparked inspiration in Phoenicians living and working in Egypt. This influence led to the development of Proto-Canaanite, a groundbreaking phonetic alphabet. Proto-Canaanite then evolved as Paleo-Hebrew and was the script used by all the peoples of the Middle East, including the Phoenicians, the Canaanites, the Moabites, and also the Hebrews. Archeologists have unearthed Paleo-Hebrew inscriptions on stone and pottery dating as far back as the twelfth century B.C.

Moabite Stone, 9th century B.C.E.

Around 800 BCE, a fascinating transformation occurred. In Babylon and surrounding areas, the Paleo-Hebrew letters were reworked, evolving into the distinct Aramaic script. Around 275 years later (circa 525 BCE), the Jews in Babylon, notably Ezra the Scribe, refined the native Aramaic letters and developed *Ashuri*, the script recognized today as *Hebrew*.

For centuries, during the Second Temple period, *Ashuri* was the dominant script used for all holy and secular purposes. However, Paleo-Hebrew was not entirely forgotten and appears on some coins of the period.[9] The last known remnant of Paleo-Hebrew writing appears on Bar Kochba coins circa 125 CE. The final known use of Paleo-Hebrew script surfaces on Bar Kochba coins, dating back to around 125 CE.

Bar Kochba[10] led the last revolt against Rome 50 years after the Second Temple had been destroyed. Rabbi Akiva considered him to be the Messiah. Bar Kochba minted his own coins by over-striking them on existing Roman coins. This was symbolic of his rebellion against Rome. He inscribed three Paleo-Hebrew letters, "*yud-hay-dalet*," *"Yehud," and* "Judea," on the face of his coins. This deliberate choice of the Paleo-Hebrew script was a bold statement –

260

a yearning for a return to the original Jewish script, a script used before foreign powers subjugated the Jews.[11]

Following the crushing of the Bar Kochba revolt, Paleo-Hebrew faded entirely from use. It became the original dead letter. Were it not for the above-mentioned discussion in the Talmud, Paleo-Hebrew would have been completely forgotten. It is virtually certain that *no one* could read it since no documents or samples of its letters survived, except for those three letters on the Bar Kocha coins.[12]

But the 20th century brought a remarkable turn of events. Archeologists began discovering buried artifacts inscribed with Paleo-Hebrew letters dating back to the times of King David, and earlier [13,] and then the Dead Sea Scrolls were found with several examples of Paleo-Hebrew text. The ancient Hebrew alphabet had been resurrected from the dead.

Why did the Jews adopt the Aramaic script?

One story as it coming from the Tower of Babel. A place Unified in speech and purpose, the people proposed to build a tower "with its top in heaven." This is interpreted to mean that they wanted to build a great edifice with a temple of idol worship at its top to "wage spiritual war against G-d." As a pre-emptive act, G-d confused their language and scattered people all over the world.[21] According to Biblical scholars, the date was 1930 BCE.

Before the episode of the Tower of Babel, Legend tells of a righteous man named Ashur, who, foreseeing the coming chaos, fled the region and established the cities of Nineveh, Rehovot, and Calah.[22] Having abandoned the region before the building of the Tower of Babel, Ashur was excluded from punishment and retained the original holy language and its script.

Thus, it became known as *Ashuri*. Over the next millennium, the holy script of *Ashuri* deteriorated and became mixed with the script of the indigenous peoples who wrote in Paleo-Hebrew. This "downgraded" script eventually emerged as the Aramaic script around 800 BC.

Aramaic sounds Arabic, but this is misleading as shown that the term Arabs and Arabia comes from H6163 עֲרָבִי Arabiy and ar-awb, which comes from 6148 עָרַב 'ârab, aw-rab,' But Aramaic actually comes from Ashur.

H804 אַשּׁוּר 'Ashshûwr, ashshoor Assyria.
H805 אַשּׁוּרִי 'Ashuwriy Asshurim, Ashurites
H806 אַשְׁחוּר 'Ashchuwr Ashur (founder of Assyria)
H839 אָשֻׁר 'Ashur Ashurites (Assyrians).

The Talmud offers this explanation as to why there are two (generally known) scripts.

According to tradition, there was one family chosen by God to retain the original holy tongue and its script: the family of Shem, one of the three sons of Noah. Through this family and its descendants, Abraham, Isaac, and Jacob, the holy tongue and the original *Ashuri* script were carefully preserved. The Talmudic view suggests that even during Egyptian captivity, the Israelites remained loyal to Ashuri, their ancestral tongue and writing system. Thus, the Torah was given in the *Ashuri* script. The year was 1480 BC *(as previously pointed out this view is incorrect, but one held by many Rabbi's and Jews)*.

After the Jews entered the land of Canaan, they were exposed to the *Ivri* writing of the people around them, and they began to read and write it alongside their holy *Ashuri* letters. This is similar to Jews today in the United States and England, who read and write English as well as Hebrew. Notably, all Torah scrolls – for roughly 750 years, from Mount Sinai to about 150 years before the destruction of Solomon's Temple – were written in Ashuri script.

However, history took a dramatic turn with King Menasseh's reign. At this juncture in history, King Menasseh[23] embraced idolatry and plotted to destroy the Torah and its leadership. He murdered the prophet Isaiah, his maternal grandfather, and caused

262

the blood of religious Jews to flow like a river through Jerusalem. It is logical to presume that he also confiscated all the Torah scrolls he could find, which, according to Rebbe Yehuda, were written in *Ashuri* and burned or buried them. At that point, the Jewish scribes would have had the opportunity to begin writing the Torah in *Ivri*, the common script of the region.

Finally, during the days of Mordecai and Esther,[24] with the Jews in exile in Babylon and Persia, Ezra wrote a Torah in the original *Ashuri* script. This scroll served as the basis for subsequent copies, ensuring the continuity of the Ashuri script in Torah scrolls right down to the present day.

The Talmud now offers a third opinion:

Rabbi Simeon ben Elazar[25] said in the name of Rabbi Eliezer ben Parta, who said in the name of Rabbi Elazar of Modin: This writing of the Torah [Ashuri] was never changed, for it is written: "The vavei ha-amudim (the hooks of the pillars).[26] "Just as the word 'pillar' (amud in Hebrew) has not changed, neither has the form of the 'vav.' Also, it is written [27] according to their script and language." "And unto the Jews, just as their language did not change, neither did their writing.

This opinion argues that the Torah has always been written in *Ashuri* script and never in *Ivri*. Rabbi Elazar offers two proofs based on logic:

The first proof is that the word for hook in the Torah written by Moses was '*vav*.' *Vav* is also the name of the sixth letter of the Hebrew alef-bet, which is shaped like a hook in *Ashuri*. Since the vav in Rabbi Elazar's days, [28] was still shaped like a hook, and his Torah was written in *Ashuri*, he concludes that the script of the Torah was always *Ashuri*. However, his logic is shown to be flawed since the letter *vav* in *Ivri* (Paleo-Hebrew) *also* resembles a hook.[29] In fact, the *vav* of *Ivri* may resemble a hook more than the vav of Ashuri.

Similarly, Rabbi Elazar's second proof is a verse in the Book of Esther, where Mordecai sends letters to the Jews throughout the kingdom, written in their "script and language." The contention is that the words "script and language" are written together and are equivalent. Rabbi Elazar reasons that the Jews did not change their language in the days of Mordecai; therefore, they also did not change their script, which was *Ashuri*.

Again, his argument does not hold up, for the fact that the Jews *did* change their language in the days of Mordecai. The Book of Daniel, written around the same time, uses Aramaic, not Hebrew, highlighting a shift in the spoken language. Why did Daniel choose Aramaic? Because Aramaic had replaced Hebrew as the language of the Jews, and it remained the primary spoken language of the Jewish people for the next millennium.

Since both proofs offered by Rabbi Elazar are rejected, we are left with two views:

1.) Moses originally wrote the Torah in Paleo-Hebrew (*Ivri-Ebro-Egelish*). It was changed to *Ashuri* script by Ezra during the Babylonian Exile and has remained so ever since.

2.) Moses wrote the Torah in *Ashuri* script. It was changed to *Ivri* towards the end of the First Temple period and then changed back again to *Ashuri* by Ezra.

This discussion is of monumental significance since it includes the writing of the Ten Commandments, "*the two Tablets of Testimony, stone tablets inscribed by the finger of G-d*" [30]. The Jerusalem Talmud [31] maintains that the Ten Commandments were written in *Ivri*. The Babylonian Talmud [32] says that they were written in *Ashuri*.

In the end, we find that the Talmudic discussion leaves us with doubt concerning which script was the original. But we can possibly resolve this by considering a ceremony performed with the *Kohen Gadol* (High Priest) and the kings of the House of David.

The *Mishna*[33] tells us that the *Kohen Gadol* must be consecrated by anointing with *shemen hamischa,* the anointing oil made by Moses. This is one of the 613 commandments of the Torah. A small amount of the oil is poured on the High Priest's head and applied between his eyes by a finger drawing the form of an X, the letter Tav, the 22nd letter of the *Alef-Bet* in *Ivri* script. And when the kings of the Davidic dynasty are anointed, the same oil is used, but applied in the shape of a crown, the vertical zigzag lines of a W, the form of the letter Shin, the 21st letter of *Ivri* script.[34] Neither of these two shapes is found in our familiar *Ashuri* script.

Since Aaron, the High Priest, and King David appear to have been anointed with forms of letters of *Ivri* script, we can presume that *Ivri* was the script used during the early generations of the Children of Israel,[35] and that *Ashuri* script was developed later. Mar Zutra suggests a thousand-year gap, placing its creation during the Babylonian Exile.

My personal reflection on this subject is to avoid the mistake of thinking that if Paleo-Hebrew was the original, then it must be the holier of the two scripts. The fact is that Ezra, the father of *Ashuri* script, was the author of three books of the Hebrew Scriptures[36] and worked with *ruach hakodesh,*[37] a form of prophecy.

The Hebrew letters that came from his hand contain some of the deepest and most mystical teachings of the Torah. These letters have sustained the Jewish people for 2500 years and will undoubtedly continue to do so in the future. However, the rediscovery of Ivri, or Paleo-Hebrew, signifies at least this: we stand

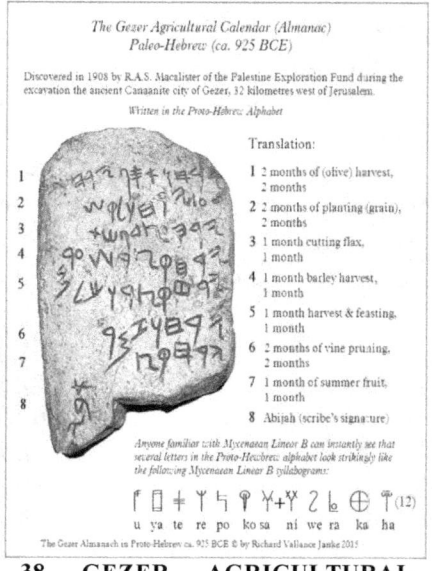

39 JERUSALEM-IN ARAMAIC-HEBREW SPELLING.

38 GEZER AGRICULTURAL CALENDAR

at the dawn of a new era, grappling to weave the past and present into a future that transcends both.

There are a number of problems with the assertion that Ivri (Paleo Hebrew) was not the original language. Clearly, archeology proves that it was. We have many inscriptions in Paleo-Hebrew, dating back to 1,000 BC, whereas the oldest Ashuri script is only 2,000 years old and dates from the second temple period. These are big problems for rabbis who are trying to protect an Aramaic square script. The earliest known Ashuri inscription is from 2nd temple period of 2000 B.C. See the section on the alphabet for more examples.

Boustrophedon or Ox-Turning.

Boustrophedon, aptly named after the "ox-turning" method, describes a fascinating writing style where lines alternate direction, going from right to left and then left to right. As we already know, the first letter of the alphabet was the ox, and this is the symbol of the covenant (British) tribe. The Greeks got their letters from the Bous=ox.

But the story takes a curious turn. We recall how God, according to scripture, spoke of turning the ox around. This caused the language to be turned around and to go from left to right while our brothers from another mother wrote from right to left!

I have surely heard Ephraim bemoaning himself *thus*, "Thou hast chastised me, and I was chastised, as a bullock ^{H5695} unaccustomed *to the yoke*: **turn thou me, and I shall be turned**; for thou *art* the LORD my God"(Jer 31:18).

Does the Bible identify the symbols of the tribes? Yes, it does, and the symbol of the Brits is the Aleph. Below shows the progression of the Aleph, the letter/symbol A Aleph r.

40 BULL

Hieroglyph	Proto-Sinaitic	Phoenician	**Archaic Etruscan**
ʖ	⌕	↑	Ⱶ
1860-1050 B.C.	1050-458 B.C,	700 B.C.	630-620 B.C.

The earliest known use of the modern A was in 1350 BC, and it's almost identical to today. Subsequent inscriptions had it rotating around until it settled down in Etruria in 620 BC.

41 ETRUSCAN ALPHABET FROM THE COCKEREL BOTTLE, 630–620 BC

A B C D E F ZH * I K L M N ? O P ? Q R S T UVWS- (SEE ALSO THE MARSILIANA TABLET (IVORY, 650 B.C.) - COURTESY WIKIPEDIA

267

The Greeks and Romans, whose alphabets formed the foundation for our Latin script, weren't the originators. That credit goes further back to the Hebrews. But the story gets more intriguing. The first actual alphabet with vowels was found in Western Greeks in 800 BC. The ancient alphabet is called an "abjab," meaning it was a consonant-only script, and as such, it is believed that the vowels (enabling correct pronunciation) had to be added.

I am not convinced that the original script did not represent vowel sounds (as said earlier) the as well as consonants. In other words, we have letters that represent A, E, I, O, U, and sometimes Y. The difficulty was it required a knowledge of the words used in order to properly pronounce the word (the use of consonants that also can stand for vowels are called *Matres lectionis*. They appear to miss one of the vowel/consonant letters, the "Ayin," Eye aᵉyin e, i, a, o, u, (see alphabet section).

When I look at the archaic/primitive Hebrew words, I'm often struck by their phonetic resemblance to modern terms. Yes, we have developed an alphabet that mostly mirrors phonetics. The problem with our modern English is that it has many archaic words and spellings that allow us to trace their roots back to Hebrew. That part is great. The difficulty is the ease of learning the language and consistency in spelling.

The Etruscans, with strong ties to both Phoenicians and Celts, were part of a network with Hebrew roots. As mentioned earlier, the Phoenicians, also linked to the Celts, disseminated the Hebrew alphabet globally.

Taken or adopted from the Israelites, and as mentioned earlier ("We are Israel"), it was first introduced to the world by Joseph. Further development came from Ephraim and Manasseh, followed by revisions from Samuel (World's Oldest Alphabet, Douglas Petrovich). It's interesting to note that Samuel was one of the greatest prophets in the Bible. He was not of the Tribe of Levi (remember, God rejected Eli's sons, and they were killed). Rather, he was of the Tribe of Ephraim (Joseph). Also, after the northern ten tribes were taken out of the land (Circa 900-721B.C.), the paleo alphabet was also removed. In fact, the Jews rejected it and switched to the Aramaic square script.

A script that the Jews adopted after the house of Omri (Cymru) was taken out.

Also, the name "Omri" (Kumri in Assyrian tables) appears to have been used in Italy. Many ancient historians attest that the area known as Umbria[175] has a variant spelling of Umbri[176], and it was a Gaulish (Celtic) name. This area was next to the Etruscans.

Why was the ox head (Aleph aka A) used for the first letter of the alphabet? Did it have a deeper significance? As always, we use the word of God as our source. Let's see what God has to say about it.

The Cowboys, aka Aleph, is a symbol of Ephraim and Manasseh. The Bible list many different names for the bull, ox, steer calf, cow, etc., and the Aleph (Eleph'ant) was the one that Joseph (God) chose to represent the vowel A.

"EGEL" is another bull term used in the Bible. Egel is **H5695 עֵגֶל '**, egel -ay-ghel; it's easy to see how this could also be pronounced **Angle** as in the Angles and Saxons, Jutes, and Normans. In Hebrew, it means bullock, calf, or a steer, and ish, H376 שׁאִי 'iysh means man or men in Hebrew, so **Egel'ish is the symbol of the covenant man (Brit'ish)** AKA Ephraim, and sometimes Manasseh are depicted at a steer, a male calf or bullock as in Deuteronomy

---

[175] They are also called *Ombrii* in some Roman sources. Ancient Roman writers thought the Umbri to be of Gaulish origin;[3] Cornelius Bocchus wrote that they were descended from an ancient Gaulish tribe.[4] Plutarch wrote that the name might be a different way of writing the name of the Celto-Germanic Ambrones, which loosely means "King of the Boii.[5] Livy suggested that the Insubres, another Gaulish tribe, might be connected; their Celtic name *Isombres* could possibly mean 'Lower Umbrians," or inhabitants of the country below Umbria.[6] Similarly Roman historian Cato the Elder, in his masterpiece Origines, defines the Gauls as "the progenitors of the Umbri".[7] The Ambrones are also mentioned, with the Lombards and the Suebi, among the tribes of Northern Europe in the poem Widsith.[8][9][10] Pliny the Elder wrote concerning the folk-etymology of the name: The Umbrian people are thought the oldest in Italy; they are believed to have been called Ombrii-Curtesy Wikipedia.

[176] Omri, Kumri h6018 עָמְרִי Omriy Khumri "pupil of Jehovah" Ancient name for Wales and a region in Italy (Umbria) next to Etruscans.

33:17 "*His glory is like the firstling of his bullock, and his horns are like the horns of unicorns: with them, he shall push (or gore) the people together to the ends of the earth*": and they *are* the ten thousands of **Ephraim**, and they *are the thousands of Manasseh*. (Psalm 29:6).

He maketh them also to skip like a calf; (H5695 Egel) Lebanon (white boy mountain) and Sirion like a young unicorn (**H7214** רְאֵם r°’êm), the unicorn is considered a wild bull or ox, also a symbol of Ephraim.

He hath not beheld iniquity in Jacob, neither hath he seen perverseness in Israel: the LORD his God *is* with him, and the shout of a king *is* among them. (Num. 23:21- 22) God brought them out of Egypt; he hath as it were, the *strength of a unicorn (wild ox).*

God predicted that the language would get turned around. Originally, languages possessed the remarkable ability to be written in both directions, left to right and right to left. The Greeks even had a name for this fascinating practice: Boustrophedon, literally meaning "ox-turning," mirroring the back-and-forth movement of an ox plowing a field.

I have surely heard Ephraim bemoaning himself thus; Thou hast chastised me, and I was chastised, as a bullock H5695 unaccustomed to the yoke: (wild bullock, a unicorn) **turn thou me, and I shall be turned**; *for thou art the LORD my God.* (Jer. 31:18).

The calf itself will be taken to Assyria (Hos. 10:6) as an offering to the great king. Ephraim will experience shame; Israel will be ashamed of its counsel. (Hos. 10:11) Ephraim is a well-trained calf that loves to thresh, but I will place a yoke on her delicate neck. I will harness Ephraim (the Ox); Judah will plow; Jacob will do the final plowing. God will use Judah and Ephraim (the Egel'ish) to accomplish his promises, and now we know how He is accomplishing His will.

Even in the last book of the Bible, God makes this promise about the Egel'ish. *[Mal 4:2 KJV] 2 But unto you that fear my name*

270

shall the Sun of righteousness arise with healing in his wings; and ye shall go forth, and grow up as calves (h5695 egel) of the stall.

Chapter 10

The Alphabet Letters

Over a century ago (1916), a renowned English scholar, Sir Alan Gardiner, made a significant discovery in Egypt. Gardiner, an Egyptologist, Linguist, and Philologist, is best known for his work in codifying Egyptian hieroglyphs into over 700 categories (see Fig, 4a), a system still used today. Discovered very early pictographic inscriptions[177] that he calls Semitic, this sparked much interest in discovering who wrote them.

The inscriptions were found at wadi el hol (meaning Wadi of Terror, basically a hell hole)and the Seribit (turquoise) mines in Egypt. The hell hole was on the Farshut[178] road and about 200 miles up the creek(nile) without a paddle. Farshut etymology is unknown, Wadi el Hol proved to be a shxty place to live. The slaves were Hebrew and had been doing hard labor for hundreds of years in Egypt.

The good old days of Joseph being in charge were long gone, and a new ruler who didn't know Joseph arose, one who really oppressed the slaves (Exo.18,13).

There's a fascinating story etched into the rocks of these regions. Slaves left behind messages in a Semitic script, yet they remained undeciphered for over a century. Enter Professor Douglas Petrovich, an Egyptologist and Philologist who finally cracked the code. He discovered that Joseph, while in charge, developed an

---

[177] Sir Alan Gardiner discovered - the B`alat inscriptions b`lt, (B`alat, לבעלת).

[178] Far'shut unknown-Proto-Germanic SHIT comes from *skit-PIE root *skei- "to cut, split." The notion is of "separation" from the body, consider SETH, H8352 substitute, set (aside), שֵׁת Shêth, shayth; from H7896; put, i.e. substituted; Sheth, third son of Adam H7896. שִׁית shîyth, sheeth; a primitive (*to set aside*) root; to place (in a very wide application) apply, appoint, array, bring, consider, lay (up or down), let alone, make, **mark**, put (on), set, shew, **be stayed**. See also H6844שָׂתָן shâthan,SATAN, urinate, piss.

272

alphabet, which was passed on to his sons Ephraim and Manasseh (covenant men-Brit'ish).

Petrovich wrote a book about his discoveries and called it "The world's oldest alphabet". It is now generally known that the ancient Hebrews invented the first alphabet, one that we, the British, disseminated to the world. Yes, this ancient Covenant man (British) alep bet is the mainstay of the world. Let me say that again, the alphabet that the British exported to the world along with our language is Hebrew!

Does God keep his promises, or what? What do you think the patriarchs, our forefathers, will say when they are resurrected and can see God's promises fulfilled in such an awesome way?

Gazing upon the pictographs of the alphabet, a spiritual certainty washed over me, confirming Petrovich's words. I also knew what the symbols associated with Joseph were and why it made perfect sense to start the alphabet out with this symbol of God's providence, a symbol that pointed to the blessings given to Abraham and Sarah and the prophetic promises given to Rebekah. Later, God prophesied that the Egel'ish would gore the nations to the end of the earth with this Aleph, ox head, and horns, both metaphorically and physically. What an awesome God.

And unto Sarah, he said, Behold, I have given thy brother a thousand (Aleph-H505) *pieces* of silver: behold, he *is* to thee **a covering of the eyes** (protection because she was drop dead gorgeous), unto all that *are* with thee, and with all *other*: thus she was reproved (Gen. 20:16).

42 SARAH EYES

Even Rebekah received the Aleph blessing; they blessed Rebekah and said unto her, Thou *art* our sister, be thou *the mother* of thousands (Aleph- H505) of millions, and let thy **seed**(Zara)[179] possess the gate of those which hate them (Gen. 24:60).

This shows that letters were used as numerals from a very early date, yet this system wasn't formally adopted till much later[180]. Essentially the Aleph was used in the story to represent a multiplier in a prophetic sense.

is that numerals were included later. But how does this reconcile with their apparent use of names like Sarah (Saria) and Rebekah?

The interesting thing about Rebekah is that in one chapter (Gen.24), the Bible encompasses the first four letters of the alphabet. We have already covered the *aleph"* in the prophecy; we also have Rebekah coming from the white house (Bet, go to my kinfolks house-Gen. 24.4), i.e., her brother L'BN (Alban-Gen. 24.33).

In Genesis 24.60-61, Rebekah receives a blessing of "millions of Alephs" and control over the "gates" (doors - Dalet) of her enemies (fulfillment explored in WAI). As soon as she gets the blessing, she mounts her camel(gamel) and leaves. Are all these signs (Zions[181]) just a coincidence? I do not think so, because it appears that Jeremiah predicted it, when he said set up waymarks (Jer 31:21).

We've covered Aleph, Bet, and Gimmel/Gimel, but what about the next letter? This would be a hey, ⍦ worship, praise exclamation (see WAI). It is what all the patriarchs did, and

---

[179]This is exactly what happened Jeremiah took the seed to Ireland and to the twin brother of Pharez, the Zaratite(seed) line, where the breach was healed and God continued the kingly line, and later we possed the gates of our enemy's.

[180] The systematic use of letters to represent numbers (gematria) is generally thought to have been formalized during the Second Temple period, influenced by Greek alphanumeric systems. The idea that this system was "invented later" is based on historical evidence showing that the formal assignment of numeric values to letters wasn't a part of the early Hebrew writing system.

[181] H6725 צִיּוּן tsiyuwn tsee-yoon (see yonder) conspicuous sign, title, waymark-tsee-yoon'; from the same as H6723 in the sense of conspicuousness (compare H5329); a monumental or guiding pillar:— sign, title, waymark.

afterward, God gave Abram and Sarai a Ha; it was a funny moment just after Isaac (It's a joke) was born. It was their Ha, Ha moment; they finally got it. They both laughed when God told them: *"This time next year Saria will give birth"* (Gen. 18).

Sarah's joyous proclamation in Genesis 21.6, "God has brought me laughter and everyone who hears it will laugh with me," with its repeated "Ha," could almost be seen as divine amusement. And it was their heyday♇. We have another hayday later (Jospeh bales of hay bowing to him and fulfillment, see WAI). This book is full of coincidences.

What are the odds of this being a random chance? It's like I keep hitting the lottery over and over. At some point, even a skeptic must start to believe!

Back to the Alpha,

A letter. Originally an ox head pictograph, it served multiple purposes. It was a symbol that both Sarah and Rebecka were given as a dowry when they married Abraham and Isaac. This was well before Egypt, so I think it's safe to say the evidence is that this was Hebrew, not Egyptian.

Below, I show the ancient Paleo Hebrew that I call Paleo English because it was invented by a man who was in charge of Egypt, The Alpha male of Israel. His symbol and the ones he passed to his kids was the Aleph/Unicorn, aka Egel, and the ish=bcy, i.e. COWBOY in Hebrew (H5695, H376).

Early Hebrew inscription going left to right.

An engraving of God's name was found on Mount Ebal (c 1400-1200 BC), it was written in a lead tablet with the name of God, it was a book of cursing from the time of Joshua. it employed a left-to-right script (boustrophedon or ox plow method, was used at this time). After this other inscriptions were found going right-to-left.

Following is the earliest known Paleo Hebrew Pictographic alphabet, and Samuel alphabet along side the modern one we use today (written left to right), after which we have an inscription going right to left.

ABCDEFZH IKLMNXOP QRST

Development of the Alphabet.

I have already shown you how the modern English alphabet is almost identical to its original over 3000 years ago, we have also said that the writing could go from left to right or right to left, and this would cause confusion in translation. Additionally, some letters have the same sound, and some letters would look the same or similar, like the Wow/Vav, and Kuf/Koph, and Resh all of which employed a lolly pop shape at one point (see section 19 for details).

276

If this wasn't bad enough some letters could take different sounds depending on how they were used in words, later changes to the alphabet tried to accommodate for this variance.

Early Hebrew pronunciation was unknown.

Due to the nature of the developing alphabet, and the variety of sounds that each letter could produce, it can only be guesses at how the original Hebrew sounded. I have taken the approach that the traceable English words in this manuscript have developed from Hebrew. In these instances, I looked at the varying permutations of sounds possible, and at times, I proposed the original Hebrew sound.

This approach in developing the appropriate sound is logical, and etymological and makes the most sense, please remember Professor Isaac Mozeson (E-Word) believes he has over 80,000 cognates linking English to Hebrew, and while he will not admit to a genetic link, the fact that he calls them real cognates says otherwise and proves this book as well as my first booth "We are Israel"

As I mentioned in the previous chapter, the early writing of the Hebrews did have vowels however they were not employed as we do today, for instance, the Aleph predominantly made an A sound, but there were other variations where it also formed other vowels (see the next section for details).

Scribal Errors

We cover the development of the Aramaic (Germain-Assyrian) Square Script in the previous chapter, this started to be introduced shortly after the captivity of the northern ten tribes (721 BC), Era and Nehemiah continued this and by around 350 BC the Jews adopted Koine Greek as their language, in fact by the time of Christ Hebrew was dead, relegated to liturgical practices. The sacred tongue of the Jews at this time was Aramaic.

Later in the 6-10 century Hebrew had a resurgence and the scribes wanted to understand how to pronounce it, so they developed diacritics, the following is a summary:

Paleo-Hebrew Script:

- As mentioned previously Paleo-Hebrew was an ancient script used for writing Hebrew before the adoption of the Aramaic square script, which is the basis for modern Hebrew. This script lacked the vowel markings and other diacritical signs that later became essential for accurate pronunciation and interpretation of the text.

Impact of the Lack of Diacritics:

- **Ambiguity in Pronunciation:** Without vowel points (Niqqud), many words would have been ambiguous, with the same consonantal root potentially representing multiple different words depending on the intended vowels. This could lead to different readings and meanings.

- **Scribal Interpretation:** Scribes copying texts without diacritical marks would have had to rely on their understanding of the language and context, which could lead to inconsistencies or errors, especially if the text was unfamiliar or if regional dialects influenced pronunciation.

- **Variations in Texts:** Over time, these potential ambiguities and the lack of standardization in pronunciation and spelling could have led to variations in the texts, especially when transcribed by different scribes in different regions.

Development of Diacritical Marks:

- The Masoretes, Jewish scholars who worked between the 6th and 10th centuries CE, developed the system of Niqqud (vowel points) and cantillation marks to preserve the correct pronunciation and chanting of the Hebrew Bible. This system helped standardize the text and reduce the likelihood

278

of errors, but by that time, many variations and interpretative traditions had already developed.

Variations and issues regarding Aramaic SS.

There are still problems with the current Hebrew script, they have several letters that can make the same sound, and here I cover a few of them.

Samech (ס) and Sin (ש) Sav (ת):

Samech is always pronounced as "s." Sin, when the dot is on the left, is also pronounced as "s." However, Shin (ש), with the dot on the right, is pronounced as "sh."

The letter Sav (also written as Tav) can be pronounced as "s" in some Ashkenazi traditions when it has no dagesh (dot) and as "t" when it does. In Modern Hebrew, it is generally pronounced as "t."

Kuf (ק), Kaf (כ), and Khet (ח):

Kuf (ק) is pronounced as a hard "k" sound. Kaf (כ) can be pronounced as "k" when it has a dagesh (dot) or as a softer "kh" (like the "ch" in German "Bach") without the dot. Khet (ח) is usually pronounced as "kh" (similar to Kaf without a dagesh).

Conclusion:

The overlap in pronunciation, particularly in older scripts or different dialects, could easily lead to scribal errors or alternative spellings. These similarities might also explain variations in transliterations and the evolution of certain words over time. It's a fascinating aspect of the language that highlights both its complexity and the challenges faced by scribes and scholars throughout history.

The lack of diacritical marks in Paleo-Hebrew would have magnified the challenges faced by scribes and readers, leading to a greater possibility of variations and errors in the transmission of the text.

Sacredness of text and orthography.

In ancient Israel, as in many other ancient cultures, the sacredness of a text was not necessarily tied to a rigid word-for-word accuracy (orthography). Instead, the meaning, message, and function of the text within the religious community were often considered more important. Variations in wording might have been seen as less significant as long as the essential message and theological truths were preserved.

The Bible was part of an oral culture where stories and teachings were transmitted verbally for centuries before being written down. In oral traditions, exact wording is often fluid, with the emphasis placed on the consistency of the message rather than the precise language. This flexibility likely carried over into the early stages of textual transmission, where scribes might have felt empowered to adapt the text to different contexts or audiences while maintaining its sacred essence.

Scribes and editors in ancient Israel had the responsibility of preserving the sacred texts, but they also played an active role in shaping them. They may have adjusted wording, clarified ambiguous passages, or harmonized texts with other traditions to ensure the text remained relevant and understandable to their communities. This process was not seen as diminishing the sacredness of the text but rather as a necessary means of preserving its relevance and authority.

The existence of multiple textual traditions, such as the Masoretic Text, the Septuagint, the Samaritan Pentateuch, and the Dead Sea Scrolls, reflects the reality that there was not a single "fixed" text in the early stages of the Bible's development. These variations were part of a dynamic process where the sacredness of the text was maintained through its adaptability to different contexts, rather than through uniformity.

Just as we have seen variations in the English text where the Old English words of Beowulf would seem almost unrecognizable today, some 1000 years later, so it would be with the ancient Hebrew, consider Aramaic and Arabic, two distinct languages that stem from the same root, as the language changed over time.

Form of Ancient Writings

Mosaic and Paleo Hebrew would have been written on velum (animal skin), and papyrus. The early writing didn't have upper and lower case letters, but just one form, additionally no spaces or diacritic marks would be placed between words, vellum (animal skin) scrolls as well as papyrus scrolls (early use) would have been used.

It is highly probable that Moses, and subsequently Joshua, then Samuel (both Joshua and Samuel were of the tribe of Ephraim the inventor of the alphabet) most likely documented the Torah on vellum, while they practiced and honed their craft on papyrus.

The cost of scrolls could be expensive (especially vellum), which could cause the scribe to conserve space and write in small print. Add to these the boustrophedon writing (change of direction) and it made it difficult to read.

At times one scribe would read while the other wrote the text. This would also cause spelling changes between copies. The rigors and discipline of the scribes would at times and over the centuries and millenniums change. In fact the attention made to the law diminished with successive kings being liberal and God-haters, it got so bad under Ahab and Jezebel that God had to send them Elijah. We could ask the question who was maintaining scriptural integrity during this time?

Well we did have two kingdoms and sometimes we see good kings in one kingdom while bad reign in the other, however after the fall of the northern kingdom, the Pentateuch (Torah-Law) fell to Judah, and it got so bad they even lost the book of the law (2 kin 22.8)!

Hilkkiah was the one who found it, probably in a pile of rubble, as they were preparing to repair the temple. They called it the "book of the covenant", where book was translated from a root word meaning to write sephar (H5612), it's where we get CIPHER from, de-cipher means to read the words or uncover. Covenant is brit (h1585 בְּרִית).

Hundreds of times throughout scripture, it calls the relationship between God and his people a covenant. For example, we have:

Brit Milah covenant of circumcision
The Ark of the Covenant
The Blood of the Covenant
The book of the Covenant.

Essentially the children of Israel were known as The Covenant People of Yah or covenant men, in Hebrew this is Brit Am Yah (Britannia) or British.

Paleo Hebrew vowels

Ancient Hebrew did have vowels just not the way we do today, there were 5 letters that could have vowel sounds, but before that, there are over 6000 discrepancies between the Samaritan Pentetuete (SP-written in Paleo Hebrew) and the Masoretic Text (MT now in Aramaic script) most are minor orthographic which today we would label as spelling. These would develop due to letters looking or sounding similar here are some, potential phonetic misspellings due to similar sounds.
V- VariationsBet/Vet Wow/Vav,
T- VariationsTet, Tav/sav, and maybe even Tzadi
K/C Variations kaf, kuf, gimel/camel Chet/Khet
S's- VariationsTzadi, (TZ SS), Samech, Sav/tav, Shin/shin
P/Ph/F- VariationsPay/Fay

Note - While the Strongs Hebrew does not list many of these known differences they do list over 20 of them. We know them because of the way the word is used and the fact we have at least one other to compare, plus often a root. Here is one example –

Biblical Orthographic[182] Variations.

Biblical Orthographic Variations Can Appear as Spelling Errors, case in point - Strong's H3321 יָצַב (Yatzav) and Strong's H3320 יָצַג (Yatzag):יָצַב both contain the same root, י-צ-ב. However, one has the ב at the end (Yatzav), while the other has ג (Yatzag). The phonetic similarity between these letters could have led to confusion during transcription. This may result in what we now call a "spelling error" because the letters ב (bet) and ג (gimel) can look somewhat similar, especially in the more ancient Paleo-Hebrew script. In particular, such an error could have been made when scribes copied manuscripts by hand.

Yom Kippur verses kafar or kapar i.e. COVER

Another orthographic variant could be the change from singular to plural. For instance, the process of atonement was a sacrifice done once a year, and as we are aware the annual festivals of the Lord were conducted once a year and point to the plan of God. We also noted that Jesus died once and for all for the sin's of the world this was a singular event not a plural event. This even is called Yom Kippur, but it should be called Yom Covar (the day of covering).

---

[182] Orthographic variation refers to different ways of writing the same word due to dialects, regional variations, or changes in script conventions over time. For example, switching from Paleo-Hebrew to Aramaic script or transitioning from one period's spelling conventions to another could have introduced orthographic variations, which we now recognize as spelling differences

We get the English word CAP from the Hebrew word KAPP. The holy day Yom Kippur (plural form) should use the singular word Kaphar meaning day of covering, when God plaid our cover charge into heaven, "cover[183]" (H3725) stems from (H3722 כָּפַר kâphar), the root word for Kippur.

Orthographic issues with Hebrew Vowels.

Another problem for Orthography and Hebrew word errors is the fact that it was a lost language, that Paleo Hebrew didn't have the multiple forms of the Aramaic Script, consider the variations for the following letters, and it was the early use of vowels.

Paleo Hebrew Vowels
1-Aleph, 2-Ayin, 3-Yud, 4-Hey, 5-Wow/Vav, all of which can make a vowel sound.

Aleph - A, E, I, O, U.
-largely A but could sound like all vowels.

Ayin - A, E, I, O, U.
-largely A but could sound like all vowels

Yud is largely Y/J as in YHW/VH or JOEY but also I, E.

Wow/Vav this letter a tent peg originally made the W sound but in modern Hebrew it only makes the V sound, at times it could UU, O, OO, E EE

Hay, was a man standing with hands to the sky as in worship like the HaLaL (HAIL, YELL), but could also make the Ha, Hi, He, ae, ea, even O, E, Y see YHWH H3068 יְהֹוָה YaHWeY we (northern ten tribes) would pronounce it JOEY. For more details see alphabetic letters.

---

[183] Etymologist completely covered over the true root for this word!

1 – A-ALEPH, A, E, I, O, U unicorn, or ox head.

Symbols– $\mathcal{V}$ $\forall$ A Aramaic Script א Value 1.

Pictograph	Ox head, two-horned bull, and wild ox unicorn.
Meaning	Strength, power, alpha male, governor, family, thousand, "aleph" highlight.
Sound	A, ah, eh, E, I, O, U Mini aleph "a" quotation silent used for highlight.
Benner	El, (Aleph), glyph-Ox head meaning strength power.
Petrovich	Eleph (aleph) Glyph Ox head.
Hebrew	ELEPH (aleph) H504 אֶלֶף 'eleph Ox kine, oxen, family.

Pictograms		Phonograms		Echograms	Aramaic Hebrew	Masoretic Hebrew
Egyptian Hieroglyphics 1859 BC		Mosaic Hieroglypic Hebrew Alphabet 1859 - 550 BC		English Modern	Square Hebrew 550 BC - 70 AD	Vowelled Hebrew 600 AD - present
Gardiner's Sign List #	Sounds Like	First Hebrew Phonogram Alphabet 1859 - 1100 BC	Paleo-Hebrew 1100-550BC	English	First Century	Vowels, dots, dashes were invented by Masoretes (600 AD) did not exist before.
🐂 (F1)	K	Aleph Cattle Note: WH = Wadi el Hol, Lahn Lahun Sinai 377	⟨	A	א	Silent stop, like the "-" in "A-ha".

As we have already stated, the very first letter in our alphabet, the two-horned ox head, holds a deeper meaning than meets the eye. Previously, we have shown that the aleph symbol was used in prophecy, and this was prior to Joseph picking it as the first letter.

In fact, God himself identifies with the Aleph, and he calls himself the Alpha and Omega, the beginning and the end. If written in Hebrew, this would be Aleph at Tav (or Tov). The Aleph ox is used to symbolize the beginning in numbers as well as the alphabet, where the Aleph indicates the number 1, also 1000 and multiples of as in prophecy[184] (לְאַלְפִּי le'Alep'eH505 thousand).

Hebrew Prefix Suffix and Infix

In Hebrew grammar, the Aleph can represent "I' in the 1st person (common) singular as in Isaiah 50:3 **I** clothe (3847 אַלְבִּישׁ 'al-bîš), the heavens with darkness and make sackcloth it's covering."

Also, when Moses wanted to know God's real name, he asked God, "Who shall I say has sent me?" And God said unto Moses, "I AM a Sir I AM", Thus shalt thou say unto the children of Israel, **I AM** hath sent me unto you.

Hebrew uses a variant of the sacred name of God in a unique way (Exo 3:14). The sacred name is YHVH or HWH, short form YaH. In these verses, it uses HiYaH. In other words, when you greet your brothers, say I HiYah, sir I HiYaH, (אֶהְיֶה אֲשֶׁר אֶהְיֶה) now we just use HiYaH, SiR!

What was God really saying? I AM, the self-existent one, I AM before time, I AM creator from Berasheet) Bera sheet, see BeT). Aleph SiR A'SiR, A'HYH, the Aleph indicates the first person singular.

Also, God says I AM the beginning and the end, the alpha and omega (Aleph and the Tov). Again, in John, we read, " In the beginning was the Word, and the Word was with God, and the Word was God. [Jhn 1:1 KJV]. God self-identifies with the Word, the Aleph Lamed = God, and god.

Later, when the Hebrews came out of Egypt and headed to the wilderness of sin (in Saudi Arabia), they stopped at Mount Horeb, and Moses climbed the mountain to meet with God and God signs (Sinai) high the tablets of the testimony. But as he came down,

---

[184] And they blessed Rebekah, and said unto her, Thou *art* our sister, be thou *the mother* of thousands of millions, and let thy seed possess the gate of those which hate them. Gen 24:60.

he encountered great shouting and revelry, and the people worshipped an Aleph, also known as a golden calf (egel[185]).

Benner says the aleph comes from the parent root EL God, god[186], which means God, god, strength power. We remember the worship of the golden calf, which the Bible calls Egel.

Petrovich believes the original word to be Elep (aleph), as the modern translation of אֶלֶף is 'eleph (H504).

Benner believes that the original Hebrew can be boiled down to what he calls parent roots, of which there are 483, with 001 being AA, which is not used in the Bible [187].

The Aleph is a bull, its worship was not new in the ancient world. Sumerian epic of Gilgamesh talks about the bulls of heaven being requested by Ishtar to defeat her foes. Even the Egyptians worshiped bulls. They are called **Apis** or **Hapis,** also known as **Hapi-ankh.** The admiration and worship of the bull come from its strength and power; in the ancient world, it was considered the kink of the beast. A bull Eleph.'ant has few, if any, predators. Even lions do not get after male elephants, although their young would be targeted. That is why the Elephs form a circle (the wagons) at night and allow the young to sleep inside.

And let us not forget that in the Bible, God had us sacrifice bulls to him, so the bull was used in worship and a red heifer[188] was holy to the lord.

---

[185] H5695 עֵגֶל 'egel   calf,
bullock from the same as 5696; a (male) calf (as frisking round), especially one nearly grown.l

[186] H410   אֵל 'ēl God,
god, power, mighty, goodly, great, idols, Immanuel, might, strong, Aleph ((אלף) comes from the parent root אל (el).

[187] The ancient Hebrew language and alphabet p. 118, Jeff Benner 2004.

[188] H6510 פָּרָה pârâh, feminine of H6499; a heifer:—cow, heifer, kine.

H6511 פָּרָה Pârâh, the same as H6510; Parah, a place in Palestine. H6499 פַּר, par; or פָּר pâr; from H6565; + a bullock (apparently as breaking forth in wild strength, or perhaps as dividing the roof):—

There were many words used in the Bible to signify bulls, cows, heifer's steers, oxen etc. The generic symbol, however, was the Aleph. Now, I need to show you additional evidence from prophecy about why this symbol became a big deal.

1When Moses gave his blessing, this is what he said about Joseph (Ephraim and Manasseh): the bull and the bush Prophecy, in majesty, he is like a firstborn bull, his horns are the horns of a wild ox, with them he will gore the nations even to the ends of the earth (Deu.33.17)!

Moses identified two bull types, a becow[189]  and a wild ox (unicorn-reem[190]) . Remember, with their horns, they will gore the nations to the end of the earth (Deu 33:17). Doesn't this sound like a fighting term like FU?

Considering that we still use the Bull's horns as a symbol of peace, victory, or war, this along with all our other idioms, symbols, motifs and memorabilia add up to substantial proof of a connection don't you think?

We remember that Joseph was in charge of Egypt and that (we) the Israelites lived there for over 400 years, they also had a V symbol, that mimics, this theme.
While there were no direct Egyptian hieroglyphs for war and peace, from Alan Garnier's Egyptian symbols list.

(+ young) bull(-ock), calf, ox.. H6509 פָּרָה pârâh,; a primitive root; to bear fruit (literally or figuratively):—bear, bring forth (fruit), (be, cause to be, make) fruitful.

[189] H1060 בְּכוֹר bᵉkôwr, bek-ore'; from H1069; first-born; hence, chief:—eldest (son), firstborn(-ling).

[190] H7214 בְּכוֹרbᵉkôwr, bek-ore'; from H1069; first-born; hence, chief:—eldest (son), firstborn(-ling).

A30 ⚇ Man with arms outstretched "praise," "adoration."

A31 ⚇ Man with arms turned behind him "turn away".

2When Israel came into the promised land, Balak hired Balaam and asked him to curse Israel. God used the Balaam donkey to speak to him and warn him not to be reckless and destroy his life by going against the Lord. Baal gave 5 oracles (Nub.23-24). Each time, he was offered more money to corrupt Israel. In his second oracle, he says, "God brought them out of Egypt, they have the strength of a wild ox, they devour nations and break their bones to pieces, with their arrow they pierce them" (Longbow and British and American military might).

3In two other instances, Ephraim is referred to as a calf: I have surely heard Ephraim bemoaning himself *thus*; Thou hast chastised me, and I was chastised, as a bullock(egel) unaccustomed *to the yoke*: turn thou me, ⋎ and I shall be turned; for thou *art* the LORD my God𝔸, (Jer.31.18).

I believe this is a prophetic statement indicating that the ox (boustrophedon ox plow method) will be turned, and the A will sit on its horns along with the direction of writing instead of going from right to left and now going from left to right. And yet again, God is identifying the cow(egel) with Ephraim. So, the Aleph ox will be turned on its head. And a mirror image like Aaron had on his head.

4In almost all the instances, as discussed earlier, the golden calf is predominantly referred to as an "egel" in the Bible, signifying a young, frisking calf. However, God said the young frisking calf would be taken to Assyria (Hos 10:11).

5He maketh them also to skip like a calf;[H5695] Lebanon and Sirion like a young unicorn. [Psa 29:6 KJV]. This imagery again suggests a potential link between the Aleph and the concept of the egel.

There are indeed more instances, but these examples should suffice to illustrate your point.

2 - B, BETH, BEYT, BAYIT-House, Value 2.

Symbolsb ⊿ ⴼ ⎡⎤ ⎡⎤ Aramaic ב

Pictograms Egyptian Hieroglyphics 1859 BC			Phonograms Mosaic Hieroglypic Hebrew Alphabet 1859 - 550 BC			Echograms English Modern	Aramaic Hebrew Square Hebrew 550 BC - 70 AD	Masoretic Hebrew Vowelled Hebrew 600 AD - present
Gardiner's Sign List #		Sounds Like	First Hebrew Phonogram Alphabet 1859 - 1100 BC		Paleo-Hebrew 1100-550BC	English	First Century	Vowels, dots, dashes were invented by Masoretes (600 AD) did not exist before.
⎡⎤ (01)	⎡⎤ (04)	Pr /H	Bayit House	⎕ Sinai 92, 115, 405, WH 1	⎕	◿	B,V	ב	ב B as in Bet (With dot) ב V as in Vet

Pictograph	House
Meaning	House, home, temple, dungeon.
Sound	B, Bh, V.
Benner	Bet (Beyt) Glyph-house, meaning house, tent, well, family
Petrovich	Bayit (bet) house.
Hebrew	H1004 בַּיִת bayit house, household, family.

Fig. 45 truncated

BET or BETH means house or tent and is uncontested. It is a truncated form of BaYiT[191] house or tent; the dominative form is also not used in the Bible as a single word (see Bethel, or El Beth'El, house of God).

H416 אל בית־אל 'El Beyth-'El Elbethel
H1008 בֵּית־אֵל Beyth-'El Bethel, non-translated variable
H1017 בֵּית הָאֱלִי BEYTH ha-'Eliy Bethelite.

We can see from the very first word here, אל, El, is composed of A and L, yet transliterated El. This seems to be a mystery since it is said there are no vowels (a, e, i, o, u) in the Bible. And then we

---

[191] H1004 בַּיִת bayit house, household, home, within, temple, prison, place, family. H1005 בַּיִת bayit house

have בּ B, yud ת T - Hyphen, א A, ל L =byt'l. This means El =God or god.

H1004 בַּיִת BAYITH, (beth, yud, sav-byt) house, household, home, within, temple, prison, place, family, families, dungeon, and misc.

3 – G/C–GIMEL-ג camel, gam, gahar (Psa. 119:17-24).

Symbols - ✓ ⌐ Aramaic ג Value 3

Pictograph	Camel head/neck, or hump, bend, throw stick, foot ⌐
Meaning	to deal well, (with me), carry the burden.
Sound	G, C.
Benner	Gam Original symbol foot, gam-meaning, gather.
Petrovich	Gather to bend, bow down.
Hebrew	H1457 גָּהַר GÂHAR.

Pictograms		Phonograms		Echograms	Aramaic Hebrew	Masoretic Hebrew
Egyptian Hieroglyphics 1859 BC		Mosaic Hieroglypic Hebrew Alphabet 1859 - 550 BC		English Modern	Square Hebrew 550 BC - 70 AD	Vowelled Hebrew 600 AD - present
Gardiner's Sign List #	Sounds Like	First Hebrew Phonogram Alphabet 1859 - 1100 BC	Paleo-Hebrew 1100-550BC	English	First Century	Vowels, dots, dashes were invented by Masoretes (600 AD) did not exist before.
⌐ (O38)	Knbt	Gahar Bend	⌐ Sinai 112 √ WH1,2	⌐	G	ג	G as in Gift

This symbol √ ✓ ⌐ ג is generally translated as a Camel or Gimel[H1581] and in Hebrew, this is a CAMEL and where the English name comes from.[192]

---

[192] h1581   גמל gamel
camel and to deal well with me, carry the burden, see 1580. The English Camel comes from this perhaps via latin/Greek. Etymologists are unsure. Old Saxon olbhunt a derivative of elephant as load bearing Old French chamelatin camelus, from Greek kamelos, from Hebrew gamal

However, the pictograph itself throws a wrench in this theory, as it doesn't automatically conjure up a resemblance. Remember the original, pictograph consisted of two parallel lines with a bend, and closed at just one end does this ⍾ look like a Camel? Others have suggested that it represents a throwing stick as a boomerang, while this was used by the ancient Egyptians, there is no evidence that it was in common use by the Hebrews.

Petrovich is leaning on the bend, stooping, for a prostrate position, this goes by the name gaher ⍾ [193] and means bend, prostrate.

Benner says it comes from foot, which he calls gam (h1571 Gam[194]), which means (when I re-orient this symbol it could look like a foot) ⬳GATHER[195]. While there is no Hebrew name for foot, to kick it in his direction, the term gather would involve walking, and the word "gam" (c), can mean "also" or "in addition," is associated with the concept of gathering or adding, reflecting movement and accumulation, which ties back to the foot imagery, maybe he is on the right track?

Note: The English word gather most likely comes from gam; see also **me'gamm'aw**, *me gather* anything, accumulate.

In analyzing Psalm 119, a common thread emerges the disconnect between most letters' pictographs and their supposed meanings. The exception might be Gimel, potentially linked to the idea of a "gamel/camel" as a load-bearing animal. However, how do

---

[193] h1457 גָּהַר gâhar, gaw-har'; a primitive root; to prostrate oneself, cast self down, stretch self., bend stoop, gam. Petrovich "The worlds oldest alphabetp.204 gimel-gahar

[194] h1571 gather גַּם gam, by contraction from an unused root meaning to gather; properly, assemblage; used only adverbially.

[195] Gather (PIE *ghedh) to collect, "to unite, join" could come from Gam H1571.

we explain the L-shaped pictograph, let take another look at it and a camel's neck.

perhaps this was a rudimentary image of the Camels, neck, after, this is also a load-bearing animal, a used for transportation and carrying stuff. At this point I have to go with this as it seems to line up.

4 – D, DALET-Door, (Psa. 119:25)

Symbols ⊂⊐ ⵂ ◁ Δ D, Aramaic ٦ value 60.

Pictograph	Door
Meaning	Door to tent or house, door two leaves. hanging, swinging.
Sound	D.
Benner	Door, Dal, later dalet – meaning- Move, Hang, Entrance
Petrovich	Door, Delet– meaning- Move, Hang, Entrance
Hebrew	H1817דֶּלֶת DELET from H1802, something swinging.

Pictograms Egyptian Hieroglyphics 1859 BC		Phonograms Mosaic Hieroglypic Hebrew Alphabet 1859 - 550 BC		Echograms English Modern	Aramaic Hebrew Square Hebrew 550 BC - 70 AD	Masoretic Hebrew Vowelled Hebrew 600 AD - present
Gardiner's Sign List #	Sounds Like	First Hebrew Phonogram Alphabet 1859 - 1100 BC	Paleo-Hebrew 1100-550BC	English	First Century	Vowels, dots, dashes were invented by Masoretes (600 AD) did not exist before.
ⵂ (031)	.	Delet Door	ⵂ ⵘ Sinai 376, 353	Δ	D	٦ ᵢ D as in Door

Most scholars accept this as a "door," which also means move, hangs, and entrance[196].

Some think it is connected to the fish[197], ⋈. We see this depicted very early on, but this could have been confused with the

---

[196] H1817דֶּלֶת delet   from
H1802; something swinging, i.e. the valve of a door,(two-leaved), gate, leaf, lid.

[197] H1709 דָּג dāḡ   fish.

293

15th letter "samekh (samech see Benner and Petrovich). It is possible this symbol got confused with the Samech.

The Biblical term for "door" is DELET, signifying something that swings, like a valve, gate, leaf, or lid. This was the original meaning, even though the symbol of the door changed over time, i.e, a tent could be a triangular opening or a square opening. In Egypt, the rich would live in houses. In fact, during the time of the exodus, we all lived in houses as we were instructed to put the blood of the lamb over the lintel.

Petrovich counters Hamilton's "fish" theory, arguing that it hinders proper reading comprehension. He finds support for the "door" interpretation in the structure of sentences using the glyph. Petrovich remains firmly locked into this view[198].

Benner again sees both the Dag (this as well as the Dalet door in use. Since the modern Hebrew meaning is Dalet and symbolizes door, he bolts for this view. The universal view of the door being the main glyph is locked in in terms of modern usage.

However, I propose that the early usage might have been more fluid. It appears to me as a true alphabet where writers occasionally employed common symbols to represent sounds (phonemes). I see no inherent issue with using a "fish" (Dag) glyph instead of a "door" (Dalet) glyph. Perhaps my perspective is simplistic, but I don't find the "fish" theory fishy at all.

Of course, over time, standardization and improvements were made, and many scholars believe (as I do) that Samuel (1050 B.C.) standardized the alphabet, including removing duplicate glyphs and improving the form of the letters. This is clear form archeology because the inscriptions changed in from. It is believed Samuel held teaching classes and had a school for the prophets.

Samuel was of the tribe of Ephraim; he was a Brit(1Sam.1.1), and as such, his forefathers invented the alphabet.

---

[198] Page 206 of TWoA.

He went to temple school at a very early age (5) and slept with God at his side.

Môsheh (one drawn from the marshes of Egypt) wrote the first five books (Levite), and then we have Joshua (Ephraim-Brit), who's life is portrayed in Joshua. He may have kept a diary that was later written into Joshua by Samuel. In addition, the book of Jasher may have been used by Samuel to piece together the details.

5-H, He, PRAISE, (Psa 119:33-40)

Symbol - 𐤄 Ψ 𐤄 Ⴈ H, E, Æ, and Aramaic ה Value 5.

Pictograph	Man standing with hands raised, praise, look here, behold, "HOLD OUT".
Meaning	Praise, worship, (HaiL), behold?
Sound	H, Hi, Ha, He, Ho, Hey Roman E Greek E, old English Æ.
Benner	Hey (Hey), glyph-Man standing with hands raised, meaning-Look, Reveal, Breath.
Petrovich	Halal (He) Glyph-hands raised, meaning-praise.
Hebrew	H'LL praise God H=praise eL=God H1984 הָלַל halal praise, glory, boast, mad, shine, foolish, fools, commended, rage.

Pictograms	Phonograms		Echograms	Aramaic Hebrew	Masoretic Hebrew
Egyptian Hieroglyphics 1859 BC	Mosaic Hieroglypic Hebrew Alphabet 1859 - 550 BC		English Modern	Square Hebrew 550 BC - 70 AD	Vowelled Hebrew 600 AD - present
Gardiner's Sign List #	Sounds Like	First Hebrew Phonogram Alphabet 1859 - 1100 BC	Paleo-Hebrew 1100-550BC	English	First Century	Vowels, dots, dashes were invented by Masoretes (600 AD) did not exist before.
(A28)	Hi	Halal Praise Sinai 92, 362 WH1,2	𐤄	H,E	ה	H as in Hay

Fig 45 condensed

The original Hebrew letter (I believe) incorporated both the H and E; hence, the Jews call it an H (Hey), and the Greeks and Romans use the letter E here.

This is another contested letter; the Hay is a picture of a man with hands raised in exclamation or worship 𐤉 in this instance, I would argue that it is the praise, *hail* and *yell*. So Hail, and Yell came from look here, attention, HLL (praise or look here) is the first part of halleluiah.

This is no accident, and it's a God thing. The name of the most prolific prophet in the old testament is Elijah. Even Jesus commented about him, saying this is just a man.

The Greek version, although the darby Bible does render praise yah as halleluiah.

Essentially, it is H'LL - YaH, let me give it to you in English. What happens when you want to definitively agree with someone? You would say H'LL'YaH. We still use it because we are in Israel, and English is Hebrew! Even the name Elijah is like a shortened version of Elohim (Hello him God) u=who Yah.

This theory suggests Elijah's Hebrew name closely resembles "H'LL eL who(u) YaH," again hinting at a deeper meaning. No co-incidence!

The psalmist does record a HeyYah. The actual name for God is Yah, and when asked by Moses who I should say has sent me, he said, "I am" has sent you in Hebrew this is "hiyah asir hiyah."

However, Benner argues this could be interpreted as "behold" ("He" in Biblical Hebrew) or "praise" ("HiYah") related to "Halal" (connected to "Hey").

The original pictographic

The unassuming Hebrew letter "Hey" (ה) boasts a rich and multifaceted history. It was also known as He and Hi, and represented a man with his arms held high like Moses, when he held out all night over the red sea and also in the morning after crossing himself setup at the opposite side and held out again (the term hold out, is from Moses). A form of worship, it is also the "hey" that was given to Abraham. Both Sarah and Abraham tee hee'd (ha, ha), and they both got a hey Ha Ha (God has a sense of humor) and then they were told to name their son Isaac, meaning laughter.

So the "Hey" means worship, praise) and it was also Abraham and Sarah's "Hey day," and their Ha Ha moment (LOL), and it is said to indicate an H that sounds like "hey", "hi," and "ha", is also said to represent the letter "e"[199]

Modern Hebrew uses "Hey" for a voiced glottal fricative sound (/ɦ/), but it's often dropped altogether (though frowned upon).

Also, the letter can represent a glottal stop in many variant Hebrew pronunciations. In word-final position, *Hei* is used to indicate an *a*-vowel, usually that of qamatz (ָ), and in this sense, functions like Aleph, Vav, and Yud as a mater lectionis indicate the presence of a long vowel.

Hei, along with Aleph, Ayin, Reish, and Khet, cannot receive a dagesh. Nonetheless, it does receive a marking identical to the dagesh to form *Hei-mappiq* (הּ). Although indistinguishable for most modern speakers or readers of Hebrew, the mapiq is placed in a word-final *Hei* to indicate that the letter is not merely a mater lectionis, but the consonant should be aspirated in that position. It is generally used in Hebrew to indicate the third-person feminine singular genitive marker. Today, such a pronunciation only occurs in religious contexts, and even then, it is often only done by careful readers of the scriptures.

The Hebrew letter "ה" (Hei or Hey) has several uses in the Hebrew language, both as a standalone letter and as a prefix, suffix or infix, in words. Here's an overview of its different functions:

1. **As a Consonant**: In its basic form, Hei serves as a consonant with a "h" sound, as in הר (har, meaning "mountain").

2. **As a Prefix**:

---

[199] H2332: Hebrew: חַוָּה (Chavvah), Transliteration: Eve, Meaning: Life, Living, H1984 הָלַל hālal ꓱleL praise, glory, boast, mad, shine, foolish, celebrate, give, marriage, renown.

- **Indicating "The"**: When used as a prefix, Hei often functions as the definite article, equivalent to "the" in English. For example, הבית (ha-bayit) means "the house."

- **Indicating a Question**: Sometimes, Hei is used as a prefix to denote a question. For example, היאכן? (ha-ye'khan?) means "where is it?"

3. **As a Suffix**:

   - **Direction or Motion Towards**: Hei at the end of a word can indicate direction or motion towards something. For example, ירושלימה (Yerushalayimah, meaning "towards Jerusalem").

   - **Feminine Noun Marker**: In many cases, Hei is used as a suffix to make a noun feminine, as in שולחן (shulchan, "table") to שולחנה (shulchanah, "her table").

4. **In the Middle of Words**: As a part of root words, Hei can be a consonant or part of the vowel structure, contributing to the word's meaning and grammatical function.

5. **In God's Name**: In a religious context, Hei is used twice in the tetragrammaton, יהוה (YHWH), the fuck name of God in Judaism.

6. **Numerical Value**: Like other Hebrew letters, Hei has a numerical value of 5. This is used in certain contexts, like Hebrew calendar years.

The humble letter Hei holds profound significance in Judaism. Within the system of gematria, Hei embodies the number five, and when used at the beginning of Hebrew years, it means 5000 (i.e., התשנ"ד in numbers would be the date 5754).

Hei, representing five in gematria, is often found on amulets, symbolizing the five fingers of a hand, a very common talismanic symbol. We are to worship Yaw with the works of our hands and our lives.

In Judaism, *Hei* is often used to represent the name of God as an abbreviation for Hashem, which means *the Name* and is a way of saying *God* without actually saying the name of God. In print, Hashem is usually written as *Hei* with a <u>geresh</u>: 'ה.

"Behold, I have graven thee upon the palms of [my] hands; thy walls [are] continually before me (Isaiah 49:16 KJV)."

H1961הָיָה *HayahHiyahI am that I am, Hiyah- a primitive root (compare H1933); to exist, i.e., be or become, come to pass*

H1961אֶהְיֶה *'eh-yeh Here we have Strong silent type A and Hey=praise Yod Praise the yud (or Yod)*

H2009הִנֵּה *hinnêh, hin-nay'prolongation for H2005; lo!:—behold, lo, see.*

H2005הֵן *hên, hâneprimitive particle; lo!; also (as expressing surprise) if:—behold, if, lo, though*

H1984הָלַלhalalpraise, glory, boast, mad, shine, foolish, fools, commended, rage, celebrate, give, marriage, renowned

6-W, V, WOW, VAU-hook-Peg, support, pillar.

Symbols .ᗐ Ⲩ=W, V,O,U, Aramaic ﹀ Value 6, (<u>Psa 119:41</u>).

Pictograph	Peg.
Meaning	Support pillar.
Sound	W, V, O, U -As in Welsh, it can form the vowel sounds O and U.
Benner	Wow, (Vav) Glyph -peg, meaning add, secure, hook.
Petrovich	Waw Support pillar is the same as (hook).
Hebrew	Wow, (vav) H2053 וָו vâv, waw VV to W.

Fig 45 condensed

Pictograms Egyptian Hieroglyphics 1859 BC	Phonograms Mosaic Hieroglypic Hebrew Alphabet 1859 - 550 BC		Echograms English Modern	Aramaic Hebrew Square Hebrew 550 BC - 70 AD	Masoretic Hebrew Vowelled Hebrew 600 AD - present
Gardiner's Sign List #	Sounds Like	First Hebrew Phonogram Alphabet 1859 - 1100 BC	Paleo-Hebrew 1100-550BC	English	First Century	Vowels, dots, dashes were invented by Masoretes (600 AD) did not exist before.
Y (O30)	Shnt	Vaw Pillar Support WH 11 Sinai 376 Sinai 381	Y	V,O,U	۱	V as in Vine Vowel "u" as in "Flute" �ۛ Vowel "o" as in "Hole" ۛۛ

Waw/Vav (*wāw* "hook") is the sixth letter of the Paleo Hebrew, including Phoenician *wāw* Υ, Aramaic *waw* ۱, Aramaic Hebrew *vav* ۱, Syriac *waw* � and Arabic *wāw* ۇ(sixth in abjadi order; 27th in modern Arabic order).

It represents the consonant [w] in original Hebrew and [v] in modern Hebrew, as well as the vowels [u] and [o]. We can see YeHoWSePH in Joseph (W) and YeHoVa (sometimes V) and YaHWaY (W).

H3084 יְהוֹסֵף yᵉhôsēp̄ Joseph
H3130 יוֹסֵף YHoWSePH, transliterated, yôsēp̄, Joseph.

In Pictographic Hebrew the Wow/Vav was a hook H2053 וָו vâv, waw, biblehub.com transliterates the W/V as a W in all 6 Bible examples—probably a hook (the name of the sixth Hebrew letter). Again originally this letter sounded like a W, but over time it could also sound like V, however, it is unique in Hebrew because it never received a Dagesh (dot indicating a sound change בַּ=Bet, ב=vet), so the V verses W, can just be guessed at, as in יהוה Y H W/V H H3058.

Finally, we get one that's actually in the bible and matches up with what we know, and experts agree.

When the word David is pronounced, they use Dā·WiD (H1732 דָּוִד Dâvid, daw-veed')where Waw/Vav is a W, i.e., the 6th letter.

The next question is why the English W symbol looks so different from the paleo-Hebrew. The answer is because it is two

VV together, and this double VV eventually became a W, ↑ ↑ Ƴ
ꓘ Y ʋ Y V VV then W

The original Semitic languages lacked the letter "W,"
although sounds similar to it existed, represented by combinations
like "WaW," "OO," or "UU." If the original sound was Wow or Vav
and looked like an F in Latin, how did the English W come to
represent this wound?

Apparently, the W started during the Middle Ages, with the
scribes of Charlemagne (768 to 814 AD) writing two 'u'u' side by
side, or two v v that eventually were joined and became a w.
separated by a space. At that time, the sound made was similar to
that of 'v.' The letter appeared in print as a unique letter 'W' in 1700.

Note that the 6th letter of Hebrew, the paleo waw/vav ↑ ↑ at
times, is identical to the quph ↑ , the 19th letter of Hebrew and
could have created some issues with translations and copying. And
indeed, the timeline (See patterns of evidence)!

7-Z - ZAIN-Psa 119:49-56 Meaning?

Symbol ⟋ ⌶ z Aramaic ɪ Value 7.

Pictograph	Two wavy lines that get joined.
Meaning	Unknow?
Sound	Z
Benner	Zan (Zayin) Glyph-mattock(pick-axe), meaning food, cut, nourish.
Petrovich	Zeah (zayin) Glyph sweat, meaning.

Pictograms Egyptian Hieroglyphics 1859 BC		Phonograms Mosaic Hieroglypic Hebrew Alphabet 1859 - 550 BC		Echograms English Modern	Aramaic Hebrew Square Hebrew 550 BC - 70 AD	Masoretic Hebrew Vowelled Hebrew 600 AD - present
Gardiner's Sign List #	Sounds Like	First Hebrew Phonogram Alphabet 1859-1100 BC	Paleo-Hebrew 1100-550BC	English	First Century	Vowels, dots, dashes were invented by Masoretes (600 AD) did not exist before
∼∼ (D13)	inh	Zeah Sweat (Brows)	⇒≋= Lat Sinai Sinai 0 346a 349	Ζ	Z	ɪ	Z as in Zechariah

301

H2102 Boil, wave זוּד zûwd, zood; or (by permutation) זִיד zîyd; a primitive root; to seethe; figuratively, to be insolent, proud, deal proudly, presume, (come) presumptuously, sod

H6864 צֹר tsôr, tsore from H6696; an (English sore and sword may come from this)stone (as if pressed hard or to a point); (by implication, of use) a **knife**, flint, sharp stone.

Benner says it's a mattock, this ✶is a pick axe and is mentioned 3 times in the Bible, with the following names *hereb, maheresa, and mader*[200] The Phoenician and Mishnaic Hebrew (oral Jewish tradition) have listed the sword as *zayin* זִין, this is not in the Bible and does not appear to resemble a mattock ⟍.

The modern Hebrew for *Zayin* זין means penis. A similar penis-type word in the Bible is *zuwb or zoob*[201].

It means discharge, as in sex, the wavy two lines may be connected. Also, *Zera*[202] means seed in Hebrew. Petrovich believes this to be *Zeah*[203] , as in sweat on the brow ⟋ I am not convinced, either way, that we know the original meaning of this glyph.

One possibility is that it is a handcuff or stock where the two parallel lines joined in the middle, which may be the origin of the zayin, i.e., the handcuffs or stocks. This aligns with the possibility

---

[200] H2719 חֶרֶב ḥereḇ sword, knife, dagger, axes, mattocks, TOOL, sword
H4281 מַחֲרֵשָׁה maḥărēšâ mattock
H4576 מַעְדֵּר maʿdēr mattock
[201] H2100 זוּב zûwb, primitive root; to flow freely (as water), i.e. (specifically) to have a (sexual) flux; figuratively

[202] H2234

זֶרַע zᵉraʿ
seed

[203] H2188 זֵעָה zēʿâ sweat, H3154 יֶזַע yezaʿ anything
that causes sweat.

302

that the "he" glyph might have been called "*ziqq*," meaning "manacle," though Biblical evidence for this is lacking.

We recall God's declaration of "I am Alpha and Omega," signifying the entirety of creation (A to Z). We know the Jews and Rabbis hated Jesus and made changes to the Bible to discredit Jews from embracing the new religious [link.]

Ultimately, the true meaning of the Zayin glyph remains elusive. Perhaps the glyph comes from a man, a male, that is exemplified by modern Hebrew as penis (dick). זָכָר It is the root of the mark, as a sign[204].

8-H, CHETH, HET-Psa 119:57

Symbols ⳩ 𐤇 𐤇 H, Ch, KHAramaic ח Value 8.

Pictograph	Courtyard (huts), rope.
Meaning	Wall, enclosure, safety, rampart, host, trench, poor, bulwark, army.
Sound	H, Ch, Kh, Hh, He, Hi, Ha, E as in Eve (חַוָּה).
Benner	Het means Outside, Divide, Half.
Petrovich	Haser/hut, het meaning enclosure.
Hebrew	H2426 חֵיל ḥayil wall.

Pictograms		Phonograms		Echograms	Aramaic Hebrew	Masoretic Hebrew
Egyptian Hieroglyphics 1859 BC		Mosaic Hieroglypic Hebrew Alphabet 1859 - 550 BC		English Modern	Square Hebrew 550 BC - 70 AD	Vowelled Hebrew 600 AD - present
Gardiner's Sign List #	Sounds Like	First Hebrew Phonogram Alphabet 1859 - 1100 BC	Paleo-Hebrew 1100-550BC	English	First Century	Vowels, dots, dashes were invented by Masoretes (600 AD) did not exist before.
(O6) / (V28)	Hwt /H	Haser/Hut Enclosure/Thread	Sinai Lahd Sinai 153	H,Ch	ח	Ch as in Bach

Fig 45 condensed

The letter shape is said to go back to a_hieroglyph for "courtyard." Another is a ⳩ rope symbol.

---

204 H2145 zâkâr, zaw-kawr'; from H2142; properly, remembered, i.e. a male (of man or animals, as being the most noteworthy sex):—× him, male, man(child, -kind)

However, the exact meaning and evolution are debated. Benner and Petrovich agree that this rope symbol originally had multiple forms. One is with a ⊟ , which benner calles a tent wall⊟ . He says the ancient name was *hhet,* meaning a string and relates it to the Hebrew word *hhets,* which he calls a wall

One form, described by Benner as a "tent wall," supposedly relates to the ancient word "hhet," meaning "string," which he connects to the Hebrew word "hhets," meaning "wall." Benner interprets this as signifying "outside, separated, divided." However, he lacks a Strongs number or Biblical Hebrew reference, making verification difficult. However, I believe he is referring to a hill (hill fort, enclosure), which in Hebrew is HaYiL[205]. Or it could be the same symbol that Petrovich talks about, a courtyard, which can also function as a wall or enclosure, chatsar, and it is most likely where we got the English word huts from, meaning cottage, village enclosure[206].

As a point of interest, the mother of all mankind was named Eve, which means life-giver. That's why we have baby showers (Chavvah or Eve). The name also means to *show*. As in, she is beginning to show she is pregnant and about to be a life-giver[207]!

9-T - TETH- Psa 119:65 ⊗ Th, T, Aramaic ט Value 9.

Symbols ⊗ Spin, weave, surround

Pictograph	Needle for spinning thread. Spinning needle collecting yarn ⊗.
Meaning	Spin, weave.
Sound	T, To, Tu, Te, Ta.
	Tet – meaning surround containing mud.

---

[205] H2426 חַיִל ḥayil wall, rampart, host, trench, poor, bulwark, army.

[206] H2690 חָצֵר chatsar a primitive root; properly, to surround with a stockade, and thus separate from the open country; but used only in the reduplicated form חֲצֹצֵר chătsôtsêr; or (2 Chronicles 5:12) חֲצֹרֵר chătsôrêr; as dem. from H2689; to trumpet, i.e. blow on that instrument.

[207] Eve H2332חַוָּה Chavvâh, khav-vaw'; causatively from H2331; life-giver; Chavvah (or Eve), the first. H2324 חֲוָא chăvâ' (Aramaic) corresponding to H2331; to show, (H2324 חֲוָא chăwâ) as in baby shower, when she starts to show..

Benner	
Petrovich	Tov tet means good.
Hebrew	Tâvâh, a primitive root; to spin[208] Tôwb, meaning *to be good*, make good[209].

Pictograms		Phonograms		Echograms	Aramaic Hebrew	Masoretic Hebrew
Egyptian Hieroglyphics 1859 BC		Mosaic Hieroglyphic Hebrew Alphabet 1859 - 550 BC		English Modern	Square Hebrew 550 BC - 70 AD	Vowelled Hebrew 600 AD - present
Gardiner's Sign List #	Sounds Like	First Hebrew Phonogram Alphabet 1859 - 1100 BC	Paleo-Hebrew 1100-550BC	English	First Century	Vowels, dots, dashes were invented by Masoretes (600 AD) did not exist before.
☥ (F35)	D	Tov Good	Sinai 112 Sinai 351 ⊕ Sinai 357	⊗	Th	ט Th as in Thin

Fig 45 condensed

The teth is currently the ninth letter of the Hebrew and has a numerical value of 9[210] (tesa). Again, we have a number or different symbols that all undoubtably were used to make the T sound.

The Hebrew Tet gave rise to the Greek theta (Θ). The sound of Teth is "T". The Phoenicians use the letter name "T" *tēth* for a wheel ⊗. Wheel in Hebrew is gheel, and it's where we get the word *wheel[211]*.

Doug Petrovich believes that the Tet means good[H2895]. **Jeff Benner** believes that this word was a pictograph of a basket and meant surround and contain mud (Hebrew word?).

It appears to me to be a needle and eye for spinning, and after it has been spun, a wheel of yarn[H2901]. Originally, hand-spinning was

---

[208] H2901 טָוָה ṭâvâh, taw-vaw'; a primitive root; to spin H2908 טְוָת ṭᵉvâth, tev-awth'; (Aramaic) from a root corresponding to H2901; hunger (as twisting):—fasting. H4299 מַטְוֶה maṭveh, mat-veh'; from H2901; something spun.

[209] H2895 טוֹב ṭôwb, tobe; a primitive root, to be (transitively, do or make) good (or well) in the widest sense be (do) better, cheer, be (do, seem) good, (make) goodly, × please, (be, do, go, play)

[210] H8672 תֵּשַׁע tēsha' nine, ninth, nineteenth, nineteen

[211] H1524 גִּיל gîyl, gheel from H1523; a revolution (of time, i.e. an age); also joy, gladness, greatly. English giddy, wheel. H1523 גִּיל gîyl; or (by permutation) גּוּל gûwl; a primitive root; properly, to spin round (under the influence of any violent emotion), i.e. usually rejoice, or (as cringing) fear,be glad, joy, be joyful, rejoice.

305

the norm. However, by Samuel's time (or possibly even earlier), a shift occurred. The symbol's change might reflect the introduction of a new tool – a foot-powered spinning wheel perhaps – that facilitated yarn collection

10-Y JOD, Yod, Yad, Yud -Psa 119:73

Symbols ﹂ﾉ ￫ ◻ ﾊ ﾅ _Aramaic ' Value 10.

Pictograph	Open handshake YOD, YARD (Myler).
Meaning	Hand, power, arm, consecrate.
Sound	Y, I, E, J, Ya, Ye (other). As in Welch, the vowel can create sounds I and E.
Benner	Yad- Work, Throw, Make, Praise- Arm and closed hand (incorrect).
Petrovich	Yad – aka yod, (yard arm) ARM.
Hebrew	H3027 יָד yād, hand, arm.

Pictograms Egyptian Hieroglyphics 1859 BC			Phonograms Mosaic Hieroglypic Hebrew Alphabet 1859 - 550 BC		Echograms English Modern	Aramaic Hebrew Square Hebrew 550 BC - 70 AD	Masoretic Hebrew Vowelled Hebrew 600 AD - present
Gardiner's Sign List #	Sounds Like		First Hebrew Phonogram Alphabet 1859 - 1100 BC	Paleo-Hebrew 1100-550BC	English	First Century	Vowels, dots, dashes were invented by Masoretes (600 AD) did not exist before.
(D36) (D47)	A		Yad Hand	Sinai 405 Sinai 376 Sinai 12 La10 Sinai 345b	ꙇ	I,Y,J	'	Y as in Yes	Vowel "i" as in machine Vowel "ey" as in "they".

Fig 45 condensed

This is another letter/word that scholars agree upon, i.e., the YaD. The hand/yard, outstretched hand as in hand shake, Yand, is used to represent consonants Y and J and vowels I and E (Yes pronounced E'es). I.e., Yah represents Yes E'es Yish in English, and other closely connected I am Haya.

The Rabbis and Jews believe the tenth letter is holy and represents God. It is the most used letter in the alphabet and is used in 11% of Hebrew words. It forms the start of Yah, YeHoVaH, and YahWaY, Yeshua (Joshua).

Yud as a prefix - The **Hebrew letter Yud** can represent various sounds, including **Y, J, I, and E**, and can serves as a prefix in names like **Jacob, Joseph**, and **Israel**. This connection highlights the link between these names and **Yah**, a short form of **YHWH** (the divine name).

The **Yud** plays a crucial role in Hebrew linguistics and theology, often symbolizing divine connection, as seen in these biblical names. The use of **Yud** in **Jacob** (Ya'akov), **Joseph** (Ycsef), and **Israel** (Yisrael) underscores their relationship to God's covenant and mission.

Yud Yard, The hand and arm were used as a means of measuring, in English we have the "hand-breadth", and the inch was a bent thumb. We also have the yard, and YARD-ARM a measuring stick. H520אַמָּה 'ammâh, prolonged from H517; properly, a mother (i.e., a unit of measure, or the fore-arm (below the elbow), i.e., a cubit;

H520 אַמָּה 'ammâ cubit, measure, post, not translated
H521 אַמָּה 'ammâ cubit
H1574 גֹּמֶד gōmed cubit
H3027 יָד yâd, yawd;

Y - YOD – Benner arm and hand closed (the original was a hand with thumb separated), Petrovich just hand (to me, it looks like the hand is open, i.e., the thumb is pointing up like a greeting as in handshake), note that the cubit unit of length was 18" this is known as the amma (arm) and comes from the length from the finger tips to the elbow, the long cubit is the amma + ½ an amma (H520 אַמָּה 'ammâh, am-maw), perhaps this is where the Yad (yard) fully stretched out, i.e., 21", it seems to me that 18 + ½ of 18 would be 22 and ½ or 23 rounded up, today this is 24".

In the Bible, body parts served as measuring tools: the long and short "amma" (cubit). the hand breadth (palm), and the finger acting as an inch. In the temple and building projects, they would have yad (yard) and footsticks, along with measurement ropes that were marked off to ensure consistency(link).

The nautical yard-arm retains the original sense of measurement.

307

Ps119.73 Your **hands** have made me and fashioned me; Give me understanding, that I may learn Your commandments.[74]

Those who **fear** You will be glad when they see me (greeting as in handshake) because I have hoped in Your word.

As Benner points out, the yod means work; we know that all hands on deck bring the workers. I have found the Yad intertwined with the verb to walk in the bible, and I feel it is where we get work and walk from, i.e., Ya'wLaK. [212]

11-K-CAPH-Psa 119:81-88, Cup, Hand, spoon, palm.

Symbol ⱏ ⱐK, Ch, Palm Ⓤ Aramaic כ Value 20.

Pictograph	Palm, hand.
Meaning	Hand, spoon, sole, palm, hollow, handful.
Sound	K, Kh. Ki, Ka, Ke.
Benner	Kaph, (kaph), open palm, meaning -bend, open, allow, tame.
Petrovich	Kap (kaf, kaph), palm.
Hebrew	H3709 כַּף kap̄ hand, spoon, sole, palm, hollow, handful, apiece, branches, breadth.

Pictograms		Phonograms		Echograms	Aramaic Hebrew	Masoretic Hebrew
Egyptian Hieroglyphics 1859 BC		Mosaic Hieroglypic Hebrew Alphabet 1859 - 550 BC		English Modern	Square Hebrew 550 BC - 70 AD	Vowelled Hebrew 600 AD - present
Gardiner's Sign List #	Sounds Like	First Hebrew Phonogram Alphabet 1859 - 1100 BC	Paleo-Hebrew 1100-550BC	English	First Century	Vowels, dots, dashes were invented by Masoretes (600 AD) did not exist before.
Ⴎ (D28)	K	Kap Palms	Ⴎ Ⴒ Ⴐ Sinai 92 WH1,2 376.349	ⱐ	K,Ch	כ,ך ⱚ K as in King (With dot) ⱚ Ch as in Bach

Fig 45 condensed

The Kaph is the 11, the letter of the Hebrew and is the palm of the hand . It is said to mean hollow, as in a cup, and also the sole of the foot(cup-H3709). This is said to come from Kawfaf H3721).

---

[212] H3207יָד yâd, yawd), used in a wide range of applications. See also H1980 s used in walk (wLK), as in the ya (wk), H3212 יָלַךְ yalak, Ya wlak- ya walk, sometimes ha wk (H1980הָלַךְ halak, ha-wlak). See also H4399, מְלָאכָה mᵉlâ'kâh, (mela, w'kaw - male work, hā·lō·wḵ, Isa. 42:24).H1983 וַהֲלָךְ wa·hă·lāḵ (Aramaic) from H1981; properly, a journey, i.e. (by implication) toll on goods at a road.

Benner says this is the open hand, the palm of the hand, and means bend, open, allow, or tame, see (H3709 כַּף kap̄)[213]

We get the English word Cap from the Hebrew word KAPP. Even the holy day Yom Kippur can be entirely explained through modern English. Similarly, the word "cover" (H3725) stems from (H3722 כָּפַר kâphar), the root word for Kippur.

There are three variants of this invented Aramaic niqud by the Tiberian <u>Masorites</u>. This was because the Aramaic had disappeared. The only known copies of the Bible today are the dead sea scrolls and then the Leningrad Codex: 1008. The Masoretic was also a dead language around 1000 AD. The early Jewish settlers in Palestine in 1915 AD, Masoretic Hebrew, (Kaph) later brought it

20	20	20
ך	כ	כ
Final Khaf 'KH'	Khaf 'KH'	Kaf 'K'

back to life.

Today, most Jews have dropped the vowels and just use the basic Aramaic 458bc. – 7CAD

K could also be used as a glottal stop and as a Kh (spirant). The final form of the letter is one of 5 Hebrew letters that have final forms. They are called <u>soffits</u> and are *kaf*/כ, *mem*/מ, *nun*/נ, *pey*/פ and *tsade*/צ.

The final forms only appear at the end of words. They do not provide a different pronunciation and are used as a calligraphic endpoint. It may have been an attempt to indicate the start of a new word, as the original Hebrew did not have spaces between words.

The Ancient form of this letter is ﺵ the hand's open palm. The meanings of this letter are "bend" and "curve", from the shape of the palm, as well as to "tame" or "subdue" as one who has been bent to another's will.

---

[213] H3709 כַּף kap̄, (Quf, Kaf, Khaf) hand, spoon, sole, palm, hollow, handful, apiece, branches, breadth, clouds, misc – BDB. Hollow, or flat of the hand, palm, sole of foot, see cap also . From H3721 כָּפַף kâphaph, kaw-faf'; a primitive root; to curve, bow down (self). So CavFF means curve in English, hello!

The modern Hebrew name for this letter is kaph, a Hebrew word meaning "palm," and it is also the ancient name for this letter. This letter is pronounced as a "k", as in the word *kaph*, when used as a stop or as a "kh" (pronounced hard like the "ch" in the German name Bach), as in the word *yalakh* (to walk) when used as a spirant.

The Early Semitic Ⓤ evolved into Ⓨ in the Middle Semitic script. This letter continued to evolve into Ⓙ in the Late Semitic script and became the Modern Hebrew ⲕand the ך (final *kaph*). The Middle Semitic Ⓨ became the Greek and Roman K (written in the reverse direction from the Hebrew).

Open palm, symbolic. Seek, and you shall find; knock, and the door will be opened. Ask, and you shall receive. Put your hand out and ask. Put your faith and trust in Yeshua/Jesus, and he will not disappoint you. Jesus puts his case forward in the first few verses and then at the end, he offer's his life for our benefit and is given to God as a sacrifice and as a result we receive salvation. So, the open palm is symbolic of service to God, who is our great reward, and salvation.

12-L, LAMED-Psa 119:89

Symbol L, 𝓵 𝓛 Aramaic ל Value 30.

Pictograph	Shepherd's staff 𝓵 .
Meaning	Teach, protect, learn, instruct, diligently, expert.
Sound	L, aL, el -L as in Learn.
Benner	Lam (Lamed), shepherd staff, meaning-teach, yoke, bind.
Petrovich	Lamed (lamed) learn.

Pictograms Egyptian Hieroglyphics 1859 BC		Phonograms Mosaic Hieroglypic Hebrew Alphabet 1859 - 550 BC		Echograms English Modern	Aramaic Hebrew Square Hebrew 550 BC - 70 AD	Masoretic Hebrew Vowelled Hebrew 600 AD - present
Gardiner's Sign List #	Sounds Like	First Hebrew Phonogram Alphabet 1859 - 1100 BC	Paleo-Hebrew 1100-550BC	English	First Century	Vowels, dots, dashes were invented by Masoretes (600 AD) did not exist before.
٦ (S39)	Wt	Lamad Teach	ل ل	L	L	ל L as in Learn

310

Hebrew	H3925 לָמַד lāmad teach, learn, instruct, diligently, expert, skillful, teachers.

Fig 45 condensed

Benner says the origin is an ox goad, a yoke, and the lamed, and Petrovich agrees that the lamed, shepherd staff, was the source of this glyph. I agree with them. The 12th letter of modern Hebrew is the lamed Aramaic.ל Also, we can see that the lamed would often have a Mem In front of it, perhaps a possession article, as in my learning.

13- M, MEM Psa 119:97

Symbol ᴡᴡ ᴡ) ᴜ Aramaic מ Value 40.

Pictograph	Water symbol.
Meaning	Water, piss, waters, springs, washing, watercourse.
Sound	M, Ma, Me, Mi (others).
Benner	Mem?, Mayim?, Mah?-Glyph water, Meaning-Chaos, Mighty, Blood.
Petrovich	Mayim (mem).
Hebrew	H4325 מַיִם mayim.

Pictograms	Phonograms			Echograms	Aramaic Hebrew	Masoretic Hebrew
Egyptian Hieroglyphics 1859 BC	Mosaic Hieroglypic Hebrew Alphabet 1859 - 550 BC			English Modern	Square Hebrew 550 BC - 70 AD	Vowelled Hebrew 600 AD - present
Gardiner's Sign List #	Sounds Like	First Hebrew Phonogram Alphabet ·850 - 1100 BC	Paleo-Hebrew 1100-550BC	English	First Century	Vowels, dots, dashes were invented by Masoretes (600 AD) did not exist before
ᴡᴡᴡᴡ (N35)	N	Mayim Water	ᴡᴡ Sinai 377 349, 353 WH1 WH2) ᴡ)	ᴡ)	M	ם, מ	M as in Memory

Fig 45 condensed

The squiggly line, in this pictograph, depicts ᴡᴡ water, most scholars agree that this means water.

Benner says the MEM, is the modern Hebrew form for water, and came from the plural form of the word i.e. mayim[H4325] meaning "water." He said the original form meant "what". And that the Hebrews feared the sea and considered it an unknown place, hence, would question it. I personally question his reasoning here, I cannot see it. Solomon had a navy with the Phoenicians who were at sea for 3 years at a time. Dan abode in ships and Ashur was by the sea shore (Jdg 5:17).

Petrovich and his colleagues all agree this is the symbol of water. In conclusion, I agree that Ma'yim is a water symbol now, but I am not sure of its origin.

The origin of the English term "WATER" Old English wæter, from Proto-Germanic *watr- from PIE *wod-or, suffixed form of root *wed- (1) "water; wet."[214], VODKA, WET, WHISKEY, WASH, WINTER (along with others) all said to come from the same root.

The origin of WATER is wet, the Yiddish is vassah וואַסער, below I list possible Hebrew from wash, and wet.

H7372 רָטַב râṭab, raw-tab'; RaDTa(V) or WRaDTa(V), a primitive root; to be moist, be wet.

7364 רָחַץ râchats, raw-khats'; (often R can turn into WR and then W as in) WR-H-TS →WT WET a primitive root; wash to lave (the whole or a part of a thing), bathe.

H4161 מוֹצָא mowtsa' mo'wtsa ~~Mo~~ WTSA*wod-or (PIE root)," Water, go out, go forth, spring, brought, water springs, bud, east, outgoings, proceeded, proceedeth, vein, come out, watercourse. The original pictograph appears to have a mem and waw

H2222 Drip ZR(z)eeP'h sprinkling of water drops see Gesenius זַרְזִיף zarzîyph, zar-zeef by reduplication from an unused root meaning to flow; a pouring rain, water.

H4325 מַיִם mayim, mah'-yim; dual of a primitive noun (but used in a singular sense); water; figuratively, juice; by euphemism, urine, semen, piss, wasting, water(-ing).

The evolution of the Hebrew language and alphabet is a fascinating story. Take the letter Mem, currently the 13th letter with a numerical value of 40. In the Bible, however, "forty" wasn't

---

[214] "WATER" Old English wæter, from Proto-Germanic *watr- (source also of Old Saxon watar, Old Frisian wetir, Dutch water, Old High German wazzar, German Wasser, Old Norse vatn, Gothic wato "water"), from PIE *wod-or, suffixed form of root *wed- (1) "water; wet."

312

denoted by Mem; they used three distinct terms[215]. Clearly, the language and numerals have changed significantly since early Bible times. And to such an extent, many of the original glyphs are no longer known!

But I feel confident that the original pictograph for water was the *Mem*. This can leave us in a dilemma as to why things change so much and if, indeed, we can trust the Bible. Well, I feel very strongly that we can trust the Bible for the most part, even though the Jews changed the script and apparently changed many of the meanings of the original pictographs.

And lost the original pronunciation of words. The Jews still retained the essential message, and while the Aramaic script made changes, and the niqqud introduced a vowel system that may or may not be correct, we still (for the most part) have a language that goes back 3000 years. This is an amazing feat and a miracle of God's providence. All the while, the Devil tried to cover up our past.

14- N, NUN - Psa 119:105-112 Snake, serpent, seed.

Symbol  N Aramaic Nun נ Value 50.

Pictograph	Snake or Seed.
Meaning	Snake, serpent.
Sound	N. Nu.
Benner	Nun, Glyph-Seed meaning -continue, hier, son.
Petrovich	Nahas (nun) serpent. Meaning crafty.
Hebrew	Nun, seed, H5126 נוּן nûn Nun, Non.

[215] H702 אַרְבַּע 'arbaʿ four, fourteen, fourteenth, fourth, forty, three score and fourteen. H705 אַרְבָּעִים 'arbāʿîm forty, fortieth. H7239 רִבּוֹא ribô' thousand, forty, etc, ten thousand.

Pictograms Egyptian Hieroglyphics 1859 BC	Phonograms Mosaic Hieroglypic Hebrew Alphabet 1859 - 550 BC		Echograms English Modern	Aramaic Hebrew Square Hebrew 550 BC - 70 AD	Masoretic Hebrew Vowelled Hebrew 600 AD - present
Gardiner's Sign List # / Sounds Like	First Hebrew Phonogram Alphabet 1859 - 1100 BC	Paleo-Hebrew 1100-550BC	English	First Century	Vowels, dots, dashes were invented by Masoretes (600 AD) did not exist before.
(19) (110) / F	Nahas Snake / Sinai 87 Sinai 360 WH1 Sinai 349		N	N as in Now	

Fig. 45 condensed

The letter "Nun" occupies the 14th position in the alphabet and holds a numerical value of 60 (though unused in the Bible).

However, its true meaning sparks debate. Petrovich argues that this is a snake because the pictograph resembles a snake, which he says corresponds to the *nahas*[216] serpent. The word actually means hiss, which means that the snake makes naw-khawsh. It seems to me the often, we truncate the original Hebrew, and it forms the real acrophobic. Let me give you an example naw-khawsh' is naw-k'hawsh', i.e, hiish the sound that a snake made back then and still makes today a hiss. I hope you get my point.

THish snake sound has not changed over the millennium, yet the word for it appears elongated in the Bible. When the actual Hebrew is נָחָשׁ nH(i)sh. So, Masoretic scribes (600A.D. H5175) added vowels when there were none. The root word comes also has the same form נָחָשׁ nHsh. THish highlights another problem the Masorites created, the niqqud, which causes Stongs to produce up to five (or more) variants for the exact same Hebrew word[217]. Thy wanted to differentiate between words, so they suggested how they should be pronounced. We don't know if this is correct, and in many cases, it is not correct. So, In this book, I'll prioritize the original Hebrew letters with their suggested pronunciations in parentheses.

Aramaic letter for N (Nun) had one form in early AH. Only after the introduction of Masoretic Hebrew did it develop into ן and

---

[216] H5175 נָחָשׁ nāḥāš serpent, nâchâsh, naw-khawsh'; from H5172; a snake (from its hiss),serpent. H5712נָחָשׁ nâchash, naw-khash'; a primitive root; properly, to hiss, i.e. whisper a (magic) spell; generally, to prognosticate:—× certainly, divine, enchanter, (use) × enchantment, learn by experience, × indeed, diligently observe.

[217] see Dabar H1697

the final nun ן. There is no practical need for two forms of the nun. The "bent" *nun* (*nun kefufah*) either begins or is in the middle of a word. The straight, or final *nun* (*nun peshutah*), is used only at a word's end. Interestingly, some interpretations assign symbolism to these forms: the bent nun signifies humility, and the straight one represents uprightness.

The pictographic form of the nun looks like this ⌐. Scholars are in disagreement about what it represents. Petrovich calls it a snake and ties it to the Egyptian Hieroglyph for the snake. Benner ties it to seed, heir, and son. Benner appears to be taking this from the modern Hebrew nun and from Joshua's family name, which is traced to seed.

There is a Nun in the Bible, and it was the father of Joshua. It is said to mean posterity or seed[218].

15 –S - SAMECH - Psa 119:113-120, Support, sustain.

Symbol ╤ ⋈ ⊞ Aramaic ס Value 60

Pictograph	Fish, grain, beam, rafters.
Meaning	Support, sustain.
Sound	S, Se, Si, Sa, Su.
Benner	Sin, (samech) glyph-thorn-meaning grab, hate, protect.
Petrovich	Sarah/sear (samek), glyph-fish, meaning stink, hair.
Hebrew	Samek H5564 סָמַךְ çâmak, to prop, sustain support.

---

[218] H5126 נוּן Nûwn, noon; or נוֹן Nôwn; (1 Chronicles 7:27), from H5125; perpetuity, Nun or Non, the father of Joshua. Scribal error, 1 Kings 16:34; Nehemiah 8:17; Greek Version of the LXX Ναυη H5125 נוּן nûwn, noon; a primitive root; to resprout, i.e., propagate by shoots; figuratively, to be perpetual, be continued

Pictograms Egyptian Hieroglyphics 1859 BC		Phonograms Mosaic Hieroglypic Hebrew Alphabet 1859 - 550 BC		Echograms English Modern	Aramaic Hebrew Square Hebrew 550 BC - 70 AD	Masoretic Hebrew Vowelled Hebrew 600 AD - present
Gardiner's Sign List #	Sounds Like	First Hebrew Phonogram Alphabet 1859 - 1100 BC	Paleo-Hebrew 1100-550BC	English	First Century	Vowels, dots, dashes were invented by Masoretes (600 AD) did not exist before.
(D3) / KS	· / Bz	Sear/Sarah Hair/Stink	‡	S,X	ם	S as in Support

Fig. 45 condensed

The SAMEK is yet another glyph that has a contested origin. It showed up as a ▷ fish, a thorn ‡, a ten peg, other times a window ⊞. Benner believes this is a thorny issue and got pricked up over it. Hence, he is strongly leaning towards a sharp object.

Petrovich raises a familiar objection to this glyph. He clashes with Benner once more, proposing a connection to "sarah" (meaning "sear," not the proper name Sarah) and "stinky hair" [219]).

Other glyphs appear to look like a fish, and Gardiner connected the dag (H1709 דָּג) to this symbol, making it a D, not an S (see Fig 4a).

Petrovich vehemently disagrees, citing his firm belief that the symbol represents an "S" based on the modern Hebrew name "Samech" (along with other reasons). Experts mostly agree that the meaning of this symbol is an S. The names he mentions for hairdo start with an S; however, currently, it ties to a sin/shin, not a samek[(H8177)].

The Hebrew word sā·mə·kê·n is used in Psalm 119.116, and meanings uphold me, sustain, support and may explain the varying signs this letter has, i.e., a grain ⟙ looking symbol and a

[219] H8177 שְׂעַר śᵊʻar hair H8181   שֵׂעָר śēʻār
hair, hairy, rough H8185 שַׂעֲרָה śaʻărâ hair.

fish⤳ symbol and then later a rafters symbol, all of which could be metaphors for support or sustain[220].

In conclusion, I am leaning towards Sameke[221] as the source, meaning support and sustain.

16- A - AYIN A, E, I, O, U, Eye, value 70

Symbol ◉ O 𐤏 ע

Pictograph	Eye
Meaning	Eye, sight, seem, color, fountain, well, face, pleased.
Sound	Silent never, A, E, I, O, U. All vowels are used in this so-called Consonantal script.
Benner	Eye-Ghah-meaning Watch, Know Shade.
Petrovich	Ayin – Eye.
Hebrew	H5869 עַיִן ʿayin eye.

Pictograms Egyptian Hieroglyphics 1859 BC		Phonograms Mosaic Hieroglyic Hebrew Alphabet 1859 - 550 BC		Echograms English Modern	Aramaic Hebrew Square Hebrew 550 BC - 70 AD	Masoretic Hebrew Vowelled Hebrew 600 AD - present
Gardiner's Sign List #	Sounds Like	First Hebrew Phonogram Alphabet 1859 - 1100 BC	Paleo-Hebrew 1100-550BC	English	First Century	Vowels, dots, dashes were invented by Masoretes (600 AD) did not exist before.
⟐ D	IR	Ayin Eye	◉ Sinai 92, 349 WH 2 / ◯ Sinai 376 346a, 363	O	0	ע	Silent guttural in the back of the throat

Fig. 45 condensed

The English EYE comes from the Hebrew, *AYiN* H5869 עַיִן,[222] and in the past had other meanings. Etymologist and I don't see eye to eye (Isa. 52.8) on this. They trace it to Proto-Germanic

---

[220] H5564 סָמַךְ çâmak, saw-mak'; a primitive root; to prop (literally or figuratively); reflexively, to lean upon or take hold of bear up, establish, (up-) hold, lay, lean, lie hard, put, rest self, set self, stand fast, stay (self), sustain.

[221] H5564 סָמַךְ çâmak, saw-mak'; a primitive root; to prop (literally or figuratively); reflexively, to lean upon or take hold of (in a favorable or unfavorable sense), bear up, establish, (up-) hold, lay, lean, lie hard, put, rest self, set self, stand fast, stay (self), sustain.

[222] H5770 עָנַן âvan eyed H5869 עַיִן ʿayin eye, sight, seem, color, fountain, well, face, pleased, presence, displeased, before, pleased, conceit, think H5870 עַיִן ʿayin eye.

*augon and PIE root *okw- which sounds like ogle to see or perceive.

Etymological Professor Isaac Mozeson says that guttural Ayin+L instead of the expected vowel Ayin + N. creates a guttural-L sight (AkL) and produces words like OCULAR and OGLE. Whereas:

Middle English Until late 14c. The English plural was in -an (ayin), which went to plural een, ene. i.e, ayim's.

If the etymologist cannot see that the old English ayin's is from ayin(s) in Hebrew, well, they must be blind! Wow, let those with ayin's see the real truth!

Additionally, the original meaning of Ayin was metaphorical, referring to colors like blue, green, hazel, and brown. In the Middle Ages, we used it for the (color) plumage of a peacock.

The (so-called experts) say there are no vowels in Biblical Hebrew. This letter sounds out all vowels, dependent on the word it joins, and it can take the form of any vowel. Again, experts say it is silent; it is never silent. They also say glottal stop, which can also forms a word dependent on how it's used.

The Scottish Aye means "I see" to perceive or agree as in "yes". Often, Hebrew verbs could be used as metaphors, see H3282 יַעַן ya'an, (perhaps pronounced eyan?; from an unused root meaning to pay attention (remember YoD can be J, Y, I or E).

17- P-Ph, F - PE - Psa 119:129-136 Mouth

Symbol ⟍ ?P Aramaic פ Value 80.

Pictograph	Mouth.
Meaning	Sentence Pay-up, mouth.

Pictograms Egyptian Hieroglyphics 1850 BC		Phonograms Mosaic Hieroglypic Hebrew Alphabet 1850 - 550 BC			Echograms English Modern	Aramaic Hebrew Square Hebrew 550 BC - 70 AD	Masoretic Hebrew Vowelled Hebrew 600 AD - present
◠ D21	R	Peh Mouth	Sinai 377 349, 375a	𝒟 WH1	?	P,Ph	ף,פ	פ P as in Power (with dot) פ Ph as in Phone

318

Sound	P, Ph, F, other sound Pə, Pê, Pe, Pi, Pa.
Benner	Mouth with a closed glyph.
Petrovich	Mouth with an open glyph.
Hebrew	H6310 פֶּה pê mouth.

The Hebrew letter Pe, supposedly meaning "mouth," possesses a glyph that curiously resembles an eye, leading to potential confusion. Experts are unsure of the original meaning. Benner likes to display the pictograph as 🦥 whereas Petrovich shows it partially open (see above).

Benner says the early glyphs don't resemble the mouth (or at least not one in a closed state). His glyph does not appear to resemble his charts.

This inconsistency raises the possibility that the original glyph differed from what we use today. Nevertheless, regardless of its exact form, the letter undoubtedly represented a "P" or "Ph" sound.

Pe or mouth appears in the Bible, which means mouth[223]. It is often used as a metaphor. It has the following translations: mouth, commandment, edge, according, word, hole, end, appointment, portion, tenor, sentence. It comes from the root to blow away, i.e make some one pay! No joke. Put you month where your mouth is and then pay-up if you fail.

18- T, tz, ts, – TZADDI, Tsadi, Tsade -Psa 119:137

Symbol ᴸ ᴦ ᴼ Aramaic צ Value 90.

Pictograph	ᴸ ᴦ or ᴼ Trail/path or sack.
Meaning	Journey, chase or bag-capture.
Sound	T, Ts, Tz, Sa, Si, Se.
Benner	Trail, journey, chase. H6654 צַד ṣaḏ side, beside, another.

---

[223] H6310 פֶּה pê mouth, commandment, edge, according, word, hole, end, appointment, portion, tenor, sentence, misc H6284 אָצְפָה pâ'âh, paw-aw'; a primitive root; to puff, i.e. blow away, scatter into corners.

Petrovich	Seror sack, with lasso (English-sore).
Hebrew	H6654 צד tsadtsad Side, from an unused root meaning to sidle off; a side.

Pictograms Egyptian Hieroglyphics 1859 BC		Phonograms Mosaic Hieroglypic Hebrew Alphabet 1859 - 550 BC		Echograms English Modern	Aramaic Hebrew Square Hebrew 550 BC - 70 AD	Masoretic Hebrew Vowelled Hebrew 600 AD - present
Gardiner's Sign List #	Sounds Like	First Hebrew Phonogram Alphabet 1859 - 1100 BC	Paleo-Hebrew 1100 - 550BC	English	First Century	Vowels, dots, dashes were invented by Masoretes (600 AD) did not exist before
𓂀 V33	Ssr	Seror Sack	Sinai 346b 𓂀 𓂀 Sinai 351 𓂀 Sinai 349	ר	Ts	ץ,צ Ts as in Sits

This is another highly contested pictograph. There appears to be two possibilities for this letter sack ∞ and path/trail (side) ᴎ. Benner goes for the tsad ᴎ, while Petrovich goes for sack. ∞

The Hebrew word that corresponds to the sack which Petro calles *seror*, is parcel, bag, H6872 צְרוֹר ts⁰rôwr, [224]. It where we get the English words SORE, SICK and SORRY from[225].

Benner fall's down the hill ᴎ and hits the trail, and tumbles over to the side. H6654 צד ṣaḏ side, contr. from an unused root meaning to sidle off; a side; figuratively, an adversary(be-) side, of man, Assyrian ṣaddu, *snare*, *trap* beside, lie alongside, one another.

Samuel probably standardized the glyph since both glyphs produce the sound Ts. It appears Sam chose to side with Benner and bagged the other glyph (see what I did there☺).

The modern Hebrew word for this letter, *tsade* does, means side. Perhaps the meaning changed over time; it is highly possible,

---

[224] H6872 צְרוֹר ts⁰rôwr, tser-ore' or (shorter) צְרֹר ts⁰rôr; from H6887; a parcel (as packed up); also a kernel or particle (as if a package), bag, × bendeth, bundle, least grain, small stone. H6887 צָרַר tsârar, tsaw-rar primitive root; to cramp, literally or figuratively, transitive or intransitive:—adversary, (be in) afflict(-ion), besiege, bind (up), (be in, bring) distress, enemy, narrower, oppress, pangs, shut up, be in a strait (trouble), vex.

[225] Sore Old English sar "painful, grievous, aching, sad, wounding," influenced in meaning by Old Norse sarr "sore, wounded," from Proto-Germanic *saira- "suffering, sick, ill" " Old High German ser "painful," Gothic sair "pain, sorrow, travail"), from PIE root *sai- (1) "suffering" (source also of Old Irish **saeth** "pain, sickness").

but today, the Jews are on Benner's side. The word is also used in English, i.e., SIDE and SLIDE[226].

19 - K, KOPH - <u>Psa 119:145</u>-152.

Symbol 𐤒 𐤒 𐤒 𐤒 Kuph, Qoph, Koph 𐤒 Aramaic ק Value 100

Pictograph	lollypop or a 𐤒, spindle, spinning yarn or sun at the horizon
Meaning	Figurative power, branch, foot, hand.
Sound	Q, K, Kh.
Benner	Sun at the horizon Hebrew?
Petrovich	Spindle hand spun H3601 כִּישׁוֹר kîyshôwr from root כשר qshr not qur or quf as he says?
Hebrew	Monkey H6971 קוֹף kofe; or קֹף qôph, Egyptian, an ape, said to mean eye of a needle. Unknown Hebrew word.

Pictograms Egyptian Hieroglyphics 1859 BC		Phonograms Mosaic Hieroglypic Hebrew Alphabet 1859 - 550 BC		Echograms English Modern	Aramaic Hebrew Square Hebrew 550 BC - 70 AD	Masoretic Hebrew Vowelled Hebrew 600 AD - present
Gardiner's Sign List #	Sounds Like	First Hebrew Phonogram Alphabet 1859 - 1100 BC	Paleo-Hebrew 1100-550BC	English	First Century	Vowels, dots, dashes were invented by Masoretes (600 AD) did not exist before
V25	Wd	Qur Spun fiber	Sinai 376.349 Sinai 353 Sinai 391	𐤒	Q	ק	C as in Cry (more guttural than Kaph)

Fig 45 condensed

Here we have the Hebrew quph, koph, kaf, khaf. Usage in Psalms Qa, qe, qi, qo, pronounced K, kh, q,qf.

This letter is again disputed by scholars. Benner says it's the sun at the horizon, or a circle, or a revolution? Petrovich says it is "spun-fiber." I.e. a stick that is spun colleting fiber with a tail. Others say it is a monkey with a tail, but apparently, this was not an animal

---

[226] Side from Old English sid "long, broad, spacious," Old Norse siðr "long, hanging down"), from PIE root *se- "long, late" (see <u>soiree</u>). Old English side "flanks of a person, the long part or aspect of anything," from Proto-Germanic *sīdō (source also of Old Saxon sida, Old Norse siða, Danish side, Swedish sida, Middle Dutch side, Dutch zidje, Old High German sita, German Seite), from adjective *sithas "long" (source of Old English sid "long, broad, spacious," Old Norse siðr "long, hanging down"), from PIE root *se- "long, late" (see <u>soiree</u>).

that the Egyptians were familiar with, so why use such an obscure object, this does not apair to be a logical choice?

The word koph in the Bible does sounds like ape H6971 קוֹף qôwph, kofe; or קֹף qôph; of foreign origin, either Indian or Egyptian a monkey, ape. Gesenius says it's an ape because it has a tail, maybe a furball with a tail, like a spinning loom? Petrovich says it is the "spun fiber" qur or qof[227]. We also have a spindle starting with a K (H3601 כִּישׁוֹר kîyshôwr), which is from the root כשר qshr.

Even though there is disagreement, I think Petrovich provides the best argument. He says the Ape wasn't in Egypt at the time. And I would add spinning yarn has been a big commodity at Goshen for millennium. Others say it is the eye of a needle, whereas they say that קוֹף (h6971) Ape and Aramaic קוֹפא both refer to the eye of a needle(link).

It's important to note that this symbol appears explicitly in the Bible, unlike its pronunciation. However, the potential for confusion exists. The symbol at times looked like a lollop pop, the wow/vav, the quf and the Resh, and at times, can look the same and cause words to be mistranslated (Fig 42 Pale Hebrew alphabet).

David Rohl says that the Bible timeline has been greatly corrupted based on translation a wow for a kuph[228], where Shoshenq I, is mistranslated for Shishaq.

Hebrew Block-Letter	Projected Proto-Hebrew Original Letter	Middle-Egyptian Hieroglyphic Exemplar (Sign-List Number)	Original Hebrew Alphabetic Name (NIVEC Number)	Hebrew Consonantals of Middle Kingdom (ca. 1842-1760 BC)	Hebrew Consonantals of New Kingdom (ca. 1560-1307 BC)	Hebrew Consonantals of Iron Age - Canaan (ca. 1150-587 BC)
ו		(O30)	wāw, וָו pillar-support (2260)			
ק		(V25)	qûr, spun-fiber קוּר (7770)			
ר		(D1)	rōʾš, רֹאשׁ head (8031)			

---

[227] H6418 פֶּלֶךְ pelek, peh'-lek; from an unused root meaning to be round; a circuit (i.e. district); also a spindle (as whirled); hence, a crutch:—(di-) staff, participle. H3787 כָּשֵׁר kâshêr, kaw-share'; a primitive root properly, to be straight or right; by implication, to be acceptable; also to succeed or prosper:—direct, be right, prosp. H3601 כִּישׁוֹר kîyshôwr, kee-shore'; from H3787; compare H6418 literally a director, i.e. the spindle or shank of a distaff, by which it is twirled, spindle.

[228] David Rohl, see 25.10 minutes into this video Pattens of evidence, he talks of campaigns into the holy land and the names of the Pharaohs Shishank, verses Shishank being corrupted because a Wow/Vav was transposed for a Kuph (or visa versa).

20 - R RESH - Head, first, top, Psa 119:153-160

Symbol  R Aramaic ר Value 200.

Pictograph	Man’s head.
Meaning	Tribe, top, head. first, beginning.
Sound	R.
Benner	Resh (resh) Glyph Man’s head, meaning-first, top, beginning.
Petrovich	Ros (res) glyph Head.
Hebrew	Head H7217 רֵאשׁ rē'š or H7218 רֹאשׁ rō'š.

Pictograms Egyptian Hieroglyphics 1859 BC		Phonograms Mosaic Hieroglypic Hebrew Alphabet 1859 - 550 BC			Echograms English Modern	Aramaic Hebrew Square Hebrew 550 BC - 70 AD	Masoretic Hebrew Vowelled Hebrew 600 AD - present
Gardiner's Sign List #	Sounds Like	First Hebrew Phonogram alphabet 1859 - 1100 BC		Paleo-Hebrew 1100-550BC	English	First Century	Vowels, dots, dashes were invented by Masoretes (600 AD) did not exist before.
 D1	Tp	Resh Head	 Sinai 405 WH1 Sinai 376		R	ר	R as in Rush

The twentieth letter of the Hebrew is a man’s head, and it is a very important symbol for Israel. We remember that Ruben is Jacob's firstborn son, and this is the sign of his strength, excelling in honor and power, but he defiled his father's bed.

Jacob said he was turbulent as water, and you shall not excel (Gen.49.3), so his birthright was the first, and a double portion was taken away. And later gave it to Joseph (the cowboy).

Despite this, Reuben retained his position as the firstborn, the "head" or leader of Israel.

Nevertheless, the symbol of the firstborn was the resh (a man’s head[229]), i.e., the lead tribe the first. We have **Rosh HaShanah,** the celebration of the Jewish New Year. As the *rosh* is the start of the year, i.e., the date of creation, the date of the first month ever.

[229] H7217 רֵאשׁ rē'š head, sum, chief H7218 רֹאשׁ rō'š head, chief, top, beginning, company captain, sum, first, principal.

However, God gave Nissan 1 as the new first month which is in the spring not the late summer/early autumn, (Exo 12:2).

21-S/SH SCHIN SHIN-Psa 119:161-168.

Symbol ∽ W Aramaic ש Value 300.

Pictograph	Breasts, teeth.
Meaning	Nurture, power.
Sound	S, Sh.
Benner	Shin (sin) glyph-Teeth, meaning, sharp, press, eat, two.
Petrovich	Breast H7699 שַׁד šaḏ, breast.
Hebrew	Sad/sadayim H7699 שַׁד šaḏ breast.

Pictograms Egyptian Hieroglyphics 1859 BC		Phonograms Mosaic Hieroglypic Hebrew Alphabet 1859 - 550 BC		Echograms English Modern	Aramaic Hebrew Square Hebrew 550 BC - 70 AD	Masoretic Hebrew Vowelled Hebrew 600 AD - present
Gardiner's Sign List #	Sounds Like	First Hebrew Phonogram Alphabet 1859 - 1100 BC	Paleo-Hebrew 1100-550BC	English	First Century	Vowels, dots, dashes were invented by Masoretes (600 AD) did not exist before.
∇∇ D27	Mnd	Sadayim Breasts	W Sinai 353 Sinai 349 ∽ Sinai 357	W	S,Sh	ש	שׁ Sh as in Shine (right dot) שׂ S as in Sun (left dot)

Fig. 45 condensed

Again, this is yet another pictograph where we appear to have lost the original meaning. Hamilton says bow, but the Hebrew for bow is qesheth, in the sense of bending. This begins with a kuph[230].

Benner says teeth[231], while Petrovich argues for breasts[232]. I am inclined to lean towards the breasts, as it's a better match for the pictograph.

22-T/S TAU, SAU-Psa 119:169

Symbol + ✕ ✗ 𐤕 Aramaic ת, Numeric 400

---

[230]H7198 קֶשֶׁת qesheth, in the original sense of bending; a bow

[231] H8127 שֵׁן šēn teeth, tooth, ivory, sharp, crag, forefront. H8128 שֵׁן šēn teeth.
[232] Petrovich TWoA p.222, H7699   שַׁד   šaḏ
breast, teat, pap, (in the sense of bulging).

Pictograph	✝ Ta-Ta goodbye, Tayis (goat), mark, draw, border. line crossed, No Middle Egytpian connection.
Meaning	Goat, mark, sign, draw border-end, goodbye.
Sound	Ta, T.
Value	400 (Bible four- h0702 אַרְבַּע 'arba' hundred, h3967 מֵאָה mê'âh,).
Benner	Taw, (tav) glyph-Crossed meaning-mark sign signal monument Tav H8420 תָּו
Petrovich	Tayis (taw) Male goat Tayis H8495 תַּיִשׁ.
Hebrew	H8420 תָּו tāv mark, desire 2nd option. H8388 תָּאַר tā'ar draw, mark out.

Pictograms	Phonograms		Echograms	Aramaic Hebrew	Masoretic Hebrew
Egyptian Hieroglyphics 1859 BC	Mosaic Hieroglypic Hebrew Alphabet 1859 - 550 BC		English Modern	Square Hebrew 550 BC - 70 AD	Vowelled Hebrew 600 AD - present
Gardiner's Sign List #	Sounds Like	First Hebrew Phonogram Alphabet 1859 - 1100 BC	Paleo-Hebrew 1100-550BC	English	First Century	Vowels, dots, dashes were invented by Masoretes (600 AD) did not exist before.
✛ M42	Wn	Tayis Male goat	Sina:92 ✕ Sina 349 ✝ Sinai 351 376 WM2	X ✝	T,Th	ת	ת T as in Time (dot) ת Th ans in Theme

Fig 45 condensed

Again, there is a lot of confusion about the meaning of this pictograph. Experts can not seem to agree. Anywhere from goat (H8495 תַּיִשׁ tayiš) to crossed sticks meaning, sign, mark[233]. Petrovich says it's a male goat, and Benner says it's crossed sticks.

I have to get cross with Pertrovich and lean on the stick's with Benner, as this seems the most likely since BDB says this is a mark, as in a sign on the forehead, and it indicates exemption from judgment! Wow, did you get that the X or cross, is a mark on the head and points to Jesus and his work on the cross to take away our sins? Wow what a savior we have!

---

[233] H8388 תָּאַר tā'ar draw, mark out D(t)a'ar=draw, Old Norse draga "to draw, drag, pull," Cld Saxon dragan "to carry,"

H8420 תָּו tāv mark, desire. H3582 תָּעָה Ta'ah, Ta-Ta Ta'ra Good bye as in leave, be out of the way (see Ta'ar). H8388 drag out the way, border..

But I would like to add that we have a similar sounding word, which means goodbye or leave wander off. i.e., end, it also is used as a border, (see next paragraph).

Well, we have come to the end of the aleph'bet and its time to say Ta-Ta, or Tarah, goodbye. This unusual sign also marks the borderline[234]. And we have Jesus saying I am the alpha and the omega, Greek for Aleph and the Ta-Ta, the beginning and the end!

The "ta ta" or "ta rah" is a common farewell word used in England, especially in the north, and common to India. The first time it's used is when Abraham exits his father's house for the promised land and makes a promise to his wife/sister Sarah.

And it came to pass, when God caused me to wander(H8582 Ta ah) from my father's house, that I said unto her(Sarah), This [is] thy kindness which thou shalt shew unto me; at every place whither we shall come, say of me, He [is] my brother. [Gen 20:13 KJV]

---

[234] And the border was drawn H8388 'taw-aw') *thence,* and compassed the corner of the sea southward (Jos 18:14).

Chapter 11

Summary

We've explored some fascinating evidence linking the British and American people to Israel. Let's solidify these connections with a quick recap, shall we?

Symbols, idioms, language, culture, artifacts, DNA, archeology, history, mythology, and even the Bible all prove that "We are Israel" and "English is Hebrew." What more can I say to convince you?

Here is a quick recap of the things written in my two books:

-

We are Israel

"We Are Israel" is more than a book; it's a captivating journey that illuminates the profound truths surrounding Israel's birthright, its kingly lineage, and offers insightful closing thoughts.

The narrative begins with Abraham's pivotal covenant. We delve into the enduring promise of a blessed lineage, destined to inherit divine favor. The fulfillment of this promise, although delayed until Abraham's advanced age, would eventually culminate in a multitude of tribes springing from his descendants. It further emphasizes the expansion of the blessing with each successive birthright child, along with the lesser-known promises that materialized as God had foretold.

This compelling narrative offers readers an enlightening exploration of key prophecies, focusing particularly on the covenant and the kingly line. Each prophecy is meticulously unpacked from the Abrahamic land promise to the blessings of Isaac and Rebekah. The book delves into the blessings bestowed on Ephraim, Manasseh, and Joseph before turning to the crucial prophecy of the kingly line.

But the journey doesn't shy away from challenges. The narrative also explores the birthright's 2,401-year delay, attributed to the consequences of sin. This delay underscores the meticulous nature of God's justice and fairness. The book sums up its wide-ranging discussions by presenting a set of critical "Keys to Finding Israel."

The narrative takes a surprising turn with a significant portion dedicated to linguistic exploration. Prepare to be amused as the book draws fascinating connections between modern idioms and their biblical origins. Phrases like "you're eighty-sixed" and "you're fired" are traced back to their biblical roots, offering surprising discoveries laced with a touch of humor.

The book embarks on a linguistic journey tracing the evolution of the ancient Hebrew language, revealing connections between our modern vocabulary and the ancient Hebrews. Word origins are tracked from the Bible to Egypt and further to Greece, Tuscany, Spain, Europe, and even into English-speaking regions. Words like 'Navy,' 'Irish,' 'His Royal Highness,' 'England,' 'Scotland,' 'Ireland,' and 'Wales,' among others, are investigated, uncovering a deep-rooted connection to the Bible, Israel, and God.

Beyond language, the text delves into the divine mission entrusted to Jeremiah, following the prophet's journey with the king's daughters to the safe haven promised by God. It discusses God's promise of building on Jacob's rock, the cornerstone of God's Covenant, and reveals the process through which Israel was uprooted and replanted in a land of security.

The exploration doesn't stop there. The book delves into the translation of sacred words, unearths new Exodus routes, and even investigates the intriguing claim that the original Jews spoke Gaelic. Ultimately, "We Are Israel" is a testament to a steadfast God who fulfills promises, affirming that the sun and stars rise and set in the patterns ordained by Him, just as the divine covenant with Israel remains unbroken."

English is Hebrew

"Unraveling the Enigma: How English Became the Hidden Language of the Hebrew Bible"

In this gripping exploration, we embark on a journey to unlock the mysteries surrounding the original Celtic language of the British Isles and its astounding connection to ancient Biblical Hebrew and other languages like Hittite, Canaanite, Etruscan, Latin, Greek, French, and the Germanic languages. Prepare to be enthralled by the interwoven tapestry of linguistic connections that have remained veiled for centuries.

This book delves into the etymological roots of words, revealing fascinating bridges like "Celtic ABER" (mouth of a river) linked to "Eber" (from over there) and the significance of names like London, Alban, and rivers like Avon, Tamer, and Thames. We discover astonishing evidence of ancient British (covenant men) mining tin in Devon, dating back 3000 years to King Solomon's time.

Navigating linguistic statistics and phenomena like cognates, word changes, Grimm's Law, Verner's Law, and vowel shifts, we unveil the complexities of tracing a language while highlighting phonetics' crucial role.

As we journey through history, we encounter intriguing revelations about the British's enigmatic connection to Egypt for over 400 years, with Egyptian mummies potentially serving as their ancestors. We'll delve into the stories of Joseph's wife Asenath (h621) and Tutankhamun, revealing a surprising 70% British link to Egypt.

Furthermore, we discover the influence of writing methods like boustrophedon, which eventually settled into left-to-right for the British and right-to-left for the Jews, accompanied by script changes from Paleo Hebrew Aleph Bet to Aramaic Square Script. Uncover the remarkable flexibility of Hebrew letters, with "bet" becoming "vet" and "waw" transforming into "vav," along with the earliest vowels generated by specific Hebrew letters like "aleph," "wow," "yod," and "ayin." Unearth the secrets of this cosmic cover-up, where experts have been deterred from exploring the connection between English and Hebrew.

With a meticulously compiled list of thousands of cognates linking English to Hebrew, we analyze the alphabet's letters and their symbolic significance in the Bible and the English-speaking world today. Each chapter peels back another layer of this extraordinary revelation, challenging our understanding of language's foundations and our connection to the ancient past.

Introduction: The Intrigue Begins

- **Chapter 1:** Language, PIE, Genesis, and How to Determine a Language Connection
- **Chapter 2:** The Story of English - Language of the Hebrew Bible?
- **Chapter 3:** Hebrew - English Names
- **Chapter 4:** Hebrew / English Names of God
- **Chapter 5:** Prophecy predicted English is Hebrew and Fake PIE root system
- **Chapter 6:** Proof the Celtic Language Is Hebrew
- **Chapter 7:** Anglo-Saxons, and Germans
- **Chapter 8:** Egyptian Connection
- **Chapter 9:** Alphabet British-Jewish
- **Chapter 10:** The Alphabet Letters
- **Chapter 11:** Summary

Prepare to be astonished and enlightened as we embark on this gripping quest to reveal the hidden connections that bind the English language to the ancient world of the Hebrew Bible.

Why has this information been sealed until now?

Until now, most of what I am saying has been sealed and locked away. We can see this when Daniel is told to WALK away because the words are sealed until the time of the end. (And he said,

"Go [your way], Daniel, for the words [are] closed up [h5640] *and sealed till the time of the end.* [Dan 12:9 NKJV]).

The Ancient Hebrew is a time capsule, that allows us to decipher (H5608-5613 ספר sepher cipher to write, tally, record, numeral)[235] and trace the root,

A few key things had to occur before, this information could be revealed, let's take a look at some of the key dates.

- Guttenberg Bible and the printing press from Germany 1454-55
- The very first translation from Hebrew into English, William Tyndale - 1494–1536
- Martin Luther (German) the Reformation -breaking from Rome 1483[2] –1546
- King James Bible, heavily using Tyndale's work 1611
- Discovery of the Rosetta Stone, inscribed circa 200 B.C., was found in 1799 by French soldiers who were rebuilding a fort in Egypt. Jean-François Champollion deciphered hieroglyphs in 1822.
- Wilhelm Gesenius, brilliant rigorous scientific method of Biblical Hebrew root hermeneutics 1829-1842, the lexicon of Biblical Hebrew and Chaldee (Aramaic) first published in 1829.
- James Strong's Exhaustive dictionary/concordance of the Hebrew and Greek Bible 1890.

---

[235]H5608-5613 ספר sepher cipher to write, tally, record, **numeral**, Origin is from Arabic sifr 'zero,' (but we show here its from Hebrew-Semitic), literally "empty, a loan-translation of Sanskrit sīnya-s **"empty**. They also say "the key to a *cipher* or secret writing" (DECIFER is the ability to read and interpret the writing a skill, that was at times possed by very few individuals)! The ZERO, & numbering system is said to come from the Arab's, yet the concept is in Hebrew consider 0 the eye symbol also stood for ZERO, h369 אין'ayin, ah'-yin; as if from a primitive root meaning to be nothing or not exist (Gen 2.5 Zero man to till the ground. PIE *oi-to-   Ayin

early and middle

- Discovery of a Paleo Hebrew Alphabet Gezer Calendar 925 B.C. – Discovered in 1908 by Irish archaeologist R. A. Stewart Macalister in the ancient Canaanite city of Gezer, 20 miles west of Jerusalem
- In 1905, Flinders Petrie, a renowned Egyptologist and pioneer in modern archeology discovered inscriptions of previously unknown symbols at Serabit el-Khadim.
- In 1916 Sir Alan H. Gardiner, another renowned Egyptologist, realized that the Serabit el-Khadim inscriptions consisted of a total of thirty-two symbols, early Hebrew inscription. Because of the limited number of symbols, Dr. Gardiner (see Fig 4a) determined that this was an alphabet.

Earliest known Paleo Hebrew inscriptions - The "Proto-Sinaitic inscriptions "were discovered in the winter of 1904–1905 in Sinai by Hilda and Flinders Petrie. To this may be added a number of short "Proto-Canaanite "inscriptions found in Canaan and dated to between the 17th and 15th centuries B.C., and more recently, the discovery in 1999 of the "Wadi El-Hol inscriptions," found in Middle Egypt by John and Deborah Darnell. The "Wadi El-Hol" (Hell Hole on the Farshut road, no joke) inscriptions strongly suggest a date of development of Proto-Sinaitic writing from the mid-19th to the 18th Century B.C.[8][9] Although Jeff Benner (Ancient Hebrew research center) says that it's as old as the 20th Century (1901-2000 B.C.)

Bible codes

And apparently, even the Bible codes give us a clue to where they are, i.e. across the river Samabtion the same places I said in my book "We Are Israel"! See below.

1. Britain is Ephraim in the "Isles of the Sea".
2. The Seed of Abraham in the Isles.
3. "Britania Rules the Waves."
4. King David and the Islands of Britain!
5. Great Britain and Ireland.
6. Great Britain, Erin (Ireland), America, and the Isles of the

Sea.
7. The Ephraimite British.
Poem: RuleBritannia

FIGURES - Illustrations - Drawings

	Proto-Canaanite	Early Phoenician	Greek		Proto-Canaanite	Early Phoenician	Greek
ʾ			A	l			Λ
b			B	m			M
g			Γ	n			N
d			Δ	s			Ξ
h			E	ʿ			O
w			Y	p			Π
z			Z	ṣ			M
ḥ			H	q			ϙ
ṭ			Θ	r			P
y			I	š			Σ
k			K	t			T

Biblical "Hebrew to English" Alphabet
Hebrew is the first and oldest alphabet: 1859 BC

Pictograms Egyptian Hieroglyphics 1859 BC		Phonograms Mosaic Hieroglypic Hebrew Alphabet 1859 - 550 BC			Echograms English Modern	Aramaic Hebrew Square Hebrew 550 BC - 70 AD	Masoretic Hebrew Vowelled Hebrew 600 AD - present
Gardiner's Sign List #	Sounds Like	First Hebrew Phonogram Alphabet 1859 - 1100 BC		Paleo-Hebrew 1100-550BC	English	First Century	Vowels, dots, dashes were invented by Masoretes (600 AD) did not exist before.
(F1)	K	Aleph Cattle			A	א	Silent stop, like the "-" in "E-ha".
(O1) (O4)	Pr /H	Bayit House			B,V	ב	B as in Bet (With dot) / V as in Vet
(O38)	Knbt	Gahar Bend			G	ג	G as in Gift
(O31)	-	Delet Door			D	ד	D as in Door
(A28)	Hi	Halal Praise			H,E	ה	H as in Hay
(O30)	Shnt	Vaw Pillar Support			V,O,U	ו	V as in Vine | Vowel "u" as in "Flute" / Vowel "o" as in "Hole"
(D13)	inh	Zeah Sweat (Brows)			Z	ז	Z as in Zechariah
(O6) (V28)	Hwt /H	Haser/Hut Enclosure/Thread			H,Ch	ח	Ch as in Bach
(F35)	D	Tov Good			Th	ט	Th as in Thin
(D36) (D47)	A	Yad Hand			I,Y,J	י	Y as in Yes | Vowel "i" as in machine / Vowel "ey" as in "they".
(D28)	K	Kap Palms			K,Ch	ך,כ	K as in King (With dot) / Ch as in Bach
(S39)	Wt	Lamad Teach			L	ל	L as in Learn
(N35)	N	Mayim Water			M	ם,מ	M as in Memory
(I9) (I10)	F	Nahas Snake			N	ן,נ	N as in Now
(D3) (K5)	- / Bz	Sear/Sarah Hair/Stink			S,X	ס	S as in Support
D	IR	Ayin Eye			O	ע	Silent guttural in the back of the throat
D21	R	Peh Mouth			P,Ph	ף,פ	P as in Power (with dot) / Ph as in Phone
V33	Ssr	Seror Sack			Ts	ץ,צ	Ts as in Sits
V25	Wd	Qur Spun fiber			Q	ק	C as in Cry (more guttural than Kaph)
DI	Tp	Resh Head			R	ר	R as in Rush
D27	Mnd	Sadayim Breasts		W	S,Sh	ש	Sh as in Shine (right dot) / S as in Sun (left dot)
M42	Wn	Tayis Male goat		X †	T,Th	ת	T as in Time (dot) / Th as in Theme

Egyptian epigraphical data in this chart, in part from "The World's Oldest Alphabet", Douglas Petrovich, 2016 AD

www.bible.ca/manuscripts

A 'a' as in water	**A** 'a' as in bat	**B** 'b' as in boat	**CH** 'ch' as in church
CH 'ch' as in loch	**D** 'd' as in dog	**E** 'e' as in money	**F** 'f as in foot.
G 'g' as in gone	**H** 'h' as in hat.	**H** 'h' as in ich.	**I** 'i' as in pin
J 'j' as in adjust	**K** 'k' as in basket	**L** 'l' as in lion	**M** 'm' as in man
N 'n' as in not	**O** . 'oo' as in zoo	**P** 'p' as in pet	**Q** 'q' as in queen
R 'r' as in right	**S** 's' as in saw	**S** 'ss' as in glass	**SH** 'sh' as in show
T 't' as in top	**U** 'u' as in glue	**V** 'v' as in viper	**W** 'w' as in win
	Y 'y' as in money	**Z** 'z' as in zebra	

www.afrostyly.com/english & www.youtube.com/egyptdecoded

A	A	B	D	E	E	F	G	H
3	c	b	d	i	y	f	g	ḥ
(G1)	(D36)	(D58)	(D46)	(M17)	(M17a)	(I9)	(w11)	(V28)
Vulture	Arm	Leg	Hand	Reed	Reed	Snake	Jar std	Wick

H	J (dj)	K	M	N	P	Q	R	S	S
h	ḏ	k	m	n	p	ḳ	r	s	s
(O4)	(I10)	(V31)	(G17)	(N35)	(Q3)	(N29)	(D21)	(S29)	(O34)
Reed shelter	Cobra	Basket	Owl	Water ripple	Stool	Hill	Mouth	Folded cloth (or)	Lock Bolt

T	U	U	TJ	KH	SH	H	N	M
t	w	w	t̠	ḫ	š	ḫ	n	m
(X1)	(G43)	(V1)	(V13)	(Aa1)	(N38)	(F32)	(S3)	(Aa15)
Bread	Chick	Rope	Cord	Sieve	Pool	Belly	Crown	Rib

339

Ancient Hebrew							Modern Hebrew		
Early	Middle	Late	Name	Picture	Meaning	Sound	Letter	Name	Sound
𐤀	✗	א	El	Ox head	Strong, Power, Leader	ah, eh	א	Aleph	silent
𐤁	𝑔	ב	Bet	Tent floorplan	Family, House, In	b, bh(v)	ב	Beyt	b, bh(v)
✓	𐤂	ג	Gam	Foot	Gather, Walk	g	ג	Gimal	g
𐤃	△	ד	Dal	Door	Move, Hang, Entrance	d	ד	Dalet	d
𐤄	𐤄	ה	Hey	Man with arms raised	Look, Reveal, Breath	h, ah	ה	Hey	h
Y	𐤅	ו	Waw	Tent peg	Add, Secure, Hook	w, o, u	ו	Vav	v
𐤆	𐤆	ז	Zan	Mattock	Food, Cut, Nourish	z	ז	Zayin	z
𐤇	𐤇	ח	Hhet	Tent wall	Outside, Divide, Half	hh	ח	Chet	hh
⊗	⊗	ט	Tet	Basket	Surround, Contain, Mud	t	ט	Tet	t
⌐	𐤉	י	Yad	Arm and closed hand	Work, Throw, Worship	y, ee	י	Yud	y
𐤊	𝑦	כ	Kaph	Open palm	Bend, Open, Allow, Tame	k, kh	כ	Kaph	k, kh
𐤋	𐤋	ל	Lam	Shepherd Staff	Teach, Yoke, To, Bind	l	ל	Lamed	l
𐤌	𝑚	מ	Mem	Water	Chaos, Mighty, Blood	m	מ	Mem	m
𐤍	𐤍	נ	Nun	Seed	Continue, Heir, Son	n	נ	Nun	n
𐤎	𐤎	ס	Sin	Thorn	Grab, Hate, Protect	s	ס	Samech	s
◉	O	ע	Ghah	Eye	Watch, Know, Shade	gh(ng)	ע	Ayin	silent
𐤐	𐤐	פ	Pey	Mouth	Blow, Scatter, Edge	p, ph(f)	פ	Pey	p, ph(f)
𐤑	𐤑	צ	Tsad	Man on his side	Wait, Chase, Snare, Hunt	ts	צ	Tsade	ts
𐤒	𐤒	ק	Quph	Sun on the horizon	Condense, Circle, Time	q	ק	Quph	q
𐤓	𐤓	ר	Resh	Head of a man	First, Top, Beginning	r	ר	Resh	r
𐤔	w	ש	Shin	Two front teeth	Sharp, Press, Eat, Two	sh	ש	Shin	sh, s
+	✗	ת	Taw	Crossed sticks	Mark, Sign, Signal, Monument	t	ת	Tav	t

Hebrew Block-Letter	Projected Proto-Hebrew Original Letter	Middle-Egyptian Hieroglyphic Exemplar (Sign-List Number)	Original Hebrew Alphabetic Name (NIVEC Number)	Hebrew Consonantals of Middle Kingdom (ca. 1842–1760 BC)	Hebrew Consonantals of New Kingdom (ca. 1560–1307 BC)	Hebrew Consonantals of Iron Age – Canaan (ca. 1150–587 BC)
א		(F1)	ʾel-f, cattle אלף (477)			
ב	Sinai 92, 405 (O1) (O4)		bayit, house בית (1074)			
ג	Sinai 112 (O38)		gāhar, bend גחר (1566)			
ד		(O31)	delet, door דלת (1946)			
ה	Sinai 92 (A28)		hēlal, praise הלל (2146)			
ו	(O30)		vāv, pillar-support וו (2260)			
ז	(D13)		zēʿah, sweat (brows) זעה (2399)			
ח	Sinai 405 (O6) h (V28) h		ḥāṣēr, חצר (2958), ḥūṭ, thread חוט (2562)	enclosure / thread		
ט	Sinai 112 (F35)		ṭōv, good טוב (3201)		Sinai 351	
י	Sinai 405 Sinai 92 (D36) (D47)		yād, hand יד (3338)		Sinai 353	
כ	Sinai 92 (D28)		kap, palm כף (4090)			
ל	(S39)		lāmad, teach למד (4340) (4913)		Sinai 349 Sinai 353	Sinai 361
מ	Sinai 405 (N35)		mayim, water מים (4784)		Sinai 349 Sinai 353 Sinai 375a	
נ	Sinai 87 (I9) (I10)		nāḥāš, snake נחש (5729)		Sinai 344b Sinai 360	
ס	Sinai 90 (D3) (K5)		śaʿār שער (8482), śrūaḥ, stink סרח (6244)	hair / stink		
ע	Sinai 92 (D4)		ʿayin, eye עין (6523)		Sinai 346a Sinai 349 Sinai 353	
פ	Sinai 92 (D21)		peh, mouth פה (7023)		Sinai 349 Sinai 349 Sinai 375a	
צ	(V33)		ṣarōr, sack צרור (7655)	© 2015 Douglas Petrovich	Sinai 346b Sinai 349 Sinai 351	
ק	(V25)		qūr, spun-fiber קור (7770)	Sinai 376	Sinai 349 Sinai 353	
ר	Sinai 405 (D1)		roʾš, head ראש (8031)		Sinai 353 Sinai 357	
ש	(D27)		šādayim, breasts שדים (8716)		Sinai 349 Sinai 353 Sinai 357	
ת	Sinai 92 (M42)		tayiš, male goat תיש (9411)		Sinai 351	

341

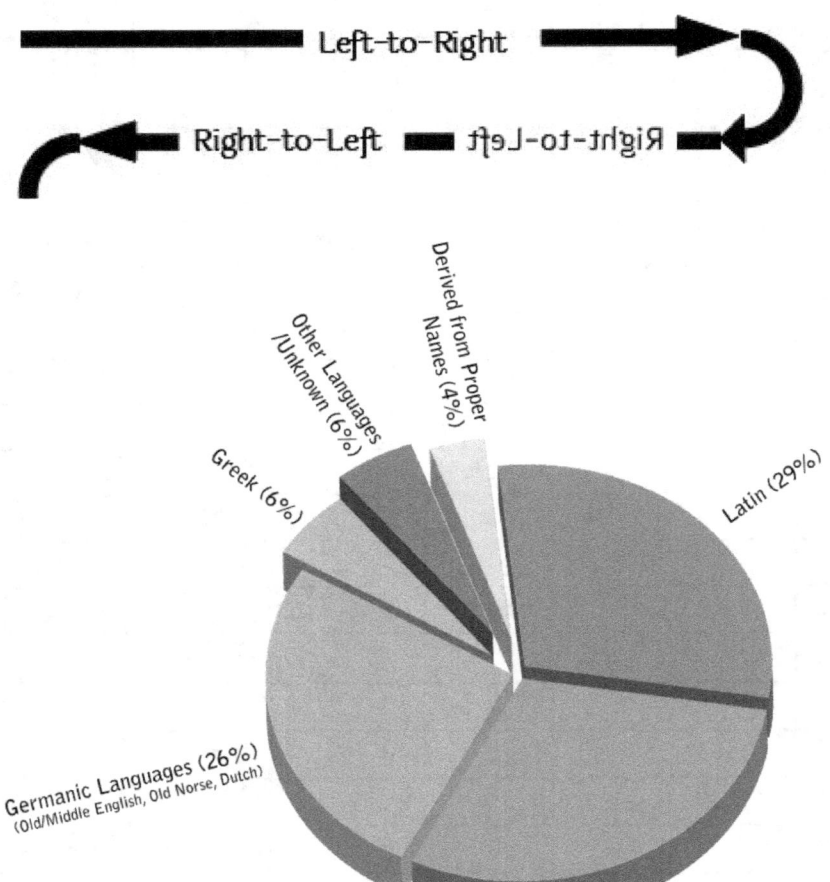

Boustrophedon
"turn like an ox (while ploughing)"

Left-to-Right

Right-to-Left

51 ENGLISH LANGUAGE PIE CHART

342

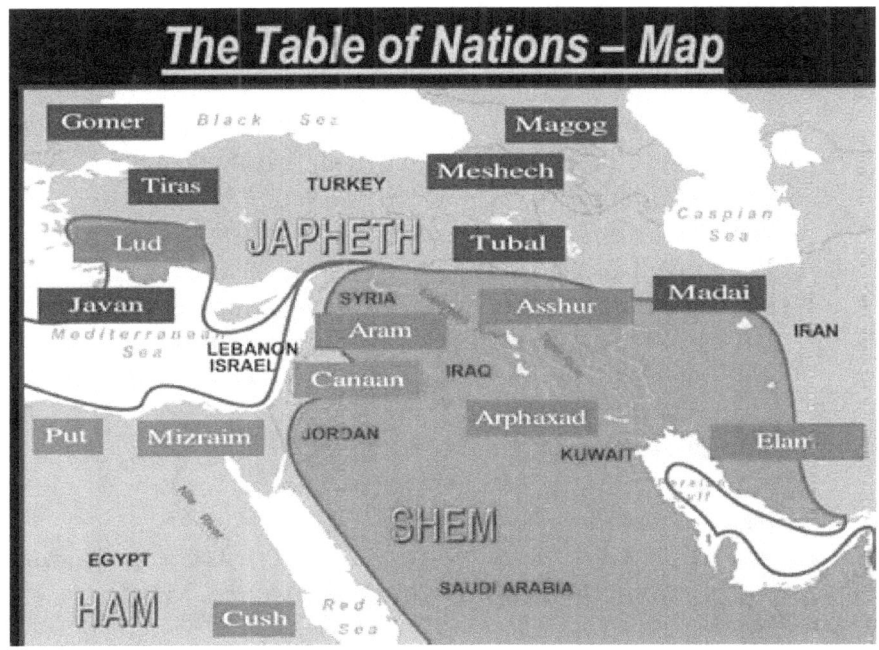

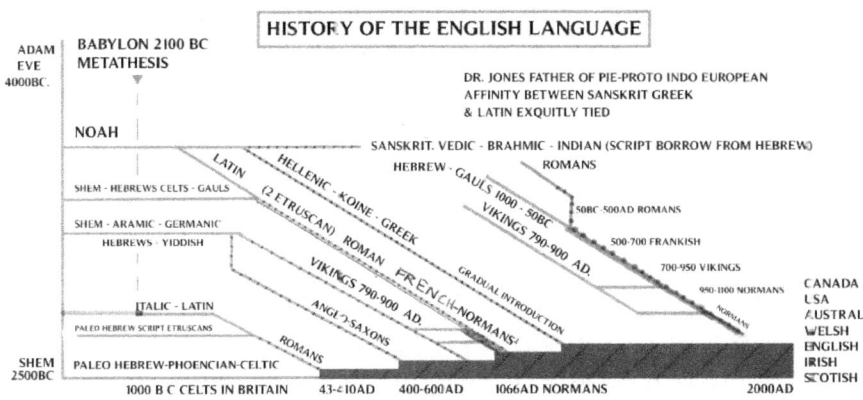

Bibliography

Books

1. Alan Gardiner - *Egyptian Grammar: Being an Introduction to the Study of Hieroglyphs*. Griffith Institute, Ashmolean Museum, 1957.
2. Bede - *Ecclesiastical History of the English People*. Penguin Classics, 1990.
3. Bradley, Henry - *The Making of English*. Macmillan, 1904.
4. Brown, Francis; Driver, S.R.; Briggs, Charles A. - *A Hebrew and English Lexicon of the Old Testament*. Oxford: Clarendon Press, 1907.
5. Cottrell, Leonard - *Anvil of Civilization*. The New American Library, 1957.
6. Crystal, David - *The Stories of English 1941-*
7. .David Down - *Unwrapping the Pharaohs: How Egyptian Archaeology Confirms the Biblical Timeline*. Master Books, 2006.
8. David M. Rohl - *Exodus: Myth or History?* Thinking Man Media, 2015.
9. David Rohl - *The Lords of Avaris: Uncovering the Legendary Origins of Western Civilization*. Arrow Books, 2003.
10. Davies, John - *A Display of Heraldry*. London: 1793.
11. Finkelstein, Israel, and Silberman, Neil Asher - *The Bible Unearthed: Archaeology's New Vision of Ancient Israel and the Origin of Its Sacred Texts*.
12. Francis Brown, S. R. Driver, and Charles A. Briggs - *Brown-Driver-Briggs Hebrew and English Lexicon*. Hendrickson Publishers, 1994.
13. Frere, Sheppard - *Britannia: A History of Roman Britain*. Routledge, 1987.
14. Gawler, J.C. - *Dan, the Pioneer of Israel*. Hodder & Stoughton, 1880.
15. Gesenius, Wilhelm. *Gesenius' Hebrew and Chaldee Lexicon to the Old Testament Scriptures*. Translated by Samuel Prideaux Tregelles, Baker Book House, 1979.

16. Gordon, Cyrus H. - *Before Columbus: Links Between the Old World and Ancient America.*

17. Heuvelmans, Bernard - *On the Track of Unknown Animals.* Routledge & Kegan Paul, 1955.

18. Higham, Nicholas J. - *Rome, Britain and the Anglo-Saxons.* Bloomsbury Academic, 1992.

19. Hislop, Alexander - *The Two Babylons.* Loizeaux Brothers, 1916.

20. Hjelmslev, Louis - *Language: An Introduction.* Madison: University of Wisconsin Press, 1970.

21. James P. Allen - *Middle Egyptian: An Introduction to the Language and Culture of Hieroglyphs.* Cambridge University Press, 2010.

22. James Strong - *Strong's Exhaustive Concordance of the Bible.* Hendrickson Publishers, 2009.

23. Jeff A. Benner - *The Ancient Hebrew Lexicon of the Bible.* Virtualbookworm Publishing, 2005.

24. Jones, Barri and Mattingly, David - *An Atlas of Roman Britain.* Blackwell Publishers, 1990.

25. Keating, Geoffrey - *History of Ireland.* Foras Feasa ar Éirinn. Translated by Dermod O'Connor, 1723.

26. Klein, Ernest - *A Comprehensive Etymological Dictionary of the English Language.* Elsevier Publishing Company, 1966.

27. Koch, John T. - *Celtic Culture: A Historical Encyclopedia.*

28. Koldewey, Robert - *The Excavation of Babylon.* Macmillan, 1914.

29. Kutscher, Eduard Yechezkel - *A History of the Hebrew Language.* The Magnes Press, The Hebrew University, 1982.

30. MacCulloch, J.A. - *The Religion of the Ancient Celts.* Dover Publications, 2003.

31. Mela, Pomponius - *De Chorographia.* Translated by F. E. Romer, University of Michigan Press, 1998.

32. Miller, Patrick D. - *The Religion of Ancient Israel.* Westminster John Knox Press, 2000.

33. Mozeson, Isaac - *The Word: The Dictionary That Reveals the Hebrew Source of English.* SPI Books, 2000.

34. Mozeson, Isaac Elchanan - *The Word: The Dictionary That Reveals the Hebrew Source of English*. New York: Jason Aronson, 1989.

35. Myler, Damian Philip. *We Are Israel: A Mystery Wrapped in an Enigma*. 2020, Chrisitan Faith Publishing. Republished as *We Are Israel*, 2024.

36. Nothaft, Carl Philipp Emanuel - *Missing Links Discovered in Assyrian Tablets*. The Macmillan Company, 1928.

37. O'Flaherty, Roderic - *Ogygia: or, a Chronological Account of Irish Events*. Translated by James Hely, 1793.

38. Olyan, Saul M. - *Asherah and the Cult of Yahweh in Israel*. Society of Biblical Literature, 1988.

39. Partridge, Eric - *Origins: A Short Etymological Dictionary of Modern English*. Routledge, 1958.

40. Petrovich, Douglas - *The World's Oldest Alphabet: Hebrew as the Language of the Proto-Consonantal Script*, Jerusalem: Carta Jerusalem, 2017.

41. Pliny the Elder - *Natural History*. Translated by H. Rackham, Harvard University Press, 1942.

42. Pritchard, James B. - *The Ancient Near East: An Anthology of Texts and Pictures*. Princeton University Press, 1958.

43. Pritchard, James Cowles. *Eastern Origin of the Celtic Nations*. London: John and Arthur Arch, 1831.

44. Ptolemy - *Geography*. Translated by J. Lennart Berggren and Alexander Jones, Princeton University Press, 2000.

45. Raymond Capt - *Missing Links Discovered in Assyrian Tablets*. Artisan Publishers, 1985.

46. Sayce, A. H. - *The Early History of the Hebrews*.

47. Smith, Mark S. - *The Early History of God: Yahweh and the Other Deities in Ancient Israel*. 2nd ed., William B. Eerdmans Publishing Company, 2002.

48. Snyder, Christopher A. - *An Age of Tyrants: Britain and the Britons A.D. 400–600*. Penn State University Press, 1998.

49. Strong, James. *Strong's Exhaustive Concordance of the Bible*. Abingdon Press, 1890.

50. Tigay, Jeffrey H. - *You Shall Have No Other Gods: Israelite Religion in the Light of Hebrew Inscriptions*. Harvard Semitic Monographs, Scholars Press, 1986.

51. Tuchman, Barbara W. - *Bible and Sword: England and Palestine from the Bronze Age to Balfour*. Ballantine Books, 1956.
52. Tyndale, William - *The Holy Bible*. Translated by William Tyndale, 1535.
53. Vennemann, Theo. - *Languages in Prehistoric Europe*. Heidelberg: Winter, 2003.
54. Worrell, William H. - *A Study of Races In The Ancient Near East*. Ann Arbor: University of Michigan Press, 1927.

Articles

1. "Deciphering the Proto-Sinaitic Script" - Journal of Near Eastern Studies Darnell, John Coleman. "The Early Alphabetic Inscriptions from Wadi el-Hol: New Evidence for the Origin of the Alphabet from the Western Desert of Egypt." Journal of Near Eastern Studies, vol. 64, no. 3 (2005): 161-180.
2. "DNA Analysis of Egyptian Mummies" - Nature Communications Schuenemann, Verena J., et al. "Ancient Egyptian mummy genomes suggest an increase of Sub-Saharan African ancestry in post-Roman periods." Nature Communications. 2017.
3. "Early Alphabetic Inscriptions" - Bulletin of the American Schools of Oriental Research Sass, Benjamin. "The Genesis of the Alphabet and Its Development in the Second Millennium BC: Twenty Years of Research." Bulletin of the American Schools of Oriental Research, no. 344 (2006): 63-75.
4. "Phoenician Alphabet Derived from Hebrew" - Journal of Semitic Studies Rollston, Christopher A. "The Phoenician Script of the Proto-Canaanite Alphabet." Journal of Semitic Studies, 2010.
5. "Saqqara Pyramid Texts" - Ancient History Encyclopedia Mark, Joshua J. "Saqqara Pyramid Texts." Ancient History Encyclopedia, 2016.
6. Independent News. "Welsh Journalists Mistaken for Israeli Spies in Libya." Link.
7. Journal of Biblical Literature - "The Development of the Early Alphabet" Accessed from: JSTOR.

8. Journal of Semitic Studies - "The Evolution of Early Semitic Alphabets". Journal of Semitic Studies, Volume 54, Issue 2, Autumn 2009.
9. The Biblical Archaeologist - "Evidence of Hebrew as the Oldest Alphabet". The Biblical Archaeologist, Vol. 59, No. 3, 1996.
10. Smithsonian Magazine - "New Discoveries on the Ancient Origins of Writing".

Web Pages
1. Ancient Hebrew Research Center - "The Ancient Hebrew Alphabet"
2. Bible Gateway - Various Translations and Lexicons of the Bible. Accessed from: Bible Gateway.
3. Blue Letter Bible - Strong's Concordance and Hebrew Lexicon. Accessed from: Blue Letter Bible.
4. Britannica - "Anglo-Saxons". Accessed from: Britannica - Anglo-Saxons.
5. British Museum - "Early Writing Tablet with Pictographs"
6. Creation Ministries International - "Revised Chronology of Egypt". Accessed from: Creation.com.
7. Douglas Harper - Online Etymology Dictionary. Accessed from: Online Etymology Dictionary.
8. Jewish Virtual Library - "Hebrew Language History". Accessed from: Jewish Virtual Library.
9. Jewish Virtual Library - "The Assyrians". Accessed from: Jewish Virtual Library.
10. The Etymology Online Dictionary - "The Origins of Various English Words". Accessed from: Etymology Online.
11. Wikipedia - "Etruscan Civilization". Accessed from: Wikipedia - Etruscan Civilization.
12. Wikipedia - "Greek Alphabet". Accessed from: Wikipedia - Greek Alphabet.
13. Wikipedia - "Pyrgi Tablets". Accessed from: Wikipedia - Pyrgi Tablets.
14. Wikipedia - "Roman Britain". Accessed from: Wikipedia - Roman Britain.
15. Wikipedia - "Serabit el-Khadim". Accessed from: Wikipedia - Serabit el-Khadim.

16. Wikipedia - "Step Pyramid of Djoser". Accessed from: Wikipedia - Step Pyramid of Djoser.
17. Wikipedia - "Wadi el-Hol". Accessed from: Wikipedia - Wadi el-Hol.
18. World History Encyclopedia - "Alan Gardiner". Accessed from: World History Encyclopedia - Alan Gardiner.
19. World History Encyclopedia - "Imhotep". Accessed from: World History Encyclopedia - Imhotep.

Etymological References

1. Brown, Francis; Driver, S. R.; Briggs, Charles A. - *A Hebrew and English Lexicon of the Old Testament*. Oxford: Clarendon Press, 1907.
2. Gesenius, Wilhelm. *Gesenius' Hebrew and Chaldee Lexicon to the Old Testament Scriptures*. Translated by Samuel Prideaux Tregelles, Baker Book House, 1979.
3. James Strong - *Strong's Exhaustive Concordance of the Bible*. Hendrickson Publishers, 2009.
4. The Etymology Online Dictionary - "The Origins of Various English Words". Accessed from: Etymology Online.
5. Douglas Harper - Online Etymology Dictionary. Accessed from: Online Etymology Dictionary.
6. Mozeson, Isaac Elchanan – *E-Word:Edenics Digital Dictionary 2023: The Dictionary That Reveals the Hebrew Source of English*.
7. Klein, Ernest - *A Comprehensive Etymological Dictionary of the English Language*. Elsevier Publishing Company, 1966.
8. Jeff A. Benner - *The Ancient Hebrew Ancient Hebrew Language and Alphabet*-Etymology of the Pictographic Alphabet.
9. Douglas Petrovich - *The World's Oldest Alphabet: Hebrew as the Language of the Proto-Consonantal Script*. Carta Jerusalem, 2016-Etymology of Pictographic Hebrew.

Abbreviation list

1. **AD** Ano Domino, - " year of the Lord"⌊ i.e. after Christ birth.
2. **AE** - Ancient English
3. **AH** - Aramaic Hebrew
4. **AL** - Ancient Latin
5. **AS** - Anglo-Saxon
6. **BC** - Before Christ
7. **BCE** Before Common Era
8. **BDB** - Brown-Driver-Briggs (Hebrew and English Lexicon)
9. **CAPITAL LETTERS,** eg. "WORD" indicate English word that comes from Hebrew
10. **C** Circa xxxx approximat date of the event.
11. **CS** - Celtic Script
12. **DNA** - DeoxyriboNucleic Acid
13. **DSC** - Dead Sea Scrolls
14. **EBD** - Etymological Biblical Dictionary
15. **EIH** - English is Hebrew
16. **EG** - Egyptian
17. **EL** - Early Latin or Etruscan (contextually relevant)
18. **Fm** – From
19. **GA** - Gaelic
20. **HE** or H-E- Hebrew-English
21. **HLL** - Halal (praise in Hebrew context)
22. **HLL-YH** - Halelujah (Praise Yah)
23. **IE** - Indo-European
24. **IEH** - Israelite Early Hebrew
25. **KJV** - King James Version (of the Bible)
26. **LXX** - Septuagint (Greek translation of Hebrew Scriptures)
27. **MW** - Middle Welsh
28. **NT** - New Testament
29. **OT** - Old Testament
30. **PE** - Paleo English
31. **PH** - Phoenician
32. **PIE** - Proto-Indo-European
33. **P.r., Prim.** – Primitive root
34. **QF** - Qoph (Hebrew letter)
35. **RV** - Revised Version (of the Bible)
36. **TE** - Tiberian English (relevant to Masoretic Hebrew)
37. **WAI** - We Are Israel

Index in Alphabetical Order

Please note that this is a truncated version of the index/matrix English-Hebrew a fuller searchable version can be found on my website rebelministry.com

Description	Strong#	Name-Pronounced	Etymology - Meaning
?	0702	arba', ar-bah'	masculine אַרְבָּעָה ' Four.
?	1438	gâda', gaw-dah'	primitive root; To fell a tree
?	1585	gᵉmar, ghem-ar'	(Aramaic) H1584:—perfect.
?	2998	Yibniyah	Ibnijah" whom Jehovah will build up"
?	3170	Yachzerah	Jahzerah, "whom God leads back"
?	3321	yᵉtsab, yets-abe'	(Aramaic) corresponding to H3320
?	3449	Yishshiyah	Isshiah, Jesiah, Ishiah, Ishijah
?	3999	mabbûwl, mab-bool'	from H2986 in the sense of flowing;
?	4396	millu'âh, mil-loo-aw'	feminine of H4394; a filling,
?	5768	'ôwlêl, o-lale' or 'ôlâl	from H5763; a suckling:—
?	6014	'âmar, aw-mar'	P.r.apparently to heap; figura... to chastise
?	6246	'ashith (Aramaic)	thought
?	6250	'eshtonah	thoughts
?	6418	pelek, peh'-lek	from an unused root meaning to be round
?	6845	tsâphan, tsaw-fan'	primitive root; to hide (by covering over
?	7554	râqa', raw-kah'	primitive root; to pound the earth
?	8226	sâphan, saw-fan'	prim. -to conceal (as a valuable), treasure
?	8264	shâqaq, shaw-kak'	run to and fro, longing,
?	8320	sâruq, saw-rook'	from H8319; bright.
? Reveal split	8176	shâ'ar, shaw-ar'	primitive root; to split or open
? Sweat	3154	yeza', yeh'-zah	From an unused root mean to ooze
?Cow Girls-	6511	Pârâh, paw-raw'	the same as H6510; place in Palestine
?Goal-net-sack-	5329	nâtsach, naw-tsakh'	Shine, be bright,a primitive root;
?Kennel, secure	7064	qên, kane	contracted from H7077; a nest
?LANGUAGE,	3937	la`az	strange language
?Last, Lease	5329	nâsah	Musician, set forward
?Monkey,	6971	qôwph, kofe	or קֹף qôph; a monkey:—ape.
?Mouth,	6310	peh	mouth, commandment
?Saw-hair,	8163	sâ'îyr, saw-eer'	or שָׂעִר see H8175; shaggy, He goat, devil
?Seven,	6235	'eser	ten, fifteen,
?Shaar	8179	sha'ar, shah'-ar	from H8176 door or gate
?Shake ah,	8248	shaqah, shaw-(k)aw'	primitive root; to quaff, to irrigate or furnish
?some say Tav	8495	tayishhe goat	he goat -
?Teeth 22nd	8127	shên, shane	from H8150; tooth (as sharp) Ivory.
?Teeth Sin/Shin	8128	shên, shane	(Aramaic) tooth
?Zion temple	5329	nâtsach, naw-tsakh'	Shine, be bright,a primitive root
10,000 X	7231	Rabab rabab	X See
10,000 X	7233	Rᵉbabah rᵉbabah	10 thousand, million, many, multiply, Rabbi
1000 Aleph	0506	alaph, 'alaph (Aramaic)	thousand
1000 x	7239	Ribbow ribbow	thousand
Ab(a) Father	0002	'ab (Aramaic)	father
Ab, Abba,	0001	'âb, awb	AwB(a) father
Âbêl	0064	'Âbêl Kᵉrâmîym, aw-bale' ker-aw-meem'	Fr-H58 plural of H3754; meadow of vineyards; a place in Palestine.
Abel-bellows	1893	Hebel heh'-bel	Abel-= "breath" as in a Bellohs
Aber (Over),	5676	'êber, Ay'-ber	Aber, fm Common Brittonic
Abigail, Abiy	0026	Âbîygayil,	or shorter אֲבִיגַל 'Âbîygal; persons name
Abram -ABRM	0087	Abram, ab-rawm	contracted from H48; high father; Abram.
Academy,	1970	hâkar, haw-kar'	primitive root to injure, make self strange
Achar	5912	Âkân, aw-kawn'	Sore as in Ache,
Ache`n, Ache	5912	Ach	Sore as in Ache,
Achen	5912	Akân-ä·kän	Son of Zerah trouble.
Actor,	6280	âthar, awt-har'	Prim. root; abundant,deceitful, multiply.
Actor,	6282	Athâr, aw-thawr'	fm H6280 to decive, act-abundant, multiply.
Adam	0120	Adam, aw-dam'	man, men
Adam	0121	Adam, aw-dam'	the same as H120; men, man.

Description	Strong#	Name-Pronounced	Etymology - Meaning
Adam see DaM,	0119	Adam, aw-dam'	to show blood (in the face),
Adamah	0127	Adâmâh, ad-aw-maw'	fm H119; redness),country, earth, ground, husband (autumn-fall),
Addown	0114	Addownad-done	Addon-' (lord Master etc) powerful
ADONIS,	0138	Ădônîyâh, ad-o-nee-yaw'	original name of three Israelites:—Adonijah.
Adorable	2981	yᶜbûwl, yeb-ool'	from H2986 crop or (figuratively) wealth.
Adore,	0142	'âdar, aw-dar'	prim. root; to expand
Ahab-brother	0256	'Ach'abakh-awb'	Ahab- once brother h215&h1
Aid,	5712	'êdâh, ay-daw'	feminine of H5707 sense of fixture
Alban	3835	lâban, law-ban	primitive root; Father of Jacobs wives White
Alban	3843	lᵉbênâh, leb-ay-naw'	from H3835; White mountain
Alban,	3836	lâbân, law-bawn'	or (Genesis 49:12) White ALP's Albine
Alban	3837	Laban	Laban White
Albion,	3837	Laban	Laban Albino, white.
Aleph-Eleph	0505	'eleph'eleph	thousand,
ALL-(adj./adv.	0352	'ayil, ah'-yil	from the same as H193;
All, kol	3605	kol kowl	or (Jeremiah 33.8) whole, all,
ALL, WHOLE, HEAL,	3605	kol kole	or (Jeremiah 33.8) whole, all, Heal, to be sound in mind and body metaphorically
Allah,	0426	'elahh (Aramaic)el'ah	God, god =
ALLAH,	0427	'allâh, al-law'	A variation of H424:—oak,
alpha	0441	'allûwph, al-loof'	,or (shortened) bullock, tame, chieftan,
ALPS LBN	3835	lâban, law-ban'	primitive root; white
Altar Et'her	6281	'Ether, eh'ther	from H6280; abundance; Ether, a place in Palestine:—Ether.
ALTAR	5849	'âṭar, aw-tar'	a primitive root;
ALTAR,	6279	'ât-har, aw-har'	a primitive root
ALUPH,	0441	'allûwph, al-loof'	; or (shortened)
Amen	0543	'amen	amen truly,
America,	5971	'am·me·ḵā Ammêka	The people of God, am=people, meka=Gods
Amon	0526	Amown, aw-mone	the same as H525; Amon, the name of three Israelites:—Amon.
Amown (Amen)	0525	'âmôwn, aw-mone'	from H539,
Anarkim,	6062	'Anaqiy, an-aw-kee'	patronymically from H6061
ANGEL King,	4397	mal'ak, ma a-wk	(see 4392 to WALK, carry message WORK
Angle	6121	'aqob	crooked, deceitful, polluted
Ani,	6060	'ânâq, aw-nawk	from H6059; Chain (around neck)
Ani,	6059	'ânaq, aw-nak'	prim. to choke neck restraint, collar
Ankel	6119	'âqêb, aw-kabe'	(feminine) עֲקֻבָּה heel, (ankle), curve bend
Ankh key of life	6060	'ânâq, aw-nawk	Egyptian hieroglyphic-Necklass, chain,
Anunnaki, Enoch	2585	Chanowk khan-oke'	Kha-noke, Anunnaki ? ANAK sons of god
ANYHOW,	2009	hinnêh, hin-nay'	prolongation for H2005; lo!, behold, lo, see.
Apple tree	8598	tappuwach, t'appuwa'ch	apple tree, apple
Arab	6148	'arab	surety, meddle, mingled, pledges, becometh,
ARAB	6160	'arabah, ar-aw-baw'	fm H6150 (in the sense of sterility); a desert
Arab or arabia	6163	'Arabiy, ar-aw-bee'	Arabian=desert wilderness
ARAM GERMAN	0758	Aram, arawm	from the same as H759;
ARAMAIC,	0762	Ărâmîyth, (Germanic)	feminine of H761 Assyrian Language
ARK box chest,	0270	'âchaz, aw-khaz'	primitive root; to seize
ARK,	0717	'ârôwn, or awr-own	'ârôn; from H717
Ark, Noah-no work	5118	nûwach, no'-akh	nôwach; No WORK, Noah, Rest
Ark, Noah-no work	5146	Noach, no'-akh	the same as H5118;
Ark, our own-Aaron	0727	'arown, aw-rone	or אָרֹן 'ârôn; Aleph Resh Wow/Vav Nun
Arm's length	0521	'ammâh, am-maw'	(Aramaic) corresponding to H520:—cubit.
Arrow, pluck bow	0717	'ârâh, aw-raw'	prim. to pluck, gather, see 3384
Arrow, y awrah	3384	yârâh, yaw-raw'	arrow, shoot
Arrow, y awrah	3372	yârê', yaw-ray'	prim. to fear; morally to revere; to frighten
ARSE,Arsehole	2048	hâthal, haw-thal	primitive root; deride, cheat At'hal
Artificial todo/make	6213	'âsâh, aw-saw'	prim. to do or make
ASAR, Ten,	6240	'âshêrâh, ash-ay-raw'	for H6235; teen; also (ordinal) -teenth
Ash color,	0806	Ashchûwr, ash-khoor'	probably from H7835;

Description	Strong#	Name-Pronounced	Etymology - Meaning
Ash pot	0830	'ashpoth	dung, dunghill as in pile up, waste
Ashteroth house	1045	Bêyth 'Ashtârôwth, bayth ash-taw-roth'	from H1004 and H6252; house of Ashtoreths
Ass Fart,	0830	sheʰphôthor ash-pohth	'ashpôth, ash-pohth'; ash-phth- filth-dung
Ass hole,	0811	'eshkowl, esh-kowl	Used Cluser of Grapes fm h810 testicles
Asshole, hat'hol,	2048	Hathal hawt'hal	Prim. deceive, mock
Asshur, Ashur,	0804	'Ashshûwr, ash-shoor	or אשר 'Ashshur; founder of Assyria-Shem
Assyria-German	0805	'Ashuwriy	Asshurim, Ashurites Aramaic-AGermanic
Assyria	0839	'ashur	Ashurites Ashurites Aramaic-AGermanic
Assyria, contend	3377	Yârêb, yaw-rabe	fm H7378 to contend, symbolic Ass'yria
Astarte, A'star	6255	'Ashtĕroth Qarnayim	Form of Ishtar (East Semitic) idle
ASTARTI TAROT,	6251	'ashtᵉrâh, ash-ter-aw'	probably from H6238; increase:—flock.
Autumn	0132	'admônîy, ad-mo-nee'	or (fully) אַדְמוֹנִי ',
BAAL	1166	bâ'al, baw-al'	prim ; Belzebub, pagan god.
Baalzebub,	1176	Ba'al Zᵉbûwb,	from H1168 and H2070; bah'-al zeb-oob'
Babble,	1680	dababdaw-bab	cause to speak root is a double BB,
Babble,	0894	babel, babble-baw el	Babylon, gate of god- Bab-el Akkadian
Babe, & Baby	0003	'êb, abebə·'ib·bê	from the same as H24;
Babel,	0894	Babelbaw-bel'	Babylon, gate of god- Bab-el Assyrian
Baby,	0024	'âbîyb, aw-beeb'	from an unused root, young sweet thing.
Babylon	0895	Babel baw-lal	Babylon , Babylonian, Babel (Aramaic)
Bagpipe	5035	nebel, neh'-bel	or נבל nêbel; from H5034; bagpipe
Bail, Bill-protector	1167	ba'al, bah'-al	from H1166; master; hence, a husband
BAIL, Bale, hay	1101	Balal, baw-lal'	Pr. to fodder to overflow, mix c-Babble
Bale of hay-	0058	'âbêl, aw-bale'	meaning to be grassy, a meadow
BALE, BALL,	1098	bᵉlîyl, bel-eel'	fm H1101 mixed, i.e. feed (for cattle)
Bale,	5034	nâbêl, naw-bale'	to wilt; generally, to fall away
Ball, he Blow	1895	Hebel heh'bel	? Blow, Abel-breath, Bellows-edenics
Ball, Cry	1892	hebel, heh'bel	emptiness or vanity;
BAR d'Var(t)	1696	dabar	speak, talk, promise, tell, commune, WORD
BAR,	1270	barzel, bar-zel'	Refined iron, pure see Persia (Per=pure)
Bar, soap-get clean	1249	bar	clean, pure, choice, clear
BAR'GAIN	6161	ărubbâh, ar-oob-baw'	feminine passive participle of H6048
BARLEY	1250	bar	Barley, grains are used for beer sold in a bar.
Barley ears	8181	se`ar see-hawr'	Hair disheveled or tossed.
Barn, Build, BEAR	1129	bânâh, baw-naw'	p. family, build, Ben, Bairn, bearn. se-Parah
BASH,	1319	bâshaç, baw-shas	p. trample down-tread.
Bashful,	3001	yabesh ye-bashe'	Bashful – to be bashful YeBashe, ashamed.
Bawl, I bawl	0056	abal aw-bal'	mourn, (by extension to cry)
BEAR PEAR,	6509	pârâh, paw-raw'	P. root bear, bring forth (fruit) see Ben (son)
Bear young,	6509	pârâh, paw-raw'	P. root bear, bring forth (fruit) IE root*bher-
Bee D'Bee	1682	dᵉbôwrâh, deb-o-raw'	r (shortened) דברה dᵉbôrâh; debby D'BEE
Beelzebub	1168	Ba'al, bah'-al	the same as H1167;
Beer, stout	0047	'abbiyrab-beer'	from H46, Mighty, stout, strong, angel, bull,
Beginning	7228	B' rê'shîyth, ray-sheeth'	from the same as H7218;
Belch or Beoch,	0889	bᵉ'oshor be(l)'och	stench, foul odour
Bellows,	5748	`uwgab	noun masculine (עוּגָב a musical instrument
Belly button	0990	Beten beh'-ten	belly button, belly, womb, body
Belteshazzar	1095	Beltᵉsha'tstsar	Belteshazzar
Ben, Bonnie	1121	bên, bane	Fm H1129; son (as a builder of the family)
Bereshiyth	7225	re'shiyth, bereshit	Head start, beginning, bear sheet blank-Resh
Bethel-	1008	Beyth-'El bayth-ale'	from H1004 and H410; house of God.
Betroth, a'troth	5854	'Atrowth beyth Yow'ab	Betroth-promise in marrage, 2houses to1
between, beyne	0996	bêyn, ba(t)yne	between (-twixt...and)
BIG (*EDENICS)	1060	BᵉKôWR, bek-ore'	from H1069; first-born
BIG COW	1060	BᵉKôWR, bek-ore'	first-born; hence, chief, eldest (son).
Biro, as in pen	0875	biro	spring of water, (fountain-pen-biro)
Birth Lady-lad(y)	3205	Ya'lady	beget, bear,
BLACK, BURN,	1814	dᵉlaq, del-ak'	p. root; to flame, to be darkened by sun
Block, clog, cowgirl	7259	Ribqâh, rib-kaw, rope cow, see Gesenius	to clog by tying up the fetlock; fettering (by beauty) Rebekah wife of Isaac.

354

Description	Strong#	Name-Pronounced	Etymology - Meaning
Blow,	1893	Hebel heh'-bel	Abel-= "breath"
Blush,	0954	Buwsh, boosh	ashamed,
Bonnie,	1121	bên, bane	from H1129 son of, builder of the family
Bonny	1129	banah baw-naw'	P.root obtain children, make, repair, set (up),
Bottom,	0992	boten bo'-ten	from 990, pistachio-nut (from its form-but)
Bow,	3721	Kaphaph, kap-haph	P. root to curve:—bow down (self).
Breach, Perez Break	6557	Perets	Pret (BREAK) or Pharez = "breach"
BREAK (free)	1272	bârach, baw-rakh'	p. root figuratively, to flee suddenly:
Break Break,	6561	paraq	break off,
Breastplate, Teets, tsits TIT, TEAT's	6731	tsîyts, tseets	tsits; fm H6692, Brests boobs, shiny object, bloom, see h4711 MaTits – brest feeding.
Britannia	1285	Brit'am'yah, See Isa 49,8	Covenant people of God 3050, 5971, 1285
British, Brit'ish	0376	'iysh (Brit)'ish	man, men, one, husband, any, misc
BRITISH, BRITS covenant people,	1285	Brits	Covenant people of God, 3050, 5971, 1285
Brit'on	0202	own or on and Brit	Covenent, strength,
BRO,	1320	bâsâr, baw-sawr'	ria H1319; flesh, brother, person, pudenda
Brother	1730	dowd	beloved, uncle, family member
Buck	0947	buwc	Trample tread (down, under (foot))
BUL BITCH.	1078	Bêl, bale	contraction H1168; Baal of the Babylonians,
Bull from Blow,	0059	Hebel heh'-bel	Abel-= "breath" as in a Bellohs,
Bull, buwl	0944	bûwl, bool	from H2981; buwl bool food stock
Bull,	2981	yᵉbûwl, yeᵓ-ool'	from H2986; produce, i.e. a crop or fruit.
Bullock Tor	6499	par, par	fm H6565; bullock-wild strength?
Bully nE p'hilly,	5303	Nᵉphîyl neᵗ-eel'	e bully, ne' feel'; to Bully, cause to fall-feller
Bush Blush	0954	Buwsh boosh	ashamed,
Buwl,	0945	bûwl, bool	"increase: (buwlshit -no increase),
Cad is,	6945	qadesh, kawd-a she'	male temple prostitute sodomite,
Cain kin folk	7014	Qayin, kah-yin	the same as H7013
Cain	7014	Qayin Cain	God left a mark on Cane, (Ken)Cain'ed him.
CAIN, stick or lance	7013	qayin, kah-yin	from H6969 stick or lance
Cainan, Kenan	7018	Qeynan	Cainan, Kenan
CALL, HOWL	6963	qowl kole	Call, to call aloud
Camel	1581	Gamel gam-el	camel and to deal well with me
Canaanites in	3669	Kᵉna anîy, ken-ah-an'ee	patrial from H3667
CANE "	7069	qânâh, kaw-naw'	primitive root
Canine,	3612	Kâlêb, kaw-lae(b)	perhaps a form of H3611,
CAP, Captor	3731	Kaphᵗ'tôr, kaf-tore'	Cap a head cover also meaning to encircle.
Capture see 3731	3290	ya'âqᵓb Jacob	yah-ak-obe'; caught his brothers heel-YANK
Capture?	3791	kâthâb, kaw-thawb'	from H3789;
Car,	3733	kar, kar	Camel saddle, (caravan-string of camels)
Cart, agalah	5699	ʿagalah	cart, wagon, chariot
Catch it, shoot at?	7198	Qeshʿeth, keh'-sheth	from H7185 bending; a bow, for shooting
Caught	2338	chuwᵗ (Aramaic)	joined, caught, to string together,
caught	5640	Çâtham caf'hm	a primitive root; keep secret:—closed up,
Caught, kuwat	2338	chûwt, khoot	caught, to string together
Change / Sin	8133	shna' (shen-aw')	alter, change,
change, chana	8132	shânâ', shaw-naw'	a primitive root; to alter, change.
Chariot	2742	chârûᵌts, khaw-roots'	a threshing-sledge (having sharp teeth); etc.
Chased, holy,	2623	chacîyd, khaw-seed'	from H2616; Holy dedicated, pious (a saint)
Cheer	2416	chay	live, life, alive, creature, running.
Cheer	2418	chaya' (Aramaic)	live, kept alive
Cheerio, cheer-hiya	2421	Chayah khaw-yaw'	Prim. root causatively, to revive, keep alive
Chet (shit-terror)	2845	Chêth, khayth	from H2865; terror; Cheth, an aboriginal Canaanite, Heth.
Chill, Curl, whirl	2342	chûwl, khool	Prim. Root to twist or whirl, dance.
Chin, cheek chiy(n)	3895	lᵉchîy, lekh-ee'	meaning to be soft; cheek or chin
Chosen,	2833	choshen, or khoshen	The high priest-chôshen, breastplate
Chosen, shozeh,	2374	chozeh	seer, see, agreement, prophets, stargazers
CIFER,	5609	çᵉphaᵣ, sef-ar'	; (Aramaic) H5608; a book, roll.
CIFER,.	5610	çᵉphâr, sef-awr'	from H5608; a census:—numbering.
Cipher,	5611	Çᵉphᵃr, seᵗ-awr'	the same as H5610;

355

Description	Strong#	Name-Pronounced	Etymology - Meaning
CIPHER,	5608	Caphar çiphar,	scribe, tell,
CIRCULAR,	2341	Chăvîylâh, khav-ee-law'	probably from H2342; circular; Chavilah
CIRCULAR,	3603	kikkâr, kik-kawr'	from H3769; a circle, i.e. (by implication) a circumjacent tract or region, also coin
CIRCULE	2343	Chûwl, khool	from H2342; circle
Cirle,	2328	chûwg, khoog	primitive root H2287 a circle, compass.
CLAP, Cap'h'k	5606	çâphaq, saw-fak'	to clap the hands compact or derision.
Cliff,	5585	çâ'îyph, saw-eef'	from H5586; branch, clift, top
Cliff,	5587	çâ'iph, saw-eef'	Fm H5586; divided (in mind),
Coat- shirt	3801	kĕthoneth, ket'h-o'-neth	coat, garment, robe -
Coat-half	3802	kâthêph, kawt-hafe'	from an unused root meaning to clothe;
Cobble together	3525	kebel, cobble	to twine or braid together; a fetter
Collie, Kâlê[b]	3612	Kâlêb, kaw-lae(b)	perhaps a form of H3611, Dog
COME to arise,	6966	qûwm, koom	(Aramaic) corresponding to H6965 arise.
COME to be,	6965	Quwm küm	Prim. rise (up), (make to) stand, set (up).
Consumption-	5486	Cuwph Cough?	a primitive root; to snatch away
Cord, khoot	2339	chûwṭ, khoot	unused root probably meaning to sew;
CORN - HORN	7161	qeren, keh'-ren	from H7160; a horn, a flask, cornet
Cotton Kaf Tav	3802	K'T'N	Linnen garment from root כתן see twot
Cough Kay(f)	6892	qe'kay	vomit-or קיא qîy'
Cough,	6958	qow'PH, kow'ph,	vomit, spue-, or קָיָה qâyâh;
Court, square	2691	châtsêr, khaw-tsare'	court, tower, village
COVER Cap,	3722	Kaphar cover	atonement, purge, reconciliation, reconcile,
Cover, Me Cover	4533	Ma'çveh, mas-veh'	apparently meaning to cover; a veil, vail.
Cover, to live,	2331	châyâh, khaw-yaw'	a primitive root
Cow, achowr rear parts	0268	'âchôwr, 'â-chôwr,	a general term for the rear parts, and could be the origin of the word cow
Crete	3731	Kaphtor Kap'h'tôwr	, kaf-tore'; or (Amos 9:7) Crete?
Crowd, gowd	1464	gûwd, goode	a primitive root (akin to H1413); Crowd
CROWDY	1471	gôwy, go'-ee	rarely (shortened) גֹּי gôy; mass of people
Cubit Span,	1574	gômed, go'-med	from an unused root
Cumri	6018	'Omriy om-ree'	Omri- from H6014; (CUMRI Welsh)
CUP,.	3709	kaph, kaf	from H3721; the hollow hand or palm
CURL COOL	2342	chûwl, khool	or חיל chîyl; (patiently), be wounded.
CUTS CAR	2782	chârats, khaw-rats'	primitive root;
Cymbri Omry,	6018	'Omrîy, om-ree'	from H6014; heaping; Omri, an Israelite.
Cyrus KYRO,	3566	Kôwresh, ko'-resh or	(Ezra 1:1-2 (last time) CYRUS
DAD Dowd	1730	dowd	beloved
Dad- POP, Pap's	1717	Dad dad	sign of ownership, her **breast** belong to him
Dad,	0111	Adad, ad-ad, a dad	Hadad, mighty man
Dad, Chadad	2301	Chadad khad-ad'	Hadad "I shall move softly; I shall love"
Dad, El dad	0419	'Eldad, el-dad'	Eldad God is love Dad -el=God
Dada,	1736	dûwday, doo-dah'-ee	mandrake ancient drugs for fertility
Dam	2457	dam- 'iyr dam-iyr	Blood, live is in the blood
Dam Husband	1818	dā-mîm, Dam	Moses called Dam husband for circumcision
Damah,ian, dimyown	1819	Dâmâh , Daw-maw	Similitude copy, Dadaian to follow God, or to be a student of Yah
Damian	1825	dimyôwn, dim-yone'	fr H1819 alike, imagination, meditation
Dan	1835	Dân, D'n, Don, Dan,	Dan means Judge
Dan Patriotic Danny	1839	Dânîy, daw-nee'	patronymically from H1835;
Dancing-	4234	machowl, maw-khole'	from H2342; a (round) dance, dance(-cing).
Dangle,	1802	dâlâh, daw-law'	Prim. root to deliver:—draw (out),
Daniel	1840	Daniye'l Daniel	Daniel
Danyan	1842	Dan Ya'an – Dan'jaan	="purposeful judgment"
DARIUS	1867	Dârᶜyâvêsh,	of Persian origin the Persian
Darius	1868	Dârᶜyâvêsh,	(Aramaic)
DARK	1815	dᵉlaq, del-ak'	(Aramaic) burnt (by sun or fire)
David Tafy	1732	David, daw-veed'	King David, H1730; loving; David,
DAY,	0116	'ĕ day in, bê·day	that day-A day-pass by, bê·day-in-29 Occ.
DAY, EON, to	3117	Yô'W'M, YoW'M; יוֹם	meaning to be hot, by sun You WarM
Debar (v.)	1703	dabbarah	intensive from H1696; a word:—word.
Debarred	1696	dabar	speak, say

356

Description	Strong#	Name-Pronounced	Etymology - Meaning
Debroah,	1683	Dᵉbôwrâh, deb-o-raw'	or (shortened)
Den,	7064	qên, kane	contracted from H7077;
Devil, evil	5760	'aviyl aw-val'	a primitive root; to stray, evil.
DINO,	8565	tan, tan	from an unused root
DINOSAUR,	8577	tannîyn, tan-neen'	or תַּנִּים tannîym;
Direct	1870	derek, deh'-rek	from H1869;
DON	0113	'âdôwn, aw-done'	or (shortened) adon Teacher Lord
Don, A don	0113	adown aw-done'	adon Teacher Lord
DON,	0136	'Adonayad-o-noy	God is our Teacher,
Door	1800	dal, dal	from H1809; door
Door Dalet D-	1817	deleth, deh'-leth	from H1802 something swinging
DOWN	1835	Dân, dawn	from H1777 Dan tibe of Judge, (policeman)
DRAG	1869	dârak, daw-rak'	a prim. root. Tread wals down, (tail) drew
DRAG	8376	ta'ah taw-aw'	Last letter Alephbet, mark, draw out (Cross)
DRAG,	1869	darak	tread, bend
DRAW,	8582	tâ'ar, taw-ar'	a primitive root; Draw, mark out
DRAW,	8388	ta'artaw-ar'	a primitive root; to drawn, mark out,
Dress, A dress	0155	addereth, ad-deh'-reth	a wide garment like a dress,
Drink, get drunk	8354	shâthâh, shaw-thaw'	p.r. to imbibe, (get drunk shitty)
Drip ZR(z)	2222	zarzîyph, zar-zeef	Flow, pounding rain
Dude,	1730	dôwd, dode	or boil, with love, love-token, lover, friend;
Dumb	1748	duwmam	silent
DUMB,	1826	dâmam, dâmam,	Meditate (silent meditation)
DUMB,	1748	duwmamcheers	silent, quietly wait, dumb
Dun Hillfort	0113	'âdôwn, aw-done'	To rule (celtic hill fort-where ruler lived?)
EAGLE,	0398	'âkal, aw-kal'	p.r. burn up eat devower
Eber or ivr -5674;	5676	'êber, ay'-ber	region beyond, OVER there, across (river)
Edom E dommy,	0123	'Edom	Edom, Edomites, Idumea-ed-ome';
Edomie,	0130	'EdomiyEdomite(s),	Syria-ed-o-mee'; or (fully) Ĕdôwmîy ;
Eglah,	5697	'eglah	heifer, cow, calf
Eglah,	5698	'Eglâh, eg-law'	the same as H5697; Cow (Davids wife)
Egypt -	4714	Mitsrayim	Egypt, Egyptian, Mizraim, Egyptians
El ALL -	0410	'elel or hell	God, god, power, mighty
ELAM,	5769	'ôwlâm, o-lawm	or עֹלָם 'ôlâm; from H5956;
Elephant,	0504	'eleph, eh'-lef	kine, oxen, family, from H502;
Elijah, El e Yah,	0452	Eliyah Elijah	Elijah, Eliah -El u Yah ot El he Yah
Elohim,	0430	'ĕlôhîym, el-o-heem'	plural of H433; Lord
English,	5695	'egel	calf, bullock see Exo 32.4
E'P'HoR	6081	'Épher, ay'-fer	Epher =calf frisking gazelle
Ephraim	0669	'Ephrayim E frawth?	ef-rawth'; e fruity double fruit
Ephraim, Fruity,	0673	'Ephrathiyef-rawth-ee'	Ephrathite, e-fruity
Esau	6215	'Esavay-sawv'	apparently a form of the passive participle
ESPY, SPY,	6822	tsâphâh, tsaw-faw	Watch tower, see far
Etruscan-Rasna rasa	7218	rô'sh, roshe	7217, Head, top, chief, race
Eve	2331	châvâh, khaw-vah'	Adams wife-Eve life giver CHEER
Evil	5760	aviyl av-eel'	from 5765; evil, deceitful
Evil Awful	5765	'ăval aw-val'	a primitive root;
Evil Devil	5766	'evel, eh'-vel	or עֶוֶל 'âvel; evil
Evil	5767	'avvâl, av-vawl'	; intensive from H5765;
Evil Eye	5770	'âvan, aw-van'	Fm H5869; to watch (with jealosy),eye
Exactly, hope so	0305	achalay, ak-ha-l-ah'ee	O that, would God (be that so)
Expel,	1892	hebel, heh'bel	emptiness or vanity, (empty) windbag
Eye Aramaic	5870	'ayin, ah'-yin	(Aramaic) corresponding to H5869; Eye
Eye fountain	5871	'Ayin, ah'-yin	the same as H5869; Eye
Eye, Eyes,	5869	Ayin ayin	Eye, sight, seem,
Fair,	3302	yâphâh, yaw-faw'	primitive root; handsome comeliness
Fall, aweful, fallen	5307	Na'phal'n-aw-fal'	fall, fall down, to cast down (cause to fall)
Fart,	0830	'ashpôth, or-ash-pohth	'ashpôth, or-ash-pohth'; smell bad, odor
FARCI see PURE	6539	Pāras פָּרַס (PHaRSi)	Persian PURE, see PURE
Feller,	5303	nᵉphîyl, nef-eel'	or נְפִל nᵉphil; from H5307; Giant, bully feller
Firstborn,	1062	bᵉkôwrâh, bek-o-raw'	(short) בְּכֹרָה bᵉkôrâh; firstborn

357

Description	Strong#	Name-Pronounced	Etymology - Meaning
Firstborn,	1069	bakar	firstborn, new fruit, firstling, first child
Firstfruit,	7225	re'shiyth, ray-sheeth'	from the same as H7218; first fruit
Firstfruit,	1061	bikkuwr	firstfruit, firstripe, firstripe figs,hasty fruit
Fruity,	0673	'Ephrathiyef-rawth-ee'	Ephrathite, Ephraimite ; p
FUCKER, A ffxx	2018	hăphêkâh, haf-ay-kaw'	fem H2016; destruction, overthrow overturn
Fuxx pack, group of	2019	hăphakpak, hafak-pak'	fm H2015; Sodom & Gomorrah deborturay
Gad,	1409	gad, gawd	fm H1464 tribe of GAD, fortune:—troop
Gadhal, got old	1419	gadowl	H1419 stately old person, great
Gael	1350	ga'al gaw-al	marry his widow primitive root, redeem
Gael, gal'h	1353	gĕullah	redeem, redemption, again, kindred, redeem,
GAEL, GAUL,	1567	Gal'êd,gal-ade'	H1530 & H5707; heap of testimony; Galed, a memorial cairn
Gag, Laag,	3932	lâ'ag, law-ag	primitive root; to delay, pause, lagg
Gagging, haw gag	2287	châgag, khaw-gag'	reel to and from drunkenness-
Gall you have	1351	gâ'al, gaw-al'	primitive root, redeem, kindsman, avenge
Gamal	1580	gâmal, gaw-mal'	primitive root; Camel
GARDEN,	1598	gânan, gaw-nan'	primitive root; garden, to hedge in or about
Garden,	1631	garzen, gar-zen'	(Gesenius), act of cutting wood, to garden
GAY	2292	Chaggay, khag-gah'-ee	Happy, joyful, from H2282;
GAZE	2372	châzâh, khaw-zaw'	primitive root; to see to look at, stair at.
GENE beget,	7069	qânâh, kaw-naw'	Prim. root; Genesis, beginning Kin, Cane
GENESIS BERSIT,	7225	re'shiyth	Beginning, clean sheet, from nothing
GENESIS,	7069	qanah, kaw-naw'	to bear, beginning, Kin, Cane, manKIND
Genetically altered	3610	kil'ayim, kil-ah'-yim	dual H3608 divers seeds, mingled (seed)
Gentiles,	1471	gôwy, go'-ee	Crowdy, mass of people (Gentiles-Israel)
GERMAN	0759	'armôwn, ar-mone'	unused root elevated - castle, palace
GERMAN	0760	'Ăram Tsôwbâh,	from H758 and H6678; son of Shem Syria
GERMAN	6019	Amrâm, am-rawm'	probably from H5971 elevated people
German,	7018	Qeynan, kay-nawn'	fm the same as H7064; Kenan antideluvian
GERMANY-	0761	'Ărammîy, ar-am-mee'	patrial fm H758; Armenian Syrian (Shem)
Gerrymandering	3379	Yarob`amYa rob am	Jeroboam = "the people will contend"
GEYSER (spring)	1521	Gîychôwn,	גִּיחוֹן Gichôwn river of paradise Gihon-spring
Ghoul, Goel,	1352	gô'el, go'-el	from H1351; profanation:
Giants, Nephily	5303	Nĕphiyl nef-eel'	or נָפַל nᵉphil; from H5307; Giant bully
Giddy, giyl'(ee)	1524	gîyl, gheel	from H1523; a revolution (spinning) time
Giddy,	2287	châgag, khaw-gag'	a festival to be giddy
GIDEON,	1441	Gid'ônîy, ghid-o-nee'	from H1438; warlike, (the Judge)
Gig, H'G'G, ha gig.	2287	châgag, khaw-gag'	a festival, religious and otherwise
Gimel,	1457	gâhar, gaw-har'	to prostrate oneself:—cast self down
Girl excitable,	1523	gîyl, gheel	to spin round with vilent emotion
Give hollow (back)	1465	gêvâh, gay-vaw'	feminine of H1460; hollow in the back
GNAW,	1641	gârar, gaw-rar'	a primitive root; ruminate
Goal, kick-ball-net	5696	aw-gole aw-gole	meaning to revolve (circle), ball
Goal, (Egla'ish) Ephraim, Leaders	5695	eglâh, eg-law';	A young bull yoked with older for 3 year training period (see hos 11.10)
God Heal, see1419	1431	gâdal, gaw-dal'	advance, boast, bring up, exceed, excellent,
GOD, is, Holy	6944	Qôdesh God'esh	Holy, self exisitant God-Exo 3:5-holy ground
Godal	1419	gadowl	or גָּדוֹל gâdôl; to get old, stately
Goddess,	6945	qadesh	sodomite, unclean
Godel, Godheal	1433	gôdel, go'-del	from H1431;
God's-set apart-holy	6942	qâdash, kaw-dash	p.r. to consecrate, sanctify, to be holy.
GOD (esHoly)	6944	Qōḏeš קֹדֶשׁ	holy, sanctuary, holiness, dedicated,
Good -tob	2896	tôḇ	good, better, from H2895
GOOD GOD (holy)	6944	God'esh God'esh	Good from God and God from Qod'esh,
Goodbye,	8582	Ta'ah Ta-Ta'rah	Good bye as in the Tav of Ps 119.176
GOSPEL, God spell	5608	**çâphar**, saw-far(cphel)	Good spell, to score with a mark, write.
Got old,	1419	gâdôwl, gaw-dole'	Stately, great, elder, See 1431
Grab,	6117	'âqab, aw-kab'	Yank, root of Jacob see Ankel, angel
Grab, heel,	6119	'âqêb, aw-kabe'	heel, footsteps,
Great Bear	5906	'Ayish, ah'-yish	or עָשׁ 'Ash; from H5789;
Grind Grain	1637	GoReN go'-ren	from an unused root meaning to smooth;

358

Description	Strong#	Name-Pronounced	Etymology - Meaning
GUARD,	1588	gan, gan	from H1598; a garden (as fenced):—garden.
GUSH GiYCH	1518	gîyach, gh ee'-akh	or (shortened) גָּח gôach; a primitive root;
GUSH,	1521	Gîychôwr -ghee-khone	(shortened) גִּיחוֹן Gichôwn; Natural spring
HAIL,	1984	halal, hal al-all hail	praise,
Hail, All hail, EL u Yah	3094	Yᵉhallel'ê , yeh-hal-lel-ale'	from H1984 and H410 proclaim, shout announce, greet
Hail,	1984	hâlal, haw-lal'	primitive root; hail, yell, proclaim announce
Hail,ᵉhaalHail,ᵉhaal	7592	shâ'al, shaw-al'	to inquire; to request; by extension
HAIR, A hair,	8185	sa`arah sah-ar-aw'	sah-ar-aw'; feminine of H8181;
Hair, se hr	8177	sᵉ'ar, se ha-' s@'ar	hair (Aramaic) corresponding to H8181;
Hair,	8181	se`ar se`a see-hawr'	Hair disheveled or tossed or שֵׂעָר sa`ar;
Hairy-Barley	8184	sᵉ'ôrâh, se-hora'	From hairy ears or שְׂעוֹרָה sᵉ'ôwrâh
Halal, Hillel see	1985	Hillel hil-layl'	from H1984; praising (namely God)
Hammer	8104	shâmar, sHawmar'	a primitive root; properly;
Handsome, fair	3303	yâpheh, ya w-feh'	from H3302 comley, handsome
HARBOR Charmer	2266	châbar, ha bar'	To Charm, to tie magic charms, unite, ally
Harbor,	3528	kâbar, kaw-bar'	P.r. extent of time, (eon); hence, long ago
Harbor Habor	2249	Châbôwr, khaw-bore';	United fm 2266, see Kebar 3529
Harbor	3529	Kᵉbâr, keb-awr';	Chebar = "far-off" H3528; length; H2249.
Harm not,	7999	shâlam, shaw-lam	a primitive root; to be safe
Have- Breath-eve	2331	châvâh, khaw-vah	p.r. tell, declare, show, make known, breath
HAZY, HAZE	2377	châzôwn, knaw-zone'	from H2372;
He,	1931	hu	He, in the following manner:
Heal, (peel)	3416	Ir'peel. yir'ɔ e hele'	Ir'peel to heal (yur peel(ed))
Heart ?	3824	lêbâb, lay-bawb'	from H3823;
Hebrew	5680	'Ibriy	Hebrew, Hebrew woman, Hebrew,
Hebrideses,	5680	'Ibriy, ib-ree or ebro	patronymic from H5677
Hebrite	5680	'Ibrîy, ib-reɔ, Eberite	patronymic from H5677;
Heckel,	2048	hathal haw-hal'	a primitive root; to deride;
Heel -	6127	'âqal, aw-kɛl'	primitive root; see edenics from ankle
Heel, see 6127	6120	'âqêb, aw-kabe'	from H6117 in its denominative sense;
HEIFER Epher	6081	'Êpher, ay'-fer	Epher steer, ox
Hell hole,	7585	shᵉ'ôwl, sheh-ole'	or שְׁאֹל shᵉ'ôl; Grave underworld, hell, pit
Hell, KHELL	3622	Kěluw hay-chelluh-c hell	from a root meaning to die to pass away
Hen, Nest,	7064	qēn kane	contracted from H7077;
Hero,	2220	zᵉrôwaʿ, zer-o'-ah or	arm (symbol of strength) forces (political & military)
HeTzR Huts,	2691	châtsêr, khaw-tsare'	(masculine and feminine);
hEVA Breath	1933	hâvâ', haw-vaw'	hâvâh; ([br]hava-breathe, exist i.e. have)
Hey-	2268	CheberHeber	kheh'-ber;
HeyBro, Eber –	5676	'êber, lɔ 'eḅ rōw — 1 Occ.	eber ay'-ber from 5674;
Hi, Hiyah,	1961	hayah	was, come to pass, came,
High five Hey	2651	chô'ph en, kho'-fen, Hey Ph'n	from an unused root of uncertain signification;
Hill Heap Tameru	8564	tamrûwr, tam-roor'	from the same root as H8558;
Him,	8034	shem	name,
Hip hip hurray,	8597	tiph'arah	to acknowledge someone -
Hiss from	5175	nâchâsh, naw-khawsh'	from H5172;
HISS,	5172	nâchash, naw-khash'	a primitive root;
Hit,	3709	kaphkaf	hollow or flat of the hand,
Hiyah ehyah	1961	'eh-yeh	Here we have Strong silent type A,
Ho Fuxx,	2017	hôphek, ho'-fek	from H2015;
HOLY father	0171	b"-holi abba ɔ-holi-ab	Fathers tent-guy who built tabernacle
Holy Judah,	0172	'Ohŏlîybâh,	(similarly with H170)
Home,	4349	Makown mak own	place, habitation, foundations
Horeb,	2717	chârab, khaw-rab'	or חֶרֶב chârêb; a primitive root;
Horeb, see buwl,	2722	Chôrêb, kho-rabe'	Horeb from H2717;
Horeb-Bull,	0944	bûwl, bool	from H2981; produce (of the earth, etc)
Horeb-Bullshxx,	0944	Buwl, shittah	Land, and produce hurting lack of rain
HORN,	7161	qeren, keh'-rɛn	from H7160; tooth tusk, horn, (elephant)
Horns,	7160	qaran	to push or gore, shine, has horns
Horrid,	2719	chereb	sword

359

Description	Strong#	Name-Pronounced	Etymology - Meaning
HORROR, Horrid	2717	chârab, khaw-rab'	or חָרֵב chărêb; a primitive root;
HORSE	2790	chârash, khaw-rash'	primitive root;
HORSE?	2392	chozeq	strength
Hosanna	1954	Hôwshêa', ho-shay'-ah	from H3467;
Hosea, Jose	1954	Hôwshêa', ho-shay'-ah	from H3467;
Hossana,	1955	Hoshayah	"Yah has saved"
HOTEL,	0168	'ohel	Tabernacle meeting place.
HOUSE court	2691	châtsêr, khaw-tsare'	Court, hamlet, surrounded by wall
House of millo,	1037	Bêyth Millôw',	or בֵּית מִלֹּא Bêyth Millô'; house of Milo
House, Bayith,	1004	Bayith bah'-yith	probably from H1129 abbreviated;
HOUSE, STORE	0214	ow'tsaro-tsaw' (our store)	treasure(s), house, store, cellar, armoury
Hug ah, haw gaw	2283	châgâ', khaw-gaw	; from an unused root meaning to revolve
Hug see ha gag	2328	chûwg, khoog	a primitive root
HUG, BOW,	2329	chûwg, khoog	from H2328; a circle, circuit, compass,
Huts,	2690	chatsar	a primitive root; surround with stockade
I saw, Haw zaw	2372	châzâh, ha zaw	a primitive root; to gaze at, to perceive.
I, AYE, YES	7069	qânâh, kaw-naw'	Primitive root; be erect, create (I am?)
Ireland,	6147	'Er luwn-d'(n)	lodge, murmur,
Irish- -	3423	Yârash yaw-rash	yârêsh; a primitive root; to occupy
Irish,	6147	'Er ish Irish	Er became the father of the Jews
Iron?	0738	'ariyar-ee'	lion, untranslated variant-
Isaac	3446	Yischâq yis-khawk	from H7831; he will laugh;
ISH, ISH SHE, HE,	0802	'ishshâh, ish-shaw'	feminine of H376 or H582;
Isle	0336	'îy, ee	probably identical with H335
Israel & Israelite	3481	Yisre'eliy	Israel, Israelite
Israel Aramaic	3479	Yisrâ'êl, yis-raw-ale'	(Aramaic) corresponding to H3478:—Israel.
Israel,	3478	Yisra'el, yis-raw-ale'	from H8280 (Sarah) and H410;
Israelite femal	3482	Yisre'eliyth	Israelitess
Jack, see Yah, or Yah see Yach (Jack)	3167	Yachz°yâh, yakh-zeh-yaw	from H2372 and H3050; Jehovah views" Yah will behold;
Jacob	3290	Ya`aqob Jacob	Father of Israel
Jehovah,	3068	Y°hovah, yeh-ho-vaw'	LORD, GOD, JEHOVAH,
Jeremiah, Im here	3414	Yirm°yah- Emhear –	Jeremiah (Amihear 'phin, gin)
Jeroboam	3379	Yarob'amYa rob am	Jeroboam (Ye Rob em)
Jeshurun just u run	3484	Y°shu rûwn,	from H3474; to grow fat (LOL)
Jewish language	3066	Y°huwdiyth	Jews' language, Jews' speech
Jezebel, Isabel	0348	'IyzebelJezebel	Jezebel
JOKE,	3446	Yischaqyis-khawk'	from H7831;
Joke,	6711	tsâchaq, tsaw-khak	primitive root;
Joke, Jake-saw joke	6711	tsachaq, tsa chok,	laugh, mock, sport, play
Joke, Joke'ab	3290	Ya`aqob	Jacob
Joke sa(w) Joke	7832	sachaq, saw-chak	to laugh (in pleasure or detraction)
Joke,	6712	ts°chôq, tse-khoke,	from H6711;
Joseph yo save	3084	Y°howceph, yeh-ho-safe'	Joseph ="Jehovah has added"-to accumulate
Joseph	3130	Yôwçêph, yo-safe'	future of H3254;
Joshua,	3442	Yeshuwa` yay-shoo'-ah	from H3091;
Joshua,	3091	Y°hôwshûwa',	Y°hôwshu'a; Ye How ShaVaH
Joshua-osheh	1954	Howshea` Howshea`	Oshea
ka pow, hit someone	3709	bə·kap·pōw b-kapow	use your hand,
Keanan, Canaan	3667	K°na'an, ken-ah'-an	from H3665;
Ken, Cain, cian	3665	kâna', kaw-nah'	primitive root;
Khumri	6018	OmriyKhumri	"pupil of Jehovah"
KIASER, Cesar, Zar	3803	kâthar, kaw-thar'	To enclose (garland) crown
Kill own?	3631	killâyôwn, kil-law-yone'	from H3615;
Kill terminate	3622	K°lûwhay, kel-oo-hah'-ee	Chelluh- from H3615 destruction, kill
Kill them,	3639	kĕlimmah, kel-im-maw'	from H3637 disgrace, to wound,
Kill them.	3637	kalamkawl-awm'	Disgrace figuratively
Kill, Whole	3632	kaliyl (Kiyl) kaw-leel'	perfect, Whole, sacrifice, perfection
Kill, weapon	3627	K°liy kel-ee'	from H3615-.vessel weapon, instrument
Killer, Kahleh,	3608	kele', keh'-leh	from H3607; a prison for killer
Killer, Kala,	3607	kâlâ', kaw-law'	Restrice (by law), hold in.
Killer, Kalah, finish	3615	kâlâh, kaw-law'	To end, cease

360

Description	Strong#	Name-Pronounced	Etymology - Meaning
Killown	3630	Kilyownki:-yone'	a form of H3631; suffer from desease.
KIND, Kin	7069	qanah, kaw-naw'	to bear, to create (like God)
KINFOLK, KIN	3669	Kěna`aniy, ken-ah-an-ee'	patrial from H3667 Cainine, (Arabic)
KINFOLK, KIN	3651	ken kane	Name of Able's brother Kane, as in cain
KIPPUR, KIPPAH,	3725	kippur, kiɼ-poor'	from H3722; Attonement, day of covering
KNOW, Knowledge	3559	kûwn, koo:1	Be erect, stand upwright
KOSHER,	3787	kâshêr, kaw-share'	To be straight or right (acceptable)
LaBaNA	3838	Lᵉbânâ', leb-aw-naw'	or לבנה H3842; Lebanon white mountain
Laban	3837	Laban L'b'n	White see also h3833-46
Lad, aw-lad	2056	valad vaw-lawd'	for 3206; a boy:--child.
Lad, boy ye led	3206	yeled	child, young man, sons, boy, fruit, variant
Lady, Girl, ya	3207	Yaldah ya l'a)dah	girl, damsel
lag, Laag,	3932	lâ'ag, law-ag	Deride as imitating
LAND,	3885	lûwn, loon	or לין lîyn; to dwell, lodge overnight
Lasha, to lash out	3962	Lesha', leh -shah	from an unused root thought to mean to break through;
Laugh, sarcastic	2049	hâthôl, haw-thole'	from H2048 derision
Laugh,	3932	lâ'ag, law-εg	derision by imitation
Laugh, Lah(f)ag	3933	la'ag, lah'-ag	from H3932; derision scoffing scorn
Law, Lawah,	8451	Towrah to-raw	Law, from H3384;
Le(v)iya Leo,	3833	lâbîy', law-ɔee'	or (Ezekiel 19:2) לביא lᵉbîyâ'; lion heart
Learner,	3925	lamad? See ꞁomo	learn, teach, instruct, shepards staff
Lᵉbânôwn	3844	Lᵉbânôwn,	from H3825; White mountain
LETTER,	8451	lǝ·ṭō·w·rāh leto w rah	Is letter for leto wrah, to write the law!
Lion Heart	3823	lêbâb, lay-bawb'	; from H3823; the heart
Lion, comes	0738	'ărîy, ar-ee'	Lion
Li-phah, lip,	8193	saphah	Lip, bank, brim, edge, language
Listen?	3961	lishshan (Aramaic)	language
Loch haim,	2421	Chayah chaw-yaw'	To live
Lock, (luwt)	3874	lûwṭ, loot	a primitive root; to wrap up:—
Lords prayer	6944	qōḏeš	ɼraiko'-desh; from H6942; sacred place
Love,	3824	lêbâb, lay-bawb'	from H3823; Heart
Love,	3825	lᵉbab, leb-ab	(Aramaic) corresponding to H3824:—heart.
LOVE,	3820	leb	heart
love, Luv -	3863	luw' luv?	pray thee,
LoVVaH, love,	3826	libbâh, lib-baw'	feminine of H3820; the heart:—heart.
Lucifer, Luciferic	1966	heylelhay-lale'	from H1984 (in the sense of brightness);
Magog	4031	Magowg, ma̵w-gogue'	from H1463; Magog, a son of Japheth;
MAHOL mak'hole	4235	Mâchôwl, m̵w-khole'	the same as H4234; circular dancing
Malachi	4401	Mal'âkîy, mal-aw-kee'	same as H4397 Messinger of God
Malarkey	4397	bǝ·mal·'â·ḵê — 1 Occ.	Message (see angel) malarkey
Malarky	4401	Mal'âkîy, m̵l-aw-kee	my messinger from the same as H4397;
Male a(t) wkaw,	4399	mᵉlâ'kâh, mel̵a wkaw'	from the same as H4397;
Male	4390	mâlê', maw-l̵y mâlâ'	Be full, pregnant, or Prophecy fulfilled
Male,	4392	male'male	full, fill, with child, multitude, worth
MAN,	4327	mîyn, meen	meaning to portion out;
MANKIND	4327	mîyn, meen	from an unused root meaning to portion out;
Mark-	8427	tav, Taw	mark, crossed sticks, last letter Hebrew/cross
Marry Yah	4179	Mowriyah Mᵉriah	Abraham offered Isaac, chosen of Yah
Mary chosen of God	4179	Mowriyah, moᵣee-yaw'	"chosen by Jehovah"- Mary-Yah
Mattock pick axe	4281	machârêshâh,	from H2790. Pick axe
Mattock, hoe	4576	ma'dêr, mah-ḏare'	from H5737; weeding hoe
Mayim	4325	mayim	water, piss
Me' no see, me	4520	Mě' nashshiy,	from H4519; forget troubles
Me' no sheah,	4519	Měnashsheh,	from H5382 forget troubles
MEASURE	4058	Madad ma dad	Metaphor compare to God, messure up
MELA,	4391	mᵉlâ', mel-aw	(Aramaic) to fill fulfill child Prophecy
Men Britam	0377	'iysh	shew yourselves men
METER, MEASURE	4058	mâdad, maw-ḏad'	To stretch, i.e. measure (see Medes, median)
Milesian	4390	mâlê', maw-l̵y'	or מלא mâlâ';Prophecy fulfilled
Mili̵h,	4390	mâlê'maw-lay'	or מלא mâlâ';
Millah speech	4405	millah	word, speach

361

Description	Strong#	Name-Pronounced	Etymology - Meaning
Millo,	4394	millu', mil-loo'	from H4390; consecration to serve
Miracle mo faith	4159	Mowpheth mo faith	mo-faith'; Miracle
Miriam Miryam	4813	Miryam, meer-yawm'	from H4805; Bitterness, rebellion
Mock	4167	Muq muck	to mock, deride
MOON, luna	3842	lᵉbânâh, leb-aw-naw'	from H3835; i.e. white the moon
Môrîyâh,	4179	Môwrîyâh, mo-ree-yaw'	or מֹרִיָה Môrîyâh; chosen of Yah, mount
Mother	0517	'em	mother, dam, parting
Mullarkey,	4397	bə·mal·'ă·ḵê — 1 Occ.	The Irish Malarkey says malarkey
Murder	4783	murdaph	persecuted-murder,
Music	4537	mâçak, maw-sak	primitive root; to mix, like wine or spices
Myler melo	4393	mᵉlô', mel-o	rarely מְלוֹא mᵉlôw'; Prophecy fulfilled
N-, Nun	5125	nûn	continued, variant
N-, Nun	5126	Nûwn, noon	or נוּן Nôwn;
Nag,	5059	nâgan, naw-gan'	Beat a tune, constant drumbeat
NASA	5375	nâsâ', naw-saw'	or נָסָה nâçâh; to lift
Naval, Bagpipe	5035	nebel, neh'-bel	or נֵבֶל nêbel; skin bag for liquids
Navy, o'nai(v)y ship	0590	oniy, on i-ee, oni(v)ee	navy, navy of ships, galley
NAZI N'Z'R	5144	nâzar, naw-zar'	primitive root; to hold aloft
NAZI, NAZARITE	5387	nâsîy', naw-see'	, or נָשִׂיא nâsi'; see nasa, dedicated
Neck,	6061	'Ânâq, aw-nawk'	the same as H6060; Anak, a Canaanite
Net off- rocks	5197	nâṭ-aph, nawt-af'	a primitive root; to ooze
NIGHT, (NaH)	3842	lᵉbânâh, leb-aw-naw'	H3835; white the moon LeBaNaH
Nimrod,	5248	Nimrôwd, nim-rode'	or נִמְרֹד Nimrôd; rebellion? Or valiant
Nine, 9	8672	tēša'	nine, ninth, nineteenth, nineteen
Nineveh	5210	Niynĕveh, nee-nev-ay	of foreign origin; capital of Assyria
No	2976	ya'ash	no hope, despair, desperate
No, all whole	3606	kol (Aramaic)	all, whole, every, because
Noah Ark	5146	Noach no'-akh	the same as H5118; no wARK rest
No'ah,	4998	nâ'âh, naw-aw'	Be at home, peace
Noon time	5125	nûwn, noon	To resprout, propagate
NOSE	5144	nâzar, naw-zar'	To hold aloof, ie. nose in air
Nuwr (Aramaic)	5135	nuwr (Aramaic)	fiery, fire
O' NO, NOT,	0369	'ayin ah'-yin	= nothing zero 0
Oath	0226	'ôwth, oth	fm H225 in the sence of appearing
Ode,	5749	'ûwd, ood	Duplicate or repeat
OMEN,	0539	'âman, aw-man'	**Believe** the sign, and trust in God Gen15.5-6
Omri see wales	6018	OmriyKhumri	"pupil of Jehovah"
Our Ma,	0520	'ammâh, am-maw'	prolonged from H517;
Our Saviour	1954	Hôw'shê'a', ho-sha'yah	; from H3467; deliverer
Over	5674	'âbar, aw-bar or awvar	to cross over; used very widely
Over, Aber	5674	'âbar, AVaR OV'R	Eber, other side H5674;
Ox turning-	5695	'egel	**calf, bullock**-Boustrophedon Aleph 1ˢᵗ letter
Ox, , Bullock	7794	showr	ox, bullock, cow, bull, wall
Ox, bull, Calf	6499	par	bullock, bulls, oxen, calves, young
Ox, Calf, Bullock	5695	'egel	calf, bullock
Ox,	8450	towr (Aramaic)	oxen, bullock
Paddy to Redeem	6299	padah	redeem, deliver, ransom, rescued, misc
Paddy,	6299	pâdâh, paw-daw'	primitive root; to redeem and God is the one
Pair leg's P'leg	6389	Peleg, peh'-leg	the same as H6388; split, water, divide
Paise Yell Hail	1984	hâlal, haw-lal'	To be clear od sound, praise
Palm,	3709	kap·pê·hem ka palm	their hands, a palm
Par(t),	6565	pârar, paw-rar'	see 6499-par-break (25x),
Peaceful, pay,	7999	Shâlam shaw-lam	a primitive root;to be safe
PEE LEG	6388	peleg, peh'-leg	from H6385 small channel of water, split
Pee,	6376	Piyshown peesh-own'	poured fourth-from 6335;
PENTITUTE,	8451	lə·ṯō·w·rāhleto w rah	Is letter for leto wrah, to write the law!
Perez	6557	Perets, Pharez, Perez	the same as H6556; breach, break forth
Pictogram, decree	6599	pithgâm, pith-gawm	of Persian origin; pictographic word
Pictogram, word	6600	pithgam, pit h-gawm'	pictographic word, Aramaic
Pision	6376	Pîyshôwn, pee-shone'	; from H6335; gush forth spring
PISS, PUSH,	6335	puwsh poosh	To spread act proundly

362

Description	Strong#	Name-Pronounced	Etymology - Meaning
Plate on Aarons	6731	tsîyts, tseets	Breast plate shiny object, see MaTzitz-6692
POOP	6832	tsᵉphûwa', tsef-oo'-ah	fm H6848; excrement
Poor	6331	pûwr, poor	primitive root; to crush
Poor,	6332	Pûwr, poor	Poor person, inferior
Priest	1419	gadowl, gâdôl	Got old-an Elder statement, from H1431;
Prophecy fulfilled	4395	mᵉlê'âh, mᵉl-ay-aw'	feminine of H4392; fill full
Puff, pah-ff	6284	pâ'âh, paw-aw'	a primitive root; to puff
PURE	1252	Bōr בֹּר	cleanness, pureness, never
PURE	1305	Bārar בָּרַר	pure, to purify, select, polish, choose,
PuRSia, PERSIA	6539	Pāras פָּרַס (see Farci)	Persian people=PURE, splendid-BAR 1249
PURIM, festival	6332	Pûwr פּוּר	also (plural) cast lost, poor,
Race people	7217	re'sh (Aramaic)	head, sum, chief
Race people	7218	ro'sh	Resh, chief, race
Rachel	7354	Rachel rä·kⁱāl'	"ewe" lamb
RAHAB	7343	Râchâb, raw-khawb'	the same as H7342; prostitute-proud
Rain, ho re ni	3384	hō·rê·nî	Teach me, (metafor rain on me lord).
Rain,	3140	Yôw'rayee, vo-rah'(n)-ee	Name, teach, rainy;
RAINBOW *	7198	qesheth, keh'-sheth	from H7185 blending
Ram, reem	7214	rᵉ'êm, reh-ame'	Unicorn, wild ox, to ram, buck, riseup.
Rash to act rashly	3423	Yarash yaw-rash'	many uses but, impoverish, ruin, drive out
Raw,	7200	râ'âh, raw-aw'	To see, behold, naked raw, everything
Raw,	6880	tsir'âh, tsi-raw'	stir from hornets stinging sharp barbes
Rebeca Rebekah	7259	ribqâ	Ribqâh, rib-kaw' Isaac wife
Rebuke	3401	yârîyb, yaw-rebe	from H7378; he will contend (reb el)
Rebuke,	7378	ryb, reeb	or רוּב rûwb; P.r. to toss (poke in ribs?)
RED HIEFER	6510	pârâh, paw-raw'	feminine of H6499; Hiefer
Region Beyond	5677	'Eber, Heber	OVER water, not from here
RIB RUB, content	7378	rîyb, reeb or rûwb	to toss, i.e. grapple; figuratively, to wrangle
Rib somone	3402	Yârîyb, yaw-rebe'	the same as H3401;
Rib, Rub as in chide	7378	rîyb, reeb	or רוּב rûwb; grapple; to wrangle
Rimmôwn, rim-mon	7417	Rimmôwn, rim-mone'	or (shorter
ROAM ROOM	7311	rûwm, room	To be high to rise or raise
ROD, cane reed	7070	qâneh, kaw-neh'	from H7069; unit of measurement rod, reed
ROME, origin?	7311	rûwm, room	To be high, to rise or raise
Room (see 7311)	0727	'arown aw-rone	or אָרֹן 'ârôn; gathering
Rope cow-girl	7259	Ribqâh, rib-kaw,	probably meaning to lasso, cowgirl, to rope
Rosh, r'osh-irish	7218	ro'sh	head, chief,
ROYAL is Royal,	3478	Yisra'el	his royal, to be princely of royal blood
Rude, Rough,	7300	Ruwd rood	a primitive root; trample about
Russia see chief	7218	ro'sh	head, chief
Russia	7220	Rô'sh, roshe	probably the same as H7218;
SACK	8242	saq, sak	from H8264;
Sack,	0810	'eshek, eh'-shek	from an unused root
Sack,	5526	çâkak, saw-kak	to entwine as a screen,
SACRED PIE	2134	zak, zak	from H2141; clean pure
SACRED PIE	2136	zâkûw, zaw-koo'	(Aramaic) from H2135; purity
SACRED,	2135	zâkâh, zaw-kaw'	primitive root to be translusent
Sad, SAG?,	7689	shad, shad	mighty:—excellent, great,
SAFE	5592	Saf,	Metaphor for saftey -
SAFE, secure	7951	shâ âh, shaw-law'	to be tranquil, i.e. secure or successful
Sag, not-sag	7689	sâgâ', saga, saggîy	To grow
Sail,	0235	'âzal, aw-zal	To go away, dissapear
Sake,	4537	mâçak, maw-sak	To mix especially wine
Samaria	8111	Shômᵉrôwn,	from the active participle of H8104;
Samaritans,	8118	Shômrônîy,	patrial from H8111;
Samek	5564	çâmak, saw-mak'	15ᵗʰ letter of Hebrew, to prop, to lean upon.
Sarah	8283	Sarah Sarah	Abrahams wife, noble woman SIR aH
Sarah princly power	8280	sârâh, saw-raw'	To have power as a prince(ess)
Satan	7853	sâtar, saw-tan'	To attack or accuse see tan (TanDinosaurus)
Satan	7854	Satan saw-tawn'	from H7853; (see 8577)opponent
Satan	8366	shâthan, shaw-than'	To make water, urinate, piss.

363

Description	Strong#	Name-Pronounced	Etymology - Meaning
SAURUS Dino'sau.	8317	shârats, shaw-rats'	P.r. swarm, wriggle, small reptiles,
SAURUS Dino'sau.	8318	sherets, sheh'-rets	fmH8317 swarm small reptiles, quadrupeds
SAVE to save	3467	yasha`	save, deliverer, help, saviour
SAVE,	7773	sheva', sheh'-vah	SAVE cry for help from H7768; a halloo.
SAVE	7768	shâva', shaw-vah'	P.r. to be free,
Savior,	1954	Hôwshêa', ho-sha(v)yah	from H3467; deliverer
Cliffe Safe,	5586	çâ'aph, saw-af'	P.r. out on branch of tree or cliff safe from
Saw or see far,	6844	tsaphiyth	watchtower
Saw,	6213	âsâh, aw-saw'	P.r.;to do or make or show
saw-hair, hairy	8163	sa`iyr	kid, goat, devil, satyr, hairy, rough
SCAR memorial	2141	zâkak, zaw-kak'	P.r. (compare H2135); to be transparent
SCAR SCORE	2145	zâkâr, zaw-kawr'	fm H2142-(to scars) remembered memorial
SCAR Z'KaR	2142	zakar	remember, memorial (etched as in scar)
Scar, a scar	0234	azkârâh, az-kaw-raw'	fm H2142; to mark (SCAR), as reminder
SCARE & CHAR	2787	chârar, khaw-rar'	P.r.to glow, melt or burn,
Scott'ish	5521	çukkâh, sook-kaw'	feminine of H5520 tent, temporary tent
Scroll,	5612	çêpher, say'-fer	or (feminine) סִפְרָה çiphrâh;
sea cow-	5520	coksuk·kōw — 2 Occ.	den,) tabernacle, pavilion, a hut
see ya,	0281.	Achiyyah a see yah	brother, or worshiper of Yah
See you	3318	way·yê·ṣǝ·'ū weye se u	Goodbye (see u)brother or worshiper of Yah
SEED	2233	zera`	seed, child, fruitful, carnal
SEED,	2234	zᵉra', zer-ah'	(Aramaic) seed, see 2233-
SEMEN,	8082	shâmên, shaw-mane'	from H8080
Serpent, sarap(nt)	8314	saraph, saraph(nt)	fiery serpent, fiery, seraphim fm H8313;
SET SIT,	3320	yâtsab, yaw-tsab'	P.r.; stand, present, set, stand still
Seth,	8352	Shêth, shayth	from H7896;
Seven, 7	7658	shib`anah	seven
Seven, 7	7659	shib`athayim	sevenfold, seven times, varian
Seven, 7	7657	shib`iymSeveYm	seventy, three score and (ten, twelve, etc...)
SEX, SCIENCE	7753	sûwk, sook	P.r.; entwin, shut in, for fornication
SEX, Saxson Knife	7906	Sêkûw, say'-koo	Surmount, cut
SEX, SHIT, Science	7915	sakkîyn, sak-keen'	to cut, divided as a knife
SHAG	7681	Shâ'ge', Shage	To err to go astray morally-
Shag,	0049	Abishag, ab-ee-shag'	Abishag Davids concubine when he was old
Shag,	7686	Shâgâh shag'	P.r.To stray, to get drunk
SHAG,	7683	shâgag, shaw-gag'	P.r.to stray to sin
SHAG,	5381	nâsag, naw-sag'	P.r. To reach lierally of fig.
Shake, shacken	8264	shâqaq, shaw-kak	P.r. To course – like beast of prey
Shaker	7931	Shakan shakan	to set down after being shaken
shaqah	8248	shaqah, shaw-(k)aw'	drink, water, butler, cupbearer, misc
Share	6238	âshar, aw-shar'	P.r.; To accumulate -
SHAVE,	7740	Shâvêh, shaw-vay'	No trees, plain, as in bald, land cleared
Shave, shef-ee	8205	shᵉphîy, shef-ee'	from H8192; Bareness, completely bare,
sheaf, handful	5995	`amiyr	sheaf, handful
Sheep	7353	Rachel raw-kale	fm root meaning to journey; ewe
Sheet, fold=2	8147	shᵉtt'ayim shᵉttayim	from fold sheet-
Shekina,	7931	shakanshakan	to set down after being shaken-
Shelah	7956	Shelah shay-law'	Shelah-the same as H7596 request.
SHELLAC,	7973	Shelach sheh'-lakh	from H7971; missile attack,
Shield	4043	Magen m'gen	shield, buckler, armed, defence, rulers.
SHIRT, a dress	7897	shîyth, sheeth	from H7896; a dress, attire.
Shit (faced) Shithiy,	8358	shᵉthîy, shet-hee'	from H8354; intoxication, drunkenness
Shit Chet	2865	châthath, khaw-thath'	cower- P.r.; Prostrate, bend down
Shit,	7896	shîyth, sheeth	P.r.; "to Bring forth", or set forth, lay
Shit,	7898	shayith, shah'-yith	from H7896; Scrub or trash, weeds
SHITTAH	2847	chittâh, khit-taw',	(SHITTAH,
Shittah, (scared)	8357	shêthâh, shayt-haw,	from H7896; fear, or terror
Shitty Drunk	8358	shâthâh, shaw-thaw	P.r.; To imbibe, get drunk.
shitty terror	2845	Chêth, khayth	from H2865; Abroriginal Cananite
Shitty	8359	shthiy shet-hee'	from 7896; warp in the weaving-inferior
SHITTY,	4960	mishteh, mish-teh'	from H8354; Drink, to get drunk, happy.

Description	Strong#	Name-Pronounced	Etymology - Meaning
SHIVA	8152	Shin'ar, shin-awr'	"country of two rivers"
SHIVER	2851	chittîyth, k'hit-teeth'	(CHIVER?) from H2865, fear, terror.
Shiver, Shower	8175	sâ'ar, saw-ar'	P.r.; to storm
Shoot	7752	shôwṭ, shcte	from H7751; Lash, (shoot out) scourge
Shove,	7589	she°âṭ, sheh-awt'	from an unused root meaning to push aside
Shovel	7725	shûwb, shoob	P.r.To turn back, back away.
Show all, naked	7758	shôwlâl, sho-lawl'	or שֵׁילָל shêvlâl; Nude (exposed)
show'	7778	shôw°êr, Shower	Door keeper for the show-Tabernacle
Show ,CHaWA	2324	chăvâ', khav-aw'	(Aramaic) H2331; to show (baby shower?)
SHOWER, *ED,	8164	sâ°îyr, saw-eer'	formed the same as H8163;
Showers, -	7769	shuwa'cry, riches	abundant, liberal
SHRIEK,	8319	shâraq, shaw-rak'	P.r. To be shrill, to whistel
SIGN ZION	6725	tsîyûwn, tsee-yoon'	fm H6723, conspicuious sign, (sign post)
SIGN, SEE Yonder	6725	tsiyuwntsee-yoon	conspicuus sign,
Sin zanuwn	2183	zanuwn	whoredoms
Sin,	8132	shana (shaw-naw')	to alter [P.r.] KJV: change.
Sinerth zěnuwth	2184	zěnuwth	whoredom
Sir	5630	çiryôn, sir-yone'	for H8302; a coat of mail, brigandine.
Sir,	8323	sârar, saw-rar'	P.r. To have, rule over, govern, lord
Sir, sarah	8282	sarah saw-raw	lady, princess, (Queen mother)
SIR,	8269	sar, sar	fm H8323; Head person, of rank, class.
Sir, sur, sar	8269	sar	prince, Chief, Ruler, Govenor.
Sirion,	8303	Shiryôwn, shir-yone'	and שִׁרְיֹן Siryôn;
Sirion,	8302	shiryôwn, shir-yone'	or שִׁרְיֹן shiryôn;
Sit,	8357	shêthâh, shay-thaw'	from H7896; the seat (of the person)buttock.
SIT,	7896	shîyth, sheet'h	P.r.To put, set in place to mark.
Sit	8352	Shêth, shayth,	from H7896; Shittah -Buttocks
SLANTE	7965	shâlôwm, shaw-lome'	Wholeness, health well being
SO LONG (goodby)	7965	shâlôwm, shaw-lome'	Wholeness, health well being
SO,	3605	kol kowl	or (Jeremiah 33:8) כּוֹל kôwl; from H3634;
Soccer, Pavilion	5521	çukkah	Tabernacle, pavilion, booth, cottage
Sod it	7704	sâdeh, saw-deh'	or שָׂדַי sâday; To spread
SOD	2086	zêd, zade'	from H2102; Arrogant, presumptuous
Sod, you sod,	2102	zûwd, zood	or (by permutation) to seeth
Sodom,	5467	Cědomse-dome'	from an unused root meaning to scorch,
SO-LONG,	7965	shâlôwm, shaw-lome'	or שָׁלֹם shâlôm; from H7999; Peace
Sore, cramp,	6887	tsârar, tsaw-rar'	P.r.; To Cramp.
Sore,	6696	tsûwr, tsoor	P.r.; To Cramp
SORE	6864	tsôr, tsore	from H6696; from pressed into a stone
Sorrow	6887	tsarar saw-rar'	sorrow, besiege, inflicted with trouble
SPAIN	8227	shâphân, shaw-fawn'	from H8226; Rock- Rabbit, fm Hidding
Speak	8193	sâphâh, Ss Phee-(T)h	Suffer, pain
Speech	8193	Sepheth, S Phee-Th	or (in dual and plural) lip, language, speech
Spindle	3601	kîyshôwr, kee-shore'	from H3787; A director, (for cotton-thread)
SPIRIT *EDEN	8314	sârâph, saw-rawf	from H8313; Burning, -poison.
SPY	6822	tsaphah tsaw-faw'	spy, to see a long way
STAIR,	0838	â' shur, aw-shoor	or אַשּׁוּר 'ashshur; A sence of stepping
STAR ESTER	0635	Eçtêr, es-tare'	of Persian A star- a Star-Jewish Heroine
STAR TARA,	8559	tâmâr, taw-mawr'	from an unused root meaning to be erect;
Star, a star,	6253	'Ashtoreth, ash-to'reth	Ashtoreth=star
Stop m	5640	Çâtham s't' am	P.r.To stop up, to repair
Store	0686	aṣar aw-tsar	store P.r.; To Store up, lay up.
Store,	6696	tsûwr, tsoor	P.r.; To Camp, Incline.
Sucker, (sometimes)	7939	sakar saw-kawr'	Wages for work done (Suck-fed by the teet)
Suffer,	8193	sâphâh, Ss Phee-(T)h	Suffer pain, termination.
Sukkot - Booth	5523	Cukkowth	Scota – Scot – Scot
Surf,	5492	cuwphah soo-faw'	5492 cuwphah soo-faw'
'Whole'am,	7965	shalowm, shaw-lome'	peace
Tall,	8524	talal taw-lal'	P.r.;To pile up, elevate.
TAMAR,	8558	tâmâr, taw-mawr'	Fm an unused root meaning to be erect;
Tar Ships -	8659	ta-šîš	Tarshîysh,

365

Description	Strong#	Name-Pronounced	Etymology - Meaning
TARA Tiarah	2918	tiyrah	castle, palace, row, habitation
Tarah	2918	tiyrah tee-raw'	Castle, habitation
Tarshihs,	8659	Taršîš, tar-sheesh'	probably the same as H8658
Tarshiysh,	8658	tarshîysh, tar-sheesh'	probably of foreign derivation
TEA TEPHI,	6827	Tsᵉphôwn, tsef-one'	probably for H6837;
Teach	8451	wǝ·tō·w·rā·tǝ·ḵā	To teach, law, wǝ·tō·w·rā·tǝ·ḵā
Teach,Write,	3384	wǝ·hō·w·rê·t̂î,	(see H8451-leto-letter)arrow,
Tears	7769	shuwaʿcry, riches	abundant, libera, opulent tears - from H7768
TEATS TITS -	4711	mâtsats, maw-tsats	that ye may milk out
Temple	0170	'Ohôlâh, o-holaw'	feminine of H168
Temple prostitute-	6948	qĕdeshah, ked-es'haw	Temple prostitute, god es whore-holy-whore
TERROR ,	8643	tᵉrûwʿâh, ter-oo-aw'	from H7321,
Teth spinning	2908	t̂ᵉvâth, tev-awth'	hunger (as twisting), fasting.
Teth spinning	4299	matveh, mat-veh'	Fm H2901; something spun.
Teth spinning	2901	t̂âvâh, taw-vaw'	P.r.; to spin, see 2904 twirl.
The interigation	0370	'ayin, ah-yin'	probably identical with H369 -Query
Them, they, these,	1992	hêm, haym	they, them, themselves, these, those, many
THEN (hane)	2005	hên, hane	Also, supprise, lo, behold, if, or if, though.
Three,	7969	shâlôwsh, shaw-loshe'	three, thirteen (H6240)
THYME,	8562	tamrûwq, tam-rook'	tamrûwq,
TIARA,	5849	ʿât̂ar, aw-tar'	P.r. To encircule for attack or protection.
TIARAH,	5850	ʿât̂ârâh, at-aw-raw'	ʿât̂ârâh, A crown (circule-wreath)
Tip Hurrah,	8597	tiph'ârâh, tif-aw-raw	fmH6286; bravery, comely, fair, glory.
Tipsee, tiyrowsh	8492	tîyrôwsh, tee-roshe'	fermented wine
Tits	6732	Tsîyts, tseets	Glissen, shine, blossom, flower, plate, wing.
Tongue strange	3956	lashown	Tongue (a whip?), languages, bay, wedge
Torah	8452	tôwrâh, to-raw'	probably feminine of H8448;
TORAH, Law	8451	towrahto-raw	fm-H3384; Law, statute, precept (teach)
TOUR,	2905	t̂ûwr, toor	To view, range, sight see
Town,	1835	Dân, dawn	fr. H1777; judge; (Hill fort of the Chief)
TRIBE,	8532	tᵉlâth, tel-awth'	(Aramaic) masculine Three (origin of Tribe)
Troth	5854	ʿĂt̂ârôwth, at-aw-roth'	betroth-two houses joined-"the crowns of"
TRUE DRUID,	1870	derek, deh'-rek	from H1869; a road as trodden, a course.
Trumpet	2690	chatsar	Sounded, trumpet, clarion
Trumpet,	2689	chatsotserah,	Fr H2690; trumpet, clarion
Tsade	6654	tsadtsad	Side, (18ᵗʰ letter of the alphabet)
Tsᵉrôr Pos 18ᵗʰ Let	6872	tsᵉrôwr, tser-ore'	fm H6887 a parcel
Tubalcain	8423	Tûwbal Qayin,	Fm 2686? offspring of Cain-Metal worker
Twirl	2904	t̂ûwl, tool	P.r.To pitch over or reel.
Two see you,	8454	tûwshîyâh,	wisdom enterprise, thing as it is (see you!)
Tyre, TOWER	6865	Tsôr, tsore	as H6864; Sore (a high rocky place)
Uncle Brother	0251	'âch, awkh	P.W Uncle, or brother, family member
Unicorn Ox, Wild,	7214	rᵉ'em re'em	unicorn (reem can bore a hole through)
Unicorn Ox, Wild,	8377	tᵉ'ow, teh-o'; (Cow?)	tᵉ'ôw, teh-o'; (Cow?)
Utter,	5790	ʿuwthoot'h	uwt'h, utter, speak
Vav Wav	2053	vâv	Hook 6ᵗʰ letter of Hebrew was a Wav-toVav
VESSEL,	0416	'Êl Bêyth-	fm H410 and H1008;House of God (vessel?)
VISION HAZY,	2383	Chezyôwn,	= "vision" from H2372; (Hazy-vision)
VISION	2384	Chiz zâyôwn,	fm H2372; khiz-zaw-yone' kids saw-visson
Walk alone	1980	halakha-wlak	To walk (with)
Walk away	3212	yalak, Ya wlak-	To carry, to work,-message of God
Walk,	4397	mâl'âk, mal'awk	Fm an unused root meaning to despatch
Walk, wk w,ork	1980	hō·w·lêḵ — 86 Occ.	akin to H3212;To walk
Wall, Mound	2426	chêyl, khale	rampart, fortress, wall
WARM U'WM,	3117	YoWM	Day, to be warmed by the sun -YoWaM
WATER	7372	râtab, raw-tab'	P.r.; rata(wata) Water, wet, moist
Water Wet,	7373	râtôb, raw-tobe'	from H7372; moist (with sap);—green.
Water (mosture)	4161	mowtsa' mo'wtsa	Water, waterspring, go out, or forth.
Welsh, lachadd	2421	châyâh, khaw-yaw'	P.r. He gave me life, revived
Wheel	5694	ʿâgîyl, a-wgheel	same as H5696 round, circular, wheel
Wheel, loop,	5696	ʿâgîyl, aw-geel'	Awheel, a gheel, (see lady giddy, gwheel))

366

Description	Strong#	Name-Pronounced	Etymology - Meaning
WHEEL	1523	gîyl, gheel	to rejoice, exult, be glad, revolve (SPIN)
White House,	3837	LabanLaban	Laban = "white"
White House,	3837	Laban	Laban
Who, you, he, she	1992	hêm, haym	they, them, themselves, these, those, **Who**
WHOLE,	7999	shalam	pay, peace, recompence, reward
whore	2181	zanah	...harlot, go a whoring,
WindBag,	1891	hâbal, haw-bal'	P.r. To act in vain, in word / expectation.
WORD UNDER	3045	yᵉda', yed-ah'	(Aramaic) certify, know,
Word	1697	dabar	**word,**
WORD,	5749	'ûwd, ood uwood	P.r.Bear witness, say aginst.
Work,	1983	wa·hã·lāk̲ wa·hã·lāk̲	(Aram.) fm H1981; a journey (walk-work)
Work,	4399	mᵉlâ'k̲âh, mela wkaw'	from the same as H4397; deputyship
Worship,	1961	hâyâh, haw-yaw	P.r. (c H1933); To exist, be
Wow (Vav)	2053	vâv, vaw (wow)	probably a hook (6ᵗʰ letter of Hebrew)
Yada	3045	yâda', yaw-dah'	P.r.; To know, ascertain.
Yah, YH	3050	Yâhh, yaw	contraction for H3068 Yahovah Lord.
Yakidah, 'Iechyd da'	3048	Yᵉda'yâh, i'kda'yah	from H3045 and H3050 "Iah has know"
Yank,	3290	Ya'aqob, Yacob	Yaacov in Ashkenazi Hebrew (grab heel)
Yarash (Irish?)	3423	yArash y'E.'shYᵉhovih	GOD, LORD-to occupy, seize, dispossess,
Ye bawl,	2986	yâbal, yaw-bal'	P.r. To flow, bring, lead, carry, conduct.
Ye hover (Lord)	3069	YHVH-Yᵉhovih	fm 1961-v. of H3068-Lord, in charge.
Ye over in charge	3068	YHVH-Yᵉhovah,	LORD, (GOD), JEHOVAH, variant
Ye sh sure,	3444	yᵉshuw'ah-YeHoWSaVaH	Ye how saviour- He is our Saviour
Yell Hail	1984	yᵊ·hal·lū,	praise God's brightness, Hail lu (el missing)
Yelled, Ye**LaD**	3206	yeled	Child, young man, son, boy, fruit.
YESH YES YEAH	3426	yêsh, yaysh	to stand out, or exist;
Yo safe, Jospeh	3130	Yowceph yow saf(e)	Yo'saf' To accumulate (to save)
Yom Kippur,	3722	Kaphar cover	Atonement (day of covering Yom Kippor)
YOU	3050	Yâhh, Yaw	contraction for H3068 (to be in agreement)
Youth yaldooth	3208	yaldûwth, yal-dooth'	abstractly from H3206 child, boy/girl.
Zayin 7ᵗʰ letter Heb?	2100	zûwb, zoob	P.r.Flow freely (as water-sweat?)
Zera Israel	2233	zera'zeh'·rah	seed, child, carnal, fruitful.
ZERO CIPHER,	5608	caphar̥çiphᵉr,	Scribe, tell, declare, number, count.
ZERUBBABEL	2216	Zᵉrubbâbel	fm H2215&H894; Child of Babble (born)
ZEUS, De, Tu, Diva	2895	t̲ôwb, tobe	P.r. do or make good, to be, go, play- well
Zion,	6723	tsîyâh, t-see-yaw'	fm an unused root meaning to parch;
Zion,	6724	tsîyôwn, tsee-yone';	fm H6723; a desert, dry place.
Zion, SIGN post	6725	tsîyûwn, tsee-yoon';	fm H6723 conspicus, guiding pillar, sign,
Zion, Capital	6726	Tsîyôwn, tsee-yone';	H6725; Tsijon a mountain of Jerusalem.

www.ingramcontent.com/pod-product-compliance
Lightning Source LLC
Chambersburg PA
CBHW060758120626
46557CB00001B/16